Worldmaking

Critic of Institutions

Roberta Kevelson
General Editor

Vol. 6

PETER LANG
New York • Washington, D.C./Baltimore
Bern • Frankfurt am Main • Berlin • Vienna • Paris

Worldmaking

Edited by

William Pencak

PETER LANG
New York • Washington, D.C./Baltimore
Bern • Frankfurt am Main • Berlin • Vienna • Paris

Library of Congress Cataloging-in-Publication Data

Worldmaking/ edited by William Pencak.
p.   cm. — (Critic of institutions; vol. 6)
1. Semiotics—Social aspects. I. Pencak, William. II. Series.
P99.4.S62W67   302.2—dc20   95–17433
ISBN 0-8204-2804-3
ISSN 1068-4689

Die Deutsche Bibliothek-CIP-Einheitsaufnahme

Pencak, William:
Worldmaking/ edited by William Pencak. – New York; Washington,
D.C./Baltimore; Bern; Frankfurt am Main; Berlin; Vienna; Paris: Lang.
(Critic of institutions; Vol. 6)
ISBN 0-8204-2804-3
NE: GT

Cover Design by Nona Reuter.

The paper in this book meets the guidelines for permanence and durability
of the Committee on Production Guidelines for Book Longevity
of the Council of Library Resources.

© 1996 Peter Lang Publishing, Inc., New York

Printed in the United States of America.

Contents

Gender

Law and Literature

Federalism

Class

History

Science

Postscript

Chapter I

Worldmaking: An Introduction

William Pencak

We are not born into the world. We create our world from an infinity of possible worlds, and recreate it as we live our lives. The critic of institutions, to whom this series is devoted, makes us aware of this. Whether philosopher, historian, statesman, or scientist, the critic presents alternatives, turning us from unconscious into conscious worldmakers. Robert Ginsberg, in his essay 'Philosophy as Worldmaking,' expresses and develops this point far more eloquently than I can.

After Ginsberg's overview of worldmaking, we move on to different ways the critic of institutions gives us our freedom. In some instances, his or her meaning is hidden; its signifiers must be interpreted semiotically for it to be revealed. In others, the critique is clear enough. In both cases, the semiotics of worldmaking texts reveals they, too, are signs of both particular contexts and of fundamental ideas, passions, and institutions which define our common humanity. This volume investigates religious, philosophical, racial, gendered, literary, legal, federalist, class-based, historical, and scientific forms of worldmaking from a variety of semiotic perspectives.

Ginsberg's essay is followed first by Edwin N. Gorsuch's equally panoramic analysis of 'Emotional Expression in an Early Medieval Manuscript.' Analyzing elaborately painted initial letters, he presents these tiny illuminations as microcosms of the Christian world-view. They not only symbolize their Biblical texts, but their colors signify both traditional scriptural imagery and the psychological reactions to particular colors put forth by modern research. This is one of three essays, the others being Fitz's and Makolkin's, which suggest humans share emotions and symbols across cultures, thereby demonstrating semiosis, the construction of signs, is grounded in reality rather than linguistic systems of particular societies. Unlike Gertrude Stein's Oakland, there is a there, a reality, 'there.'

Two articles on eastern philosophy further demonstrate that the most apparently abstract learning may serve as a sign of contemporary problems. Wei Yuan, as On-cho Ng demonstrates, was concerned with more than reviving ancient Chinese texts: he hoped that by so doing he could regenerate a moribund society along conservative lines. Steven Heine's account of modern Japanese philosophy emphatically argues that the 'place' of absolute nothingness, the supreme goal of an important strain in Japanese Buddhism, is indeed a 'place' intimately linked to debates over the nation's militarism and expansion in the early twentieth century.

Race, unfortunately, as Ann Makolkin writes in 'From Gene Fund to Genocide: Semiotics of Otherness and Exclusion,' is far too often the basis of worldmaking. From Plato to chauvinists in the recently liberated republics of the former Soviet Union, myths of chosen peoples and pseudo-scientific theories of racial inferiority have merged to brand the 'other' as not merely different, but as inhuman. Stephen Fitz's study of African American slave religion shows racial worldmaking not only victimizes the stigmatized 'inferior,' but the self-deluding 'master race' as well. White southerners found themselves moved by the genuine emotionalism of slave Christianity, but then rejected such passion in themselves because of reason and upbringing. Borrowing from psychologist Carl Jung's theory of the collective unconscious, Fitz stresses that certain emotions and symbols are rooted in our basic humanity, not to be denied even by those who attempt to push them aside.

Fitz's essay performs the double duty of showing how exploited peoples, using signs they understand among themselves but which are concealed from their rulers, can construct alternative worlds through folk tales, music, and religious ritual. James Smith Allen's account of French feminist Utopian thinker Céline Renooz shows how this nineteenth-century woman, seeking to liberate women from masculine domination, also created an elaborate cosmology through an eccentric mixture of science, philosophy, and history. Yet her conclusions that nature should be modelled on cooperative plants rather than competitive animals, that feminine intuitive understanding should replace fallacious masculine reasoning, and that the gods drove out the goddesses in ancient times are plausible even if her methodology and writings are bizarre. Jeffrey Polizzotto describes another path a woman seeking liberation could take. Transforming the song 'John Brown's Body' into a 'Battle Hymn' about the American Civil War's sacred mission to free the slaves, Julia Ward Howe elevated herself into the interpreter who gave men's war a transcendent purpose. Later in life, she would find similar cosmic significance in the peace movement and struggle for women's rights.

Coincidentally, legal and literary worlds merge in two more essays centering on the nineteenth century. Thomas O. Beebee shows marriage to be a complex, changing sign in German thought and law, a shifting fulcrum at which authority, emotion, tradition, sexuality, and contract meet. Diana Royer views Nathaniel Hawthorne's Puritan characters and tales as signs of his dissatisfaction with the conformist, hypocritical, and — when the American Civil War began — stridently nationalistic mid-nineteenth century world in which he took a keen interest.

Nationalism is criticized also by Virginia Black in her essay 'Natural Society: The World of Federalism.' She powerfully argues that mutual trust and a conversation about the public good must underwrite any successful polity. Far from being outdated in a world of centralized nation-states, federalism is the solution to problems they have created yet cannot solve.

Class should no more be taken for granted than the nation-state. Both belong to worlds which are constructed — and thus can be deconstructed. Angela Leonard tells of how new perceptions of exploiters and exploited arose in early nineteenth-century Britain during the campaign to repeal the Corn Laws that forbade and then limited importation of grain. Landed aristocrats who profited from the act were signified as 'chuckle-headed fox hunters' opposed by virtuous, industrious workers and consumers. Natalie Isser shows conservatives were as adept at demonizing their enemies as were reformers. The government of Napoleon III in France created a 'Red Specter,' advertised in a widely-circulated pamphlet of that name, to drum up support for the new, precarious regime. Almost exactly a century before the McCarthy trials in the United States, the Bonaparte restoration created an imaginary world of subversive Communists, thereby obtaining support from a gullible, paranoid public.

Historical writing, that pack of commonly accepted tricks we play on the dead, as Voltaire described it, has not been immune from biased worldmaking. In 'Soviet Historiography and the Problem of Myth,' George Enteen explains how Stalinist historical writing depicted a Soviet Communist party at bay from enemies within and without, valiantly reacting to successive crises. Such mythmaking became so pervasive that new enemies and crises continually had to be found: historical myth thus created historical reality, with disastrous consequences for millions of purged 'traitors.' My own essay argues that twentieth-century post-historicist intellectuals, generalizing their own privileged existence to all humankind, have declared history at an end and the bourgeois civilization whose comforts they enjoy the culmination, the final stage of human development.

Historically, they will eventually become signs of their time rather than live on as its legitimate interpreters.

The 'etherial semiotics' of David Zeeman prove that natural scientists are no more the 'objective' observers of a given world than so-called social scientists. 'Ether,' a word that signifies the medium through which electromagnetic charges move, became defined first as 'place' and then as 'property' as radio broadcasting technology developed. The way scientists view the world, and how the public views and adapts scientific research, have been shaped by the economic and political imperatives of technology.

Are these humanly constructed worlds compatible? Perhaps not, but many can coexist peacefully in an atmosphere of mutual respect, as outlined in John C. Calhoun's theory of the 'concurrent majority.' However, as I note in my postscript, few worldmakers are willing to grant others equal tolerance. Illustrating varieties of worldmaking, this volume looks forward to a new millennium in which the perniciousness of exclusionary and demonizing ideologies will become evident to all, and the virtues of open and tolerant worlds celebrated and implemented.

In addition to documenting the worldmaking of others, this volume testifies to the intellectual world of the annual Round Table symposia of the Penn State Center for Semiotic Research directed by its founder, Distinguished Professor of Philosophy, Roberta Kevelson. As a regular participant, I began to preach the semiotic gospel to my colleagues and students in the Penn State History Department. Many of them have responded with curiosity and enthusiasm, incorporating a semiotic approach if not semiotic jargon into their own work. Their essays, which form roughly half of this volume, thus signify a new world of semiotic inquiry which has evolved from the Round Table. I am deeply grateful to Professor Kevelson for the privilege of editing this volume. Great thanks are also due to Cindy Palecek and her staff at 'A Perfect Secretary' in Reading, Pennsylvania, for superbly preparing this volume, their third book for me. Nona Reuter, Christopher Myers, and Peter Lang Publishing are to be highly praised for having faith in this project and in 'The Critic of Institutions' series. My greatest thanks are for the contributors, my colleagues and students, whose patience with a curmudgeonly and demanding editor stands as a model of tolerant worldmaking in itself.

Chapter II

Philosophy as Worldmaking

Robert Ginsberg*

Philosophy is the art of re-making the world with the power of the mind informed by the insight of the heart.

For the philosopher, the world is not given; it is encountered. For others, the world is taken as given; it is the context, the structure, the complex, the stricture in which they work. Often people awaken to the world in which they find they live and work. The philosopher awakens the world by showing what we make of it, what we take from it, what we give to it. The world is fixed, according to the mundane view, while we move and change within it. We are the movers and changers, the shakers and makers of the world, according to the philosopher. That world dwells within us.

What in the world are we talking about? The world that is the intersubjectivity of humanity. The inner world, what each of us as human being lives, is intimately connected to the rest of the world which is shot through with human subjectivity. The outer world thereby is our world. It enters within who we are. We extend ourselves as persons throughout it. Hence, the world is our home. The phrase 'human world' is redundant, for the word 'world' is derived from the Germanic 'wer-ald,' the 'age of man.' The world we mean is the human presence on earth.

The planet earth is the objective realm. For much of its rapidly changing existence, it had no human presence. Shortly, it will be disburdened of any human presence. At present, we contribute our world to the earth. We have made a human realm on the surface of a planet, and for a time we are integrating that objective body into our world.

At first, the human presence was but another natural feature of the planet. Like crocodiles and cockroaches, our heirs apparent, we were inhabitants of the earth. The earth was experienced as given; we had to struggle to survive on its terms. The world was fighting with the earth.

The human adventure completed its first volume when we were able to sufficiently overcome the objective hazards of living on the planet to dwell in our humanity.

In several languages, two words have been needed for this difference between planetary body and intersubjective world, because two different experiences are involved, two different ways of being. On the earth (Ger. *die Erde*; Fr. *la terre*), I am a human animal, a biological being. In the world (Ger. *die Welt*; Fr. *le monde*), I am a moral participant, a human being.

Volume Two of our story is the working out in full of the world, our shared identity, the global community. The philosopher is taking a hand in the writing of those chapters.

Volume Three is for getting the whole world back down to earth, harmonizing the planetary existence with human being-with (*Mitsein*). In those chapters, for which philosophers are preparing the outlines, the earth joins our world; it comes into our care rather than our control. Here in three acts we have the main *History of Humanity in the Universe*:

1. The triumph of humanity over the earth: making the earth home to the world.
2. The triumph of the world over our inhumanity: making our world home to everyone.
3. The triumph of humanity over its separation from the earth: making the world and earth grow together.

The last act, no. 4, is the defeat of humanity, the destruction of the world, by either inhumanity or natural causes: making the earth go on without us.

The drama is initially played between protagonist humanity and antagonist nature, but their roles will shift, and the protagonist is presently still struggling with itself. The moral consciousness arises in the initial struggle against nature. The struggle in which we are now engaged is almost entirely a moral one among ourselves. 'Moral' means much more than right principles or proper actions; it is a shaping awareness of others, a lived presence with others, an insistent connectedness with others, such that we are really We.

Who are We? The philosopher wakes up the world each morning to figure out who We are and what We are to make of ourselves. The question is always the same. It is the eternal task for our mortal species.

Others get up each morning to do their tasks as if this were the same world as the day before. Their contributions may make that world a little better. Yet what they miss seeing and shaping is the world. Hence, they have not awakened.

The philosopher must see the world anew, must seize the world anew, undistracted and undistressed by the program of our daily tasks. Others conscientiously labor to make their place in the world, while the philosopher, through the labors of conscience, re-makes the world.

Heartfelt thought remakes the world. Thinking is not simply about something, as when we think about the earth and obtain objective information concerning it. The 'ob' prefixed to 'obtain' and 'objective' signal an apposition, an opposition of the thinking subject and the thinging object. But thinking, if heartfelt, may also be the interpretive, evaluative, purposive, participatory, transformative engagement in the subject under consideration. The 'sub' signals something underlying. Thus, the subject as thinker and the subject as thought share something in common. They throw themselves ('ject,' as in the verb-noun, 'project') into each other. What do you think of that?

I think that you are wandering from the subject with too many interjections. You began with the serious topic of the world, but now you are amusing yourself with words.

Musing is the philosopher's prerogative; it is the mental passport to wander from place to place in the effort to find our place. Reader, we may well find the worth of our world in our words.

Reader: The philosopher's duty, I have been told, is to follow where the argument leads. That may throw light on the world. That is why I am reading this book.

Author: Arguments have a way of misleading us. Every philosopher is betrayed into giving the full powers of reason to the development of a wrong line of thought. Philosophers need to be saved from their arguments. Insight is needed first — and last — to initiate, redirect, or turn away from an argument. I have been seeking insight about what the world means to us.

Reader: Why in the world don't you just answer that question in plain words?

Author: I will try, now that you have arrived on the scene to help me. The world is what we mean to ourselves.

Reader: Who do you mean by 'we'?

Author: That is precisely the question!

Reader: I want the answer.

Author: The answer is We.

Reader: Circular, redundant, tautological, pedantic, insignificant! No insight in sight.

Author: Why, you too allow words to play upon your understanding!

Reader: I am catching the disease of verbiage from you. Let's get down to substance.

Author: Another 'sub' word for what stands at the bottom of things.

Reader: What is the difference, at bottom, between we and We?

Author: The we is the grammatical subject; it stands at the bottom of the sentence. It is the base of operation in some expressions. The We is the human intersubjectivity; it stands at the core of everyone's existence. Grammatically, we can be divided into I and you and any number of others. Each is independent and may come into association. Existentially, I, just like you, and everyone else, is indissolubly conjoined.

Reader: I don't know about you, but I can speak for myself. I am myself. I can join with others, and I can keep others out of my life. I am free to be apart from the world rather than a part of the world. The world is nothing more than a set of free and changing associations of more or less sociable individuals.

Author: Such individualism at the personal level spells a dividualism at the level of the world. Your argument, which promotes the dignity and freedom of the person, demotes the place of the world in the life of persons. A divided world, a world of many worlds, fails to be the world. Thereby individuals are shortchanged in their own substance.

Reader: Is the world, then, to be conceived of as some uniform body, an authoritarian whole, a totalitarian system, a global government? Let's save the world from such mad dreams. If that is what you are making into the world, then I stand against the world.

Author: Because you are standing up for . . . ?

Reader: The supreme value of personhood.

Author: I stand with you in that, shoulder to shoulder, person to person. But may I ask you a question?

Reader: Please feel free to do so; it is the prerogative of the author.

Author: Thank you for your courtesy. You are responding as best you can, and that is the real task of the reader. Now, whose personhood are we defending against oppression?

Reader: My personhood.

Author: Only yours?

Reader: To begin with mine and that of my loved ones and neighbors.

Author: And to end with?

Reader: That suffices for a good life.

Author: For your good life?

Reader: I can't answer for others beyond my circle. You may ask other readers about their lives, if you wish.

Author: They have a concern in the matter, indeed, everybody in the world is involved.

Reader: How can you know anything about everybody or speak on their behalf?

Author: Because if we allowed that some of those people could be excluded on some grounds from protection as free human beings, then we are opening the case against you to be denied protection on yet other grounds. Do you see that to deny anyone's humanity, anywhere in the world, is to potentially deny everyone's humanity?

Reader: That's what it may come to in theory, although in practice we can be free in our community even though others in distant lands are oppressed.

Author: Your freedom, and my freedom, is not fully assured until we have assured that everyone else's freedom is protected. Freedom in being self-affirming affirms its self-protection, but this is inescapably bound with the protection of others.

Reader: You and I may enjoy our freedom and neglect others who are oppressed, as long as we have sufficient power to resist being oppressed by others. We may even have an interest in oppressing others in order to be strong enough not to be oppressed by others.

Author: If we prepare to oppress others in the name of our freedom, then others may with equal right prepare to oppress us in the name of their freedom. Sooner or later we may all be deprived of freedom. We would all be losers that way. But if we prepare to liberate all others, then all others are encouraged to respect our freedom. We would all be winners that way. Oppression is ultimately self-destructive. Freedom is inherently expansive.

Reader: Well, for my benefit I am willing to recognize the rights of others. If we all stand for freedom, then we will all benefit.

Author: Starting from 'I,' you are coming to recognize the 'We.' Self and world are interdependent.

Reader: I wouldn't say that. I started from 'I' and arrived at a strategy for treating others, or 'we' with the small letter, for my benefit. The world is only the field of life for persons. We (again with small letter) do have to take account of others in order to lead our own life. But nothing mystical occurs between myself and others.

Author: Don't miss the mystical as you work out the logic of human life. The world is at heart mystical. The tie which binds us to one another is not the afterthought meant to strategically protect our individual freedoms, but it is the groundthought of our inseparability which mandates freedom for all.

Reader: Mystical, metaphysical, magical, mythical talk! I stick to that thinking which is grounded in the self, 'I think, therefore I am,' as was said by one of your famous predecessors in philosophy. As I make way for myself in the world, I see, upon reflection, that other people come into consideration. 'I would be free, therefore others should be free.' That is the practical formula.

Author: Cartesian thinking needs rethinking. Marvin Farber, the American philosopher of Naturalism and a leading scholar of Phenomenology, once assigned me as a student to write a naturalistic meditation to replace, if I could, Descartes's *Meditations* and Husserl's *Cartesian Meditations*. I found that an enormous amount of mental preparation was required before I even got to the *cogito*. A good part of the mental work was also social, emotional, and physical. Everything that Descartes and Husserl held in suspension drew my attention. What they would close off, I opened up.

The world makes way for itself within our thinking. Descartes had left out the world only to bring it back in through the thinking self, while Husserl never got back the world. But when, in my Meditations, I was about to say, 'I think . . . ,' the world had already spoken through me, in me, to me, with me. The monologue I was trying to conduct was at bottom a dialogue with the world. These very words by which we think are socially shaped and shared. The self that I assert, the 'I' presupposed as conducting the thinking, is a human being, so that its being is bonded to humanity. 'I think, because we are human.'

Reader: That is a lot to think about. But let's get back to the world. Isn't the world nothing other than the human collectivity, each member of it deserving of freedom, or do you conceive the world to be an organic whole which takes precedence over individuals and therefore might oppress some of us?

Author: The world is more than the sum of its individuals. And the consummate individual has a good part of the world within. The trouble is that you are inclined to see the world as outside, as environment, while what counts for you is the inner world of the person. But the world is in there. It is the innerment of who we are. The world does not surround us; it abounds within us. The world is not the detached exterior field through which we move, but the interior forcefield in which we dwell. Even the hermit finds the furnishings of humanity ever present in thought and feeling. Even in meditation the thinker faces the world. Even as I write, you, the other, pop up out of these pages and refuse to melt away.

Reader: Since you are writing for me, I have the right to inform you of where your thinking is mistaken. The major fault with your thinking about the world is that is it merely thinking. You think that if you think about the world then you are doing something about it, for it, with it. Idle thoughts . . . , idyl thoughts . . . , idol thoughts. Didn't Marx criticize you philosophers for being mere interpreters of the world, while others go about changing it?

Author: Marx's projected *Theses on Feuerbach*, which he did not get to write because he busied himself otherwise in changing the world, are themselves interpretations that thereby change the world that is within understanding. This is the quintessential task of the philosopher: re-visioning the world through better understanding.

Reader: Aren't you mistaking Weltanschauung for philosophy? A world-view may be an individual's integrated outlook on life that helps get that person through the world, but philosophy, so far as I can see it in practice, is an impersonal discipline of offering and testing arguments. The world of you philosophers is the ivory tower. Philosophy traditionally has nothing whatsoever to do with the real world.

Author: A Weltanschauung is what everybody in the world needs. It is not simply a philosophy, but it is an affective grasp and a chosen path. A Weltanschauung is not just a way of seeing the world; it is a way of being in the world. World-commitments are operative in Weltanschauungen. Freud and Jung recognized these as deeper than philosophies. But the practice of philosophy as an essential human discipline means more than having a philosophy. *A philosophy*, or, if you prefer, a Weltanschauung, is a package, something that you take with you to conduct your life. But *philosophy* is conduct; it is the opening up and critical examination of all such packages. Philosophy is philosophizing upon philosophies.

Reader: For what purpose? Why do we need philosophy when we each have a philosophy?

Author: For the purpose of harmonizing our vision with the world by clarifying the human-centeredness of our individual lives. Philosophizing is this corrective, restorative, creative, reflective art of improving self-and-world.

Reader: Philosophy as you practice it seems to be the art of gratuitous hyphenation. Self and world are distinct. 'Self-world' might be acceptable as the world of the self, the self with its accompaniments, extensions, and world-view. 'World-Self' may be a mystical notion of organic unity. 'Self-and-world' is an impossible locution, a clump of jargon, a philosophical chimera.

Author: I cannot be fully myself as human being unless I address humanity fully. I can't look at humanity properly without being human. The hyphenation is intersubjectivity.

Reader: We come back to that. We are going in circles.

Author: We always have to come back to that. It is our core. We circle it to understand it. It always pushes itself out past the circumference of our attention. Each day as philosopher, as human being, I try to circle in on it, to work it out, to get it all out into the open, to open it up.

Reader: Do you ever get anywhere, or is such philosophizing futile? Philosophers claim to be beating the bush to flush out the truth, but when I see what they are doing it looks more like beating around the bush. Upon closer examination, they often turn out to be beating a dead horse.

Author: You are making philosophers take quite a beating! Each day I make a little progress. Some days I make a little regress. But this is a project never to be finished. For each day brings a new world. The world comes fresh each time we awaken to it. What our humanity is, what it means, what we should do about it, is not a lesson simply taught and finally learned. It is the ongoing, interactive, unfolding process of living with the world. The world is revised daily. And every day I am obliged to remake myself.

Reader: Why all this heavy endless work? Take my case for freedom. Get up in the morning and be free!

Author: I take your case for freedom of everyone. That means that I get up in the morning to figure out how to liberate others. This is a question of taking action on behalf of those evidently oppressed. It is also a matter of discovering the oppression inflicted on others which hitherto has not even been seen as oppression, and of which I may unknowingly be a perpetrator.

Reader: I may concede that we ought to come to the aid of people who are being enslaved, tortured, or killed, if giving such aid does not put us at great risk. But how can we have any obligation toward those whose deprivation of freedom is unapparent?

Author: That is the right question again. You have a talent in raising good questions.

Reader: Thanks. How about your giving the answer that settles the question?

Author: That's not easy. Some answers make their questions disappear. Answers released from questioning may be questionable. Some questions need to be repeatedly applied to the answers. This is such a question. It requires me to rethink my life. 'Are others being oppressed in ways I have missed? How might I unknowingly be depriving others of freedom?' is a subject for daily investigation. Every once in a while, an answer breaks through, as I discover my self-deception. This was the case for me with sexism, ageism, and heterosexism. I must leave myself open to uncovering the next ism.

Reader: If each day you review your soul and assess the world, then that does not leave much time to do anything else. You would have the whole world on your shoulders. Your freedom would be overwhelmed by the weight of the world.

Author: But if I get up and take a stroll in the garden while my neighbor cries out in being murdered, am I truly free? Or is it a caprice and not freedom to continue my stroll without giving some assistance? My freedom is not diminished by interrupting the stroll, but it would be diminished by allowing my neighbor to be murdered. Our freedom is at stake. The potential joy I might take in the world is outweighed by the potential joy to be taken in our humanity.

Freedom is liberation. I liberate the other whose freedom is as worthwhile as mine; thereby I liberate myself in affirming humanity. So freedom is not a given, nor is it an attribute or instrument with which you do this or that.   As Sartre put it, we are freedom. Freedom is living in such a way as to liberate your humanity — which is our humanity. Freedom is what We are together.

Reader: I concede that no loss in freedom occurs in rushing to the aid of a neighbor, assuming that you run no grave risk. But my neighbors are never attacked.

Author: What, never?

Reader: Well, hardly ever.

Author: Your neighbors are under attack this very moment, though you have not noticed that.

Reader: I would certainly have noticed the outcry of my neighbors. Because I am reading this crazy chapter in an otherwise fine book does not mean that I am insensible to what is going on around me.

Author: What is going on within you may be keeping you from seeing who your neighbors really are.

Reader: Well, if you think that you know better than me who my neighbors are, then please tell me: who are they?

Author: Everybody.

Reader: The street on which I live does not have enough dwellings for that many neighbors.

Author: But the world in which you dwell has enough room.   You would rush to the aid of your neighbor down the street just as you would to the one just next door.

Reader: Down the street, yes, and perhaps over on the next street. But my neighborhood does not extend throughout the city, the country, or the whole world. By 'neighbor' we mean someone in close proximity for whom we have a special care. Perforce, the whole world cannot be my neighbors.

Author: The special care you will find within you, and you will discover that you can effectively reach out to those seemingly a world apart. It's a small world. This discovery comes from asking yourself that question of how you may have been deceiving yourself about oppression. When you wake up to everyone being your neighbor, the world changes.   Then you manage to hear those cries from every corner of the world to which you are obliged to respond in the name of freedom.

Reader: I can't possibly help everyone in the world who needs help.

Author: Yes, you can. In these ways. First, redirect your life in the light of the enlarged consciousness of the world. You will be enhanced in your personhood, empowered in your humanity, by discovering six billion neighbors. Second, take a hand in reshaping the world, including assisting others to enlarge their understanding as well. Why, if each enlightened person were to assist one other neighbor to grasp world-neighborliness, then everybody in the world would soon be converted to such neighborliness.

Reader: While you are at it, are there any other tasks you would assign me in order to save the world?

Author: You would assign yourself those tasks each morning.
Reader: Thank you, but how on earth am I to do that?

Author: Excellent question. You have to raise that question each day. In the course of re-examining your/our humanity you will come upon promising actions. Each day you will act to save the world.

Reader: Nice assignment. But how will I know which are the right things to do, especially since anything I do has minimal affect on the world? You are placing me in a condition of indecision, ineffectuality, and finally, despair.

Author: Logically speaking that sounds like an accurate picture. Yet our humanity cries out for taking action. So we must overcome the seeming impossibility of our situation by doing our best.

Reader: Our best is not good enough to save everybody.

Author: Probably. But then, upon further reflection, we may find a way to do better. That's something marvelous about being human: our best may not finally be our best.

Reader: While we try daily to do better than our best on behalf of freedom throughout the world, we have no time to enjoy the freedom of strolling in the garden. The obligation that you discover embedded in freedom overrides your freedom. This is a sacrifice of freedom by those who presently are free for the sake of the freedom of others in the future. A perverse line of reasoning. I am willing to help others, even my far-flung neighbors, but not at the cost of my freedom. I cannot liberate everyone, probably not even anyone. But I can live with what freedom I have. The garden stroll you mentioned calls me away from the despair of the world.

Author: Answer that call. You will be a better person for it. Drink deeply of the joy of life. Affirm in your living the value of such enjoyments. And liberate all others so that they too may enjoy life.

Reader: I'm glad that you allow me some time to enjoy life even though I have to liberate everyone else in the world. But the questions then are: When, and how long, and in what ways should I choose to pursue such private enjoyments, given the unceasing calls for help from the outside world?

Author: Yes, those are the very questions to which each of us must daily answer. The outside world is another mode of ourselves; the inner world is also a mode of access to everyone. No one can give you the formula for life whereby you properly apportion your time in serving others or fulfilling self, in serving self or fulfilling others. Take your daily stroll in the garden of life. Do not miss it. But do not miss the rest of the world, including the hidden link between this garden and the oppression of distant neighbors. Make the world a garden for all of us.

Reader: I will reflect upon that in my next stroll. But now I wish to return to the history of the world that you were so pretentiously writing before I stepped into the chapter. You mentioned that if we ever make our world triumphant then new room for the biological realm would be found. Would you explain that?

Author: We have made some opening efforts along that line in the course of struggling with world problems such as hunger, population explosion, pollution, and exhaustion of resources. We see now that human beings have to tackle the geosphere, the biosphere, the ecosphere, if we are to succeed in our struggle to forge the humanosphere — the planetary home for *homo sapiens*. As humanity recognizes it is a global community in which all are neighbors, then it has to manage global problems confronting us as a species. The feeling that humanity is everything that counts, while nature is merely material for our use, must give way to the experience of nature as informing our humanity. Our identity as terrestrians is being discovered not simply as a factual matter but as a spiritual adventure. We are opening our hearts to the subjectivity of nature.

The Tao that underlies the flow of the river is the Tao in the riverbed of my life. To become in tune with the force, flux, form of nature is to tune up our hearts. One heart in tune with nature is a heart in tune with humanity. Do you get the tune? Your love of the garden brings nature back into your life and into the life of the world. Self-Humanity-Nature; World-Earth: the creative hyphenations that seem logically impossible.

Reader: I see many people in the world awakening to the earth in the spirit of humility and responsibility, of sharing and saving, rather than the old exploitive mastery of nature. I hope it is not too late. But supposing that we do succeed as loyal stewards of the earth, yet your last volume for humanity announced destruction.

Author: Death is built into the story. No tale of humanity can be meaningful without it. In the stage of the biological struggle against nature, death usually took away the human players before they could make much meaning of life. But when humanity held off death long enough by concentrated effort, the world came into being as the value of human life.

The struggle against inhumanity to extend freedom to everyone on earth often leads to horrible death. Yet we can speak of a meaning to human life in that sacrifice, that affirmation, that advance on behalf of our humanity.

We seem to be acting in time to save the planet from depleting its oxygen and its other life-support systems. But no use our deceiving ourselves about the end of the story. The world, to speak frankly, is doomed.

Reader: Aren't you making the mistaken claim of inevitability, giving up on action to save the world because of a rigid notion that it must be destroyed? Who or what will cause this?

Author: We are the prime candidate for extinction of the human species as well as for destruction of all life on earth. The suicidal, speciescidal, biocidal weapons that may bring this about have been under development since 1945.

Reader: Are you still worried about a nuclear holocaust? Humanity has managed to deter nuclear war even though tens of thousands of such weapons were distributed. A nuclear war would be unethical, and it is outlawed. The Cold War is over. The nuclear test-ban and non-proliferation treaties are in effect among many parties. A program for dismantling nuclear weapons is in process. A World Authority may soon be designated to control such weapons and the means to manufacture them. No party would find it to its interest to initiate a nuclear war. Even if such a war broke out, defenses exist to protect some parties. No party would prolong a nuclear war to the total destruction of itself and the rest of the world. Even in a nuclear holocaust people can be counted upon to survive in clusters. And should the surface of the earth be burned away, microbes in the ocean depths would survive to get the march of evolution going again with new life.

Author: These are the thoughts by which we deceive ourselves into thinking that we are not threatening ourselves with extinction. Though the nuclear holocaust is unthinkable, we are likely to fall victim to it. If not in the next year, then perhaps in five years. If not in five years, then perhaps in 50 years. The threat lies not so much in the weapon as in the condition of the world. We are engaged in a race to fully make this a world with freedom for all before we break out again into world war with the aim of killing millions for the sake of our freedom. As long as the world is not realized as one-world, then we are threatened by world-destruction. No peace (Rus. *mir*) is whole without world (Rus. *mir*) peace. Nuclear weapons are only one means of speciescide. Other means will be available.

Reader: But that such self-destruction will occur is not necessary.

Author: To be human is to insist that it is not necessary as well as not desirable. It is to take action to save the world from self-destruction.

Reader: Then we have hope.

Author: Hope is the other name for being human.

Reader: So if we succeed in changing our world-destructive ways while we engage in world-making, then the story of humanity on earth will sign off with, 'They lived happily ever after!'

Author: Don't deceive yourself. Though we are becoming a moral community, yet we remain a mortal species. Just as the individual human life — mine as well as yours — must assuredly end, so must the life of the human species. The world, which we are in the process of saving, is on its way out. It will become out of fashion on the earth.

The world is our measure of all things. We measure the earth and the universe by the time scale of our world, but humanity is only a few moments in the whirl of Being. Our mission to humanize ourselves means humanizing the universe, putting a human face on Being. But Being soon will be done with us. To be human or not to be human? That is the question Being has been asking itself.

Nothing lives forever. We will go the way of all flesh. We brought distinction to the universe; in turn it will bring extinction to us. We created moral meaning for Being. But that means nothing to the impersonal forces of Being. We see ourselves as making all the difference in the world to the universe. But the universe remains stolidly indifferent to us.

Several endings are being drafted for the story. In the end, so far as the universe goes, it is all the same. We may destroy ourselves, fall victim to a pandemic, be extinguished in a new ice age. The earth may be hit by a comet, drawn into the sun, or torn out of orbit. The sun will explode, implode, or burn out. The probable astronomical, terrestrial, biological, and human causes are many.

Reader: But none of them is certain. Each may be countered. By the exercise of freedom we may save ourselves. Travel to other planets is within reach. Colonies in space. Unlimited nuclear energy, genetic cloning, computerized generation of raw materials, synthetic body organs, the new millennium, . . .

Author: Do not deceive yourself. The ingenuity and dedication in keeping a human presence in the universe are admirable. I am all for the effort. Our moral necessity is to continue the world in the face of its destruction. But we must also see that sooner or later we must fail. The universe is not a permanent home to our world. Our world, which makes a moral difference to Being, is alien to Being.

Reader: You condemn us to despair. No point in bothering to help one another in making this a better world if the world is doomed. All the sacrifice, all that responsibility, that hard work, on which moments ago you were insisting, now appear senseless. Each person might as well live against the world, enjoying whatever freedom is accessible, without caring a whit for the liberation of others. Your doomsday vision of world destruction itself threatens the world by depriving it of meaning and hope.

Author: On the contrary. Mortality brings with it the fullest possibility of meaning because we insist on morality. Immortality would relieve us of responsibility because everything would be taken care of. Hope may thrive only without guarantees. The world is endangered by the very denial of the threat to its existence. We must work to save what is most worthy in the universe and what cannot be permanently saved — the world. That is most worthy in ourselves, of ourselves, for ourselves. The world *is* ourselves, stronger than hyphenation, indivisibly plural. We make worth by working for the world. We are the value-givers in the universe.

What counts is the quality of our commitment and the creativity of our work, not their final result. Though in the end we are the losers in the universe, before the end we will have won our way to being who we should be. We will have made a world for ourselves in a universe that cares nothing.

Reader: Absurd, self-contradictory, pointless, unrealistic!

Author: The reality is that we are moral beings while Being itself is amoral. The point is that we take charge of the world despite the non-humanity of the universe. Self-assertion, self-confirmation, self-creation is how we answer the universe in which we find ourselves. The surd is the unanalyzable core, the irreducible identity of our heart: intersubjectivity. The world viewed from the eyes of the universe is absurd:

incomprehensible, inexplicable, inconsequential. The world viewed from the world is worth our love.

Reader: Love? For all the world, I don't see how love gets into this discussion.

Author: Why, you know that love makes the world go round. Being in love is what makes us fully human beings. Love makes us think the world of one another. Love is that fullest freedom that bonds us. Love is the consolation for mortality. Love is the world in a nutshell. When we are in love we are sitting on top of the world. Without love we would be dead to the world.

Reader: Whose love? Love of what? What kind of love?

Author: Love of life, love of others, love of the world. Love as the overflowing of one being to another. Love as finding the whole world in your arms. Love as the oneness of two beings. Love as the perfection of the human person. Love as the passionate openness to Being. It is love which affirms that human life, a life distinctively and responsibly human, is worthwhile, though we are all to die, those who love as well as those who are loved. Death may be the grim reaper, but love is the joyous sower.

One love whereof I speak is the love for a special other. So special is that other that in loving that one with all our heart we rise up beyond time, distance, and dying. Another love may extend to the whole wide-world, world-transforming love, that grasps the whole not by reason but by affection. This is the discovery of universal neighborliness. To experience these forms of love before we die is worth everything in the world. We are doomed, we are dying, by that's not the end of the world. For we are alive. Rejoice!

Reader: You are crying out with passion in what started as a philosophical chapter in a scholarly book. How in the world did I get mixed up in this?

Author: I have drawn you into the mystical, metaphysical, magical, mythical experience. I have drawn you out into the world, throwing you off balance with play upon words, shock to reason, and call to passion. Welcome to the world!

Reader: But where in the world are we?

Author: Dear neighbor, We are the world. The world is our intersubjectivity, our humanity, our mortality-and-morality, our freedom, our responsibility, our dialogue, our meaning, our hope, our heart, our home, and our love.

Reader: And where do we go from here, we who are all doomed?

Author: Everywhere in the world worth going, in these golden moments of our life.

* Robert Ginsberg is Professor of Philosophy, Penn State, Delaware County Campus.

Chapter III

Emotional Expression in an Early Medieval Manuscript: British Library, Cotton Vespasian A I

Edwin N. Gorsuch*

I

Early Anglo-Saxon illuminated manuscripts have long fascinated scholars. The Lindisfarne Gospels, for example, have intrigued students for a variety of reasons, including not only the painstaking effort undertaken by the illuminator to render the manuscript's exquisite detail, but also its complicated and balanced patterns.

On a more general level the distinguished art historian J. J. G. Alexander (1975), in an influential article, observed that: 'The earlier [insular] period from c. 650 to the later ninth century . . . saw the northern peoples in Ireland and England translating the illusionistic figural art of the classical Mediterranean world into their own language of non-figural, abstract pattern.' Alexander's article explores a point made by N. E. Barley (1974) concerning the differences of modern aesthetic taste and the Anglo-Saxon color vocabulary. Barley stresses the greater importance in Anglo-Saxon aesthetics of the light-dark continuum in color use (1974). In light of Barley's observation, Alexander shows that the insular period used color for its decorative design and illustrative pattern rather than to serve illusionistic needs. He discusses the Lindisfarne manuscript specifically and contrasts it with the later Codex Amiatinus, a work produced at nearby Wearmouth-Jarrow a few decades later. The earlier artist emphasized complex and balanced ornamental decoration; he served this end by using different colors to balance the composition rather than to achieve representational likenesses. In contrast, the later Codex Amiatinus harks back stylistically to a sixth-century Mediterranean prototype, presumably one of the numerous Latin manuscripts brought to Wearmouth-Jarrow from Rome by the monastery's founder, Benedict Biscop. This example maintains an illusionistic aesthetic sense as the artist attempted to render the book cabinet in the Ezra portrait, for instance, in representational terms. Color works to a different end where the artist, influenced by a Mediterranean and late antique aesthetic sense, attempted to create the illusion of realism in his depiction.

Alexander highlights another important point regarding the use of color in insular manuscripts. He cites the observation of Carl Nordenfalk (1957) that insular artists used multi-colored ink drawings to connect titles and initials within texts, and then points out that illuminators further illustrated the meaning of texts with artistic decoration, citing the Leofric Missal (late 9th c.) as 'probably the earliest surviving example of this technique.'

A precedent for the practice noted by Alexander may exist in certain insular manuscripts of the late seventh and early eighth centuries. The argument can be made that there correspondence exists between the emotions expressed in the handling of capital initials and the affective content of the manuscripts' written material. To be sure, this harmony of sentiment may not have resulted from the artist's deliberate and conscious intent. Rather, the consonance of meaning may follow from subconscious mental processes as the illuminator chose designs and colors to render the capitals. On the other hand, the artist possibly chose his designs and colors for the capitals consciously to complement and enhance the accompanying textual material, although I do not make this claim. If colors in fact conveyed specific meanings, then thematic linking of artistic decoration and text predates by several hundred years the tenth and eleventh century examples discussed by Alexander. These initials are not pen and ink drawings of the type noted by Alexander, and substantial differences exist between the Leofric Missal and the British Library psalter, Cotton Vespasian A I (c. 700). Still, that correspondences of meaning between artistic decoration and text manifest themselves in this latter work is significant. In any case, this paper attempts to demonstrate the more modest claim.

My analysis draws upon the foregoing observations to explore the emotional meaning of certain capital initials in Cotton Vespasian A I. The initials in question use an artistic design that appears in numerous early insular manuscripts: the 'eared cat' motif. My article in *Semiotica* (1991) identified this motif and explored the way a mid-eighth-century scribe employed it in a manuscript of Bede's *Historia Ecclesiastica* — British Library Cotton Tiberius A XIV (731b). This study will examine not only the illuminator of the psalter's use of the motif, but also the meaning implications of contiguous decorative material. I will borrow an interpretive method akin to that initially employed to interpret twentieth century art, a powerful methodology that works just as well for other eras. It seems particularly suited for achieving new perspectives on early medieval art, where abstraction and decorative color use characterize insular manuscript illumination much as they do twentieth century abstract expressionism.

In addition, this essay will analyze the emotional meaning of each of the psalms begun by one of the capital initials that is the subject of artistic analysis. I hope thereby to identify the important emotions that emerge from the psalm texts. Next the paper will assess the consistency between the emotional expression set forth in the artistic decoration and that of the psalms' texts. My final task interprets the relationships between the illumination and the textual material.

II
The Theoretical Context of the Research

The theoretical base for this investigation rests largely on the phenomenological approach taken toward criticism by the art historian Richard Moore (1968). He distinguishes at least two levels of organization that characterize a picture (or any other artistic representation, for that matter). First, the explicit level is the narrative or other pictorial content of the painting, the subject matter of the artistic creation. In the case of Tommaso Masaccio's *Tribute Money* (c.1427), to take a famous example, Jesus, after being confronted by the tax collector, tells Peter to look in the fish's mouth to find the coin that will be used to satisfy Caesar's representative. Then, in another scene on the right of the composition, St. Peter gives the coin to the tax collector. Much traditional artistic criticism focuses at this level, which is entirely appropriate. Important questions relating to theme, iconography, and symbolism can be addressed by considering the explicit content of the artistic object.

But another level of meaning exists as well: exploration of the structural relationships within the total field of the composition. This examines the way elements in a creative work relate to one another in an organizational sense. The role of hand and arm postures in *Tribute Money* illustrates this approach. Such gestures perform several important functions. First, the hand positions of the figures in the central group have a rhythm. This can be seen in both the right and left hand postures of the tribute collector, as well as in the right hand-pointing gestures of Jesus and St. Peter. The left hand of Peter also performs a rhythmic compositional function, while the tax collector's right hand connects the figure furthest to the viewer's right within this central group. His left hand, similarly, points to link him to the Christ in the center of the composition as it focuses artistic energy at that point. The right hand gestures of Jesus and Peter, however, reposition this dynamic force on the second depiction of Peter as he kneels at the seashore and takes the required coin from the fish's mouth. At the same time in this central grouping, Peter's left hand connects with Jesus's pointing hand to transmit the line's energy. The artist, however, controls this force and keeps it from overwhelming the central grouping by two other gestures: the downward thrust of Jesus's left hand and its mirror image in the extreme outside figure in the central grouping, who appears on our left. The mirroring postures not only forcefully unify the central group; they also create an implied oval when we view the human figures in the foreground against the background of the mountainous landscape.

This tentatively suggested oval form is not an accident. Whether produced consciously or unconsciously, it suits the total meaning of the composition. The oval represents the egg that symbolizes the regenerative powers of the universe, the life force inherent in the world that comes to be identified with the divine power of the spirit. Appropriately, the head of Christ should be located at or near one of the focal points of the ellipse implied by the juxtaposition of forms.

This interpretation has implications for semiotic research. Each of the configurative planes constitutes a sign system, as does the integrated compositional whole that incorporates the several meaning fields into one overarching entity. Each level can be profitably analyzed to decode its meaning. Even the creator may not have been aware that he or she placed this information in the composition. Sometimes creation is intuitive, reaching into the unconscious for its inspiration. Thus explicit conscious awareness of everything in a composition escapes the direct understanding of the creator. The entire effort, however, reveals much about the artist, the time, and his milieu. To understand this articulation on the rational and analytic level requires that these individual sign systems be analyzed to break them into their component parts. The result represents an enhanced appreciation of the artist's creativity on both conscious and unconscious levels. This, then, represents the system of interpretation used to analyze several of the capitals that appear in British Library, Cotton Vespasian A I, an Anglo-Saxon psalter dating from about 700 A.D.

III
The 'Eared Cat' Motif

Before proceeding further, the component parts of the classic 'eared cat' motif should be described. The decoration generally requires a letter such as V, I, H, J, and U suited to the use of one or more dominant vertical strokes. Employing a vertical with a body capable of carrying a defining outline, the artist typically distorts the stroke's top corners to suggest 'cat ears' together with the outline of a face, and manipulates the bottom corners to hint at a tail or possibly feet. At top center, just below the 'cat ear' extensions, the artist often places a circle containing a center dot. This, in conjunction with the 'cat ears' and an attendant concave indentation across the top of the letter, produces the effect of a cat face, with a little imagination. Black is the most usual color employed in both the body and outline of the initial. Sometimes no distinction exists between the periphery and the body of the form, and the same color carries over and tints both areas. In the case of the circle at top center, variations prevail: some might be colored red or yellow and have a black dot or no dot at all, while other examples might be left in the natural vellum. When executed in its most dramatic fashion, the form gives the effect of a cat, perhaps on its hind legs, confronting the viewer in a rather menacing way. This, then, represents a classic handling of a decoration that can reasonably be described as the 'eared cat' motif.

Figure 1

British Library, Ms. Cotton Vespasian A I
folio 91n

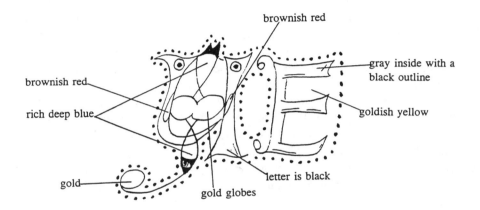

Sketch by Edwin N. Gorsuch with the
assistance of Thomas R. Shields

Figure 2

British Library Ms. Cotton Vespasian A I
fol. III V.

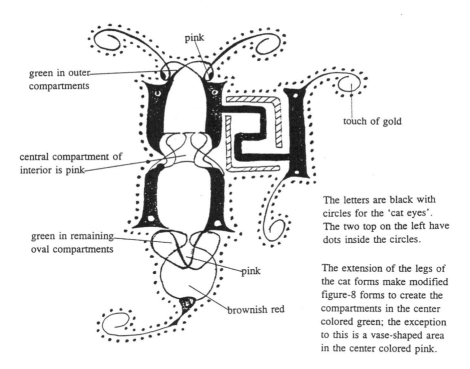

pink

green in outer
compartments

touch of gold

central compartment of
interior is pink

green in remaining
oval compartments

pink

brownish red

The letters are black with
circles for the 'cat eyes'.
The two top on the left have
dots inside the circles.

The extension of the legs of
the cat forms make modified
figure-8 forms to create the
compartments in the center
colored green; the exception
to this is a vase-shaped area
in the center colored pink.

Sketch by Edwin N. Gorsuch with the
assistance of Thomas R. Shields

Figure 3

British Library Ms. Cotton Vespasian A I
fol. 134.V.

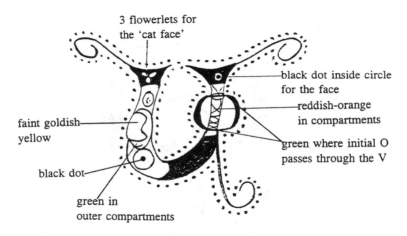

First letters of 'voce'

3 flowerlets for
the 'cat face'

black dot inside circle
for the face

reddish-orange
in compartments

faint goldish
yellow

green where initial O
passes through the V

black dot

green in
outer compartments

Sketch by Edwin N. Gorsuch with the
assistance of Thomas R. Shields

IV
Selected Capitals from British Library,
Cotton Vespasian A I:
Descriptions of fol. 91 r., fol. 111 v., and fol. 134 v.

The joined letters 'V and E' that open the psalm beginning *Venite exultemus domino salutari nostro* (Come let us exult in the Lord of our salvation), Psalm 94(95), provide an excellent example of the 'eared cat' motif in which the artist combines several characteristic elements of a revealing artistic vocabulary (see Figure 1). In this instance the two verticals of the letter 'U' provide individual vehicles for carrying the cat shape; the ears and cat visage appear on both of the vertical lines, which the artist characteristically rendered in black ink. In the space between the two ascenders, two circles intersect on a horizontal to create what can be seen as one of the arms of a cross. In the vertical direction, completing the cross, two ovals suggest fish images. And a third, although covered by the intersecting gold circles, links up with the ones at the top and bottom. On the ends of the respective figures that are closest to the horizontally placed goldish-yellow circles, the curved lines tracing the oval extend slightly beyond their point of intersection to give the suggestion of fish tails; continuing, they lead into the obscured oval design. To the extent that this oval is visible, it reveals the same pinkish-red color as that of the encircling dots. This reddish-pink also appears on the right and left borders of the gold circles where it obscures or encroaches upon the black outline of the 'eared cat's' middle. At the top of the upper fish abstraction the lines do not completely close to give the further intimation of a piscine mouth. These two tips have a black color and link up with the inner two 'cat's ears' through a slight extension of line that also serves to create the stylized hint of fish gills. As alluded to earlier, the horizontal arm of the cross, generated by the intersecting circles, carries a goldish-yellow color. The oval fish forms providing the vertical element have a rich deep blue color. Interestingly, at the bottom of the lower oval, the circle of the 'cat's face' appears and the shape finds its completion in a tail that curves down and to the left and up again to create a gold-colored circle. The letter 'E' seems an afterthought with the outline of the letter in black to provide borders for an interior gray line that carries through both the vertical arm and the three horizontals. Between the horizontals the artist repeats the goldish-yellow to complete the basic rectangular design of the letter in three colors. Finally, a series of reddish-pink dots surrounds the whole decoration. Two short tails reach back from the upper and lower horizontals of the 'E,' extending leftward to form two small circles to suggest closure between the 'V' and the 'E.'

The combined letters 'IN,' introducing the psalm beginning *In exitu Israel ex Aegypto domus Jacob domine populo barbaro facta est* (When Israel went out of Egypt, the house of Jacob from a people of strange language), Psalm 113(114), provide a good example of the 'eared cat' motif (see Figure 2). No less than six 'eared cat' heads appear at the top and bottom of the initials' verticals. The top and bottom of the two left strokes are black with the center being broken up into a complicated figure-eight design in which the tails of the cat forms extend to provide the boundaries for an area colored in green and pink. The pink appears in an interior vase-shaped space while the right and left compartments of this section breaking the verticals receive the green color.

Above, the faces' interior 'ears' provide a staging point for interlacing curves that, at the top, circle twice and culminate in two globes hovering over the 'eared cat' ornaments to the right and the left. At the bottom, the staging results in the repetition of the figure-eight patterns that, in turn, lead into an oval. Next, that oval culminates in a small circle reminiscent of the cat visage, and finally ends with a tail circling off to the left at the top. The cat faces are formed either by small circles surrounded by the black of the letter or, as in the case of the two on the left at the top, by the addition of black dots within the circles. The oval at the bottom is brownish-red while the continuation of the figure-eight just above it repeats the use of the green and pink colors as seen above. On the 'N' side of the composition, three horizontal and two vertical lines work their way to the third 'eared cat' vertical furthest to the right. The form taken by this connection is almost imagelike, especially since these lines are balanced off by rich blue lines that would form a rectangle but for the breaks for the connections of the black lines at upper left and bottom right with the 'eared cat' verticals. The 'eared cat' at the right likewise has tails going off of the upper right and lower left 'cat ears' to culminate once again in circles. Finally, pinkish-red dots surround the entire composition.

The letters 'VO,' the initial letters of *voce* in the psalm beginning *Voce mea ad dominum clamavi voce me ad dominum depreaecatus sum* (I cried unto the Lord with my voice; with my voice unto the Lord did I make my supplication), Psalm 141(142), also provide an illustration of the 'eared cat' motif (see Figure 3). The motif appears at the top of the two verticals with curved antennae arching to the left and right of the outer 'cat ears' to culminate in circles to the upper left and right of the initial. The cat visages each receive distinctive treatment with the face on the left being composed of three floret petals, two of them angling to the upper left and right, while the third proceeds downward, all working together, to suggest a face. For the 'eared cat' face at the top of the right vertical, a black dot inside a circle formed by the black of the initial accomplishes the same task in a more familiar fashion. Beneath the floret visage on the left, two small circles enclosing black dots frame two outer green compartments that surround, on the inside of the vertical, a gold center. From the bottom circle containing the black dot, the black of the initialing continues around to the right and up the right vertical to the point where it intersects the 'O,' which straddles the right vertical from just below the 'eared cat' at the top. At the points of the intersection the artist uses the color green where the line of the 'O' passes through the right vertical as a framing device. Between the two points where the intersections take place, reddish-orange is used in compartments framed by black lines. At the bottom of the right vertical a tail proceeds downward to circle up to the right. Finally, pinkish-red dots surround the composition in a familiar manner.

V
Emotional Expression in the Psalm Texts

Psalm 94(95) articulates emotions that derive from expression of love for God, together with fear of the consequences of failing to obey Him. The psalmist begins by calling his listeners to rejoice in the Lord who provides salvation by coming into his presence, praising Him, and offering Him songs. The next stanzas emphasize the greatness and power of the creator God who, having formed the physical world, stands above all other gods. People should kneel before this creator God, and the writer likens His followers to sheep watched over and protected by the shepherd. The last verses of the psalm warn that failure to listen to the divine voice leads to the same punishment borne by an earlier generation that wandered in the wilderness for forty years after it had turned away from godly ways.

The psalmist conveys positive emotions in this poetry through use of such words as exult, acclaim, salvation, praise, and songs, and negative or opposite ones through reference to hardened hearts, temptation, testing, weariness, swearing, and wrath. First, the type of love that involves dependence of the less powerful on a protector emerges from terms such as exult, acclaim, and salvation. Followers exult in the Lord and thereby are conjoined with the divine. The Latin word *exsulto* carries the meaning of leaping up for joy. The individual undergoes transformation by the movement involved in joyful expression. Similarly, *acclamo* means crying out in approval. Here too, raising one's voice in approbation connects the individual with God, the object of this expression. Meanings for *laus* include not only praise, but also glory, fame, and commendation. Thus transforming physical and vocal actions not only commend the creator God, but also celebrate His glory and fame through these actions of praise.

It should be emphasized that the offering of psalms or songs involves more than ecstatic expression. Rather, it requires the discipline needed to perform a song from beginning to end. Discipline is consistent with another emotional orientation expressed by the psalmist: the importance of listening to and obeying the divine word. Acting in this way requires discipline, which represents a quality suggested by singing melodies of divine praise. Singing a song requires discipline both to articulate the appropriately pitched sound and to place that sound suitably in time. There is an analogy suggested here with the discipline involved in obeying the divine will. Not only are appropriate vocal actions required for carrying out God's wishes, but these must also be appropriately placed in a time frame. The intoning of divine praises, mentioned in the first part of the psalm, therefore, reinforces the warning set forth in the last stanzas.

The emotional message that comes through here involves, first, the fear of divine wrath that should motivate followers of the Lord. When disobeyed, God becomes wrathful, He acts on this anger, and this potential produces the emotion of fear on the part of His followers. Just as this psalm conveys the primary emotion of fear, it also suggests the subordinate affective orientation towards the development of an appropriate discipline so that a person can obey the divine will. Fear and an orientation to valuing discipline as a positive way to relieve it represent the two emotional orientations that emerge from the warning element in the psalmist's work.

On the other hand, the psalmist also emphasizes a positive emotional orientation through the word salvation, which defines love between unequals; it is that of the weak for the omnipotent, of the dependent on the all-competent. This affect involves the actions of exultation and praise that transform and connect the believer with the divine; this sentiment is not altruistic since each party has certain expectations of the other. The divine party expects, indeed demands, the most exacting obedience; the subordinate, on the other hand, looks to benefit from the supernal power. The believer expects this power to be tangibly shown in this world as he thinks the Lord's salvation includes an earthly component. This expectation is suggested by the reference to the people in the wilderness who, even though they had seen godly works, had turned away from them and were separated from the Lord for forty years. Both the temporal allusion and mention of godly works indicate that God provides earthly benefits for those who know and follow His ways. The love that person and God each extend to the other, therefore, has a conditional quality that depends on actions they carry out in the world.

The conditional nature of the love that the psalm expresses acquires further definition through the poet's language. The people in the wilderness hardened their hearts and both tempted and tested God even though they had seen His works. The actions implied by the phrase hardening of hearts suggest a breaking of the connection between God and humans that had existed when they exulted in and praised the Lord. As it broke, the people tempted and tested the Lord by ceasing their songs of rejoicing for the creator God who controls all of the world. Lack of attention to God represents the hardening of hearts, and that which first tempted and tested the Lord, then made Him weary, and finally provoked His wrathful vengeance. This sequence of emotions defines both the nature of the psalmist's God and the nature of the divine love. This God has a mercurial temperament; He can be pushed only so far.

Psalm 113(114) likewise expresses the contrasting emotions of love for the Lord and fear of His power, together with a hatred of evil. The love expressed here, however, has its own unique emphases that contrast with Psalm 94. The psalmist first expresses love by stressing the human initiative taken by the nation of Israel in going out from the barbarous evil of Egypt to enter the sanctuary of Judah.

The people of Jacob expressed their love of God by leaving behind the iniquity of the heathen Egypt. God thereby not only rewarded their faithfulness, but the Exodus also strengthened the bond between the Lord and His people. The Lord confirmed their faith not only by causing the sea to part and the Jordan to reverse its course, but He also made pools of water and fountains appear from the rock and from the stony hill. The poet goes on to speak of mountains and hills that skipped like rams and lambs as a result of the divine will. But this Lord should also be feared. The psalmist warns that all should tremble in the presence of such a power. The first stanzas of the psalm emphasize, however, the love between this powerful God and his people. The Lord recognized their initial act of love for Him in leaving the barbarous land of Egypt, and responded by using His awesome power to protect them in their flight and subsequent wandering. God's bestowal of these blessings, in turn, led His people to thank Him for His glory, mercy, and faithfulness. God was worthy of love and of increased fame because of His trustworthiness. This faithfulness involved having mercy on His people when they required assistance. His tenderness of heart allowed the exercise of His power out of pity for their condition.

The psalmist then contrasts the heathen with the followers of the Lord while bringing out affective orientations that recognize God's glory by focusing on the dignity of His human handiwork. He marvels that the heathen should wonder where the Hebrew God was when they only needed to look around and see the wonders of His creation. The psalmist makes an interesting contrast between the heathen gods and his own. The former, crafted by men and made of metal, were dumb, motionless, blind, and lacking in feeling. But more important, perhaps, the adherents of those gods exhibited similar characteristics of insensitivity. The psalmist speaks, here, on a spiritual level as he points up the special gifts provided by the Lord to His people. The Hebrew God had created His followers to trust Him, and to know they could communicate with this unseen but all-encompassing power. This ability to relate to their Lord carried over into their daily earthly lives, where they then applied trust and empathy in interactions with other believers. In a very special sense they had the ability, within their own group, to communicate because the Lord participated in this process with them. A qualitative difference existed between the interchanges of the heathen, which might even be described as the utterances of animals, and the higher exchanges of the children of Israel. They acquired a special sensitivity for speech, sight, feeling, and action. Trust in the Lord not only enabled Him to act as their helper, but also to work as their shield in adverse times. But this emotion of trust carried with it the additional affect of fear in recognition of the divine punitive power. When the Hebrews trusted in the Lord, albeit with a tinge of fearfulness in their motivation, He demonstrated His mindfulness of them by extending His blessing. In return the Lord's followers blessed Him in recognizing their good fortune in having such guidance and protection.

The rest of the poem brings out other affective dimensions and amplifies some already expressed. First, there is the social or community nature of the trust in the Lord. Not only one individual or the psalmist himself worships, but rather the entire House of Israel. While the Lord speaks directly to an isolated individual, he also reveals His will through aiding the community as it pursues its collective activities. Furthermore, God makes no distinction on the basis of earthly position, status, or rank. All are equal in the Lord's eyes whether they are great or small in those of the world. All that matters is that their fear of the divine power leads them to act in ways that will ensure extension of the Lord's blessing. The poet reiterates, here, the motivating emotion of fear as the most important position in the affective dynamics governing the human relationship with the divine power.

Another affective orientation related to the community emphasis present in this psalm is the affirmation of procreation and, by implication, sexuality and family life. The blessing of the Lord would permit the house of Israel to multiply both in this and in succeeding generations. The conditions of life in the ancient world created substantial pressures for reproduction since disease, death in child birth, infant mortality, and warfare constantly threatened to decimate the community. Thus physical regeneration of the group loomed as a matter of great concern and brought with it an affirmation of sexuality and family life in the context of the era's pastoral tribal culture.

Worthy of emphasis too in this part of the poem is the psalmist's division of God's creation into Heaven, which belongs to the Lord, and earth, which He gave to human beings. The psalm affirms earthly life, which humans should engage, embrace, and pursue with vigor. God provided the earth to be used by humans so long as they trusted in Him to provide His blessing.

Finally, the psalmist concludes with a statement that can be understood on several levels. He contrasts the dead who cannot praise the Lord with the houses of Israel and Aaron who bless the Lord forevermore. In a literal sense this means that the earth is for the quick, and living in its fullest sense involves praising the divine power. The heathen dead enter the underworld and have foregone, for eternity, the capacity to praise the Lord. In another sense, though, the terms 'dead' and 'underworld' refer to followers of other gods living in this world. They lack the connection with the vitalizing higher power of the divine. Those who trust in God, however, possess the link that enables them to communicate in a transformed way both with the Lord and their fellows who are the children of Israel. In contrast with the walking dead, they live, move, and exist in a transformed and transcendent milieu, in the shimmering and translucent realm illuminated by divine power. Their trust in God connects them to an energizing electric force that vitalizes all aspects of their being. The walking corpses are the spiritually inert who seem to be wooden caricatures of God's children. The energizing sap of life no longer feeds such people. Like the metal gods they craft with their own hands, they may shine on the outside as do gold and silver, but they lack any vitalizing force beneath the shimmering surface sheen. Those who trust in God, in contrast, bless the Lord both in this world and in eternity. They may die, but they never enter the gloomy underworld. The Lord, their helper and shield, enables them to transcend the mortal life.

To summarize, this poem sets forth emotions explaining how their trust in God allowed a community to escape from an evil environment. This reliance derived in part from a respect for an awesome divine power that not only controlled the earth and the heavens, but also inspired a healthy measure of fear. This faith in the Lord came back to those who praised and rejoiced in the divine power in the form of aid and protection in times of danger. Contempt for the gods of the heathen represents the polar emotion to this confidence in the unseen God. The images of gold and silver, gleam and shimmer though they might, lack the energizing power of the one true God.

Psalm 141(142) likewise expresses profound emotional sentiments that reflect not only the psalmist's sense of self, but also a relationship with the divinity and other human beings. The torment in the author's life appears at once. He feels a profound agony and isolation in this dangerous period. He finds himself overwhelmed by the treachery of his foes and unconcern of his fellow humans. He clings to the tenuous thread of flickering hope for refuge in the Lord. Words such as distress, anxiety, misery, and imprisonment define the emotional state perceived by this forlorn man. He expresses his distress openly before the Lord from whom he now feels a profoundly troubling sense of separation. In the past, the Lord had provided him with strength in times of need. Now, however, things seem overwhelmingly different as he faces his threatening enemies totally alone. Even his God, who had aided him in the past, seems so remote as to stimulate the fear that He, too, has abandoned him.

Distress in this dangerous situation gives rise to the fear-based anxiety that paralyzes the poet from any action save calling out in a loud voice to the Lord. Given the danger at hand — if in fact David composed the psalm while hiding from enemies bent on his death — the fear giving rise to anxiety is a realistic emotional response. Fear often expresses itself in anxiety, and the poet at this time could only cry out to the Lord for assistance. He could not yet mobilize his own internal resources; before he could do this he not only needed the Lord to provide him with the energizing force to rouse him from his hopeless state, but also help from elsewhere to fight his enemies. In his misery the psalmist could not confront his adversaries without help from beyond his meager and compromised being. His agony derived in large part from his isolation; he felt cut off not only from his God, but also from other human beings. He likened this isolation to an imprisonment where the captive finds himself cut off from outside sustenance.

Just as the poet expresses emotions involving solitude, a second striking affective orientation concerns his act of crying out to the Lord. He cries, not in the sense of whining, but rather, as the Latin version expresses it, with a great voice. He sets his anguish forthrightly before the Lord in the Latin translation, and expects that the Lord will act to rectify his concerns. The Latin manuscript text uses *deprecatus sum* (I have plead for intercession) to convey the sense of earnest prayer, approaching even an insistent and demanding entreaty when the petitioner cries out. In his state of anxiety and isolation, the Latin version allows him to muster the capacity to cry out in order to set forth his troubles. Added to the insistent tone of this petition is the highly charged emotional sense in which the term crying may be understood. The psalmist pours out his complaint in a fashion that again suggests the overwhelming nature of the emotion that affects him. He also makes use of cry when he refers to the Lord as his 'refuge' and 'portion in the land of the living.' When he pours out (*effundo*) his complaint, he addresses his isolation and anxiety by making contact with something outside of himself.

As the psalmist's concerns change by being uttered in spoken words, they take on a different and more manageable form simply because they are taken from the inside and placed on the outside. Speaking of troubles which had festered inside him and produced his torment, the psalmist speaks of how they come from a weblike, entangling darkness. They then emerge into the light where, at the very least, they may be clearly examined thanks to the Lord. After the poet finishes speaking the sequence of words that symbolically represent his complaints, he finds himself in a new place. Not only have his tangled feelings been brought to light, but the discrete element of the word facilitates the process. His overwhelming emotion is broken up and placed in a new configuration that he can better handle. By this process, the psalmist also communicates something outside of himself. He sets forth a message that he believes was heard by a higher power. His puzzlement comes from the perception that his God seems to have abandoned him in his crisis.

In the same verse where the psalmist speaks of pouring out his complaint, he also opens up his distress to divine inspection. The King James translation says that he 'shewed before him my trouble.' The Latin uses the verb *pando*, which has the figurative meaning of 'opening up' or 'throwing open' its object. This is reasonably close to the sense conveyed by the King James's use of 'shewed' as the verb. Interestingly, however, the Latin *pando* carries the primary meaning of 'stretching out or extending,' which has special significance in this context. Similarly, the Latin term translated in the King James version as 'trouble' is *angustia*, which may mean not only difficulty and distress, but also — when speaking of circumstances — a 'straightened condition' or 'poverty.' Again, however, the primary meaning provides us with an interesting perspective that indicates a secondary one. In its primary sense *angustia* means 'narrowness.' *Pando* coupled with *angustia* suggests that the poet stretched out himself to open up the narrowness of his impoverished and distressed condition to the Lord.

In this psalm, the author acted beyond simply raising his voice to articulate his distress. The sense of extending and stretching out is of utmost importance since it begins his entering into transcendence. He was not in a closed condition when he raised his cry, but rather beginning to extend and open up himself to the outside power. Exposure of distress to the Lord will start to dissolve the discomfort and overcome the perceived narrowness by breaking down boundaries between God and man. However, we may interpret this dynamic in another way. By opening and extending himself the psalmist exposed his distress and entered into a state whereby the narrowness could give way to contact, participation, and an empowerment. In the psalm the poet feels an affinity with the Lord, he cries out to the Lord, and he extends and opens up his distress to the divine entity in the hope that God might strengthen him to deal with his highly potent enemies. That energy would flow from the Lord to the petitioner was the hope, although there does not appear to be a potential flow of power in the opposite direction.

The psalmist does not, apparently, see his love of the Lord as an action that awakens the divine power. He conceives of a division between God and human, the closure of which depends solely upon the divine will. Emphasis rests strongly on a godly grace that is all powerful and all determining. The omnipotent and omniscient Lord commands the capability to end the poet's distress, He can rescue him from isolation, and He can overwhelm his enemies who have such daunting strength. Little in this poem shows that the psalmist's love of the Lord goes beyond dependence on divine power. Such love lacks adult mutuality and partakes more of a child-adult emotional dynamic. The energizing power flows in only one direction — from the Lord to the human.

In another verse where the poet uses the word cries, he labels the Lord both as his 'refuge' and as his 'portion in the land of the living.' Here too he conveys interesting emotional viewpoints. We may again achieve additional insight through the Latin. Crucial is the notion of flight conveyed by *refugium*, which derives from the verb *refugio* and has 'to take flight' as one of its meanings. Flight implies at least two places, one of danger, the other of security. The Lord represents, then, the place where the poet flees to escape his peril. Existing with the Lord, in other words, is not perpetual for the poet; rather, it occurs when he feels secure. On other occasions he lives in a state of danger and attempts to alleviate it by flying to the Lord to secure his refuge. That a condition of apartness and danger contrasts with one of closeness and safety is suggested by the phrase 'refuge in the Lord.' The peril is so compelling that only flight will lead to sanctuary.

To summarize the emotions conveyed in this psalm. They are complex and speak to the human condition because of the somewhat exaggerated nature, bordering on dysfunction, of the psalmist's emotions. These emotions are then highlighted to express our own experience. In his crisis the author feels an emotion of agonizing abandonment that he expresses by crying or shouting out as he stretches himself to the divine power. The affect of forlornness follows in part from the way the poet defines both his own and the divine identity. A gulf separates him from the Lord, and only the latter can breach this division. This estrangement leads, then, to the expression of an emotion that borders on anger. It becomes evident in the act of shouting out and imploring the Lord to rescue him from his distress. The psalmist fails to understand why the Lord will not respond. That the poet's emotion comes close to anger, but must be distinguished from that affect, requires emphasis. The energy of anger is present, but it is frustrated. The Lord has rescued the psalmist before, his hope for assistance endures, and his dependence remains so complete that he cannot afford to allow real anger to surface. Simultaneous with the affect of abandonment, hope appears and works to contain the anger.

Just as the boundaries used by the poet to define both his own and the divine identities have implications for the affects of abandonment and hope, so also do they affect his conception of love. Both his own love for the Lord and the latter's love for him obtain their meanings, in part, from these limits. The psalmist's love for the Lord is fundamental, but inconsistent. Focus on worldly matters crowds out attention to the divine will on occasion and according to a predictable cycle. When the poet finds himself in difficulty he gives his attention to the divine, expresses his allegiance, and calls for assistance. This is the love of the wayward and dependent child who, when faced with the frightening and dangerous, runs back to the protection of the all-powerful parent. Similarly, the love of the Lord is conditional for a poet who must act in prescribed ways to receive it. Not to comply with those strictures brings a fate worse than abandonment and isolation; it brings destruction and annihilation.

VI
Problems of Interpretation

Thus far we have reviewed the theoretical context of this research as derived from an approach to the interpretation of twentieth century art. We also have described the capital initials beginning three psalms in British Library, Cotton Vespasian A I. In addition, we have examined the emotional content of the three relevant psalms using textual analysis. Before analyzing the emotional values that these initials may convey, prudence requires attention to three problems: (1) the stylistic context within which the capitals fit; (2) the ability of color to express emotion; and (3) certain symbolic equations important in the interpretation of this material.

To answer the first of these questions, a stylistic context fits the decoration of these capitals. A cursory glance at J. J. G. Alexander's *Insular Manuscripts* (1978) shows numerous examples of variants of the 'eared cat' motif. Beginning with the early seventh century it appears as part of the letter D in a Dublin, Royal Irish Academy, Psalter f. 12 (c. 625) (mistakenly identified as the verso in Alexander 1978: ill. 2), and at the top of the upright of the letter Q in the Trier Domschatz Cod. 61, f. 126 v. (c. 740) (Alexander 1978: ill. 127). In both instances, however, only the basic outline of the decoration resembles the 'eared cat' motif in Cotton Vespasian A I. More like those in the latter ms. are the examples found in Gotha, Forschungsbibl., Cod. Memb. I. 18, fs. 1, 78, and 126 (c. 750) printed in Alexander as illustrations 128, 129, and 132. This Gospel book dates from the mid-eighth century. Each of these initials' use of the motif strikingly resembles that in the British Library ms. The Gotha ms., however, incorporates additional decoration. Preliminary analysis does not show a clear and obvious connection between the motif and the written text's emotional meaning. Further study might well reveal, though, that such relationships exist in an iconographic program. To determine this program would require a minute examination of the physical manuscript. Use of the motif occurs at the beginning of the Gospels of St. Mark and St. Luke, while the illuminator employs it a third time in a preface. Another variant appears in the B initial of New York, Pierpont Morgan Lib. M 776, f. 66 (c. 750) (Alexander 1978: ill. 151). In contrast with the Gotha examples, here the top of the letter shows the general outline of the motif. It begins Psalm 118, and the manuscript itself dates from the mid-eighth century.

Finally, London, Lambeth Palace Lib., 1370, f. 2, f. 5, and f. 172 (c. 875) (Alexander 1978: ills. 321, 322, and 324) shows three illuminations using the motif. These renderings are closer in conception to those in British Library, Cotton Vespasian A I, except that the cat's face is triangular rather than round. This manuscript probably dates from the second half of the ninth century, possibly from Armagh, Ireland. Here too it may be possible to show that the motif fits into a comprehensive iconographic program in the text. What can certainly be said, however, is that the motif occurs in insular manuscript decoration not only a century before, but also contemporaneously with and more than a century after its use in British Library, Cotton Vespasian A I. Whether all these uses of the motif carry the same meaning cannot be clearly proven at this stage of the research. Finally, illuminators almost always combine the motif with at least one other stylistic element, so that study of these combinations may reveal hitherto unsuspected hidden meanings as their codes are cracked.

A second question is the ability of color to convey emotional information. A clear relationship exists between color and the communication codes of a culture. Colors serve as vocabulary elements within a language and transmit meaning and information. This includes affective data as well as other types of knowledge. Probably a substantial component of the set meanings associated with colors is cultural. But some color associations exist independently of culture and derive from the generic humanly physiological response to exposure to a particular color or color combination. Deborah T. Sharpe (1974) cites a study by R. Gerard (1957) that shows red has a more arousing physiological effect than blue. Similarly, Alexander Schauss (1979) reported that use of bright pink reduces aggression and increases relaxation. J. Gordon Nelson (1984) presented evidence confirming that seekers of high and low stimulation respectively preferred the colors red and blue. And Bernard I. Levy (1984) secured results showing a relationship between color and emotional response as subjects reacted to six colors and equated different emotional states with each. Sharpe also notes that many cultures employ black to symbolize evil, and white for goodness and purity. This is certainly true of the medieval period, as Bede's *Historia Ecclesiastica* (731a) illustrates. In Book V, Chapter 12, he offers an account of Drycthelm's vision. Reportedly, just before he was revived from death, Drycthelm passed through the dark, black, and stench-filled environs of Hell on a journey to the bright outer precincts close to Heaven where he saw happy people dressed in white robes. Bede associates black with the tortured souls and evil spirits of Hell, while he identifies white with the heavenly harmony. Bede's writing suggests we may look to the colors illuminating the contemporary medieval psalters as having important emotional meanings.

One more preliminary point requires discussion: identification of the 'eared cat' motif — and by extension — the cat itself with evil or satanic forces. There is a long tradition in English and Scottish folk belief that witches typically possessed cats as their familiars. Having entered into the service of the devil, the witch secured the services of a demon that took the form of a cat or other domestic animal. The familiar not only advised the witch by communicating the devil's wishes, but also acted as an agent in carrying out mischievous acts (Robbins 1959: 190 ff.). James Frazer (1951) offers an additional perspective concerning the relation between cats and evil. Celtic peoples held fire festivals in which animals having an association with the devil were enclosed in wicker baskets and burned in bonfires. These rituals continued into modern times, with cats frequently sacrificed in the ceremonies. Not only animals, but also humans deemed witches or warlocks were condemned to the horrible fate of being burned alive. Celtic peoples apparently believed that fire was the most powerful method available for eliminating these manifestations of evil from the world. The Celts thought they were purging evil from their midst when they burned cats in these sacrificial rites. In the cultural tradition current in the early eighth century cats, witches, and evil were all associated with one another.

VII
Emotional Expression in the Capitals: An Interpretation

Having described the initials that begin Psalms 94(95), 113(114), and 141(142) in British Library, Cotton Vespasian A I and explained the emotional content of these psalms, the next step in this discussion is to relate the two phenomena. With Psalm 94(95), several suggestive motifs are immediately apparent. These include: the 'eared cat,' the gold globe, the 'fish,' and the cross (see Figure 1). The artist uses the 'fish' and globe forms to construct the cross. In addition, several other features of the initials' decoration might yield important information upon detailed examination. The predominant emotions set forth in the psalm's text emphasize praising and exulting the Lord, on the one hand, and, on the other, fearing the consequences of failing to hear and obey the divine word by succumbing to the ways of temptation and incurring divine wrath. Reading the combination of fish forms and globes as a cross, it seems clear that here a symbol perfectly illustrates the emotional component of the text that involves exultation in and praise of the Lord as the 'rock of salvation.' First note the vertical orientation of this part of the composition. The thrust of the three 'fish' forms splits the two globes where they come together. The cross acquires a dominant upward focus; the cross as the topmost 'fish' is both larger than the lower ones, and extends above the rest of the composition including the 'eared cat' motifs to the right and left. The inclusion of the 'fish' forms emphasizes, in an Old Testament writing, the central role played by the Christ. Medieval Christians saw the Christ prefigured in references in the Old Testament to the Lord as the 'rock of our salvation.' The fish, of course, served as an ancient Christian symbol since the letters of the Greek word for fish spelled out the beginning initials of Jesus Christ, Son of God, and Savior. Use of the fish form thus underlined the meaning of the cross itself in the composition. Of further interest are the globes that the artist used to construct the horizontal of the cross. From ancient times orbs had been used as symbols to denote the domains controlled by the rulers of the world. Here their incorporation into the cross both underlines the subordination of all things to the divine power and refers to the section of the psalm praising God as the creator and master of all the world. The effect of this part of the artistic composition is to convey the same praise and exultation of the Lord as the psalm. The gold color used in the globes similarly emphasizes this praiseworthy theme.

In the space between the 'V' and the 'E' the artist produces an interesting effect through the two short tails emanating from the top and bottom of the 'E's' vertical. These, in combination with the dots that surround the perimeter of the two letters, suggest another fish form, albeit conceived in a slightly different way from the earlier described examples. These fish forms almost envelop or sandwich the 'eared cat' that constitutes the right vertical of the 'V.' The emotional message conveyed suggests that the divine power can control evil forces. Concerning the handling of the 'E' itself, the use of gray inside the black outline for the horizontals and the vertical of the letter, combined with the repetition of the goldish-yellow in the open rectangular areas, may carry symbolic meaning. Although the tips of the horizontals are somewhat attenuated and do not clearly articulate the 'eared cat' motif, still the repetition and carrying over of the black outline suggests the same emotional significance as in the evil of the 'eared cat' motif. This, however, is balanced off by the color gray used inside the outline. Perhaps more significant, the application of the goldish-yellow color in the rectangular areas between the horizontals suggests an expansive presence of the divine power. When we recall that the psalmist refers to his group as 'the people of his pasture, and the sheep of his land' the decoration takes on a suggestive meaning. The openness of the goldish-yellow rectangles suggests the vistas of the Lord's pasture lands in which the people of God dwell to their benefit. Just as the Lord maintains his dominion over the orb of the world, so also does he extend his protection to the pastures in which his people, or sheep, find themselves protected by the divine shepherd. The emotional message conveyed by this seemingly innocuous combination of forms and colors, then, taken in the context of the psalm's text, might be substantially more significant than mere beautiful ornamentation. That message may, in fact, tell the viewer that divine power manifests itself in the world, protects those living in the world who praise and exult in the Lord, and calls upon those who love the Lord to express that emotion in the joyousness of praiseful song. Although evil exists, those who exult in the Lord and praise him will have the strength to turn away from temptations that inevitably bring disaster.

To turn now to the 'eared cat' motif. It appears in this letter combination three times in somewhat different forms, first in a classic formulation, second where one of the cat ears is distorted to suggest a bird beak, and third where the artist attenuated the 'cat body' to the extent of making it pure line and provided the form with a circular tail. (Perhaps it may be stretching a point to call the 'bird beak' an example of the motif, as will become clear in a moment.) The motif shows itself in its classic form, however, in the right vertical of the 'V.' The left vertical is another matter, as it carries over into the horizontal that links up with the right vertical to complete the initial's basic outline. As indicated earlier, the artist has articulated the form's visage in such a way as to suggest a bird profile with the bird beak facing left, as much or more than the profile of an 'eared cat.' Combined with this ambiguity, the extension of the vertical into the horizontal in the form of a curve first slightly out to the left and then down and back to the right gives the impression of some sort of water fowl, perhaps even a duck.

The ambiguity of this decoration, and indeed the close artistic relationship between the two almost indistinguishable forms, provides some interesting clues concerning underlying emotional meanings. The protean character of the two forms becomes clear when we understand that alteration of several small curves produces the alternate motif. This suggests that at some level there might be a close connection as well between the two renderings. Other available evidence supports the existence of some sort of relationship. First, the 'eared cat' motif suggests the symbolism of evil, association with the devil, and a threatening sexuality. Evidence for these associations includes, as we have seen, the widespread belief among Celtic peoples that cats served as witches' familiars. While these obviously pagan celebrations were perhaps not countenanced by Christian leaders, still the association between cats and evil doubtless persisted. It is well to remember that this part of the world maintained vigorous pagan traditions at this time, which required continued Christian missionary activities in northern Europe well into the medieval period. But the illuminators producing these works may not have consciously thought they were creating 'eared cats.' On a conscious level perhaps they simply thought they were producing decoration; the unconscious produced motifs carrying dense concatenations of submerged and inaccessible meaning. Drawing inspiration, then, from the ambient environment, the illuminator perhaps found this symbolism at an unconscious level and gave it the form we observe today in the manuscripts. Whether consciously devised or produced by a submerged understanding, the 'eared cat' motif for this and other compelling reasons may be said to convey a fear of evil as its emotional message. The evil symbolized in the motif acquires its definition in relation to the mischief and licentious sexuality associated with witches, their familiars, and finally the devil.

The 'sitting duck' image relates to the 'eared cat' motif in its symbolism and emotional meaning analogously to their physical resemblance. First, the 'duck' occupies, in the decorated initial, a position analogous or parallel to the one occupied by the 'eared cat' motif. Each fills the position of a vertical in the 'V,' even though the 'sitting duck' form does more and provides the horizontal as well. Each form, moreover, consists of an abstract head containing a circle with a dot in its center. The artist formed the differences in the heads, as already noted, by small changes in line strokes after having created the initial suggestion of head shapes by distorting the line of the top portion of the verticals. In addition, each of the 'bodies' of the forms is elongated in some ways reminiscent of a snake, at least in the case of the 'sitting duck' and other examples of the 'eared cat.' This includes the 'eared cat' at the bottom of the cross form in this ensemble that has a curved body, attenuated completely to the limiting extreme of line, culminating in the circular tail. The curved elongated body is the element shared by the three forms, and deserves special note because of its primordial significance as a root symbol. At its most basic level the form suggests male sexuality in reference to the fundamental shape of the male penis. The form appears again, very clearly, in the serpent of the Old Testament Adam and Eve story. The narrative equates the serpent with evil and the 'tree of knowledge' carries with it an implication of guilt about sexuality. Adam's and Eve's need to cover their genitals with fig leaves illustrates the guilty emotion.

In the case of the decorative initials introducing Psalm 113(114) on fol. 111 v. of Cotton Vespasian A I, several suggestive motifs, it might be argued, convey emotional messages consistent with the psalm's affective import (see Figure 2). First, an extraordinary number of 'eared cats' appear in these two initials. If this motif at some level symbolizes a fear of evil, then the same type of emotion appears in the poem. The evil represented in the song emerges in the reference to the barbarous people of Egypt that the house of Jacob put behind as they escaped from that horrid land. Israel's formidable captivity and the evil endured in Egypt visually appear in the repeated use of the 'eared cat' motif.

The globe motif also conveys important emotional information. It is repeatedly employed in this composition to balance and contain the implications of evil suggested by the 'eared cat.' In three of the four instances where the globe form appears, it hovers above and outside the 'eared cat.' Further, at least one of the globes is colored with some gold, inviting the conclusion that these forms encompass and contain the evil represented by the 'eared cats.' Positioned not only above, but also to the right and the left of the upward oriented 'eared cats,' the location of the globes suggests that cosmic powers will not allow evil to rule unhindered. The curved lines that lead from the 'eared cats' to the globes seem to be a tether allowing the supreme power focused in the globes to restrain the mischievous evil forces represented by the 'eared cats.' The same sort of dynamic artistic relationship characterizes the two downward-oriented globes that likewise are part of the composition; they too play an encompassing role in the artist's design. The emotion involving faith and trust in divine power certainly appears in the psalm. The Lord facilitated the escape of the house of Jacob from the evils of Egypt by causing the sea to recede and producing other natural wonders.

The figure-eight forms that both make up the horizontal of the 'I' and proceed downward off of the inverted 'eared cat' motifs at the bottom of the letter are noteworthy, too. The tails of the 'eared cats' lead into a vortex of activity that conveys constraint. Despite the curvature of line that suggests intense movement, the tails turn in upon themselves and ultimately become knots that are blocked in their quest for release. The velocity indicated by the line's directional change seems ultimately illusory. The tails of the top and bottom 'eared cats' lead into each other through the agency of the figure-eights. The composition suggests the limited and material rather than the transcendent.

A green color interestingly appears in the framing compartments around the pink vase shape that sits in the center of the field formed by the figure-eight design. This balances the bounded quality conveyed by the pink vase. The more soothing green and pink colors seem to provide an escape from the constraint of the figure-eight's inward oriented curving direction. The pink that accentuates the vase shape seems important in that the vase receives definition from the contrast of colors. The form itself conveys meaning in that it receives, envelops, and brings to rest that which needs containment. The artist finds a repository for the swirling energy of the figure-eight motif by using color values superimposed upon the composition's linear design. A different order of reality comes into play in achieving this result while the coloric dimension must be distinguished from the linear one.

In relating this interpretation to the emotions conveyed in the psalm's text, the escape of the people of Jacob from Egypt is an important reference. They were surrounded by evil and relied on their faith and love of God to deliver them.   Similarly, the 'eared cats,' with their encompassing and bounding figure-eight tails, function as artistic representations of that fearful evil; the barbarity of the captors is contained just as the vase in the composition provides an analogous outlet for the linear energy of the design.

Beneath the downward-oriented 'eared cats' in this part of the initial another pair of figure-eights leads off of the inner 'ears' of the respective verticals. These, in turn, transmute into a fish form further down culminating in a circle with a dot inside that suggests a fish eye. The artist conveys a sense of boundedness here, too, with the qualification that the energy of the figure-eight curves finds resolution and containment more readily in the oval that constitutes their extensions. The artist uses a brownish-red color for the interior of the oval while also employing pink and green in the comparable sections of the figure-eights. Thus a pink vase form appears in the tail region of the fish-like oval. Choice of the brownish-red hue for the fish motif may suggest the blood of the Christ that provided deliverance for all believers.

This combination of forms reinforces the emotional significance of the artistic decoration. If we accept the oval as a fish representation, then the emotional meaning of the vase shape is confirmed. Here the fish motif essentially elaborates the vase. Clearly the linear energy of the figure-eights feeds into the oval and secures containment and encapsulation. The intense evil activity emanating from the cat 'ears' disperses and is absorbed in the combination of vase and fish motifs. The evil of the Egyptian captors of the people of Israel is offset and directed to where it can do no harm by the God of Jacob who turned back the sea and altered the course of the River Jordan. In the Christian era it seems entirely consistent that the divine power should be symbolized by the fish, perhaps the most widely used symbol of the Christ.

Another major element of the initial's artistic structure is the handling of the lines leading to the right side of the composition. Here a segmented black line connects the 'eared cat' verticals of the 'I' and 'N' parts of the design. Composed of five segments, it not only links the right two 'eared cat' verticals, it also accentuates their potency as a design element. The black line magnifies the effect of the individual 'eared cat' verticals, like an artery that transmits nourishment and strength from one side to the other to increase the motif's formidable evil and menacing qualities. Balancing off this impact to some degree are the four blue lines that almost surround the segmented connecting black line.

The segmented black line ties in directly with the center and right 'eared cat' verticals, interrupting the outer blue square formation in two places — at upper left where it joins the center 'eared cat' vertical and at bottom right where it connects with the right one. The blue lines of the square design enclose a field comparable to the domain encompassed by the globes in the initial accompanying Psalm 94(95). The contained space appears, however, in a more central area of the composition, and significantly, the black segmented connecting strand breaks its boundary lines. If we interpret the 'eared cats' to suggest the evil forces at work in the world, then the broken blue square stands as a defense against this danger, but a limited one since the blue square is not completely   closed. The segmented black line penetrates it at the two noted points. In relating these design elements to the psalm's text, the interpretation emerges that the forces of evil operating in the world are indeed formidable. The Egyptians who held the people of Israel in slavery are not only barbarians, but wield great power. This force, however, is partially balanced by the resources of the people of Judah. These include the initiative they take to escape and their faith in the Lord who protected them. The broken blue square symbolizes one of the elements in Israel's arsenal for counteracting the awesome strength of their barbarous and evil enemies. Fear of the Egyptian captors, hope for deliverance, and faith in the Lord as their protector come through both the text and the artistic decoration as characteristic emotions in this context.

A final element in the artistic design of these initials conveys an important emotional message: the series of pink dots that surrounds the entire composition. Although appearing frequently in the decorations of Anglo-Saxon manuscripts, it nonetheless has meaning that extends beyond the realm of artistic convention. Here it establishes a boundary containing all of the artistic expression pertaining to the initial; it sets up a defined field of activity. Significantly, the artist establishes this set of limits as a porous series of dots rather than an impenetrable solid line. The perimeter appears to establish the normal boundary between two areas, but interaction from one side to the other remains an infrequent although distinct possibility. Upon reflection, this describes exactly the relationship medievals believed existed between the intangible spiritual realm, on the one hand, and the material world, on the other. The series of encapsulating dots, then, reminds us that the spiritual and material worlds intersect; they are not completely severed realms. The fear of evil embodied in the 'eared cat' motif is not only limited by the encircling boundary, but power from outside this material realm may also dull this evil force. The design, therefore, conveys an emotion of hope that derives from faith in transcendent divine power, which can interject itself into the material world and protect the faithful.

To summarize the relationship between the emotional messages conveyed by the artistic decoration and the text of Psalm 113(114) in Cotton Vespasian A I: the repeated use of the 'eared cat' motif artistically transmits the fear of evil that appears in the poem's text in the form of the barbarous Egyptian captors of the Hebrew people. The figure-eight forms protruding from the 'eared cats' accentuate this emotion as does employment of the segmented black line that connects two of the 'eared cats' and reinforces the intensity of their impact. The menacing nature of the 'eared cats,' together with the frenetic sense of motion suggested by the figure-eights, accords well with the sense of fear and apprehension expressed by the poet as the people of Israel mustered the courage to take action and escape their captivity.

The faith in the Lord that gave the chosen people confidence likewise receives expression both in the artistic decoration and in the psalm's text. The globe forms, the encompassing boundary of pink dots, and — to a lesser extent — the blue-lined rectangle, convey that the Lord will contain the forces of evil. Further, the green and pink colors accentuate the vase shape that inheres in the figure-eights, imparting the sense that some receptacle will contain the frenetic agitation of the evil forces. Finally, the fish form in the composition suggests the deliverance and salvation that believers might expect as a result of their faith in the Christ. Faith, hope, and trust in the protective power of the unseen Lord — in contrast with the material gods of the heathen — represent the positive emotions that offset the fear of evil. Both text and art work transmit this full complement of emotions.

In the case of fol. 134 v. of Cotton Vespasian A I, which begins Psalm 141(142), the decorative initials 'VO' show a close relationship to the psalm's text given the common emotions conveyed by each (see Figure 3). First, the song's words impart a sense that the poet is in a dangerous, fearful, and isolated condition. No man would know him, and his enemies stealthily laid traps for him. He was forlorn, abandoned, and filled with such anxiety that he could only cry out his complaint to the Lord. The figure-eight interlacing in the right vertical of the 'V' and enclosed by the 'O' conveys just this emotional message. The twisting and circling back of the entwining pattern suggest the sense of entrapment, bondage, and isolation that the author expressed in his verse; the reddish-orange color accentuates this message as its harshness transmits a sense of menace. In addition, that the 'O' letter encompasses this tangled interlacing — which may indicate the psalmist's troubled condition — suggests an additional level of restriction. He feels confined not only by his excruciating emotional condition, but also by other external constraints. In contrast, however, the artist uses the color green at the two points where the circle of the 'O' intersect with the right vertical of the 'V' initial. The grating red-orange employed in the interlacing on the right 'V' vertical inside the 'O' gives way to green at the two junctures of the 'O' with the vertical. Green may suggest openings where the poet might escape from his painful and anguished state. He is severely compromised, but not completely trapped since he has the Lord as his potential refuge. Similarly, the 'eared cat' forms at the top of each of the 'V's' verticals both carry an emotional meaning suggesting fear of evil. But significantly different messages seem characteristic of these two 'eared cats' because of the contrasting way the artist handles their faces. A dot within a circle defines the face on the right, as in similar examples, and may symbolize the devil's evil. However, florets form the 'cat' visage at the top of the left vertical, connecting the motif to the world of nature. One of the words used in the Latin version of the psalm, *laqueum*, suggests that the psalmist's enemies are hunting him down as they would pursue wild quarry in nature. They lay snares for him, and he feels subjected to the unforgiving perils of the natural world. *Laqueus* has the meaning of snare, trap, or noose, and at least two of these terms point to stalking of prey.

Balancing off these emotional messages that project menace and conjure up fear are the several images conveying an emotional orientation towards faith in the protective power of the Lord. Most striking is the visage visible on the left vertical of the 'V' viewed from a 270 degree orientation. Looking at the vertical from the left side in this way, the two framing circles with center dots, combined with the green and goldish-yellow interior compartments, work together to form a visage with the goldish-yellow heart-shaped compartment indicating the face's mouth. This particular hue in the heart form, combined with the other compositional elements just noted, is important. This tint used in conjunction with this form suggests divine love, both because of the universal sovereignty symbolized by the gold color and because the heart form means love. Employment of the softer green shade in the outer framing compartments of the heart conveys divine connection with the verdant natural environment where a transcendent protectiveness operates. The color green here both balances its use on the right vertical of the 'V' and imparts a compatible symbolic message. It seems as though a divine face looks out from its perch on the vertical and surveys the surrounding scene. However, that visage both faces opposite the tangled figure-eight segment in the right vertical and projects its surveillance away from the 'eared cat' forms at the composition's top. This symbolic turning away may well connect with the emotions of abandonment, isolation, and fear expressed in the psalm's text.

Finally, encirclement of the composition with pink dots establishes a boundary not just with this one letter, but with many of these initials. The circle of dots appears, therefore, to be a convention that resonates with symbolic potential. First, it creates a border that permits influence from the outside. While defining a circumscribed universe for the artistic composition and for its emotional meaning, the convention allows transcendence of normal limits since the dots form a broken rather than a continuous line. It limns a negotiable frontier that allows for interaction between the greater universe outside and the lesser one described by the artistic notation. Ultimately, divine power can enter into and affect the events within the universe symbolized by the composition's design.

Several conclusions now seem reasonable. First, analysis of the illuminated manuscript artist's expressive vocabulary appears to be rewarding. Application of the method to the emotional content of psalms confirms and deepens understandings achieved using other interpretive procedures. More specifically, the artist shows emotions relating to the presence of evil and fear of hostile enemies by using the 'eared cat' motif, black and reddish-brown colors, a distinctive rendering of the 'cat's tail,' and the 'sitting duck' form. He also depicts emotions showing faith in religious truth, love of God, and devotion to spiritual values by employing harmonious pastel colors as well as the stylized cross, the golden globe, and fish forms. Finally, use of the color green promises that the psalmist's emotional commitment to his faith will let him escape from his confinement.

Second, the illuminator's decorative elements need to be imaginatively viewed both as a totality and in relation to one another, a method of interpretation requiring application of a certain type of imagination and mental flexibility without permitting complete license. Rather, the artist's total expressive vocabulary establishes a boundary to provide an interpretive context. Within these limits imagination may uncover what the artist may have buried and obscured. In the case of the illuminator of British Library, Cotton Vespasian A I, this vocabulary includes the relatively limited number of elements discussed in this essay, which he employs with workmanlike skill. Shapes, forms, and colors constitute the medium through which he transmits emotional messages. In their entirety, these establish the parameters within which the viewer may reasonably apprehend the images' meanings. Art conveys emotion, but to understand the nature of the emotional message requires application of relatively unfamiliar interpretive methods. When properly employed they deepen our understanding. The letters are not simply fanciful decoration; rather, they impart a significant emotional message. They symbolically encapsulate the fears and hopes of early eighth century British Christianity for those with the empathy and imagination to search for that world, if not in a grain of sand, in a small patch of illuminated vellum.

Edwin N. Gorsuch is Associate Professor of History at Georgia State University. This study was supported by the Office of the Vice-President for Research at Georgia State University.

REFERENCES

Alexander, J. J. G., *Insular Manuscripts Sixth to the Ninth Century* (London: H. Miller, 1978).

_____, 'Some aesthetic principles in the use of colour in Anglo-Saxon art,' *Anglo-Saxon England* 4 1975, 145-154.

Barley, Nigel F., 'Old English colour classification: where do matters stand?' *Anglo-Saxon England* 3 1974, 15-28.

Bede, c. 710, *De Tropis*, in *The Complete Works of Venerable Bede*, ed. J. A. Giles, vol. 6. (London: Whittaker and Co., 1843-1844).

_____, c. 715, *Commentaries on the Scriptures*, in *The Complete Works of Venerable Bede*, ed. J. A. Giles, vols. 9-11. (London: Whittaker and Co., 1843-1844).

_____, 731a, *Bede's Ecclesiastical History of the English People*, eds. B. Colgrve and R. A. B. Mynors (Oxford: Clarendon Press, 1969).

_____, 731b, British Library, Manuscript Collection, Cotton Tiberius A XIV, London c. 750.

Dublin, Royal Irish Academy, Psalter, c. 625.

Evans, Jonathan, 'Medieval studies and semiotics: Perspectives on research,' *Semiotics 1984*, ed. John Deely (Lanham, Maryland: University Press of America, 1985) 511-521.

Frazer, James G., *The Golden Bough* (New York: Macmillan, 1951).

Gerard, R., 'The differential effects of colored lights on physiological functions,' unpublished Ph.D. dissertation, University of California at Los Angeles, 1957.

Gorsuch, Edwin N., 'Emotional expression in a manuscript of Bede's *Historia Ecclesiastica*: British Library Cotton Tiberius A XIV,' *Semiotica* 83 1991 (3/4), 227-249.

Gotha, Forschungsbibl., Cod. Memb. I. 18 (c. 750).

Levy, Bernard I., 'Research into the psychological meaning of color,' *American Journal of Art Therapy* 23 1984 (2), 58-62.

London, British Library, Manuscript Collection, Cotton Vespasian A I (c. 700).

_____, Cotton Nero D IV, (c. 698).

Moore, Richard A., *The Dialectical Norm of Nineteenth and Twentieth Century Art*, (Atlanta: Georgia State College, 1968).

Nelson, J. Gordon, 'Color preference and stimulation seeking,' *Perceptual and Motor Skills* 59 1984 (3), 913-914.

New York, Pierpont Morgan Library M 776, (c. 750).

Nordenfalk, Carl, *Early Medieval Painting* (Geneva, 1957).

Robbins, Russel Hope, *The Encyclopedia of Witchcraft and Demonology* (New York: Crown, 1959).

Schauss, Alexander G., 'Tranquilizing effect of color reduces aggressive behavior and potential violence,' *Journal of Orthomolecular Psychiatry*, 8 1979 (4), 218-221.

Sharpe, Deborah T., *The Psychology of Color and Design* (Chicago: Nelson-Hall, 1974).

Todorov, Tzvetan, *Theories of the Symbol* (Ithaca, NY: Cornell University Press, 1982).

Trier, Domschatz Cod. 61, (c. 740).

Chapter IV

Worldmaking, *Habitus* and Hermeneutics: A Re-reading of Wei Yuan's (1794-1856) New Script (*chin-wen*) Classicism

On-cho Ng*

Worldmaking as we know it always starts from worlds already on hand; the making is a remaking.

Nelson Goodman, *Ways of Worldmaking*

The progress of knowledge presupposes progress in our knowledge of the conditions of knowledge. That is why it requires one to return persistently to the same objects . . . ; each doubling-back is another opportunity to objectify more completely one's objective and subjective relation to the object.

Pierre Bourdieu, *The Logic of Practice*

That Wei Yuan was an important intellectual figure in the first half of the nineteenth century needs no belaboring. Much has been written about him and the significance of his works.[1] He voiced the concerns of his time and advocated remedies to the besetting problems of a Ch'ing dynasty (1644-1911) in decline, problems such as lax central control, bureaucratic inefficiency and malfeasance, local instability, intensified Sino-Western contacts, and the related growth of the illicit opium trade. In an age of internal degeneration and external challenge, Wei purposefully shaped his intellectual endeavor so that it was devoted to envisioning and rehearsing in imagination what could and should be readily realized in action. Scholarship was never really disinterested, disengaged from the practical world. To that end, Wei compiled the famous voluminous *Collected Treatises on Statecraft in the Ch'ing Dynasty (Huang-ch'ao ching-shih wen-pien)*, which is an anthology of some two thousand essays written by Ch'ing officials and scholars on various aspects of the imperial bureaucracy and administration. The work, first published in 1827, comprises eight sections, the first two of which are respectively theoretical discussions on learning and governance. The other six sections are organized in terms of the the Six Ministries of the imperial Chinese government (Ministries of Civil Service, Finance, Rites, War, Punishments, and Public Works), with particular emphasis on fiscal issues, public works, and military affairs.   Wei's goal was to make available a definitive corpus of writings on the theory and practice of statecraft.   The central point he hammered home in the preface of this anthology was that scholarlship must have practical import.   Just as José Ortega y Gasset has said that all significant teaching was 'social pedagogy,' that culture was 'labor, the production of human things,'[2] so too Wei claimed that *wen* (scholarship) was 'rooted in ethics and consigned to statecraft,'[3] that 'those who are adept in discussing the mind must seek corroboration in events.'[4]   They both desired to see the drama of their thoughts writ large in the socio-political life of their community.

As a scholar based in the lower Yangtze area, Wei had actual experience with and wrote about a host of administrative problems.   Serving as advisor to important provincial officials, he was actively involved in plans for improving transport of grain tribute to the capital by using the sea route instead of relying on the increasingly inefficient Grand Canal.   He was also a crucial player in moves to reorgainze the salt monopoly system in the Liang-huai region, making it a more profitable generator of tax revenue. Wei also devoted considerable energy to drafting proposals for shoring up China's defences, both along the land and maritime frontiers.   Between 1829 and 1831, when Wei landed a position as a clerk in the Grand Secretariat in Peking, he had access to the imperial archives and developed a even stronger interest in military affairs and history.   He began writing the *Record of Imperial Military Exploits (Sheng-wu chi)*, which was a celebratory history of the successful campaigns of the Ch'ing period. Ironically, it was hurriedly finished when China suffered the disastrous defeat at the hands of the British in the Opium War (1839-42).   In this work, Wei, while retelling the impressive Ch'ing past military record, also pointed to the problem of military weakening in the early nineteenth century.

Perhaps Wei's best known work was his *Illustrated Gazetteer of Maritime Countries (Hai-kuo t'u-chih)* in which he strove to provide a detailed portrayal of the eastward expansion of the West and its impact on Southeast Asia, which culminated in the great disorder on the China coast. Consisting of four general parts and some fifty fascicles (later expanded to one hundred fascicles in the 1852 edition), the 1844 work studied the geography, history, recent developments, practical arts, and military technologies of the West, and suggested that China must strengthen its maritime power by borrowing the Western means of weaponery, ships, and training. Coupled with the policies of leading the South-east Asian countries to resist the West and of making the Westerners check one another, China would achieve the end of warding off further Western intrusion.[5]

Wei Yuan was also well-known as a proponent of the New Script (*chin-wen*) Classics. These Classics were so called because originally, they were written in the new script of the Western Han dynasty (202 B.C.-A.D. 9), as opposed to the old script used in the Chou dynasty (1122?-256 B.C.). These were texts reconstituted and reconstructed in the Western Han period, since many of the original classical texts were destroyed or lost in the Ch'in dynasty (221-207 B.C.) and in the Ch'in-Han transition. As the Classics were being reconstructed, primarily through the memory of the elderly scholars who had studied them in the pre-Ch'in days, a commentarial tradition also came into being. Before long, however, the Chou classical texts began to resurface, written in the old script. Hence the coexistence of the New Script and Old Script Classics. Both textually and interpretively, the two versions could vary significantly. In the Han times, controversies raged as to which corpus of Classics was authentic. The Old Script Classics would be attacked by the New Script partisans as forgeries, while the Old Script supporters would brand the New Script Classcis as flawed reproductions of faulty memories. By and large, the New Script texts held sway in the Western Han, but by the Eastern Han dynasty (A. D. 25-220), the Old Script tradition gradually became dominant. It was to remain so until the eighteenth and early nineteenth centuries, when the New Script Classics reemerged as an important subject for classical studies, thanks first to the fact that in the late seventeenth century, the Old Script *Classic of Documents* was proven to be a forgery. The Old Script-New Script controversy once again reared its polemical head.[6] With the exegetical works of Chuang Ts'un-yü (1719-1788) and then of his maternal grandson, Liu Feng-lu (1776-1829), the New Script tradition finally reestablished a distinct voice in the the Ch'ing intellectual world.[7]

Wei Yuan studied for a period of time with Liu Feng-lu and claimed him as a mentor. However, while Wei, as a classical scholar, staunchly touted the superiority of the New Script classical tradition as the true repository of the wisdom of the ancient sages, he did not embark on an essentially mimetic project of simply explicating and elaborating what his predecessors had done. Wei went beyond the tradition. He employed the major New Script notions and terminology in a highly selective and discriminating fashion, integrating them into his own grand conceptual scheme of Chinese history and culture. Wei was not a New Script epigone in the strict sense of the word. His thoughts on the Classics were unmistakably syncretic, or even idiosyncratic, although encased in them were unmistakable New Script elements.

Still, why do we need another discourse on the familiar figure of Wei Yuan? To undertake once more a study of Wei here is to use him as a narrow aperture to gain entry into the broader question of intellectual pursuit as worldmaking. Wei, always advancing and making sense of ideas by tapping them out on the pulses of socio-political realities, was in fact engaged perpetually in a reformist project to remake and reshape the world he inhabited. By investing a practical meaning in his writings and by reinventing an exegetical tradition to which he declared scholarly allegiance, Wei produced texts that beg to be read as efforts of worldmaking. As Wei strove to articulate the central problems of his time, he drew from available cultural resources and manufactured texts that were out of the ordinary but yet compelling to a wide audience. His works and thoughts also merit attention by scholars outside the the field of Chinese studies, for they provoke profound reflection as to how the world made, or in the making, is ensconced in texts, which in turn raises the issues of the production of texts and the way how these texts should be read.

In short, I propose to weave three interrelated theoretical and methodological issues into an analysis of Wei's scholarship on the New Script Confucian Classics. First, primarily in terms of Nelson Goodman's famous hypothesis on the processes of worldmaking, the processes that went into the making of Wei Yuan's world of classical truths and values are examined.[8] How did Wei come to grips with and modify the given tradition, and consequently generate a multiple understanding of the New Text? Second, with reference to Pierre Bourdieu's theory of *habitus*, the boundedness and inventiveness of Wei's intellectual activity, governed as it was by available cultural resources, is explored. In other words, given the cultural 'dispositions,' to use Bourdieu's term, of Wei's own time and space, his rendering of the New Script classical was highly sensible, a proleptic adjustment to the demands of realities.[9] Third, I ponder the inescapable question of the reading of canonical texts, the hermeneutic problem of interpreting Wei Yuan's classical writings, which were interpretations that he posed as the reality of experience and consciousness of his time. In fact, Wei's hermeneutics were part of his habitus. This essay thus has two dimensions: provincial and universal. Provincially, it addresses in detail an aspect of Wei Yuan's thought, that is, his New Script classicism which, albeit often noted, is generally given laconic treatment in the current literature. Universally, in coming to terms with some of the theories on cultural production and text-reading through Wei Yuan's work, this essay is a meditation on the writing and practice of intellectual history.

Nelson Goodman's philosophic theory of worldmaking starts with the premise that barring any theological assertion of the certitude of a universal beginning, no world is created *ex nihilo*. Any world made is perforce a world (or worlds) remade.[10] To put it another way, following Stephen Pepper, all intellectual exercises begin with a 'root metaphor' in 'an area of empirical observation' which provides the analytic order and evaluative categories for the relevant evidence at hand. The root metaphor, as the goal-seeking and goal-directing originating point, furnishes the 'purposive structure' in which meaningful hypothesis can be formulated to explicate the problems at hand.[11] Wei Yuan's world of classicism was a world remade from the Han and the Ch'ing worlds of New Script exegeses. When Chuang Shou-chia (1774-1828), Chuang Ts'un-yü's grandson, decided to publish his grandfather's collected works, he asked Wei Yuan to contribute a foreword.[12] In this short 1829 tribute to Chuang and his *oeuvre*, Wei identified and defined his root metaphor, the world already on hand, one upon which he was to build another world.

Wei began his discourse with a quote from a Western Han New Script version of the *Classic of Odes*, the *Exoteric Commentary on Han's Odes* (*Han-shih wai-chuan*):[13] 'As for the righteous loyalty between ruler and official, the closeness between father and son, and the distinction between woman and man, one daily acts on [them] without pause.' Wei then quoted from *Luxuriant Gems of the Spring and Autumn Annals* (*Ch'un-ch'iu fan-lu*) by Tung Chung-shu (179?-104?B.C.), a Western Han dynasty masterpiece of exegesis in the New Script tradition:

> What the sages intended to expound was not the ability to discuss species of animals and birds. What the sages intended to expound were humaneness and righteousness and their rationale. As they [i. e. the virtues] are thoroughly outlined and delineated, we get to their meanings so that there are no doubts and questions. . . . Meanings come from the Classics and their commentaries; the Classics and their commentaries are the profound origin.

Here, Wei sought his root metaphor in two master texts in the ancient New Script corpus, pointing to the central fact that the pursuit of the Classics ought to be essentially the quest for meanings of virtuous living. What Wei wanted to do was to rebuild a world of classical scholarship purposefully in search of the profound meanings residing in the sages' words.[14]

Wei then referred to the great Han historian, Pan Ku (A. D. 32-92), for his criticism of the degeneration of learning in the Eastern Han dynasty:

> Those who pursue broad learning fail to ponder the principle of careful hearing [of truths] and of casting out ideas that are doubtful. Instead, [they] pursue the trivial and petty principles and eschew the difficult . . . , using twenty or thirty thousand words to explain a text of five characters.

To bolster his point, Wei further cited Hsü Kan (an Eastern Han scholar):

> Therefore, a scholar should first [study] the great principles. Names and their referents (*ming-wu*) come last. . . . The petty Confucians' pursuit of broad learning focuses on names and their referents, and is detailed with regard to implements, but is wanting in the explication of ancient lessons. [They] study selectively sentences and phrases, unable to sum up their profound meaning in order to grasp the minds of the sage-kings.[15]

Wei's reference to the degeneration of classical study in the Eastern Han was in fact a denouncement of his contemporaries' equally otiose scholastic pursuit of the Classics that only served to confuse, obfuscate, and trivialize the deep meanings of the ancient words. Indeed, from the eighteenth century onward, philological and textual studies of the ancient Classics, generally known as *k'ao-cheng hsueh* or *k'ao-chü hsueh* (literally, scholarship of investigation and verification), or sometimes known as *Han-hsueh* (literally, Han learning, i. e., scholarship that harked back to the Han dynasty's preoccupation with the Classics), became the dominant mode of learning. The initial salutary goal of these studies had been to retrieve the undistorted and untainted messages of the ancient sages by redeciphering and reestablishing the meanings of the Classics through rigorous philological investigations. But in time, such scholarship regressed into a kind of finicky textualism, preoccupied with words in and of themselves. As the original interpretive hermeneutic impulses receded into the background, classical commentaries became encyclopedias or dictionaries.[16]

Then fortunately came Chuang Ts'un-yü, whose profound learning, according to Wei Yuan, illustrated 'the mutually complementary relation between heaven and humanity,' 'expounded on morals and virtues' and 'discussed comprehensively the past and present,' 'never undertaking trivial and hairsplitting scholarship.' Chuang, therefore, could truly escape the strictures voiced by Han dynasty scholars such as Master Han, Tung Chung-shu, Pan Ku, and Hsü Kan. Regrettably, as Wei took pains to point out, Chuang was seldom appreciated by his contemporaries. Even though he was a genuine Han-learning scholar who recaptured the original Han spirit of classical studies, he was neglected by his colleagues of the *k'ao-cheng* persuasion in his time.[17]

To sum up, in the 1829 foreword dedicated to Chuang Ts'un-yü, the acknowledged progenitor of New Script classical learning in the Ch'ing dynasty, Wei Yuan's hammered home a three-fold message: first, the Western Han classical study of the New Script tradition was superior to its successor in the Eastern Han period when the Old Script school predominated; second, classical study in his own time failed exactly because of its similarity to the Eastern Han approach, philosophically sterile, strategically onerous, and practically feckless; third, Chuang's New Script learning recaptured the spirit of the Western Han classicism, probing the Way and the profound meanings of the Classics. Repudiating the dominant world of *k'ao-cheng*, Wei embraced the world of New Script hermeneutic tradition, a world he was to remake into his philosophic universe.

After Liu's death in 1829, Wei helped edit and collate Liu Feng-lu's collected work and wrote the preface in 1830, in which he once again promoted the New Script exegetical tradition.[18] In particular, Wei saluted the long-acknowledged *raison d'être* of this tradition, namely, the revealing of 'profound principles [concealed] in subtle language' (*wei-yen ta-i*). It was their greatest accomplishment that the Western Han New Script classical masters inherited the great principles embodied in cryptic language transmitted by the seventy disciples of Confucius. Using *wei-yen ta-i* as the purposive guide, the masters dealt not only in words, facts, and events, but more importantly in their meanings and realization in the practical world. Wei listed the various New Script schools and masters of some of the Classics. He pinpointed their respective merits. The masters of the *Classic of the Changes* 'observed the changes in the cosmic signs and emblems and thus knew the future.' Those of the *Classic of Documents* were able 'to save and aid the rulers by referring to the 'Great Plan' [the chapter on governance].' Those of the *Classic of Odes* 'treated the three hundred and five odes as remonstrances.' Those who studied the *Spring and Autumn*

Annals could employ that work 'to decide court cases.' Those of the *Classic of Rites* 'deliberated on institutions.' Others referred to the *Analects* and the *Classic of Filial Piety* 'to safeguard the teachings and abet the Way.' In all, the New Script masters of the different Classics were able 'to describe the systematic workings of yin and yang, employ the teachings of the sages, and circumscribe the boundary of the Royal Perfection (*huang-chi*) [i.e., ultimate rulership].' Their scholarship was 'distinguished, resembling the mode of learning in the Three Dynasties [i.e., Hsia (2205?-1766 B.C., Shang (1766?-1122? B.C.) and Chou (1122?-771 B.C.].' But such practices and approaches that apprehended the deep meaning of the sages' words had disappeared in the Eastern Han dynasty as the Old Script tradition came to hold sway.[19] No doubt, Wei Yuan's identification with the New Script tradition stemmed from its quest for meaning which in turn legitimated and explained human actions. He would have heartily agreed with Coleridge who once said, 'What a mean thing a mere fact is if it is not related to a comprehensive truth.' In other words, in the process of 'weighting' or finding 'emphasis,' a crucial step in worldmaking according to Nelson Goodman,[20] Wei Yuan settled upon the New Script commentarial goal of revealing great principles in arcane classical language.

In paying homage to the works of his mentor Liu Feng-lu, Wei called for the revival of New Script learning. He did so first by surveying the changing modes of classical exegesis in the past. He began by lamenting that fellow-scholars of his time almost invariably regarded the Eastern Han Old Script learning as superior to Western Han learning, not realizing that putative Old Script masters like Hsü Shen (A.D. 98-147) and Cheng Hsuan (A.D. 127-200) actually incorporated much of New Script scholarship in their commentaries. As Cheng Hsuan's Old Script commentaries prospered and became the officially endorsed texts of the Eastern Han period, the New Script schools and traditions lost their independence and distinctivenes. In time, they were either lost or eclipsed. In Wei's view, it was high time that New Script learning be brought back as it was the means whereby the sages' Way could be retrieved. He explained:

> The learning of the profound principles revealed in subtle language of the Western Han crumbled in the Eastern Han. The learning of laws, regulations and institutions of the Eastern Han died out in the Sui (581-618) and T'ang (618-907). The learning of philology and phonology of the Two Han dynasties was extinguished in the Wei (220-266) and Chin (266-316). Did not their ways rise and fall in succession? Moreover, simplicity and refinement invariably

alternate and appear in the world. The way of heaven is such that three insignificant [successions] make one pronounced [system]. The main point about today's effort to revive antiquity is to progress from philology and phonology to the laws, regulations, and institutions of the Eastern Han. This is like the way in which the state of Ch'i gave way to the state of Lu.[21] From the laws, regulations and institutions, [we] went further backwards to the profound principles revealed in subtle language of the Western Han, which linked classical scholarship, matters of administration, and literature as one. This is like the manner in which the state of Lu proceeded to the Way.[22]

Here, Wei, in charting the changes in classical studies throughout the ages and in calling for a return to the good old days of antiquity, referred to two principal notions in the New Script exegetical tradition, namely, the notion of alternation between 'simplicity (*chih*)' and 'refinement (*wen*),' and the notion of the succession of the 'three systems (*san-t'ung*).' A word of explanation is in order, although a detailed exposition of the complicated meanings of these New Script notions need not concern us here. The succession of the 'three systems,' in New Script reading of the Classics, referred actually to the succession of the first three dynasties in Chinese history, each of which exemplified a specific culture (simplicity or refinement) and way of governance. In its simplest form, this notion explains dynastic change. Expanded and elaborated in New Script exegeses, it also seeks to elucidate the principle of political legitimacy and historico-cultural evolution in antiquity. This tripartite successive scheme is sometimes reduced to the notion of the alternating cycle of 'simplicity' and 'refinement.' The beginning of a dynasty witnessed the institution of simplicity, a culture that emphasized the spirit and sentiment behind rites and ceremonies. As these rites and ceremonies grew, refinement occurred and a culture of conspicuous ornamentation came into being. Preoccupation with external appearance and artificial grandiloquence finally yielded decadence. Decay, however, would lay the groundwork for the regeneration of simplicity. Summoning these New Script ideas on the pattern of changing history and shifting cultural imperatives, Wei hinted that his own time was on the threshold of a new cycle, ripe for change.

To further advance the argument that he was living on the edge of a new epoch to be marked by the rebirth of New Script learning, Wei sought justification in the New Script notion of the 'three ages (*san-shih*).' Specifically, this notion explained the way Confucius recorded events of different 'ages' with felicitous language in the Classic, *Spring and Autumn*

Annals. Events of the first age he heard and knew of through transmitted records (*so-ch'uan-wen*); events of the second he heard through contemporary accounts by the elders still alive (*so-wen*); those of the third he personally witnessed. Different phraeseology and language style must be employed to bring out the significance, particularly the moral import, of these events of different ages.[23] Indeed, it may not be far-fetched to bring to mind Vico's linguistic historicism which identified each of the four stages of cyclical development of civilizations — age of the gods, age of heroes, age of men, and age of decadence and dissolution — with the four respective linguistic tropes — metaphor, metonymy, synedoche, and irony.[24] While the New Script notion of 'three ages,' with its overt moral purport, is professedly different from Vico's scheme of analysis which saw language as the bedrock of a universal order, both saw the unavoidable intervention of language in the effort to recapture the past.

Wei Yuan likened his time to the age in which events were personally witnessed, when his contemporaries busied themselves with the pursuit of learning *à la* the Eastern Han. Now it was time for them to proceed backwards to the learning of the Western Han, the age whose events could be known through accounts by elders. No doubt, these elders would have been Liu Feng-lu and Chuang Ts'un-yü. The Ch'ing scholars should then hark all the way back to the age whose events could only be known through transmitted records, namely, the traceable exegetical tradition from Tung Chung-shu's commentary on the Annals, through the bequests of Confucius's seventy disciples, to the sages' words themselves. Ultimately, 'from the Six Classics (Classics of *Changes, Odes, Documents, Rites, Music and Annals*) are sought the universal order of the sages.'[25]

In both quasi-hagiographic prefaces to Chuang Ts'un-yü and Liu Feng-lu's collected works, Wei faithfully attested to his subscription to the New Script tenets, which nonetheless, he used in an idiosyncratic way. Instead of expatiating these tenets in terms of their original meanings, he primarily employed them to fix the beginning point of yet another continuum in which classical scholarship would unfold and develop. Inasmuch as 'ordering' is an inevitable process in worldmaking, according to Nelson Goodman,[26] Wei manipulated the tenets precisely to construct 'order' in the sense of a chronologico-historical order. He was able to establish his own time-span as a historic present whence the three-system/three-age/simplicity-refinement succession was to begin anew. While in these two prefatory essay Wei placed within his order only the changing forms of classical scholarship, in his other writings, the sense of his present as a historic beginning would be fully developed into a statement of how the contemporary cultural condition was on the verge of change.

In 1829, Wei wrote a work of seven fascicles (*chuan*), entitled *An exposition of the subtleties of Tung Chung-shu's study of the Spring and Autumn Annals (Tung-tzu Ch'un-ch'iu fa-wei)*. Although it is no longer extant, the preface and the table of contents have survived. In the preface, Wei compared the works of Tung Chung-shu and Ho Hsiu (A.D. 129-82), another New Script master, and made manifest his preference for Tung's exegesis to Ho's because of the former's success in comprehensively illuminating all the major tenets of the New Script tradition. None, in Wei's view, was able to match Tung's ability 'to select the good in the Classics, to grasp the authority of the sages and to implement the way of the world.' He bemoaned that even his teacher, Liu Feng-lu, tended to focus on Ho and neglected Tung. It was therefore necessary to redress the balance and direct attention to Tung's superior learning. Judging from the table of contents, Wei, unlike his rather narrow treatment of the New Script precepts in the prefatory pieces, presumably tackled in a comprehensive way the 'great principles concealed in subtle language' of the New Script tradition in light of Tung Chung-shu's insights.[27]

Around the same time, Wei Yuan wrote a two-part piece on the New Script version of the *Spring and Autumn Annals* entitled *A Discourse on the Kung-yang Annals (Ch'un-ch'iu lun)* in which he boldly claimed that 'had there been no [New Script] Kung-yang [commentary to the *Annals*], the *Annals* would have been nothing.'[28] It was only in the New Script text that the *Annals*'s paramount goals 'to illuminate the rules of rulership in accordance with the history of [the state of] Lu and to reform the Chou institutions with the anticipated arrival of a latter-day sage' were fully expounded. Thanks to the New Script text, the *Annals*'s trans-historical teachings on rulership, the 'methods of the hundred rulers' (*pai-wang-chih fa*), found clear expression, specifically in the interrelated notions of the 'three ages' and 'three successions.'

Thus, in this piece, Wei Yuan referred to these two central New Script notions as embodiments of universal truths. Confucius in the *Annals* established the methods of recording historical events in the 'three ages' so as to dispense proper moral judgments: 'For the age whose events were personally witnessed [by Confucius], [he] used subtle language; for the age whose events were heard through contemporary accounts by living elders,

[he] expressed his pain and sorrow over calamities; for the age whose events were known through transmitted records, [he] vanquished his feelings of sympathy [and wrote dispassionately].'[29]   In this delicate process of intermixing stylistic recording and substantive teaching through history, he revealed the universal way of governance for those in positions of power. In other words, rulers of all ages should study carefully Confucius's *Annals*, a history which praised the moral and condemned the wicked.   Learning from this historical exemplar, rulers would act morally and refrain from evil deeds.

The 'three ages,' in the New Script commentarial tradition, also epitomized three different kinds of worlds.   As an ideal construct, the remote age which Confucius knew through transmitted records was a world that witnessed the 'attainment of order after regulating disorder;' the closer age which he knew through the contemporary accounts of living elders witnessed 'peace arising out of attained order;' the age which Confucius experienced himself witnessed 'universal peace.'   Whereas in Wei's prefaces to Chuang Ts'un yü and Liu Feng-lu's works, he used the notion of the 'three ages' as an analogical device to depict the evolution of Ch'ing scholarship, here, he pointed to it simply as a historical schema, a pattern of historical change from 'attained peace' (*chih-p'ing*) through 'arising peace' (*sheng-p'ing*) to 'universal peace' (*t'ai-p'ing*).[30]   This New Script historicism would furnish the basis for Wei to construct his own model of historical movement in terms of epochal change.

Undoubtedly, Wei's most important work on the New Script tradition was contained in two pieces of writings, one on the *Classic of Odes*, the other the *Classic of Documents*: the *Ancient Subtle Meanings of the [Classic of] Odes (Shih ku-wei) and Ancient Subtle Meanings of the [Classic of] Documents (Shu ku-wei)*.   The first draft of the former work was completed in 1829.   The final revised version came out in 1840.   The primary goal of this volume was 'to elaborate the profound principles revealed in the subtle language of the three [New Script] schools of the *Odes* — Han, Lu and Ch'i — filling in their lacunae and illuminating their abstruseness and obtuseness, so that the Duke of Chou's and Confucius's intent to benefit posterity by instituting rites and rectifying music is revealed.'[31]   Wei's work differed significantly from the previous works on the same subject, such as the ones by Feng Teng-fu (1783-1841) and Ch'en Shou-ch'i (1771-1834), in that it questioned the reliability of the dominant Old Script Mao text of the *Classic of Odes*, whereas the earlier writings rested content with examining the methods and teachings of the New Script commentaries. Wei suggested that the Mao version was unreliable and might well be spurious as it appeared later than the three New Script counterparts, even though Wei did not want to totally abandon the Mao text because it could serve as a supplement.[32]

Principally, Wei took issue with the Old Script Mao text for its rigid interpretive categorizations of the songs and poems in the Classic. According to the Mao text, the *feng* (folk) and *ya* (patrician) odes were classified either as 'orthodox' (*cheng*) or 'changed' (*pien*), the former written in times of prosperity, the latter in times of decay. Moreover, there was in every ode, so the Mao text said, the practice and purpose of *mei* (glorification, celebration or praise) or *tz'u* (criticism or vituperation). Wei Yuan excoriated this sort of mechanical reading as 'obstinate rules' (*chih-li*) and averred that if

> . . . the rules of 'orthodox' and 'changed' were not broken, then the merits of the *ya* and *sung* (sacrificial) odes would not have been illuminated, and rites and music would have been rendered useless. If the rules of 'glorification' and 'criticism' were not broken, then the sincerity and innocence of the *feng* odes would not have been manifested and the *Spring and Autumn Annals* need not have been written.

What Wei sought in the *Odes* was the 'deep and subtle' (*shen-wei*), not the punctilious adherence to the obstinate rules laid down in the Old Script Mao tradition. In touch with the deep and subtle, one came to know that the poems were capable of 'stimulating the mind' (*hsing*), 'inspiring self-contemplation' (*kuan*), 'teaching sociability' (*ch'ün*) and 'regulating feelings of resentment' (*yuan*). Otherwise, one would be reading 'odes of mere words and phrases' (*chang-chü chih shih*).[33] Wei was deeply dissatisfied with the Mao text's contrivance of the rules of 'criticism' and 'glorification' exactly because they rendered the poetic into mere words and phrases. He explained why these rules were arbitrary and artificial:

> As for the *Classic of Odes*, there were the minds of those who wrote the odes. There were the minds of those who collected and edited the odes. There were principles of discussing the odes. There were principles of narrative odes and reflective odes. Those who wrote the odes expressed their own sentiments, stopping when those sentiments had been fulfilled. They did not calculate how the listeners would respond. [They] composed odes in response to the events happening at the time, without seeking to know how and where the events originated. [They] composed odes to satirize those who ruled from above,

seeking only to fulfill their own dreams, not to admonish and punish on behalf of others.

The odes were written first and foremost as expressions of sentiments, the artistic shaping and rendition of emotions and feelings. But when the officials collected the odes and presented them to the rulers, they

> . . . used the words of the authors to proclaim the goals of the listeners. [They] used the odes composed in response to the events happening at the time [of composition] to deduce the causes and origins of the events. . . . [They] used an ode which satirized one person as an ode which satirized many. . . . In the preface of the [New Script] Han version of the Odes which is still extant, only four odes . . . were [considered to be] for 'glorification' and 'criticism.' All the rest were composed for the authors themselves. . . . The Lu version of the Odes also did not contain one ode for 'glorification' or 'criticism.'

The practice of the Mao text to turn personal expressions into universal espousals, Wei Yuan said in jest, was like 'moaning and groaning on behalf of one who was not sick.'[34]

Given Wei's enormous respect for the *Spring and Autumn Annals*, it is small wonder that he discerned a most intimate relation between the *Classic of Odes* and the *Annals*, maintaining that the folk songs (*feng*) with virtuous transformative power could be understood only after one had read the *Annals*. They both revealed the alternation between simplicity and refinement. The rites and music celebrated in the *Odes* contributed to 'establishing orderly government and forestalling disorder.' The *Classic of Odes* illustrated how a government proceeded 'from simplicity to refinement.' On the other hand, the *Annals* showed how a regime 'broke loose from disorder and returned to orderly government,' how it 'reverted to simplicity from refinement.'[35]

It should be noted that Wei Yuan's focused study on the *Odes* as a means to promote the New Script tradition was in fact quite out of the ordinary. For most partisans of this tradition generally seized upon the *Spring and Autumn Annals* as their exegetical and discursive foothold. Wei had broadened the Ch'ing New Script textual horizon by involving the other Classics. Late in his life, in 1855, one year or so before he died, Wei completed his exploration of the *Classic of Documents*, entitled the *Ancient Subtle Meanings of the [Classic of] Documents*. It may be considered a product of his lifelong interest and endeavor in restoring the Western Han

New Script classical tradition.[36] At the beginning of his preface, Wei stated the aim of his study, 'Why is the *Ancient Subtleties of the Classic of Documents* written? It is to expound and illuminate the profound principles revealed in subtle language in the Western Han New and Old Script versions of the *Documents*, and to expose the unsubstantiated creations and absence of the transmission of teachings of the masters in the Old Script versions by Ma [Jung] (96-166) and Cheng [Hsuan] in the Eastern Han Dynasty.'

Wei then went on to describe how the Old Script versions of the *Documents* came to be the predominant canonical texts. Initially, it was Fu-sheng's twenty-nine chapters, transmitted by Ou-yang and Hsia-hou, which constituted the standard New Script *Documents*. Then K'ung An-kuo (156-74? B.C.) recovered forty-five chapters hidden in the wall of Confucius's old residence. This Old Script version had an additional sixteen chapters. Kung studied with Ou-yang and in fact accommodated both the New Script and Old Script texts. Ssu-ma Ch'ien (145-87 B.C.) had also studied with K'ung. Therefore, in the Western Han dynasty, the Old and New Script texts were really one, with only minor differences. But in the Eastern Han time, Tu Lin recovered another Old Text version which was then transmitted by Wei Hung. Chia K'uei, Ma Jung, and Cheng Hsuan all wrote commentaries and annotations to this version which gradually became the dominant version, deliberately setting it apart from the New Script versions. With the appearance of the forged Old Script version in the Eastern Chin dynasty, even the texts embraced by Ma and Cheng became defunct.

In Wei Yuan's day, it had been generally accepted that the Old Script *Documents* which appeared in the Eastern Chin was spurious. This work was often attacked and criticized as apocryphal. But much to the Wei's dissatisfaction, many scholars of his time still accepted the Ma and Cheng versions as genuine transmissions of the authentic text recovered by K'ung An-kuo. According to Wei, the discrepancies between the K'ung and Ma-Cheng texts were glaring. It was like comparing 'a horse and a cow.' Wei listed five reasons why the Ma-Cheng versions could not have been a faithful representation of K'ung's version.

First, the so-called Old Script *Documents* on which the Ma-Cheng versions were based was written on bamboo sheets. Each sheet could hold very few characters. If all the forty five chapters were included, then a great number of sheets had to have been used. However, it was recorded that this bamboo-sheet version comprised only one fascicle, and therefore it could not have been complete. Second, the history of the transmission of the additional sixteen chapters was entirely lacking. Wei wondered why scholars such as Ma Jung and Cheng Hsuan were unable to say even one word on this matter. Third, the various chapters of the *Documents* recorded in Ssu-ma Ch'ien's work were radically different from those included in the Ma-Cheng texts. Ssu-ma had studied with K'ung An-kuo and thus it was highly plausible that he would have transmitted the latter's version. How was it then that Ssu-ma's text was drastically at variance with the Ma-Cheng texts which supposedly inherited the authentic K'ung version? Fourth, the history of the transmissions of the New Script tradition could be readily traced, and their contents demonstrated a coherence and consistency not found in the Old Script schools: 'Ma Jung differed from Chia K'uei. Chia k'uei differed from Liu Hsin (45 B.C.-A.D. 23). Cheng Hsuan again differed from Ma Jung.' Their interpretations were so varied that it was hard to determine which was the authentic version and which was not. Fifth, the origin of the Tu Lin Old Script version could not be ascertained, and the information of its transmission by the masters was completing wanting. In constrast, on both these scores, the Fu-sheng and K'ung An-kuo versions received their corroborations in ancient writings and histories.

Wei criticized some of the prominent Ch'ing scholars who had studied the *Documents*, such as Chiang Sheng (1721-1799) and Wang Ming-sheng (1722-1798) who followed Ma and Cheng, Sun Hsing-yen (1753-1818) who adopted both the Old and New Script texts, and Tuan Yü-ts'ai (1735-1815) who regarded whatever in Ssu-ma Ch'ien's book that was different from Ma's and Cheng's texts as New Script. Because of their works, Wei lamented that the profound principles revealed in subtle language in Fu-sheng's, Ou-yang's, Hsia-hou's, and K'ung An-kuo's texts were destroyed. He concluded that the Old Script versions, whether the Eastern Han Tu Lin, Ma Yung, Cheng Hsuan texts, or the Eastern Chin Mei Tse text, were all unreliable.[37] Wei urged scholars to return to the authentic New Script text:

> Aware of the spuriousness of Mei Tse's [Old Script version] in the Eastern Chin, [we] return to the Old Script texts of Ma and Cheng. This is like the way in which the state of Ch'i gave way to the state of Lu. Knowing and proving that the Old Script espousals of Ma and Cheng were concoctions lacking any tradition of teachings of the schools, [we] return to the teachings of Fu-sheng, Ou-yang, Hsia-hou, Ssu-ma Ch'ien and K'ung An-kuo, which examined

antiquity. This is like the manner in which the state of Lu yielded to the *tao* (the Way).[38]

Wei here again alluded to the New Script notion of the successive 'three systems,' that is, the backward progression from Eastern Chin through Eastern Han to Western Han.

Wei more directly dealt with the notion of the 'three systems' when he explicated the cryptic first two lines of the 'Yao-tien' (The canon of Yao) in the *Documents*: 'Examining into antiquity, we find that the emperor Yao was called Fang-hsün:'

> Cheng's commentary claims that the *Classic of Odes* has the article (*t'iao*) of the three categories (*san-k'o*) and the teaching (*chiao*) of the five families (*wu-chia*). The five families are T'ang, Yü, Hsia, Shang and Chou. The three categories are Yü and Hsia as one category, Shang as one category, and Chou as one category. . . . The three categories are the three systems (*san-t'ung*). The Chou, including the Hsia and Shang, formed the three systems. What came before the three systems are called the three antiquities (*san-ku*). Therefore, when the history of the Chou was again compiled, they were distinguished by using the phrase 'examining into antiquity.'[39]

Wei then went on to describe the ancient practice of 'linking together the three systems,' in large part following Tung Chung-shu's discussion in the *Luxuriant Gems of the Spring and Autumn Annals*. Wei maintained that this practice constituted the profound principle revealed in subtle language in the *Documents*, a principle fully grasped by Tung but missed by the Eastern Han exegetes such as Ma Yung and Cheng Hsuan. The principle was, in concrete terms, that previous dynasties must be honored because heaven did not bestow the mandate to rule on just one family.[40]

To be sure, Wei Yuan wrote his commentary on the *Classic of Documents* in large part to drive home the message that the New Script tradition's stress on revealing the profound principles residing in the Classics was the only correct spirit in which to approach the words of the sages. But his effort should not be narrowly viewed as a partisan move to champion the New Script school. The larger point he made was the lamentable degeneration of genuine learning striving for truths into piecemeal, trivial, calculated efforts to seek fame and fortune through pedantic valorization of scholastic worth, a phenomenon that recurred time and again in history. In the ancient Han period, for instance, the initial earnest goal to search for truths in the Classics became a preoccupation with words. As the study of the Classics became the avenue for success in the officialdom, both New Script and Old Script scholars sought only to further careers by immersing themselves in finicky semantic and philological pursuits.

In the Sung (1127-1279) times, the Confucian masters focused on the *Four Books* (i.e. the *Analects*, *Mencius*, *Great Learning* and *Doctrine of the Mean*) so as to provide a clear path to the sages' original teachings. They recognized that the textual catholicity so often associated with classical studies easily became diverted from its experiential and philosophical basis. But unfortunately, Wei contended, once the *Four Books* were ensconced as centerpieces in the examination system, commenteries on them proliferated, all devoted to achieving success in the examinations. Learning once again became pedantic, scholastic, and oriented toward securing personal interests. Scholars 'forgot the original sagely teachings and meretriciously sold the sacral Classics so as to enrich their attire and meals.'[41]

Wei's promotion of the New Script tradition was no mean and small-minded sectarian endeavor. Although his method was often philological, using meticulous textual evidentiary investigative techniques to prove the authenticity of the New Script texts, his goal was always the recovery of the profound principles of the sages. While he decidedly sided with the New Script school, he did not uncritically embrace it. As we have seen, he still valued the Old Script Mao version of the *Odes*. In addition, Wei did not wholeheartedly accept the New Script view that Confucius created the Classics. Rather, he adhered to the Old Script contention that it was the Duke of Chou (c. twelve century B.C.) who created the Classics, which were later edited and transmitted by Confucius. The Classics, except the *Spring and Autumn Annals*, came from the Duke of Chou:

> Therefore Confucius himself said, 'I transmit but do not create.' The one who created was described as the sage; the one who transmitted was described as the enlightened. . . . Even if one is in a position to rule but does not have the virtue to rule, then one does not dare to create rites and music. Even if one has the virtue to rule but is not in a position to rule, one also does not dare to create rites and music. One indeed cannot do that if one does not have the position and virtue as exalted as the Duke of Chou's.[42]

That Wei Yuan refused to be constricted by narrow sectarian definitions was a result of his primary goal to recover the truths encased in the Classics. His works done in the New Script tradition were in many ways indictments of his contemporaries' obsession with philology and their neglect of classical learning's philosophic and experiential relationship to the whole of China's cultural condition. His New Script scholarship was devoted to laying bare the truths of the Classics so that once again, the literati would know what to make of the past and how to act in the present. Wei, in his preface to Liu Feng-lu's collected works, as we have seen, called for 'linking together classical study, administrative affairs and literature as one,' by learning from the profound principles revealed in subtle language. It is hardly any wonder that in one of his works on economic and military policies, Wei employed the idea of 'three systems' to validate his argument that the present Ch'ing dynasty should study the previous Ming dynasty and learn selectively from it. At the very beginning of this 1855 study, *A Record of the Ming Economic and Military Policies (Ming-tai shih-ping-cheng lu)*, Wei explained the correct present usage of the past:

> The Three Dynasties were prosperous because the Yin followed the rites and rituals of the Hsia, and the Chou followed the rites and rituals of the Yin. Therefore the *Analects* has the statement of 'surveying the previous two dynasties' and Hsun-tzu has the statement of 'emulating the later kings.' All kings invariably honor the descendants of the previous two dynasties. Is it not because what has occurred before is invariably the teacher with respect to the continuation, alteration, modification, and addition of laws and institutions?[43]

The Ming, as a matter of historical truism, was the teacher of the Ch'ing.

In his study of the *Odes*, Wei explained that Confucius edited the Classics because he wanted to revive and perpetuate the achievements of the ancient sages, specifically those of King Wen and Duke of Chou, by preserving and transmitting them in words:

> Therefore [Confucius] said, 'Since King Wen is no longer alive, does not his culture rest with me?' [He] also said, 'For long I have not dreamed as of yore that I saw the Duke of Chou.' The commenting on the *Changes*, the editing of the *Documents*, the compiling of the *Annals* and the rectifying of rites and rituals, all revolved around the [Duke of] Chou. . . . [He] wished to follow King Wen but was unable to realize it, and so he pursued Duke of Chou's institutions. [He] wished to implement the ways of the Duke of Chou but was unable to realize it, and so he invested his ways in words to reveal them to posterity.[44]

In short, scholarship was no idle business. It recorded the great deeds as guides to action for posterity.

In this piece of writing on the *Classic of Odes*, Wei also saw a close relation between good government in antiquity and its ability to expound the odes:

> As for [maintaining] the authority of the king in ruling the world, none was more important than the [king's] tours of inspection and hunts, and the feudal lords' appearance in the court once every six years. The Son of Heaven collected the folk odes. The feudal lords presented the folk songs. The Grand Commander expounded on them in order to see the successes and failures of administration and government. The practices of celebrating the humble and degrading the inefficient were implemented. Therefore, the feudal lords dared not act with impunity, and the livelihood of the people was thereby sustained. The exposition of the odes was the greatest institution of a monarchy. The chastisement of the inefficient was the greatest authority of the Son of Heaven.

The central message was that since the songs and odes came from the people, reading them carefully would yield correct insights into the state of affairs in the country. In conjunction with the other institutions such as the tours and hunts on the part of the king, and paying tribute to the court on the part of the feudal lords, the entire regime achieved orderly rule. That was exactly what occurred in the Western Chou. But toward the end of the Eastern Chou, the situation became radically different:

> The Son of Heaven no longer toured his domain. The feudal lords no longer paid tribute to the court. The institution of expounding odes was discarded. The celebration of the humble no longer occurred in the monarchy. Traces [of these practices] disappeared and the odes were no more. The feudal lords acted with impunity. Therefore, it was said that there was no king in the world. Since there was no king in the world, the uncrowned king must be relied upon. Therefore it was said that the *Annals* was the affairs of the Son of Heaven.

The odes, as an integral part of the way of governance, were irrevocably tied to the fortune of the regime as a whole. Wei here also alluded to the concept of the 'uncrowned king,' that is, Confucius, in connection with the *Annals*. This Classic dealt with nothing but the affairs of the state. Confucius was the uncrowned king by virtue of his compiling the *Annals*, which filled the political vacuum in an age of ineffective and immoral kings. In the *Annals*, Wei held, Confucius bemoaned the dismal fact that 'the chastisement of the inefficient was replaced by the invasion by force, which succeeded the way of reward and punishment prescribed in the institutions of tours of inspection, hunts, and expositions of the odes.'[45]

Similarly, in his study of the *Documents*, Wei did not merely occupy himself with explicating words and phrases, but he also expressed his practical preoccupations with reforming the government. Since ancient times, laws and institutions inexorably changed. For instance, with regard to laws, corporal punishments were changed in the age of the *Annals*, when Confucius advocated a more humane government. With respect to institutions, the system of selecting people to join the government had to be changed so that priority and preference would not always be given to the hereditary nobles. Moreover, the feudal system of the antique world inevitably also must change. The displacement of other states by the Ch'in dynasty which eventually unified China was a necessary development. It was 'the general tendency of the world. Even if the sage did not bring along the change, the feudal system would have changed on its own.' Wei's study of the *Documents* also convinced him that in antiquity, 'rulership by heaven' (*t'ien-chih*) was supplanted 'the rulership by humans' (*jen-chih*). 'Even heaven and earth could not fail to heed this self-regulated change.' Moreover, from 'the way of the king,' antiquity moved to 'the way of the hegemon.'[46] 'This was the direction toward which fortune tended. Even the ancestors could not fail to heed this self-regulated change.' In sum, knowledge of the Classics and the ancient world led Wei to place a high valuation on change. Since change had been the rule of life since antiquity, his own age must then also embark on adjustments to suit the needs of the time.[47]

As Wei's followed the New Script tradition to probe the pristine truths of the Classics as practical guides to action, he also formulated and developed his own thoughts in various writings on the cultural conditions of his time. Summoning and incorporating New Script tenets, Wei embarked on worldmaking as a critic of the institutions of the late Ch'ing dynasty. The New Script historicist scheme of the 'three ages' and 'three systems' provided him with the basic outline for his vision of change, but in the words of Nelson Goodman, the processes of 'deletion,' 'supplementation,' and finally 'deformation' would occur,[48] as Wei Yuan strove to forge his own intellectual universe while accommodating New Script precepts.

Wei Yuan's engagement with the tenets of the New Script tradition was highly selective. He certainly excised a large portion of the tradition's 'three categories and nine principles,' choosing to explore only the notions of 'three ages,' 'three systems,' and the alternation between 'simplicity' and 'refinement.' But while he deleted elements of the New Script corpus of precepts, he also added significantly to the corpus by bringing it to bear on a variety of texts. It was no longer discussed solely in the context of classical exegesis. The New Script ideas would be supplemented as Wei applied them to other domains of discourse, for instance, classical Taoist philosophical teachings. By deleting from and supplementing the New Script classicism, reshaping or deformation of its credos would result.

Wei Yuan's thought was permeated throughout by the *leitmotif* of the inevitability and the necessity of change, a truism he illustrated not only using the Classics but also other ancient texts like the Taoist canon, *The Book of Lao-tzu* (third century B.C.), and the military philosophy, *The Book of Sun-tzu* (fourth century B.C.): 'Their way embodies everything; their spirit illumines the entire cosmos; their method is in accord with heaven and earth. They understand thoroughly the constancy of change.'[49] Wei's philosophy of change was most systematically advanced in his *Mo's [i.e., Wei Yuan's] Writing-tablet (Mo-ku)*, a collection of his philosophic ruminations, completed before his death and published posthumously in 1878. In it, Wei depicted a cosmic-human world constantly in flux, propelled by the 'transformative material force' (*ch'i-hua*): 'Not for a moment is there no change in transformative material force. That which does not change is the Way. Circumstances change from day to day and are irrecoverable.'[50] Nature and History vouched for the inexorability of change. Heaven and earth of old were not the same as their counterparts now. Stars died and were born; rivers altered courses; topography permutated, so that steep cliffs became valleys and mountains were submerged in seas; flora and fauna evolved. Likewise, cultures of the human historical world changed: diet, attire, music, dance, punishment, governmental institution, military strategy, so on and so forth.[51] Wei metaphorically saw 'the cosmos from the ancient time to the present' as 'a great chess game.' What the historical records contained were 'the moves in a chess game, hither and tither, repeating and reverting, so that there are myriad possibilities.'[52] Wei thus concluded that whereas 'antiquity had its own ancient [ways], to adhere inflexibly to the old so as to guide the present is to betray the present; to adhere inflexibly to the present so as to define the past is to betray the past.'[53]

History revealed that much progress had been made since the Three Dynasties in antiquity, Wei affirmed. To begin with, the abolition of corporal punishments at the beginning of the Han dynasty meant that government at that time became more humane. Second, when the system of an imperial administration consisting of prefectures and districts supplanted the feudal system, government became more open to the public. Third, in antiquity, the aristocracy monopolized the officialdom. But with the rise of examinations to recruit officials, the principle of heredity no longer excluded the talented of lowly background from public service. Wei boldly claimed that the later ages, in expanding the public (*kung*) domain, were actually superior to the antique Three Dynasties, which embraced the feudal principle of maintaining private (*ssu*) authority.[54]

Adducing institutional changes since antiquity as illustrations, Wei contended that even if the ancient sages were resurrected to undertake reforms, they would not have undone those changes. Revival of antiquity was a form of pernicious wishful thinking. When the Taoist followers of the Chin dynasty attempted to revive the supposed simplicity and naturalness of the ancient spirit, they succeeded only in 'flouting the rules of propriety and doing great harm to the established teachings of the world.' The Sung Confucians also took great delight in touting the greatness of the Three Dynasties, but antiquity's institutions, such as 'communal farming, the feudal system and the recommendation system of bureaucratic recruitment must not be revived.' If they were, it would mean that 'Confucian statecraft would be harmed by obdurate antiquarian preoccupations.' Wei Yuan bluntly stated that 'the more ancient practices are changed, the more the people would be benefited.'[55] Indeed, all of Wei's writings on reforming the politico-economic structure of the imperial government were inspired by the conviction that 'under heaven, there is no method that can remain unchanged for hundreds of years.' There was 'no infinite immutable method.'[56] The only historical constant was that 'as problems arise as entrenched laws become old, there would have to be institutional changes in accord with time.'[57]

Wei Yuan's perception of history as change stemmed from his ontological conception of ultimate reality as 'oneness' (*i*) which was the vital source of change: 'Oneness begets change; changes beget transformations; transformations beget the infinite.' Nothing existed alone; all beings were dialectically involved: 'All things under heaven do not exist alone but must have their opposites. But it should be said that no two heights can be coupled, no two greats can be accommodated, no two nobles can be paired, no two circumstances can be duplicated. Coupling, accommodating, pairing, and duplicating must lead to conflicts of interest.' However, conflict need not occur if the opposites assumed unequal status in their unavoidable dialectic engagement: 'In the relation between the opposites, there must be one as the principal, the other the auxiliary. In this way, the opposites will not fail to become one. [The cosmic symbol of] *ch'ien* is elevated, while [supplementary cosmic symbol of] *k'un* is lowly. Thus, heaven and earth establish their own places, and the myriad things follow suit.'[58] The antinomic contradiction that is implied and inherent in every being and its opposite can be overcome through the continuous complementary interplay between them as principal and auxiliary.

Thus, Wei Yuan asserted that each era and every person must come into the truth in its or one's own manner, engaging and resolving problems in a timely fashion. History was no static formation but a process given over to circumstances, constantly in traffic with the particular needs of segments of time as they succeeded one another. Nonetheless, it was not Wei's goal to render history into sheer contingency and circumstantiality. Far from it. Inherent in his idea of change was a clear sense of constancy. Underlying the flux of transformative material force was the unchanging Way (*tao*), the fundamental anchor of reality. As pointed out above, Wei likened history to a game of chess consisting of everchanging moves. But the rules of a chess game did not change, and one could learn the ways in which a game could be won. As Wei put it, a skilled chess-player was one who, 'while engaged in the game, has the knowledge that rises above the immediate game.' In other words, there was supra-historical or trans-historical insights that ensured one's effective encounter with historical contingencies. There was certainly 'change as in alteration and change,' (*pien-i-chih i*), but there was also 'change in the midst of constancy' (*pu-i-chih i*).[59]

This sense of constancy was also manifested in the sense of a holistic oneness. After all, changes grew out of the primal oneness, as mentioned earlier. This oneness was the Way: 'The profound person, approaching the Way, begins with oneness, conceals himself in oneness, praises oneness, and takes delight travelling in oneness.' The dialectic antinomy of opposites was dissolved in oneness, as in the reconciliation of the anatomical dualities of the limbs, the eyes, the ears and the nostrils: 'Although there are two [of each of them], they are one body part.'[60] In his *Lao-tzu pen-i* (The Fundamental Meanings of *Lao-tzu*) of 1840, an explication of classical

Taoist philosophy, Wei elaborated the meaning of this all-encompassing oneness in terms of the Taoist sense of ultimate universal nothingness. Wei began: 'Why is it that the opposites of high nobility and lowly masses are really one? Those who are called dukes and kings are so because of people's opinion. . . . At the very beginning of creation, there was no nobility to speak of. . . . If we can consider ourselves unworthy and lowly, the world will become righteous. This is the result of apprehending oneness (*te-i*).' Wei went on to say that to collapse the distinction between high and low is to 'obliterate oneself' (*wu-wo*). 'When my self does not exist, things also do not exist. There is then neither high nor low, neither nobility nor lowliness. High and low are one, the noble and the lowly are one, you and I are one. As there is nothingness everywhere, there is oneness everywhere.'[61] In this undifferentiated oneness-nothingness, change as such could not have any real ontological status.

Wei's often sanguine advocacy of the inevitability of change is also counterbalanced by his conception of reversion, revival, or return. To the extent that the oneness of the Way, the ultimate truth, is immutable, all changes must return to it. It was true that 'even the ancient sage-kings' could not reverse the tides of history. They could not destroy military strifes in the 'age of military strifes;' nor could they preclude punishments in the 'age of punishments.' Yet, according to Wei, it was also true that if the principle of rulership modelled on the sage-kings were pursued, then in the natural course of time, there would be rulership that 'returns to the origin and revives the beginning.'[62]

In the 'Fourth Essay on Learning' in his *Mo's Writing-Tablet*, Wei argued that the key to effecting such return rested in purging selfish desires (*yü*) so that there would be 'no desires' (*wu-yü*), as taught by Confucius. To purge desires was to follow the Way. But as Wei lamented, 'ordinary people fear learning about the Way because they are intimidated by the fact that it is at odds with the body.' To follow the Way meant constantly battling the body and curbing desires stemming from it. But since 'stifling anger is like destroying a mountain and curbing desires is like reclaiming a valley,' Wei plaintively asked, 'Are there those who can persist in the prolonged efforts of destroying a mountain and reclaiming a valley?' To overcome this sense of antagonism between the Way and the body, one must appeal to the mind-heart (*hsin*). Instead of positing an antithetical relationship between the internal Way and the external body, one bridged the two by seeing life as the process of return (*fu*) to the mind-heart.[63] For 'the mind-heart of humanity is the mind-heart of heaven-earth,' and as 'the body is within the mind-heart, myriad things are replete within my own self.'[64]

Propounding this ultimate holistic vision of the ontological plenitude of the self, which united heaven and humanity, Wei's ideas on contingent change, in the final analysis, found dissolution. Viewed against this classic Confucian (and Taoist) time-transcending and space-nullifying scheme of universal oneness, history merely presented spectacles of change, forms and structures, or in Wei's term, circumstances (*shih*), that human life had experienced; it would not alter or affect the cosmic-human imperatives which stood above, that is, the one Way manifested in the human mind-heart.

Wei's complex philosophic weaving brought into one fabric two different threads of thinking: inevitable circumstantial institutional changes in accordance with time, and inexorable historicist return dictated by ontological constancy and universal oneness. This fabric was Wei's historicist scheme of the 'three ages,' inspired by the New Script version, yet also different from it. In his *Fundamental Meanings of the Lao-tzu*, Wei expounded what he called the 'three ages:' the age of *t'ai-ku* (high antiquity), the age of *chung-ku* (middle antiquity) and the age of *mo-shih* (the ending age). But just as change and movement were represented by this tripartite diachronicity, so too was constancy represented by the synchronic ideal of non-action (*wu-wei*). Wei used the analogy of the growth of an infant to denote change within constancy:

> When a newly born infant is suckling, its knowledge has not yet been developed. Breathing, speechless, and not exerting effort, this is non-action of high antiquity. As it gradually grows, naive innocence has not taken leave, and so there will not yet be corrupt tendency toward indulgence in desires and the development of cunning. This is non-action in middle antiquity. As it commits mistakes, it gradually gets to know them and to understand them, without being hasty in making decisive breaks with them. This is non-action in the ending age.

Thus, as with the developmental changes that an infant experienced, a historical age also sported its own attributes. But the constant ideal of non-action, first realized in high antiquity, persisted as the ultimate criterion of excellence, albeit manifested differently: 'As time changes, non-action also changes. But the spirit of high antiquity is not abandoned even for one day.' To put it another way, 'circumstances change but the Way remains the same. Can it be said that the ending age and high antiquity, as with being asleep and awake, are at odds with each other?'[65]

In terms of actual history, according to Wei, the age of the sage-rulers Huang-ti (reign, 2697?-? B.C.), Yao (reign, 2357?-2256? B.C.) and Shun (reign, 2255?-2205? B.C.) constituted the age of high antiquity; the three dynasties of Hsia, Shang and Chou made up the age of middle antiquity; the successive tripartition was finally complete with the ending age, which coincided with the Spring and Autumn period (722-481 B.C.): 'Peaceful rule began with Huang-ti and was continued by Yao; [It] was complete in the New Dynasties but was destroyed in the Ch'in.'[66] But in the ending age of decay, there were already seeds of rebirth: 'As the Chou declined, problems abounded in the refined culture and the ideal of simplicity was completely extirpated. Without the great Way, people could not be swayed so that they would again return to the feelings of moral nature and mandate. . . . Therefore, there would inevitably be the return to the rule of high antiquity.'[67] With reference to the New Script notions of the alternation between simplicity and refinement as the dynamic force of historical movement, Wei praised both Confucius and Lao-tzu as harbingers of the necessary reversal of fortune:

> Simplicity and refinement reliably succeed each other so as to rectify problems. When problems become the worst, there will be reversion to the origin. Confucius established frugality and moderation as the foundations of rituals, desiring to rescue the extravagances of refinement with the faith in simplicity. This was also the teaching of Lao-tzu on innocence and trustworthiness. We cannot but say that in their time, the preconditions [for revival] in the Western Han had already been planted. [68]

As the 'flux of material force was remade' (*ch'i-yün tsai-tsao*) in the Han dynasty, 'the people were liberated from sufferings,' and so 'it could well be said that the Han was high antiquity.'[69]

In another context, in his *Mo's Writing-Tablet*, Wei, using the term *ch'i-yün* (the flux of material force), divided Chinese history into three periods. The first stage began after the legendary 'Three Emperors' (i.e., Huang-ti, Yao and Shun) and ended before the Ch'in period. From the Han onward until the Yuan dynasty, there was another stage, thereby hinting that from the Ming to the Ch'ing, that is, Wei's own time, there was the third stage of history. In light of his three-age historicist scheme, it is not hard to see that Wei conceived his time as the ending age which, although rife with problems, presaged the arrival of another high antiquity of great peaceful rule.[70] Hence his faith in reforms. The vital human efforts in history would correspondence to the supra-human demands of the transhistorical movement of time. Inherent in the ending age were the seeds of regeneration, the potentiality to achieve return to the age of high antiquity when the Way would again reign supreme.

In sum, in the dynamic flux of material force, simplicity and refinement alternated, circumstances changed, and the three ages appeared. But the constant Way, the 'pure and simple' (*shun-p'u*) 'mind-heart of high antiquity' (*t'ai-ku-hsin*), persisted. 'Just as there is nothing that does not eventually return to its origin, so too there is not one day when high antiquity is not present.'[71] As Wei saw it, one is obliged to live in history, in time-bound circumstances that were mutable, obdurately demanding change. But the Way of high antiquity provided the immutability and unity of ultimate meaning. Each historical age, in its own circumstantiality and contingency, as a facet or perspective of the total truth, discovered, realized, and returned to the ultimate truth.

It should also be remarked that Wei's three-age schema was regressive and devolutionary, descending from the idyllic age of high antiquity characterized by simplicity to the decadent ending age distinguished by its ostentatious refinement. It differed significantly from the progressive and upward-moving schema of the New Script three ages, from the age of approaching peace, through the age of rising peace, to the age of universal peace. Ostensibly then, Wei's design was informed by a certain pessimism, as opposed to the sense of optimism, improvement, and eventual fulfillment evident in the New Script model. But in fact, Wei's scheme was not without a ground for a sense of well-being, perpetually renewable. Perhaps this could be explained in terms of what Arthur O. Lovejoy has described as 'the paradox of the fortunate Fall.' In studying Milton's *Paradise Lost*, Lovejoy advanced the idea that implicit in this poem was the view that the Fall, though highly sinful and lamentable, was a fortunate occurrence. For if it had not taken place, the Incarnation and Redemption could never have occurred, and the omnipotent divine goodness could not have been so magnificently manifested.[72] In a similar way, Wei's ending age of preponderant decay and degeneration was after all a necessary stage in the redemptive process of human history which would see its consummation in the age of high antiquity. The ending age, seen in light of Paul Tillich's terms, could be described as Kairos, the 'fullness of time,' the fate of time, a moment of crisis, a point in time filled with significance derived from its relation to both an end and beginning.[73] The ending age rang the death knell of an unhappy age and was about to usher in the beatific age of high antiquity. At a time when symptoms of dynastic decline became evident, the vision of renewal of, and return to, greatness was a comforting and inspiring historicism that imbued Wei Yuan's reformism with emotional resonances.

Thus, Wei Yuan's reformism was unmistakably grounded on a historicism which was in turn derived from a classicism. Why were there such connections? After all, if his foremost goal was to help China ward off internal disaster and external threats, why did he not confine himself to his practical and reformist advocacy? Why did he elaborately gild his politico-economic proposals with historicist-classicist messages? This brings forth the question of a thinker's *habitus*, to borrow Pierre Bourdieu's theory. Although we rightly confer significance upon Wei Yuan as an epoch-making thinker who, as a sagacious historical actor, provided crucial glue to the tone and tenor of a place and time, his cultural *habitus* itself embodied a significance of its own, represented in academic conventions, scholarly customs, intellectual habits, and moral prescriptions. (Culture is here defined in the narrow non-anthropological sense as the sum-total of moral, religious, aesthetic, and intellectual products of a community at a particular place and time.) In other words, it was in the interplay between the larger cultural meanings of late imperial China and the particular individual excogitations of Wei Yuan that his historical role can be ascertained.

Wei Yuan's thought can be seen as an outgrowth of a particular *habitus*, a durable system of dispositions constituted historically by the cultural and social conditions of a particular social group: the Chinese literati. As Bourdieu explains, the dispositions are 'structured structures predisposed to function as structuring structures, that is, as principles of the generation and structuring of practices and representations.' Yet, this process of structuring or being structured is by no means teleologically determined 'obedience to rules' or 'conscious aiming at ends.'[74] Rather, as a historically acquired system of 'generative schemes,' it enables the 'free production of all thoughts' that are 'inherent in the particular conditions' of the production of the *habitus*. In other words, ideas and thoughts are never free-wheeling or free-floating. The historically and socially situated conditions of their germination set certain definable limits so that they are not capricious and surprising novelties. On the other hand, they are far from a simple 'mechanical reproduction of the original conditioning.' What the *habitus* makes possible is the generation of all the 'reasonable' and 'common-sense' ideas that are congruent with the objective historical conditions, while, without violence, excluding those that are at odds with the historical characteristics of a place and time. *Habitus* is 'embodied history, internalized as a second nature and so forgotten as history.' The past is the 'accumulated capital' which, although being enacted, is also acting in the production of ideas. In this way, it 'produces history on the basis of history and so ensures the permanence of change.' But since such change is delimited, generated within the *habitus*, it is immediately recognizable and foreseeable. In brief, *habitus* involves the 'art of assessing likelihoods;' it provides the 'sense of realities.'[75]

What was the *habitus* out of which Wei Yuan's thought was wrought? Or what were the dispositions that lent his thought the power of a particular cultural logic, that gave it intelligibility, that imbued it with proleptic insights? Wei Yuan was a typical Confucian literatus, an ethico-religious being whose ultimate concern was the realization of the Way of heaven as the Way of humanity. His New Script thought is inspired by the constant process of moral renewal guided by the immutable Way, variously expressed as the 'mind-heart of high antiquity' and 'oneness.' He was also a scholar who was engaged in learning through which he came to grips with facets of reality. He appreciated the poetic quality of the written word, as evidenced by his study of the *Odes*, which he saw as enlivening and enlightening for the mind and the heart. He affirmed the intimate relationship between socio-political well-being and morality, and placed the onus of governance squarely on individuals who must curtail and extirpate desires. As a learned scholar of the Classics, he nonetheless wrote prolifically on many aspects of statecraft. He was a historian, a philosopher of history, who charted the ebb and flow of history in terms of a morally meaningful historicism. He was a metaphysician who probed the ultimate import of the cosmos in relation to human destiny. His ideas on change and the universally embodying mind-heart were ponderings on the transcendent meta- and supra-material nature of human existence. He was lastly, a political being, confronting head-on the practical problems of his day, and offering concrete counsel as to how state and society could be ameliorated. In short, his works and thought were realizations of the cultural dispostions of a Confucian literatus, products of the Confucian *habitus*.[76]

But still, the paramount fact cannot be forgotten that Wei was a Confucian literatus in late imperial China, a particular time in Chinese history. The study of the Classics and the ultimate goal to retrieve the meanings of the sages' words through painstaking philological investigations dominated the Ch'ing world of learning. What specifically constituted his cultural *habitus* in the first half of the nineteenth century was perhaps an unprecedented form of Confucian 'intellectualism,' to employ Yü Ying-shih's terminology, in which classical texts and words, in and of themselves, became integral parts of ultimate truth.[77] Although it was true that Wei Yuan and others had begun to react against the sterile scholastic form of intellectualism and had jettisoned pure textual classical scholarship in favor of practical reformist advocacy and ethico-moral discourse, classical studies remained the principal arena in which ideas were contested and truths expounded.[78] It is little wonder that this period's two towering intellectual figures, Wei Yuan and his friend Kung Tzu-chen (1792-1841), embraced New Script Confucian classicism. Its central tenet of revealing the profound principles of the Classics concealed in cryptic language stood in sharp relief to the scholastic erudition of their contemporaries, which Wei saw as knowledge without wisdom, technique without understanding.[79] Nonetheless, both Wei Yuan and Kung Tzu-chen were themselves contributors to Ch'ing intellectualism. For the most intelligible and taken-for-granted means to propound truths was classicist exposition.

What Wei Yuan sought to accomplish, then, was nothing out of the ordinary in late imperial China. There was no perceived disjunction between the objective order and his aspirations, and so there was no violation of the sense of limit or sense of reality, that is, the established order. In fact, this mode of engagement with the existing world was, in Bourdieu's term, an experience of '*doxa*,' distinguished from orthodox or heterodox beliefs that after all imply 'awareness and recognition of the possibility of different or antagonistic beliefs.' Wei's reformist, historicist and classicist thinking was '*doxic*,' beyond any questioning of legitimacy; it actualized the structuring dispositions in his *habitus*. Hence its matter-of-fact and self-evident qualities.[80]

Unquestionably, Wei was prompted to advance his reformist thought in a classicist-historicist guise by the deteriorating conditions of his time. Indeed, according to Bourdieu, a crisis is the precondition for generating a critical discourse that 'brings the undiscussed into discussion, the unformulated into formulation.' But this crisis must break 'the immediate fit between the subjective structures and the objective structures.' That did not happen in Wei's day. Insofar as the Classics (the subjective aspirations of change) continued to supply the rhetoric and symbolic resources, the socio-political world (the objective structure) would remain conventional and natural in the eyes of Wei Yuan.[81] Therefore, despite all his talk about change, he balked at fundamental wholesale changes of institutions: 'A profound person does not lightly advocate reforming institutions, but focuses on removing the flaws surrounding institutions. When the flaws are removed, the institutions will return to their origin.'[82]

The language of the Classics was then the language that commanded the most attention in Wei's time. It was an 'authorized language,' as Bourdieu puts it, 'invested with the authority of a group,' and 'the things it designates are not simply expressed but also authorized and legitimated.[83] To put it another way, in the case of Wei Yuan, the authorized language was the language of hermeneutics, an integral part of his *habitus*. John Henderson, in his recent comparative work on the Confucian and Western exegetical traditions, states that in imperial China, as in other premodern cultures, the quest for and affirmation of truth were undertaken in the context of hermeneutics and assumed the form of the commentary.[84] Similarly, Steven Van Zoeren, in his focused study on the hermeneutical history of the *Classic of Odes*, avers that 'the interpretation and exegesis of canonical texts were occasions for normative, political and speculative teaching and thinking.'[85] Thus, exegetical endeavors and philosophic excogitations assumed a most intimate relationship. How a Classic was read was very much a function of the interpreter's ingrained philosophic view. Seen in this light, classical exegesis was in a general sense no different from much of twentieth-century interpretive hermeneutics as the subjective interpenetration of the writerly (the text) and readerly (the interpreter).[86] Of course, there is the notable difference: in China, the ultimate universality of the values embodied in the Classics was not subject to questioning. Therefore, while individual authorial imprints and historico-cultural conditions yielded interpretive latitude, the timeless authority of the classical texts themselves formed the bedrock of the hermeneutic order.[87]

The Confucian Classics, in the broadest sense, were not simply repositories of universal values; they served, in a hermeneutic sense, as the encompassing framework which imbued individual phenomena with meaning and significance. On this score, Confucian exegesis was similar to the Western hermeneutic tradition which has also sought to understand particular phenomena in terms of a larger framework of universal meaning. Secondly, Confucian hermeneutics saw understanding as integrally tied to action and commitment. It regarded the comprehension and elucidation of texts as an existentialist encounter with the living vital messages of the Classics. In this respect, Confucian hermeneutics resembles in particular Hans-Georg Gadamer's philosophical hermeneutics, which rejects the sort of programmatic hermeneutics that reads literal meanings out of texts by treating them as objects in themselves, to be approached without preconceptions of the interpreter, thereby bridging the historico-chronological gap between the reader and the text. Supposedly pruned of presentist prejudices, the interpreter thus intrudes himself/herself into the objectified text. Gadamer, on the contrary, affirms our own biases in the hermeneutic enterprise and sees the fusing of our own historical horizons with that of the texts as the ontological basis of understanding, yielding in the end what he calls 'effective history.' Our cognizance of the historical role of the texts is the very condition of our understanding of the texts. For instance, it will be quite a futile effort to attempt to understand the Bible without prior knowledge of the paramount influence of the Scripture in the historical life of the West. Gadamer says:

> What is reconstructed, a life brought back from the lost past, is not the original. In its continuance in an estranged state it acquires only a secondary, cultural, existence. . . . Similarly, a hermeneutics that regarded understanding as the reconstruction of the original would be no more than the recovery of a dead meaning. . . . The essential nature of the historical spirit does not consist in the restoration of the past, but in thoughtful mediation with contemporary life.[88]

Understanding any texts results from the dynamic fusion of our own horizon of meaning and that of the text.

Confucian, as with Gadamer's, hermeneutics read the Classics as texts which embodied a living and vital cultural tradition. The Confucian literati's hermeneutic reflections on the Classics were their engagement with and participation in a cultural tradition. The literati, as subjects in history, were not simply mouthpieces of transhistoric classical messages. Humanity was creativity, a constant working out of the Classics' ideals.[89] No programmatic methodology dictated Confucian exegesis, notwithstanding certain discernible common strategies and assumptions.[90] Thus, a New Script follower like Wei could readily diverge from his teachers' reading of the Classics. Armed with his notion of change-within-constancy as reality's ontological center of gravity and his goal of socio-political reform as the experiential locus of understanding, Wei communicated with the Classics. His hermeneutic project achieved the intended agreement with the Classics, and vice versa, about a shared reality, a reality defined by the primacy of change and the ultimate return to the Way. Confucian exegesis was an interactive dialogue with a living past ensconced in the Classics. Hermeneutics led not only to a better understanding of the words of the sages but also to their integration in the interpreter's philosophy and life. Wei Yuan would have agreed with Gamader's assertion that 'understanding belongs to the being of that which is understood.'[91]

Further, if we follow Dominick LaCapra's understanding of text-reading, Wei Yuan was a maker of texts in his own cultural world. While many Ch'ing classicist philologists engaged only what LaCapra calls the 'documentary' aspect of the texts, so that they merely conveyed the putative empirical data in the texts, Wei Yuan interacted with the 'work-like' dimensions of the great texts, so that he went beyond the immediate contexts of the Classics and wrought critical and transformative ideas that directly addressed the exigencies of his time.[92] His New Text classicism was thus animated with practical transformative ideas. Wei Yuan was a creative participant in the hermeneutic project. In his dialogic interaction with New Script classicism, he brought to the fore the multivocal and polysemic qualities of the Classics, which he in turn utilized in his confrontation with his present. Wei Yuan saw the interpretation of texts as both a sign of the polity's moral well-being and an important way in which a society was inculcated with correct values. In the end, perhaps this is the authentic legacy of Wei Yuan in a postmodern age: in retelling a master tale of the past, the endeavor is not simply to reconstitute the textual facts in their provincial historical contexts; it is also to reformulate them as vital ingredients in a preferred narrative germane to present needs.

On-cho Ng is Associate Professor of History, Penn State.

ENDNOTES

1. Much has been written on Wei Yuan. The following works are particularly useful for researching the themes of the present essay: Liu Kuang-ching, 'Wei Yuan chih che-hsueh yü ching-shih ssu-hsiang' (The Philosohpy and Theory of Statecraft of Wei Yuan), in The Institute of Modern History, Academia Sinica, ed., *Proceedings*

of the Conference on the Theory of Statecraft of Modern China (Taipei: The Institute of Modern History, Academia Sinica, 1983), pp. 359-90, Wu Tse, 'Wei Yuan ti pien-i ssu-hsiang ho li-shih chin-hua kuan-tien' (The Idea of Change and the View of Historical Evolution in the Philosophy of Wei Yuan), *Li-shih yen-chiu* 9.5(October 1962):33-59, Hsü Kuan-san, 'Kung Wei chih Li-shih che-hsueh yü pien-fa ssu-hsiang' (Kunag Tzu-chen and Wei Yuan's Philosophy of History and Their Ideas of Political Reform), *Chung-hua wen-shih lun-ts'ung* 1st series 13 (January 1980):69-104, Ch'en Yao-nan, *Wei Yuan yen-chiu* (A Study of Wei Yuan) (Hong Kong: Ch'ien-t'i shu-wu, 1979), Ch'i Ssu-ho, 'Wei Yuan yü wan-Ch'ing hsueh-feng' (Wei Yuan and the Intellectual Trends in the Late Ch'ing), *Yen-ching hsueh-pao* 39(December 1950):177-226, Ôtani Toshio, 'Gi Gen keisei shisô ko' (An Investigation of Wei Yuan's Statecraft Thought), *Shirin* 54.6(November 1971)33-75 and Sato Shinji, 'Gi Gen no gakumon to shisô' (The Learning and Thought of Wei Yuan), *Chûgoku koten kenkyû* 12(December 1964):24-40. While Ch'i and Otani stress the centrality of the *chin-wen* (New Text) classical tradition in Wei's thought, both Liu and Sato emphasize its syncretic nature. A good chronological account of Wei's life and scholarship is Wang Chia-chien, *Wei Yuan nien-p'u* (a Chronological Biography of Wei Yuan) (Taipei: Institute of Modern History, Academia Sinica, 1967). As regards English-language works, the following are particularly notable: Peter Mitchell, 'The Limits of Reformism: Wei Yuan's Reaction to Western Intrusion,' *Modern Asian Studies* 6.2 (April 1972):175-204, Jane Kate Leonard, *Wei Yuan and China's Rediscovery of the Maritime World* (Cambridge, Mass.: Harvard Unviersity Press, 1984) and Benjamin Elman, 'The Relevance of Sung Learning in the Late Ch'ing: Wei Yuan and the *Huang-ch'ao ching-shih wen-pien*,' *Late Imperial China* 9.2(December 1988):56-85.

2. On this idea, see Rockwell Gray, *The Imperative of Modernity: An Intellectual Biography of José Ortega y Gasset* (Berkeley, 1989), pp. 81-83.

3. Wei Yuan, *Wei Yuan chi* [Collected Works of Wei Yuan] (Peking, 1983), p. 8. This source is hereafter cited as WYC. All translations of quotes from Chinese-language sources are mine.

4. *Huang-ch'ao ching-shih wen-pien* [Collected Treatises on Statecraft of the Ch'ing Dynasty] (Taipei, fascimile reproduction of 1873 edition, 1976), preface, p. 1. For descriptions on the contents of this collection, see Frederic Wakeman, 'The Huang-ch'ao ching-shih wen-pien,' *Ch'ing-shih wen-t'i* 1.10(Feb. 1969)8-22, Peter Mitchell, 'Futher Notes on the HCCSWP,' *Ch'ing-shih wen-t'i* 2.3(July 1970):40-6 and Leonard, pp. 19-24. On Wei's conceptions on 'statecraft,' see Elman.

5. A succinct summary of Wei's statecraft writings can be found in Leonard, pp. 18-31.

6. Benjamin A. Elman, *From Philosophy to Philology: Intellectual and Social Aspects of Change in late Imperial China* (Cambridge, MA: Harvard University Press, 1984), pp. 177-80.

7. On the rise of the New Text learning in the Ch'ing period in the Ch'ang-chou area in central China in the Yangtze delta, see Benjamin A. Elman, *Classicism, Politics, and Kinship: The Ch'ang-chou School of New Text Confucianism in Late Imperial China* (Berkeley, 1990). More specifically on Chuang Ts'un-yü and Liu Feng-lu's New Text ideas and their relationship to the original New Text notions of the Han Dynasty (206 B.C.-A.D. 220), see my 'Mid Ch'ing New Text (*chin-wen*) Classical Learning and Its Han Provenance: The Dynamics of a Tradition of Ideas,' *East Asian History*, forthcoming in December 1994.

8. Nelson Goodman, *Ways of Worldmaking* (Indianapolis, 1978). For critiques of and discussions on Goodman's thesis, see L. Aagaard-Mogensen, R. Pinxten and F. Vandamme, eds., *Worldmaking's Ways* (Ghent, 1987).

9. Bourdieu spells out the notion of *habitus* at great length in two theoretical treatises: *Outline of a Theory of Practice*, Richard Nice, trans. (Cambridge, 1977) and *The Logic of Practice*, Richard Nice, trans. (Stanford, 1990).

10. Goodman, pp. 6-7.

11. Stephen C. Pepper, *Concept and Quality: A World Hypothesis* (La Salle, 1967), pp. 1-34.

12. The preface was entitled 'Wu-chin Chuang hsiao-tsung-po i-shu hsü' (Preface to the Bequeathed Works of Chuang, Lineage Head of Wu-chin), collected in WYC, pp. 236-8.

13. On this particular text and the general question of the New Script and Old Script versions of this Confucian classic, see Steven Van Zoeren, *Poetry and Personality: Reading, Exegesis, and Hermeneutics in Traditional China* (Stanford, 1991), pp. 80-90.

14. WYC, p. 236.

15. WYC, pp. 237.

16. On the rise and development of *k'ao-cheng* in the Ch'ing period, see Yü Ying-shih, 'Some Preliminary Observations on the Rise of Ch'ing Confucian Intelectualism,' *Tsing Hua Journal of Chinese Studies* 11.1&2(Dec. 1975):105-46, and Elman, *From Philosophy, passim*.

17. WYC, pp. 237-8.

18. 'Liu li-pu i-shu hsü' (Preface to Liu Feng-lu's Bequeathed Works), collected in WYC, pp. 241-3.

19. WYC, p. 241.

20. Goodman, pp. 10-12.

21. The idea here is that although Ch'i was a dominant feudal state in the Chou dynasty that ruled at one time on behalf on the royal Chou house, it must yield to the culturally and morally superior state of Lu, the home state of Confucius. In other words, the military leadership of Ch'i must be supplanted by the moral and spiritual leadership of Lu.

22. WYC, p. 242.

23. For a more detailed discussion on the varied elaborate expressions of these New Script notions, see Ng, 'Mid Ch'ing.'

24. Cf. Hayden White, 'Foucault Decoded: Notes from Underground,' *History and Theory* 12.1(1973):48.

25. WYC, pp. 242-3.

26. Goodman, pp. 12-14.

27. WYC, pp. 134-6.

28. WYC, p. 133.

29. WYC, p. 134.

30. WYC, p. 133.

31. WYC, pp. 119-120.

32. Wang Chia-chien, p. 40. See also HCCCHP, 1292:1a-b.

33. WYC, pp. 119-21.

34. This work is collected in *Huang-ch'ing ching-chieh hsü-pien* (Additions to *The Classical Exegeses of the Imperial Ch'ing*) (Taipei: I-wen yin-shu-kuan, 1961 reprint), 1292:6a-b. This voluminous collection of writings on the ancient Classics was compiled by Wang Hsien-ch'ien (1842-1918). It is hereafter cited as HCCCHP.

35. WYC, p. 120

36. Note that there was another work by Wei Yuan on the New Script Classics which he wrote late in his life, but it is no longer extant. He completed *An Investigation of the Methods and Teachings of the New and Old Script Classical Masters in the Two Han Dynasties* (Liang-Han ching-shih chin-ku-wen chia-fa k'ao) in 1855, a year or so before his death. Glimpses of this work can be caught in the survived preface. In the first part of the preface, Wei re-presented verbatim the contentions he had made in the preface to Liu Feng-lu's collected works. In the second half, Wei told of his plan to delineate the transmission of the teachings of the masters and schools of the various Classics. His ultimate aim was to recover the teachings of the New

Script masters. The work appeared in large part to be the reconstruction of the corpus of New Script Classics by 'culling what was recorded in the histories and treatises' and 'evidential verification of each individual's [works].' See WYC, pp. 151-3.

37. WYC, pp. 109-14.

38. WYC, pp. 116.

39. HCCCHP, 1280:1a-b.

40. HCCCHP, 1280:2a-5a.

41. WYC, pp. 117-8.

42. Quoted in Ch'en Yao-nan, p. 52.

43. WYC, p. 161.

44. Quoted in Lu Pao-ch'ien, *Ch'ing-tai ssu-hsiang-shih* (A History of Ch'ing Thought) (Taipei: Kuang-wen shu-chu, 1978), p. 256.

45. *Ibid.*, p. 256.

46. 'The way of hegemon' referred to a period (722-481 B.C.) in the Chou dynasty when, because of royal weakness, a succession of powerful feudal lords, given the title of *pa* (hegemon) by the Chou imperial house, ruled China on behalf of the Chou kings.

47. The quotes are found in Wu Tse, pp. 45-6.

48. Goodman, pp. 14-17.

49. WYC, p. 227.

50. WYC, p. 48.

51. For a more detailed parade of the examples that Wei Yuan used, see Hsü Kuan-san, pp. 89-91.

52. WYC, pp. 78-9.

53. WYC, p. 48.

54. WYC, pp. 60-1.

55. WYC, pp. 48-9.

56. This statement appears in Wei's *An Essay on the Planning of the Salt Monopoly (Ch'ou-ts'o pien)*. See WYC, p. 432.

57. This statement appears in another of Wei's reformist writing, *A Record of Sea Transport in 1826 (Tao-kuang ping-shu hai-yün chi)*. See WYC, p. 418.

58. WYC, pp. 26-27.

59. WYC, pp. 78-79.

60. WYC, pp. 26-27.

61. *Lao-tzu pen-i* (Shanghai: Commercial Press, 1947 reprint), p. 47.

62. WYC, p. 72.

63. WYC, pp. 10-11.

64. WYC, pp. 12-13.

65. WYC, p. 258.

66. *Laot-tzu pen-i*, p. 3 and WYC, p. 254.

67. *Lao-tzu pen-i*, p. 93.

68. WYC, p. 257.

69. WYC, p. 258.

70. WYC, p. 43.

71. WYC, p. 256.

72. Cf. Arthur O. Lovejoy, 'Milton and the Paradox of the Fortunate Fall,' in Marcus Klein and Robert Pack, eds., *Innocence and Experience* (Boston and Toronto: Little, Brown and Company, 1966), pp. 64-72.

73. Cf. Roger L. Shinn, 'Tillich as Interpreter and Disturber of Contemporary Civilization,' in James Luther Adams, Wilhelm Pauck and Roger Lincoln Shinn, eds., *The Thought of Paul Tillich* (San Francisco: Harper and Row, 1985), pp. 52-3 and also James Luther Adams, 'Introduction: The Storms of Our Times and *Starry Nights*,' in *ibid.*, p. 13.

74. Bourdieu, *Outline*, pp. 71-2.

75. Bourdieu, *Logic*, pp. 55-58.

76. I am describing these paradigmatic attributes of Wei Yuan as a Confucian literatus in accordance with those of an ideal-type Confucian intellectual, as depicted by Tu Wei-ming. See 'The Way, Learning, and Politics in Classical Confucian Humanism,' in Tu Wei-ming, *Way, Learning, and Politics: Essays on the Confucian Intellectual* (Albany: State University of New York Press, 1993), pp. 1-12.

77. For a definitiion of the term as used by Yü, see Yü, p. 137.

78. On the 'fracturing' of the Ch'ing philological classical learning, see Elman, *Philology*, pp. 233-48. On Wei Yuan's dissatisfaction with *k'ao-cheng* philology, see Elman, 'Relevance of Sung Learning,' pp. 56-85.

79. On Kung's New Script thought, see my 'Revisiting Kung Tzu-chen's (1792-1841) New Text (*chin-wen*) Thought: An Excursion in the History of Ideas,' *Journal of Oriental Studies* Vol. 33, forthcoming.

80. Cf. Bourdieu, *Outline*, pp. 164-68.

81. Cf. Bourdieu, *Outline*, pp. 168-9.

82. WYC, p. 46.

83. Bourdieu, *Outline*, p. 170.

84. John B. Henderson, *Scripture, Canon, and Commentary: A Comparison of Confucian Western Exegesis* (Princeton: Princeton University Press, 1992), pp. 3-4.

85. Steven Van Zoeren, *Poetry and Personality: Reading, Exegesis and Hermeneutics in Traditional China* (Stanford: Stanford University Press, 1991), p. 2.

86. On the 'contemporary' hermeneutic implications of traditional Chinese exegesis, see Van Zoeren, pp. 3-7.

87. It may be instructive to look at American socio-politico-legal culture today. People debate social questions by interpreting and with reference to the American consitituion, but almost no one questions the constitution itself. If Wei Yuan is characterized as 'conservative,' a staunch defender of the Confucian *habitus*, then even many of our 'liberals' are in fact quite conservative, to the extent that they are timid guardians of the constitutional principles.

88. Gadamer, *Truth and Method*, W. Glyn-Doerpel, trans. (London, 1975), pp. 149-50.

89. On the existentialist dimensions of the Confucian literatus, see Tu Wei-ming, *passim*.

90. Henderson, *passim*.

91. Gadamer., xix.

92. Cf. LaCapra, *Rethinking Intellectual History: Texts, Contexts, Language* (Ithaca: Cornell University Press, 1983), pp. 26-30.

Chapter V

Is the Place of Nothingness Not a Place?: Worldmaking and Criticism in Modern Japanese Philosophy

Steven Heine*

> 'Space is nowhere. Space is inside it like honey in a hive.'
> Joë Bousquet[1]

I
Japanese Conceptions of Time and Space

Philosophical worldmaking can be said to consist of the constructing, or the reconstructing, of the fundamental elements of time and space. Typically, traditional and modern Japanese thinkers argue for a synthetic, nondualistic outlook which emphasizes the inseparability and ultimate identity of these two elements, for '(t)he 'now' of immediacy is always a 'here' as well.'[2] That is, the categories of time and space are equalizable and interchangeable. A prime example of a view of the unity of time and space is Nishida Kitarô's (1870-1945) notion of the 'logic of place' (*basho no ronri*) based on a 'contradictory self-identity' (*mujunteki jiko dôitsu*) that characterizes 'absolute nothingness' (*zettai mu*), which refers to the interdependence, ultimate insubstantiality, and thus the absolute mediation of nonobjectifiable opposites. Nishida, the founder of the Kyoto School of modern Japanese philosophy, seeks to reconcile conceptual polarities and dichotomies based on traditional Zen Buddhist doctrines that situate enlightenment in terms of the nonduality of ultimate (*nirvana*) and mundane (*samsara*) reality, and in a way that recalls the Western monistic tradition expressed in Gnostic and Neo-Platonic sources. 'In my view,' he writes, 'the phenomenal world is spatial in the form 'from many to one' . . . and yet is temporal in the form 'from one to many'. . . .   This is the self-contradictory structure of the conscious act.'[3] For Nishida and the Kyoto School, oppositions and contradictions involving temporality and spatiality are illusory ideations which can and must be overcome through contemplative philosophical insight, often supported by meditation experience.

Nishida's notion of place represents the culmination of his lifelong philosophical quest to discern the ground of pure experience by drawing on East Asian sources, especially Zen thought, from which basis he engages in dialogue with a variety of Western philosophical standpoints, including classical Greek philosophy and medieval mysticism as well as modern American pragmatism, German idealism, and continental phenomenology. For Nishida, place does not refer to an idea of utopia or heterotopia, but functions as a metaphor for the transformative matrix that lies at the basis of all perceptions of consciousness and acts of judgment. Nishida's position has long had its critics, including Buddhists, who feel that place reifies and objectifies nonsubstantive, impermanent reality, and non-Buddhists, who maintain that Nishida has failed to address concrete social and ethical issues. In particular, the social critics suggest that Nishida, at least in part, may have developed the notion of place, which he tends to associate in some passages with imperial hegemony, in support of Japanese nationalist ideology before World War II.

My aim in this paper is to review critically Nishida's philosophical writings that express the notion of place as well as the various criticisms that have emerged both prior to and since the war. I will argue, however, that the problematics in Nishida's philosophical worldmaking do not stem so much from the kinds of metaphysical or socio-ethical limitations suggested by most critics, but rather from the fact that his modern logical style of thought and writing fails to capture the traditional Zen form of expression that uses irony and paradox to undermine its own assertions. In other words, the reification of place which critics point to in Nishida derives from the absence in his writings of the kinds of rhetorical devices that are found in the medieval Sino-Japanese Zen records that he seeks to convey to a twentieth-century audience which try to insure that all conceptualizations are seen as provisional pedagogical tools rather than objectified, hypostatized entities.

I will begin with a brief overview of traditional Japanese thought concerning time and space and of Nishida's role as its primary modern interpreter.

The modern Japanese sense of worldmaking based on establishing an identity of time and space is the result of the historical interplay and theoretical resolution of two conceptual currents: the Buddhist view of impermanence (*mujô*) as the key manifestation and symbol of the insubstantiality of reality experienced during times of loss, uncertainty, instability, death, and dissolution; and the indigenous Shinto emphasis on the sacrality of spaces understood in terms of the 'betweenness,' gaps, or intervals (*ma*) lurking betwixt and between conventional sites, such as shadows, openings, hollows, crevices, etc. An interesting poetic expression of the unity of impermanence and spatial gaps evoking the aesthetic ideal of 'profound mystery' (*yûgen*) is the following 5-line, 31-syllable verse (*waka*) by the medieval Buddhist poet, Saigyô:

> A heart subdued (*kokoro naki*)
> Yet poignant sadness (*aware*)
> Is so deeply felt;
> A crane flying over the marsh
> As autumn dusk descends.

Here, Saigyô depicts the experience of a transcendental emotion, deeper than and enriching the usual sense of Buddhist detachment suggested in the opening line, based on the contemplation of a deceptively simple natural scene: the bird flying off at the time of transition in the daily and seasonal cycles symbolized by the twilight sky. In the image of the 'autumn dusk,' an example of *yûgen* frequently used in medieval literature, temporal and spatial qualities converge to suggest movement, ephemerality, and distance in a physical as well as a spiritual sense.

Nevertheless, despite persistent claims of nonduality, there is a tendency for Japanese thinkers to give a preference or priority to one side of the identity, either to the side of temporality or to the side of spatiality, while subsuming the other side within the dominant one. For example, the thirteenth century Zen thinker Dôgen formulates a cluster of doctrines stressing the unity of time and space, including 'being-time' (*uji*, or all beings are time and all times are being), 'here-and-now enlightenment' (*genjôkôan*), and 'impermanence-Buddha-nature' (*mujô-busshô*, or the equality of transiency and ultimate reality). In an effort to restore the significance of the basic Buddhist doctrine of impermanence, which he felt was distorted by disguised assumptions of eternalism among his contemporary philosophers, Dôgen tends to give priority to temporality and to view spatiality as an extension of it. He argues, 'The mountain is time and the sea is time. If they were not time, there would be no mountain or sea. You must realize that the time of the mountain and sea occurs right now. If time should deteriorate, the mountain and sea will deteriorate as well; and if time does not deteriorate, neither will the mountain or sea.'[4] In this case, the identity of time and space (or beings) is argued from the standpoint of the former rather than the latter, as mountains and seas are defined by their innate link to temporality.

On the other hand, some Japanese thinkers exhibit the reverse tendency of emphasizing the identity of time and space from the standpoint of spatiality, thereby subsuming temporality within it. For example, traditional Pure Land Buddhist thinkers such as Genshin portray enlightenment as a spiritual rebirth (*ôjô*) in the 'western Paradise' that is described in exquisitely vivid language as a realm filled with timelessly precious and beautiful objects. Also, both esoteric Buddhist and Shinto priests have built temples and shrines following the occult law of geomancy, according to which there are sacred spiritual-physical energies or force-fields linking sacred mountains and other natural locations. An interesting modern example of giving priority to space is found in the critique of Martin Heidegger by Watsuji Tetsurô. Watsuji, a Kyoto School intellectual historian and anthropologist known for initiating cross-cultural philosophical interpetations of Dôgen's view of time in comparison with Hegel, Bergson, and others, also was critical of Heidegger for overemphasizing temporality at the expense of a clear focus on spatiality. In his work *Climate and Culture*, written in the late 1920s when Heidegger was first being translated and interpreted in Japan, Watsuji begins by arguing that Heidegger's analysis in *Being and Time* of Dasein (or Being-there) as Being-in-the-world tends to neglect the side of 'worldhood' or 'there-ness.' These notions are introduced and discussed by Heidegger, but they are given relatively little attention when compared to the way he highlights the existential issues of anxiety, guilt, and death that are crucial to the formation of temporality. Watsuji goes on to examine the climatic roots of various cultural ideologies and religious traditions, including the monsoon, temperate, and desert climate mentalities.

Nishida Kitarô also seems to give priority to space in formulating his primary metaphysical principle of 'place' (*basho*), or the place of absolute nothingness (*zettai mu*). The notion of place, which can also be translated as field, context, locus, or topos (Nishida was influenced by Plato's notion of *topos*), refers not to a specific location or site but to the 'where' of ultimate reality ruled by the principle of contradictory self-identity, 'an undifferentiated . . . arena where all things arise, except that it is not a place or arena, but an aperture or opening.'[5] Place remains beyond yet functions through particular locations in space. Therefore, Nishida frequently stresses that place 'has a spatial character in respect of the one negating the many in the order of coexistence, and is temporal in respect of the many negating the one in the order of occurrence. Time and space are not independent forms, but only dimensions of the self-transforming matrix of space-time.'[6] Nishida also extensively examines temporality in developing the notion of the 'continuity of discontinuity' (*hirenzoku no renzoku*), which clarifies the significance of the eternal now in relation to the passage of time. Yet, in the culminating stage of the development of 'Nishida philosophy' (or 'Nishida *tetsugaku*') he choses a spatial rather than a temporal metaphor, in large part to demonstrate that absolute nothingness is not an abstract, ethereal realm, but is invariably manifested in concrete reality. Nevertheless, '(t)he Platonic analogy . . . breaks down quickly, for its spatial character presupposes the complete externality of the *Topos* with respect to that which abides within it.'[7]

The title of Jonathan Z. Smith's book, *Map is Not Territory*,[8] which deals largely with the encounter between universal and local religious traditions, suggests that spaces and places are not to be understood only as literal sites but as conceptual lattices shaped in large part by ideological assumptions and bids for power. While this is partly the case for Nishida, he also emphasizes the contrary view, that is, that place is not only conceptual but occurs right here-and-now in the concrete world. Yet, Nishida's view is different than Gaston Bachelard's topo-analysis in *The Poetics of Space*,[9] which analyzes quaint microcosmic locations, especially in the home environment. Nishida focuses on the macrocosmic, or, rather, on the 'where' that is beyond the distinction of macrocosm and microcosm, or universal and particular. Nishida, who was very much influenced by Husserlian phenomenology, may not have been familiar with Heidegger's work, especially the post-*Being and Time* writings. But his use of the image of place recalls the later Heidegger's turn to spatial metaphors, such as 'clearing,' 'region,' and 'fourfold,' though Heidegger also frequently writes of Being in a temporal sense as an 'event' (*Eriegnis*) or 'event of appropriation.'

It is important to recognize that, although almost always translated as the 'logic of place' (or field, context, locus, topos, etc.), Nishida's approach is actually a 'topological or contextual logic,' based on his use of the adjectival form in Japanese (*bashoteki ronri*) rather than the prepositional (*basho no ronri*, or 'logic *of* place').[10] Thus, Nishida's topological logic (sometimes referred to as predicative logic), in contrast to objective, subjective, or even dialectical logic, neither proposes a formal logical analysis of place in contrast to other categories such as the void nor intends either a reification of place as an other-worldly absolute or a hypostatization of it as a particular locale. Nishida's view is not a utopia in the sense of a perfect place (literally 'no place,' *u-topos*) or a heterotopia as a collection of multiple individuated locations. Although influenced by traditional Japanese notions of sacrality, he does not wish to identify place with holy mountains, geomantic forces, or ritual symbols such as mandalas (circular symbols used in meditation) or stupas (shrines commemorating burial or other sacred sites). Nor does he resurrect the traditional Buddhist notion of pure space (*akasa*) as a symbol of *nirvana* that resolves the problematics of the world of *samsara* characterized by the incessant flux of time.

Yet, the question naturally arises: Where is this place, and why does Nishida refer to its process of 'self-determination'? If the place of nothingness is not a place, why use spatial imagery? And if it is potentially any and every place, how can the appropriate sites be located and distinguished from those that do not disclose the absolute? Nishida's philosophy has received persistent criticism from a variety of sources raising such questions, from Zen and Pure Land Buddhists as well as from Marxists and other non-Buddhists, and for philosophical, religious, and, very frequently, political reasons. Nishida's two foremost disciples, Tanabe Hajime (influenced by Pure Land theology) and Nishitani Keiji (deriving from Zen meditation), are among his sharpest critics who argue for understanding place in a more metaphorical, existential sense as an interior capacity for fulfilled subjectivity. At the same time, both before and after the second world war, Marxists and leftists, who apparently originally coined the moniker 'Kyoto School' in the 1930s as a negative term, have taken Nishida to task for the nationalist implications they find in his wartime writings — a Hegelian-Heideggerian tendency to identify the place of the absolute with the state, in this case, imperial Japan.

Nishida's writings during this period, in addition to his professional and personal activities, are multifaceted and very complex. He was primarily a pure philosopher although he did participate in discussions and debates about national ideology. It is important to point out that there can be no easy judgments either condemning him for fanatical nationalism or dismissing a political criticism altogther. Rather, as Pierre Bourdieu suggests in his discussion of *The Political Ontology of Martin Heidegger*,[11] who was similarly involved in a philosophical worldmaking which became entangled with fascist political ideology before World War II, there may be no such thing as autonomous philosophy independent of a socio-political environment so that it is necessary to recognize a dual reading of Nishida: the primary one philosophical, and the secondary one ideological. Furthermore, the distinction between an existential and a political criticism is not so clear-cut, because some of the Buddhist criticism has also focused on political issues, ranging from a right-wing perspective in the prewar writings of Tanabe, who at that time may have felt that Nishida was not sufficiently supportive of nationalism, to a left-wing perspective in the prewar work of Ichikawa Hakugen and the recent methodology known as Critical Buddhism (*hihan bukkyô*), both of which challenge the tacit complicity of Kyoto School thinkers with the emperor system.

In the next two sections, I will explain the formation of Nishida's philosophy of the place of absolute nothingness and assess the various criticisms, Buddhist and non-Buddhist, which suggest that Nishida portrays place in a way that is alternatively either too abstract or too specific. In the concluding section, I argue that the limitation in Nishida's philosophical worldmaking is not so much based on existential or political grounds, which reflect contemporary issues, but rather on the way he overlooks or at least chooses not to use key elements of the traditional Zen Buddhist discursive style, such as ironic wordplays, tautologies, and paradoxes, although he seeks to articulate Zen thought in modern perspectives. The medieval Zen records often include what can be referred to as rhetorical safeguard devices against overly literal or transcendental interpretations of sacred space by employing a paradoxical methodology of at once evoking and refuting, or constructing and deconstructing, supernatural imagery from an ironic standpoint.

II
The Formation of Nishida's Philosophy of Place

Nishida's thought developed through four stages of a complex, lifelong philosophical project, with the philosophy of place emerging prominently in the final two stages. The underlying goal of his project is a systematic disclosure of the unified ground of all forms of experiential reality, encompassing the intuitive and rational, aesthetic and moral, contemplative and active, religious and secular, and metaphysical and mathematical. This ground is disclosed in a manner that attempts to be faithful to Japanese spirituality, particularly Zen, yet borrows from Western logical rigor, especially Aristotelian logic and Kantian epistemology. Although references to Western thought, from the classics through medieval and modern philosophers, are actually frequently more abundant than Buddhist sources, it is clear from both the philosophical content of his work and recorded private remarks to colleagues that Zen meditation lies at the root of Nishida's philosophy. Yet Nishida is by no means a Zen apologist. Nor does he engage in comparative philosophy as an end in itself or to assert the supremacy of Buddhism — a delicate but critical standpoint not always perfectly upheld by his disciples. Rather, comparison is used as a philosophical methodology for uncovering the universal logical-ontological foundations of the multiple manifestations and dimensions of the unity of experience.

The initial stage of Nishida's philosophy is manifested in his first major work, *An Inquiry into the Good* (1911),[12] which analyzes reality in terms of the notion of pure experience, the direct and immediate givenness or presentness of reality. Pure experience, identified with the 'good' (*zen*) as a unity of will and spirit, knowledge and action, is the fundamental moment of perception prior to thought, reflection, or judgment. It is the universal intentionality, not a passive perception, to 'know events as they truly are' without hesitation or deliberation. In this work, Nishida is influenced by William James's radical empirical methodology which seeks to get at things as they are, though with mystical or contemplative implications based on a sense of primordial harmony, rather than James's pragmatist moral imperative. The next stage, *Intuition and Reflection in Self-Consciousness* (1917),[13] marks an attempt, later acknowledged by Nishida to be unsuccessful, to overcome the psychologism or overtly subjectivistic tone of the earlier work. Here, Nishida seeks to escape from referring primarily to the self or the human subject and to find a neutral vantage point that encompasses subject and object, self and other, without giving priority to either side. He synthesizes Henri Bergson's 'pure duration' with neo-Kantian categories to eliminate psychological terminology and formulate an epistemological notion of self-consciousness as a transcendental ego at the foundation of experience.

The third stage, beginning with *From the Acting to the Seeing* (1927), marks Nishida's breakthough or radical reversal from the subjectivist tendencies of his previous writings toward a neutral determination of reality beyond subject/object, internal/external, psychological/metaphysical dichotomies. This results in the logic of place of absolute nothingness, or, rather, in a topological or contextual logic articulating the meaning of nothingness. This can also be referred to as the 'logic of truly Subjective Self-awakening,' keeping in mind that '(t)he logic of place, however, neither confronts objective logic nor excludes it.'[14] According to one interpreter, 'The logic of place enabled [Nishida] to organize the whole of the efforts of philosophy — perceptual judgment, phenomenology of consciousness, enlightenment — in a single systematic whole . . .'[15]

Absolute nothingness is rooted in the Mahayana Buddhist doctrine of emptiness as the nondifferentiable and nonsubstantive ground of reality. Genuine emptiness or nothingness, though unsupported by any prior ontological condition, remains the basis of all phenomena, in contrast to the Western category of mere nonexistence or absence, for which the Japanese term *kyomu* (literally 'hollow nothingness') is used. According to Nishida, Western thought, with the exception of Neo-Platonic mystics like Meister Eckhart, Nicholas Cusanus, and Jakob Boehme, has generally been preoccupied with the opposition between being (*u*) and nonbeing (*kyomu*) and has failed to penetrate to absolute nothingness. Place is influenced by Plato's concept of *topos* as the 'receptacle of ideas' as well as Husserlian phenomenology and perhaps even quantum physics, the latter two representing modern standpoints that view the world from a synthetic and dynamic contextual perspective. The notion of place (*basho*) highlights the Zen emphasis that emptiness not be seen as an abstract transcendental realm detached from concrete existence but as perpetually realized in the ever-varying manifestations of the fullness of being, thus according with the famous *Heart Sutra* dictum: 'Form is none other than emptiness; emptiness is none other than form.'

Place as a unifying principle can be understood provisionally in terms of three dimensions. The first dimension is the physical world of objectifiable being corresponding to the noematic realm in Husserl's terminology. The second is the world of human reality, the subjective or noetic aspect of experience, that is, the realm of consciousness which perceives and evaluates objective entities. This realm was given priority in Nishida's early writings, but is seen now as an aspect of the topological self-determination of nothingness on a relative level which is experienced as a no-thing that makes possible our perception of and judgments concerning objects. The third dimension is the intelligible world of absolute nothingness, the nonsubstantive synthetic context for all appearances and judgments encompassing but unrestricted by the noetic and noematic, which are not independent entities linked together but a single inseparable event. The intelligible world is the basis of the good, the true, and the beautiful, and it is realizable only through the 'dazzling obscurity' of sudden and selfless illumination. Here, Nishida's work has significant affinities with a variety of sources which function on the fringes of mainstream Western discourse, including mystics who experience the unity-in-differentiation of the Godhead as expressed in Gnostic, Neo-Platonic, or Kabbalistic writings, and modern poststructuralist and deconstructive philosophers who seek to overcome logocentric tendencies in conventional Western thought and language by highlighting the infinite variety of signifiers without a single, transcendental signified standing substantively in the background.

The final stage of Nishida's work, culminating in his last major essay written at the end of World War II just before his death, 'Topological Logic and the Religious Worldview' (1945),[16] is a clarification of the central tenets of the previous stage in terms of two interrelated topics: the spiritual or existential in addition to the metaphysical or epistemological implications of place; and the temporal-historical foundations of culture and, in particular, the distinctiveness of Japanese culture in contrast to the West. Nishida shows that place is not a simple oneness but the dialectical interplay of antithetical, contradictory forces manifested in time as the Eternal Now embracing past/future in the absolute presencing of each and every complete moment. Religion, the cultural dimension that alone deals with the ultimate concern of life and death, can be transformed into a new foundation for world society through a synthesizing of Christian morality and Buddhist meditation on the basis of absolute nothingness that allows for the integrity and self-determination of each tradition as oppositions that are reconciled as part of the principle of contradictory self-identity. But during this last stage, perhaps under pressure from the government which he may or may not have been trying to resist,[17] and despite an otherwise international perspective, Nishida rather chauvinistically stresses how the unique features of Japanese spirituality realized in the imperial state are necessary for the overcoming of the Western scientific, mechanistic worldview. For example, Nishida suggests that the superiority of the imperial system over its Western rivals is due to the governing of the Japanese nation on the principle of nothingness rather than being.

III
Nishida's Critics

Nishida's philosophy of place, or the unity of subject and object in the acts of perception and judgment, has clearly dominated Japanese thought for the last two-thirds of the twentieth century, but, like any prevailing perspective, it has received criticism from a variety of sources, including his own disciples and other Zen Buddhist scholars and thinkers, as well as non-Buddhist philosophers, particularly Marxists and poststructuralists. This criticism was initiated before the Second World War, while Nishida was alive and at the peak of his creativity and influence on Japanese society. It continues to the present time as questions are increasingly being raised about the prewar role of Nishida and the Kyoto School as a whole, which is accused of contributing to nationalist ideology and political fanaticism in a way that recalls the questions raised about the involvement of Heidegger, de Man, and Eliade in European Nazism and Fascism.

Kyoto School Criticism: Tanabe and Nishitani

The philosophy of Tanabe Hajime developed both under the sway of and as a critical response to Nishida's thought. Tanabe considered Nishida overtly mystical or contemplative in tone, neglecting the importance of social experience or one's interaction with the Thou (both vertically with God and horizontally with community). Tanabe's standpoint was influenced by his training in the other-power (*tariki*) tradition of Pure Land Buddhist faith rather than the self-power (*jiriki*) path of Zen meditation. He was also affected by the personal experience of his wife's sacrificial suicide on his behalf and the need to reconcile and redeem his own philosophical development in light of the Japanese military defeat and subsequent antinationalist criticism. Whereas Nishida identifies absolute nothingness with the transcendental good as the logical-ontological unity of opposites, Tanabe views nothingness in terms of the spiritual power of love in the social-ethical mission of repentance (*zange*) and resurrection. Nishida stresses action-intuition operating logically in the Eternal Now, while Tanabe focuses on the perpetual existential function of action-faith through the blind alleys and fundamental ignorance of the pathways of history.

The prewar critique of Nishida by Tanabe, whose earliest work was in the field of mathematics, is based on the notion of the 'logic of species' (*shu no ronri*) as a correction of topological logic or logic of place. According to Tanabe, Nishida's philosophy emphasizes the primacy of the universal encompassing the particular, or of the individual subsumed by the universal, and overlooks the crucial intermediary role of the category of species operating in logic and history. During this stage, Tanabe more or less equated species with the state and became known as the most virulent Kyoto School supporter of imperialism, a view for which he was attacked by progressives and later felt a deep sense of remorse.

At the end of the war, Tanabe responded to this challenge by formulating the philosophy of continuing self-criticism or absolute criticism, a total self-negation that can only come from the side of the Absolute, which appears as the power of self-negating love. In *Philosophy as Metanoetics* (1946, but written in 1944)[18] and other works, he argues that absolute criticism requires a transformational or profound change-of-heart experience based on a spiritual turning, metanoesis (*zangedô*), or repentance. Metanoesis, in turn, involves a resurrection through existential dying or relinquishing of one's former self to be reawakened on the basis of nothingness-as-love. In this light, Tanabe reinterprets the Zen doctrine of the 'identity of life-death' (*shôji ichinyo*) as the unified experiential moment of simultaneous self-negation and redemption in an age in which the total destruction of and by humankind has become a real, if not necessarily imminent, possibility. In the last but no doubt most important stage of his career, Tanabe bypasses the debate between place and species, and his criticism of Nishida seems to be that if these notions are left, even if unintentionally, on a strictly metaphysical level of discourse, rather than brought to an intensely existential level of personal repentance, they will fail to penetrate to the fundamentally experiential realm of absolute nothingness.

Nishida's second main disciple, Nishitani Keiji, who was purged after the war and regained prominence beginning in the mid-1950s as the head of the Philosophy Department of Kyoto University, continues some of the nationalist tendencies in both Nishida and Tanabe as well as the existentialist critique of Nishida by Tanabe. However, in contrast to Tanabe's Pure Land-based approach, Nishitani seeks to deepen Kyoto School philosophy based on Zen meditation and Mahayana Buddhist compassion. Nishitani critically reviews 'the criticisms of Nishida's philosophy by Tanabe from the standpoint of the logic of species, by Takahashi [Satomi] from the perspective of finitude and becoming, and by Yamanouchi [Tokuryû] from the claims of a process dialectic . . .'[19] Like these critics, Nishitani feels that Nishida overlooks the process-oriented quality of the unfolding of history that characterizes the absolute, and he directs his attention to an overcoming of the nihilistic and scientific trends in the modern era. Nishitani's approach to the connection between philosophy and religion seems to bear an inverse relation to Nishida's concerns and methods. The starting point for Nishida is the philosophical query, 'What is the nature of pure experience?,' that eventually led him to proclaim that mystical insight alone discloses the fundamental structure of the topological logic of reality. Nishitani's leading question is 'What is religion?' (the title of one of his main works published in 1961 and translated under the title, *Religion and Nothingness*[20]), which involves an examination of the metaphysical foundations of religious experience. Both thinkers, however, appear to view the relationship between absolute and relative, I and Thou, subject and object, not from the standpoint of one side or the other of an irreconcilable opposition, but from the transcendental perspective of the 'and,' which constitutes the conjunctive process itself. The self-negating 'and' represents the place or context of absolute nothingness.

On the other hand, Nishitani, influenced by Nietzsche and Heidegger, is not so much interested in defining the nature of place as in using absolute nothingness as a tool by which to criticize and overcome the nihilistic tendencies in modern Western science which have infected the globe with a world-weary destructiveness and the potential for a catastrophic conflagration. Nishitani employs a threefold distinction in this cultural-epistemological critique: being, relative nothingness, and absolute nothingness. He accuses modern science of a fixation on the realm of being which belies an underlying fascination with nonbeing in the sense of hollowness or absence as well as an inability to understand genuine nothingness. This deficiency is based in part on the way science absorbs and reacts against the Christian monotheistic ideal in which humans gain fulfillment only through a self-negation of their humanity when contrasted with the divinity of God, a view that reinforces the scientific tendency to be oblivious to human needs. Yet science, which lacks a theological, or a teleological, background for its stance is, according to Nishitani, less in tune with the meaning of nothingness than is Christianity. Nishitani maintains that numerous Western thinkers, especially Western mystics and modern existentialists (he seems to prefer Nietzsche's 'innocence of becoming' to the analysis of nothingness in Heideggerian or Sartrean phenomenology), have realized the standpoint of relative nothingness, a partial understanding limited by the attempt to conceptualize nonbeing as an antithesis to being.

Absolute nothingness overcomes this duality, but for Nishitani this overcoming can only by attained by virtue of a bodhisattva-like change-of-heart rather than through logical analysis, as in the case of Nishida (at least prior to his final essay on 'Topological Logic and the Religious Worldview').

Other Buddhist Criticisms: Critical Buddhism
Criticism of the nationalist implications in Nishida's philosophy of place from within the Zen sect stem from the 1930s writings of Ichikawa Hakugen, who remained a forceful critic of the militarist-nationalist trends in samurai-influenced Zen practice through the Vietnam War period by both highlighting the ideals and exposing the weakness of traditional Sino-Japanese recorded sayings of the great masters.[21] Another Zen-based critique which sets up a contrast between the Kyoto School and the doctrines of early Buddhism expressed in Indian Sanskrit sources has come from the recent Critical Buddhism methodology,[22] which to some extent can be seen as a Tokyo-based effort of the Sôtô Zen sect to challenge the philosophical dominance of the Kyoto thinkers including Nishida and Nishitani who are associated with the Rinzai Zen sect.   The Critical Buddhists make a refutation of Nishida's notion of place part of a larger criticism of an underlying problematic standpoint in Mahayana Buddhist metaphysics in China and Japan, leading to the contemporary problems of social discrimination and extreme nationalism.

First, the Critical Buddhists are deeply troubled by the Zen sect's discriminatory practices against outcastes (the so-called *burakumin* or special status community who often work in occupations involving some form of death, which is considered impure, such as crematorium workers, butchers, leather workers, etc.).   One of the main social functions of Zen is the performance of funeral ceremonies for the lay community, including *burakumin*, who are given ceremonial names that reveal their outcaste status while Zen rhetoric continues to stress nonduality, nondiscrimination, and harmony.   In order to understand this dilemma, the Critical Buddhist thinkers set up a contrast between two forms of Buddhism: critical philosophy based on a realization of the early Buddhist doctrine of moral causality (karma) liberated from substantiality; and the substantive, logocentric (which they term '*dhatu-vada*') or topological philosophy that violates causality by seeking a single source or locus of reality.   They argue that Nishida's doctrine of 'place' is a throwback to medieval 'original enlightenment' (*hongaku*) thought, which, by denying causality, tends to foster a false sense of equality that mitigates the need for social responsibility. Original enlightenment and related doctrines such as the universal Buddha-nature (*busshô*) espouse an uncritical tolerance and syncretism that fosters in the name of universal love such problematic viewpoints as the notion of demanding societal harmony (*wa*) at the expense of individuality and a tacit compliance with militarism. These attitudes are in turn supported politically by totalitarian and nationalist ideologies as well as intellectually by *nihonjinron* (cultural exceptionalism or 'Japanese-ism') rhetoric that ends up abetting social discrimination.

The basic weakness of original enlightenment thought is that because, ontologically, it does not allow for the existence of the Other since all things are considered to arise on the basis of the single, undifferentiated primordial 'dhatu' (place or locus), epistemologically and ethically it is rendered incapable of dealing with the inevitably complex manifestations of otherness that force concrete ethical choices. That is, the original enlightenment -influenced topological, *dhatu-vada* doctrines lack a basis and precedent for developing a mechanism for situationally specific, ethically evaluative judgments, and the result is an unreflective endorsement of the *status quo*. According to Hakamaya Noriaki's Critical Buddhist analysis of how epistemological non-discrimination (*musabetsu*) results in social discrimination (*sabetsu*), 'although some interpret the doctrine of original enlightenment as a theory of equality because it claims to recognize the fundamental universal enlightenment of all people, in reality . . . the doctrine of original enlightenment, which in a facile way requires seeking out the fundamental unified ground of enlightenment, must be considered the primary source of [social] discrimination.'[23] In Japan, this results in an acceptance and even support, rather than resistance, for the 'myth of Japanese uniqueness' and related nationalist and nativist ideology that has pervaded post-Tokugawa, especially prewar, intellectual life.[24] Zen, in particular, has often hidden its support for the status quo behind what becomes an elitist aestheticism based on the notion that everything reflects the Buddha Dharma.[25] The criticism suggested here is that Nishida's philosophy of place is one more example of asserting a logocentric basis of reality that renders various individuated appearances somewhat illusory and devalued, thereby resulting in an indifference to and even exploitation of the plight of outcastes who are seen as merely a part of the illusory realm.

Non-Buddhist Criticism: Asada Akira

Leftist criticism of Nishida's philosophy of place as a right-wing ideology began as early as 1932, the year after the Manchurian incident, when the term Kyoto School (Kyoto *gaku-ha*) was coined by Tosaka Jun.[26] From Tosaka's anti-nationalist perspective, recalling Ichikawa's Buddhist criticism, Nishida and his disciples were reactionary romantics idealizing the Japanese tradition while remaining blind to — or even covertly (and by the war more overtly) supporting — the hegemony of imperial ideology (*tennô ideorogii*). This criticism recalls a comment by Michel Serres that any theory of the priority of a single space is imperialistic. Tosaka acknowledged that there was a left-wing slant to some of the Kyoto School thinkers, but he felt that the orientation of the entire group drifted drastically to the right as the wartime approached, ensnaring even the progressives.

A more recent leftist critique of the Kyoto School is suggested by Asada Akira, who gained instant fame (referred to as the 'AA phenomenon') in the early 1980s for his book, *Structure and Power: Beyond Semiotics*,[27] which introduced French poststructuralist theories to Japan from a Marxist perspective. Asada points out that in the prewar work, *The Problems of Japanese Culture*, Nishida distinguishes between two forms of national power: power based on being (*u*) reflected in European kings and nations, which contains conflict between individuals and the whole; and power based on nothingness (*mu*) as in the case of the Japanese emperor which, via the principle of absolute contradictory self-identity, unifies particularism and universalism, atomism and holism from a 'holonic' (*zentaishi*) standpoint ever capable of harmonizing differences. Ironically, the political power of the place of nothingness, according to Asada's critique, is perhaps best symbolized by the 'empty space' of the imperial palace gardens in central Tokyo. Asada remarks that Nishida's philosophy seems at first to be peaceful and pluralistic. But, he argues sardonically, 'When this [power of place] spontaneously spreads, the "Great East Asian Co-Prosperity Sphere" — is this the absolute contradictory self-identity between liberation from European imperialism and aggression by Japanese imperialism — will be formed.'[28]

It must be pointed out, however, that by no means all scholars and commentators on the Kyoto School agree with Asada's view of Nishida. Some view Nishida as a pure philosopher uninvolved in politics, whereas Michiko Yusa argues that Nishida was actually working effectively behind the scenes to challenge militarist orthodoxy. According to Yusa, 'Far from being a recluse or an armchair philosopher, [Nishida] was actively involved in the preservation of freedom of learning and education in opposition to the domestic policies of the nationalistic and militaristic government . . . .which had no little impact on the public.'[29] The questions raised in this debate, as in the controversies involving the participation by Heidegger, Paul de Man, and Mircea Eliade in European Nazi and Fascist ideology, are whether a thinker can be judged and held accountable for every possible implication, consequence, or by-product in his thought or methods. Furthermore, how can he be forgiven for past indiscretions, misjudgments, or mistakes? While a fuller analysis of these issues is beyond the scope of the present paper, it is important to point out that, unlike Nishitani and Heidegger, Tanabe, at least on a philosophical level, did offer a repentance for his pre-war activities, but Nishida died before he had the opportunity to explain and reckon with his own understanding of the relation between his philosophy and politics. Yet, Bourdieu's suggestion, mentioned above, of a dual reading that is simultaneously and ambiguously philosophical and ideological, seems as relevant to the case of Nishida and Japan as it is to Heidegger and the West.

IV
Conclusions: Whither Place

The criticisms of Nishida's philosophy of place have focused primarily on two issues. Kyoto School disciples, who are either Zen or Pure Land Buddhists, suggest that Nishida overlooks the meaning of time in the sense of the unfolding processes of history, which demand personal decision-making or existential choice in the encounter with human destructiveness and nihilism. For Tanabe, coming to terms with this issue is the key to understanding the error of excessive support for nationalism he felt that he and his colleagues committed before the war. Non-Buddhist leftist arguments deal mainly with the issues of militarism and imperialism, and offer a critical voice which in some cases also comes from Buddhists, including the postwar Tanabe as well as Ichikawa and Critical Buddhism. This criticism maintains that Nishida posits the category of place as an independent (non-)entity that is nevertheless located in a particular space, the contradictory space-less space of the imperial palace. Both Buddhists and leftists agree that the social aspect of Nishida's thought is not as well developed as the metaphysical dimension. For the Buddhists, especially Critical Buddhism, correcting Nishida requires rethinking the meaning of tradition and recovering the doctrine of moral causality or karma that was subverted by East Asian notions of original enlightenment. For the non-Buddhists, particularly Asada, the task is to deconstruct the power relations underlying Nishida's ideology.

However, I will point to a problem in Nishida's philosophy from a different angle, which pertains to the question of his use of language and rhetoric in constructing the world based on place, in particular, to his overreliance on Western-style logical formulations at the expense of losing touch with the style of discourse in the Zen Buddhist tradition. As indicated above, some of his translators and interpreters have probably done Nishida a disservice in misrepresenting 'topological logic' as the 'logic *of* place,' thereby hypostatizing the 'where' of nothingness. But part of the problem lies in Nishida's preoccupation with developing a Western logic that lacks some key discursive elements, particularly the use of irony and paradoxical wordplay, in the tradition of medieval Zen records, which he is trying to recapture in a contemporary context. In discussions of sacred places in medieval Zen texts, the commentators move in two directions simultaneously, both of which are generally missing in Nishida's texts (except when he cites these sources) as well as the texts of other Kyoto School thinkers: an ironic refutation of supernatural beliefs concerning the sacrality of space, which is intertwined with a rhetorical flirtation with those same beliefs. Medieval Zen in China and Japan developed in an intellectual climate of competing with popular religions, especially Taoism, Shinto, and folk beliefs, for defining the meaning of spaces populated by local demonic and protective gods or dominated by universal principles such as causality.[30] The Zen rhetorical strategy is to explore yet avoid a commitment to either perspective — that is, either to a popular belief in deities or to a philosophical view of causality — through the construction and deconstruction, mythologization and demythologization that continually plays the opposing beliefs off of one another.

A key example is a Zen *kôan* (spiritual puzzle) record concerning the pilgrimage site of Mt. Wu-t'ai, one of four sacred mountains in medieval China where bodhisattvas were said to appear to those who came seeking visions. This mountain was the abode of the bodhisattva Manjusri, who revealed himself in visions and performed miracles for devout pilgrims. Generally, the Zen anti-ritual, demythological approach shunned such popular symbols, and Rinzai, the founder of one of the main sub-sects within Zen, directly refuted and forbade Mt. Wu-t'ai pilgrimages.[31] Yet, other Zen records are less severe than Rinzai's, and make their point by a playful and ironic rhetorical style. In the *Blue Cliff Record kôan* collection commentary (case no. 35), monk Wu Cho is said to visit the mountain and engage in a dialogue with Manjusri, who, like a typical Zen master, outsmarts the pilgrim. Manjusri asks the monk about the size of the congregations in his monastery, and Wu Cho offers a literal response, 'Some are three hundred, some are five hundred.' When asked the same question in return, Manjusri resorts to a Zen tautology, 'In front, three by three; in back, three by three.' Manjusri, a supernatural ruler of the sacred mountain, 'wins' this round of the dialogue, but the commentary makes it clear that we are not to take too seriously his exploits.

According to the verse commentary:

> Extending throughout the world is the beautiful monastery:
> The Manjusri that fills the eyes is the one conversing.
> Not knowing to open the ˀuddha-eye at his words,
> (Wu Cho) turned his head and saw only the blue mountain crags.[32]

The final line can be read as a criticism of the monk for not paying attention to the vision and words of the bodhisattva who 'fills the eyes' and ears, but it can also be interpreted as a simple, descriptive expression of nature that counteracts the supernatural claims: the mountain crags alone make up the universal/local place of nothingness for Wu Cho, who no longer needs to rely on visions or dialogues with other-worldly beings to experience the true nature of the world. The effectiveness of the last line lies in a double-edged quality that has been deleted in Nishida's attempt at logical worldmaking, even in his unique topological logic. The passage in the Zen record reflects an ability to construct and deconstruct the multiple meanings of place, perhaps thereby leaving less of a target for criticism.

Therefore, this example of traditional Zen discourse points out a limitation in Nishida's philsophical worldmaking that has been overlooked by his critics based on the role of language in expressing the meaning of nothingness. Nishida has chosen a metaphor, the image of place, to represent the function of nothingness. His critics, whether on philosophical or political grounds, suggest that place is something static and objectifiable. However, the problem is not with the metaphor of place *per se*, but rather with the fact that Nishida has not built into his analysis of place an ironic sense of displacement or self-negation of the metaphor. He examines the place of nothingness but does not convey the nothingness of place. One of

Nishida's Kyoto School disciples, Masao Abe, has argued that nothingness, which is fundamentally nonconceptualizable and inexpressible, could be written with an X appearing over it, much as Heidegger has done in some writings with the word Being (*Sein*). Such a device might insure that readers would not understand the term as a objectifiable entity. But traditional Zen discourse makes this point even more effectively by referring to the sacred mountain as 'only the blue mountain crags.' It seems that the notion of place could rise above criticism if Nishida had developed a way of simultaneously deconstructing and constructing its metaphorical status.

*Steven Heine is Associate Professor of Religious Studies, Penn State.

ENDNOTES

1. From *La neige d'un autre âge,* commenting on the spatial qualities of a tree, cited in Gaston Bachelard, *The Poetics of Space*, trans. Maria Jolas (Boston: Beacon Press, 1964), p. 202.

2. Robert E. Carter, *The Nothingness Beyond God: An Introduction to the Philosophy of Nishida Kitarô* (New York: Paragon House, 1989), p. 1. This idea is conveyed in a wordplay suggested by Stephane Mallarmé, 'Nothing shall have taken place but place,' cited in Jonathan Z. Smith, *To Take Place: Toward Theory in Ritual* (Chicago: University of Chicago Press), p. 96.

3. Nishida Kitarô, *Last Writings: Nothingness and the Religious Worldview,* trans. David A. Dilworth (Honolulu: University of Hawaii Press, 1987), p. 61; see n. 16 below.

4. Dôgen, *Shôbôgenzô* 'Uji,' trans. in Steven Heine, *Existential and Ontological Dimensions of Time in Heidegger and Dôgen* (Albany: SUNY Press, 1985), p. 160.

5. Carter, *The Nothingness Beyond God*, p. 84.

6. Nishida, *Last Writings,* p. 62 (parenthesis on last sentence deleted).

7. Andrew Feenberg and Yoko Arisaka, 'Experiential Ontology: The Origins of the Nishida Philosophy in the Doctrine of Pure Experience,' *International Philosophical Quarterly* 30/2 (1990): 196.

8. Smith, *Map is Not Territory: Studies in the History of Religions* (Leiden: Brill, 1978).

9. Gaston Bachelard, *The Poetics of Space,* trans. Maria Jolas (Boston: Beacon, 1969).

10. This comment requires two qualifications: first, 'logic of place' is technically an accurate translation, though somewhat misleading in this particular context; second, I am referring primarily to Nishida's final philosophical essay written before his death in 1945 (see n. 16 below), although there are exceptions to this usage in his writings.

11. Pierre Bourdieu, *The Political Ontology of Martin Heidegger,* trans. Peter Collier (Cambridge: Polity Press, 1991), esp. p. 3: 'Thus we must abandon the opposition between a political reading and a philosophical reading, and undertake a simultaneously political and philosophical dual reading of writings which are defined by their fundamental *ambiguity,* that is, by their reference to two social spaces, which correspond to two mental spaces.'

12. There are several English translations, including *An Inquiry into the Good,* trans. Masao Abe and Christopher Ives (New Haven: Yale University Press, 1990).

13. Nishida, *Intuition and Reflection in Self-Consciousness,* trans. Valdo Viglielmo, Takeuchi Yoshinori, and Joseph S. O'Leary (Albany: SUNY Press, 1987).

14. Abe, 'Nishida's Philosophy of 'Place,'' *International Philosophical Quarterly* 28/4 (1988): 371.

15. James W. Heisig, 'The Religious Philosophy of the Kyoto School: An Overview,' *Japanese Journal of Religious Studies* 17/1 (1990): 69.

16. This essay, 'Bashoteki ronri to shûkyôteki sekaikan,' is in Nishida's 19-volume collected works, *Nishida Kitarô zenshû* (Tokyo: Iwanami shoten, 1979), 11:371-464. The two translations are: 'The Logic of *Topos* and the Religious Worldview,' trans. Michiko Yusa, *Eastern Buddhist* 19/2 (1986): 1-29, and 20/1 (1987): 81-119; and *Last Writings: Nothingness and the Religious Worldview,* trans. Dilworth, pp. 47-123.

17. Pierre Lavelle, 'The Political Thought of Nishida Kitarô,' *Monumenta Nipponica* 49/2 (1994): 139-65.

18. Tanabe Hajime, *Philosophy as Metanoetics,* trans. Takeuchi Yoshinori, Valdo Viglielmo, and James W. Heisig (Berkeley: University of California Press, 1986).

19. Nishitani Keiji, *Nishida Kitarô,* trans. Yamamoto Seisaku and James W. Heisig (Berkeley: University of California Press, 1991), p. 228.   Takahashi and

Yamanouchi were both considered Kyoto School philosophers though the former taught at Tohoku University rather than Kyoto University.

20. Nishitani, *Religion and Nothingness,* trans. Jan van Bragt (Berkeley: University of California Press, 1982).

21. Ichikawa Hakugen, *Bukkyôsha no sensô-sekinin* (Tokyo: Shunjûsha, 1970).

22. See Heine, 'Critical Buddhism and the Debate Concerning the 75-Fascicle and 12-Fascicle Shôbôgenzô Texts,' *Japanese Journal of Religious Studies* 21/1 (1994): 37-72.

23. Hakamaya Noriaki, *Hongaku shisô hihan* (Tokyo: Daizô shuppan), p. 142.

24. See Peter N. Dale, *The Myth of Japanese Uniqueness* (New York: St. Martin's Press, 1986).

25. Hakamaya, *Hihan bukkyô* (Tokyo: Daizô shuppan, 1990), pp. 47-92, esp. 77-80.

26. Heisig, 'The Religious Philosophy of the Kyoto School,' p. 52.

27. Asada Akira, *Kôzô to chikara: kigôron o koete* (Tokyo: Keisô shobô, 1983).

28. Asada, 'Infantile Capitalism and Japan's Postmoderism: A Fairy Tale,' in *Postmodernism and Japan,* eds. Masao Miyoshi and H. D. Harootunian (Durham: Duke University Press, 1988), p. 277.

29. Yusa, 'Nishida and the Question of Nationalism,' *Monumenta Nipponica* 46/2 (1991): 204.

30. See Bernard Faure, *Chan Insights and Oversights: An Epistemological Critique of the Chan Tradition* (Princeton: Princeton University Press, 1993), pp. 155-74.

31. *Rinzai roku,* ed. Iriya Yoshitaka (Tokyo: Iwanami shoten, 1991), p. 65; Robert M. Gimello, 'Chang Shang-ying on Wu-t'ai Shan,' in *Pilgrims and Sacred Sites in China,* eds. Susan Naquin and Chün-fang Yü (Berkeley: University of California Press, 1992), pp. 119-24.

32. *The Blue Cliff Record,* 3 vols., trans. Thomas and J. C. Cleary (Boulder: Shambala, 1977), 1:219-20; original in *Taishô shinshû daizôkyô* (Tokyo: 1905-12), 48:174a.

Chapter VI

From Gene Fund to Genocide:
Semiotics of Otherness and Exclusion

Anna Makolkin*

Universal is that which is common
Aristotle, *Metaphysics*

I
Introduction

Among the numerous common cultural products which transcend our differences are our myths (Malinowski, 1926; Lévi-Strauss, 1978; Hirschman, 1987; Makolkin, 1992). Myths may reflect the common existential physical reality, such as the myths of creation and the myths of the cosmogonic perception. The collective representations of our shared environment are often explained as common archetypes (Jung, 1967; Frye, 1968). However, myths can also point to a level beyond nature and have a sociological function, validating a particular organizational structure and order. Such are the collective perceptions of the Self, the Other, and their interrelationships which fall into the category of *social mythologies*. Despite the contextual differences, all collective perceptions of the Self, be they concepts of race, religion, ethnic group, class, or professional affiliation, share common operative techniques, a similar mythical narrative, and tend to evoke similar responses outside this context. Myths of exclusion and uniqueness play key roles in the basic mechanism and the dynamics between the 'I' and the 'Other'. Emotions of dislike or even hatred of the 'Other' reveal themselves as predictable strategies of exclusion on the basis of mythical assumptions about superiority and inferiority, health and sickness, barbarism and civility. These recurrent mythological motifs, the repeated structural polarities, happen to constitute the universal deep structure of any societal myths (Aaron, 1952; Chomsky, 1968).

High and low, barbaric and civilized, strong and weak are persistent polarities, or what Umberto Eco labelled 'ratios,' which sustain the ongoing myth-making about the Self and the Other and substantiate the ideology, ethics, morality, and politics of exclusion. This process of exclusion throughout global history demonstrates a steady pattern and a uniform mythical basis. The signs of otherness and exclusion are what Aristotle defined as *recognizable signs,* reaffirming the universal conflict between the 'I' and the 'Other'.

The characteristic feature of such myth-making or semiosis of exclusion is the invariable archetypal appeal to the vital signs and exploitation of the universal preoccupation with health and anxiety about death. The 'Other' is traditionally a *dangerous sign,* a potential source of disorder, chaos, and decay. Each new cultural layer and new discursive period may reinvent the ways of manipulating the same familiar notions, icons, and signs; but the basic founding, mythical elements never change. The 'Other' is the unchangeably *dangerous sign* and 'I' is invariably a victim to be protected. This paper will demonstrate the common semiotic interplay of various signs of exclusion in different times, spaces, and mythopoetic environments. Manipulating the survival instinct and popular medical and biological knowledge, the Chernobyl disaster became still another mythmaking occasion, an opportunity to revive the icons of hate and exclusion and resuscitate the dormant *dominant signs* in a new context.

II
Gene and Gene Fund

The sign 'Gene,' originating in the Greek icon 'genos' and meaning race, has had an interrupted history of usage. The Greeks preferred to operate within the barbarian/civilized paradigm when comparing themselves to the non-Greeks. For many centuries, the myths about collective identity operated with icons such as blood, race, barbarian, and civilized. In the nineteenth century, Gregor Mendel's study of peas inspired an epistemological metaphor for future ethnopolitics founded on his hypothetical genetics. The term 'genetics,' allegedly coined by William Bateson in 1906, referred to the transmission of biological traits. Prior to that the foundation for genetics was laid by Charles Darwin, whose concept of species and evolutionary pattern of human development was appropriated by various social, political, and literary discourses out of its original scientific context. The universal archetypal mythmaking and the myth of otherness thus obtained pseudo-scientific support. The idea of a strong Darwinian species or a defective gene among certain ethnic groups became a new collective obsession. The hate of a particular 'Other' could now be legitimized through an alleged biological signification. (It is not only we as a group who believe so, Social Darwinists could claim, but biologists and geneticists as well.) The scientific hypothesis was transplanted onto the mythopoetic ground of mythmaking so that the myth of the 'Other' flourished in the new environment. The Darwinian notion of a species — and ultimately of man versus animal — had been extended to man versus the 'Other human.' Exciting gene research was appropriated by the popular mythmakers of hatred who conceived their own idea of the defective gene pool and arbitrarily applied it to the hated Other.

If Victorians referred to the Slavs as barbarians in nineteenth-century England, the German National Socialists were already armed with Darwinian theory and genetics as a reputable science in order to construct and defend the myth of Aryan superiority. Their policy of genocide evolved from the myths of social equality, hatred of the capitalists, and contamination by other ethnic groups to the ultimate myth of the superior genetic fund represented by Aryan Germans.

The ideal German Nazi republic appealed to *familiar signs* such as Health and Illness, Life and Death. Hitler's intended genocide policy was first presented as a protective health measure. It began with euthanasia laws followed by propaganda of hatred directed towards the Jews and Gypsies as sources of contamination and degeneracy. The final solution was ultimately justified as a protective measure against the alarming damage to the Nordic gene fund. The victims of this ethnopolitics were turned into genotargets. The National Socialists presented themselves first and foremost as the protectors of the collective German gene fund (Proctor, 1988). The carriers of the destructive diseases were, of course, 'impure Germans' contaminated with non-German blood in their paternal line (Rosenberg, 1970).

This use and abuse of knowledge for the fulfillment of the delusional will comes to mind in another historical context: the Chernobyl disaster. Despite the acknowledged impact of Chernobyl's radioactivity in Great Britain, France, Italy, and Finland (countries which openly admit it), some Western journalists presented it to the public as a unique product of faulty Communist industry, a purely local event. Some Ukrainian journalists used Chernobyl to point out the danger of collaboration with Moscow. Some even presented the disaster as a deliberate 'Moscow plot,' matching Hitler's plot against the Jews. Others used it as an opportunity to defend Ukrainian separation as a health measure. To remain united with Moscow meant to have more Chernobyls and be completely physically destroyed. The semiotic strategy worked as follows:

Life	**Death**
Away from Moscow	With Moscow
Radiation free	Endangered
Genetically safe	Genetically unsafe

The Chernobyl disaster evoked intense popular medical discourse about the potential danger posed by radiation to the genetic pool of the residents close to Chernobyl. Precise scientific knowledge was appropriated by the popular myth-makers who acquired a new myth-making territory. The damage of the DNA of the human cell was replaced by the intended damage to the restricted pool of DNA belonging to the ethnic Ukrainians. Thus the myth of the *genofond* (genetic fund) was put forth (Pyrig, 1993).

This myth, conceived in the complex post-Chernobyl period of genuine concerns about the health of all humans, was reduced to the so-called 'national egotistic concern' of the surviving Ukrainians. In January, 1993 Tatiana Myshutina informed the readers of *Ukraina* about the genetic fund program, interviewing the Chairman of the Preservation of the Ukrainian Genetic Fund Commission, Dr. Liubomyr Pyrig. This member of the Ukrainian Academy of Sciences informed her that 'the notion of genetic fund is more than mortality and birth, but involves the transmittance of the particular biological and intellectual qualities of previous generations to the future ones' (Pyrig, 1993:20). Quoting geneticists, Pyrig claimed that culture is primarily a biological process. He expressed concern with more than health, but with the declining birth rate among Ukrainians along with the brain drain of Ukrainian intellectuals to the West and loss of the Ukrainian language. 'Ukraine without Ukrainians,' — he lamented, without explaining his meaning exactly. Later in the interview, Pryig touched on the concept of the soul and national physiognomy. For him, the national soul means a national psychology created and formed under particular geographic, historic, and developmental conditions, 'the psycho-emotional state transmitted through genes.' Here already biology and mythology, nature and culture, knowledge and hypothesis are fused into one single pseudo-scientific mythology. The readers obtain pseudo-knowledge from a person who allegedly possesses knowledge but is actually creating a myth, a myth of the glorified particularity:

What are the features of the Ukrainian soul, 'Ukrainian national physiognomy?' One may refer to kindness, hospitality, patience, and tolerance. Those particularly could be sometimes harmful because during certain historical national periods — for self-preservation — a national egoism must be displayed (Pyrig, 1993:21).

Such a concept of national egoism is not new. The National Socialist ideologies also blamed the decline of the German culture and nation on the excessive kindness of the Germans. Pyrig's loving criticism of the Ukrainians' alleged collective selflessness actually resurrects Alfred Rosenberg, the philosophical authority of the National Socialists:

This eternal kindness, kowtowing in front of the others (God forbid lest somebody might be offended and we always sacrifice ourselves) has brought the nation to its present state (Pyrig, 1993:21).

Similarly, Rosenberg blamed the mythical kindness of the Germans for the 'degenerative state of the Weimar Republic.'

A naive beginning with the collective kindness myth eventually brought Germany to the policy of national egoism, the pathway of resurrecting the mythical German soul. Thus Germany came to ethnopolitics and genocide. Given the fact that Germans as a group embraced the myth and policy of national egoism in much more favorable cultural conditions (protected language, culture, and frontiers), Ukraine shows less cultural immunity to withstand the dangerous modern ethno-mythology. The propaganda of safety in the post-Chernobyl Ukraine has been already successfully tied to the myth of purity and glorified particularity. Post-Chernobyl meditations have imagined a nation as an endangered species. Health and death anxiety are being manipulated again to sell the mythical endangered genetic fund idea. The Chernobyl tragedy contributed to the anxiety of an undefined collective entity which seeks its own identity. In the absence of a clear identity, mythical constructs are used and abused, masking a dangerous though familiar climate of intolerance. Pyrig and his colleagues are taking advantage of the post-Chernobyl momentum and disseminating the recognizable signs of exclusion and hate. Their appeal to the collective psyche and collective mentality is not new, nor are the visible and detectable signs of intolerance that accompany it.

III
Rosenberg's National Egoism

The appeal to the exceptional qualities of the group and its collective ego was successfully used by the chief myth-maker behind Nazi ethnopolitics, Alfred Rosenberg. Rosenberg maintained that the 'doctrine of love' and the innate German kindness had failed Germany as a nation and all of civilized northern Europe. Instead of the traditional German kindness and generous acceptance of the 'Other,' he proposed that Germans adopt a new spiritual essence revolving around duty and honor rather than love. The alleged exceptional kindness of the German soul had caused the pitiful state of national health which could be improved with the new myth: — 'Today a new belief is arising; the mythus of blood' — uttered Rosenberg. Only through the purification of blood, i.e. the improved genetic fund, and the peculiar physiognomy accompanying it, could the German and European Nordic soul be saved:

> Today, it has become clear to every upright German that with the doctrine of love, one which embraces in equal measure all the creatures of the world, a sensitive blow has been struck against the soul of the northern Europe (Rosenberg, 1970:105).

The tragic state of European affairs in the thirties was presumably due to 'embracing the "Other",' mixing the blood and contaminating the genetic pool.

Historically, the main justification for indiscriminate embracing the 'Other' was the premise of Christian love. It needed to be replaced by a new spiritual essence, to legitimize not love but hate. Rosenberg's Nordic religion became such a successful replacement. Instead of universal brotherly love, the Nordic dogma offered a particular love, love of the Nordic man and resurrection of the Nordic/German *Volk*-soul. Instead of loving the world and 'any creature,' Rosenberg insisted on loving only the next of kin, the German *Volk* gene carrier, and the transmittance of his innate kindness and generosity only within the blood-related community or the particularly selected genetic pool.

Rosenberg successfully replaced the presumably harmful doctrine of universal love with the doctrines of blood and self-preservation, or self-love, to form the new seductive myth. Instead of the human soul, Rosenberg's Nordic religion promised to take care of the German *Volk*-soul which had been presumably tortured for millennia by the inferior 'Other.' This very convenient shift from the Christian utopia to the Nordic myth rejected traditional Judaeo-Christian morality and ethics, with their unconditional 'embrace of the Other,' and adopted the strategy of exclusion for the sake of self-love and preservation of the Nordic genetic pool. Christian love had presumably brought the Nordic man into a harmful liaison with the non-Nordic population and turned him into an endangered species. To pave the way to the final solution, the mythical solution had to take place first through this simple substitution of the mythopoetic components and *dominant signs*.

This Nordic religion would not revolve around love but around pride and the Nordic soul. Love consciousness would be supplanted by honor and glory consciousness. The familiar high/low, weak/strong dichotomies would be employed to promote this new superior spiritual essence:

Judaeo-Christian	**Nordic**
Universal love	Particular love
Love	Pride
Pity	Honour
Failure	Victory
Weakness	Strength
Low	High
Harmful	Healthy
Other	I
Non-Aryan	Aryan
Non-Nordic	Nordic
Non-German	German

The Nazis' system of beliefs philosophically conceptualized the strategy of ethnopolitics for their future mythological justification, which ultimately led to hatred and genocide. Armed with Darwinism and genetics, skepticism of the Enlightenment, Lutheran protest against the Church, and the Marxist precedent of rejecting religion, Rosenberg conveniently constructed a myth which combined fact and fiction, knowledge and ignorance, and substituted hate for love. Rosenberg's mythus and Nordic religion were the epistemological tools for giving ethnopolitics a firm mythical foundation. Representing the upper layers in the mythological structure, Rosenberg's mythus triumphantly exploited the universal fear of the 'Other' and all the subsequent mythical and real differences between the 'I' and the 'Other.'

The idea of a nation as an endangered species would be recycled again in the twentieth century along with the myths of purity, uniqueness, and the mythical 'cultural center'. Rosenberg anticipated the blood and gene discourse which indeed became key modern preoccupations, along with national and ethnic competition for 'the cultural center.' The center/periphery dichotomy would later be appropriated by the contemporary ideologies of Russian nationalism and even by members of the former Tartu-Moscow semiotic school in their typologies of culture. The mythical semiosis of popular culture and cultural ideology can be found in semiotician

Yuri Lotman's hierarchy of cultural texts and religion (Lotman, 1977; Lotman, 1990).

Echoing Rosenberg, Lotman placed Catholicism with its alleged pragmatism beneath Russian Orthodoxy (Lotman, 1990:228). It is appropriate to recall that Rosenberg also dismissed the Roman Catholicism as an Etruscan-Jewish-Roman system and that his idea of genetic fund protection began with the modification of this mythical system (Rosenberg, 1970:34). Lotman has openly spoken about 'cultural boundaries,' 'nomads,' and 'cultural infection':

> On the frontiers of China, of the Roman Empire, of Byzantium, we see the same thing: the technical achievements of the settled civilization pass into hands of the nomads who turn them against their inventors (Lotman, 1990:142, 147).

Who are those 'nomads'? Who were they in the past and who are they in the present? Who are the present nomads in the cradles of the former Byzantine, Roman, or Austro-Hungarian Empires? Who were the 'nomads' among the Vikings and their heirs? Curiously enough, the term 'nomads' has been applied in the post-*perestroika* discourse when newly-formed Baltic states labelled millions of non-Balto-Slavs as 'nomads.' They introduced citizenship laws to exclude them from their new 'democratic' societies based on their allegedly nomadic origin, and relegated them to the status of aliens.

Lotman acknowledges that the cultural 'infection' is not a completely invasive procedure. It begins with the 'mutual attraction' to the cultural organization, to its semiotic structure:

> The process of 'infection' needs certain external conditions to bring it about and needs to be felt to be necessary and desirable. As with any dialogue a situation of mutual attraction must precede the actual contact (Lotman, 1990:147).

Lotman's notion of 'medical or health' considerations in contact with the allegedly different cultural system echoes the protectionist slogans of the cultural guardians of Nordic culture, who in turn reiterated the identical concerns of Plato and Gobineau (Lotman, 1990; Makolkin, 1993). To these we now turn.

IV
Plato — the Ancient Advocate of the Genetic Fund

Rosenberg's mythical Nordic man and his 'cultural centre' were not constructed independently and originally. As with all Europeans he was indebted to the Greco-Roman cultural legacy. To elevate the Germans Rosenberg had to accept their kinship with the Greeks, their gods, and their heroes. Greek philosophy and science persistently promoted the notions of Greek uniqueness and centricity in the world. The germs of intolerance and hate also permeate ancient Greek mythology and metadiscourse. Racist, discriminatory politics is not a German invention. A precursor may be found in Plato, in his *Republic* and *Laws*. The ideas of segregation and proto-concentration camps are clearly formulated in Plato's *Laws*. Book VIII of the *Laws* mentions the restricted sale of food to foreigners and provides the best ancient account of artificial hunger created consciously in society to force the undesirable 'Other' away from the privileged cultural center. Foreigners would be encouraged to trade only bread and wine while they had to purchase the rest of their goods from the local traders on certain specific days of the month. According to Plato:

> On the last market day a foreigner should buy for himself his entire monthly food ration in advance. On the tenth day of the month, the sale of liquid food products, a monthly ration, would take place. (Plato, 1972:335).

Thus, the biological survival of foreigners was controlled by the local population through the trade laws, which revealed an ancient attempt to protect the desired ethnic and genetic pool through restrictive laws. In addition to food and shelter, housing, another basic condition for survival, would also be controlled by the privileged locals. Plato's *Laws* stipulated a controlled distribution of shelter to preserve the social class division and an ethnic differentiation of urban space. The *Laws* ultimately aimed to expel all foreigners from the city state:

> A foreigner, if he possesses a skill, may obtain a home and remain in the country for no more than twenty years. After twenty years of living he should take his possessions and leave. (Plato, 1972:336)

Foreigners who had made exceptional contributions to ancient Greek society could ask for an extension, but under no circumstances could they apply for permanent residence.

Plato's *Laws* would be appropriated by the legal codes of many modern European countries which still continue to pursue covert policies to preserve the indigenous stock. The German, Israeli, and Swiss citizenship and immigration laws exemplify the original, essentially segregationist goal of the Platonian *Laws*. The current Estonian legal measure largely emulates the *Laws* and demonstrates how the power of the simplistic endangered species myth prevails over the acceptance of a far more complex reality and history shaped by the interaction of different cultural texts and peoples.

The idea behind Plato's *Laws* was both mythical and impossible. It exemplified a prototypical genetic fund concern expressed within the ancient epistemological paradigm of the civilized Athenian 'I' and the barbarian 'Other.' Athens was the center of the ancient world; anything beyond it was a space inhabited by the less civilized.

V
Gobineau Revising Plato

Plato's segregationist and discriminatory laws would be re-articulated and re-applied in modern times. In the nineteenth century, Arthur Gobineau lamented the failure of the Greco-Roman rulers to follow and implement Plato's *Laws* to prevent their societies' decline. Guided by mythological nostalgia and driven by the forces of the archetypal mythopoesis, Gobineau proposed to amend what he thought were Plato's too liberal laws to suit his more rigid racial theory.

If Plato simply feared foreigners and wanted to resettle them outside his ideal state, Gobineau intended to stop all foreign contact to prevent biological and cultural degradation. Gobineau insisted that 'societies perish because they are degenerate' and the cause of degeneration is the 'influx of foreign elements' (1967:59). He maintained that the decline of all past civilizations is an eloquent argument proving secret revulsion against the crossing of blood:

> But if, like the Greeks and the Romans of the later Empire, the people has been absolutely drained of its original blood and the qualities conferred by the blood, then the day of its defeat will be the day of its death (1967:64).

Gobineau manipulated the same icons which usually seduce the collective 'I' of any group:

Life	Death
Health	Illness
Pure Blood	Crossed Blood
Rise	Fall

To enforce his racist delusions Gobineau employed the canonical semiotic device of fear, and appealed to the biological instincts of self-preservation: 'The intermixture of all these decadent ethnic varieties will inevitably give birth to further ethnic chaos' (1967:161). The *life/death* paradigm supports the familiar *order/chaos* structural paradigm. Life is metaphorically represented by the order of the superior white race while the black and yellow races stand for disease and decay. The triad of white, yellow, and black embodies the heroic hierarchy, the ladder of civilization where 'the negroid variety is the lowest, and stands at the foot of the ladder' (1967: 134).

Anticipating future hierarchies and pseudo-scientific theories, Gobineau puts forward his anthropological observations which distinguish the three basic varieties among the human species. Skull comparisons did not start in Nazi Germany. Nineteenth-century phrenologists perfected Gobineau's physiological parameters which he established in his nearly-forgotten *Essay on the Inequality of Human Races.*

In Gobineau's mythical world, the negro appears as a 'human machine' that kills willingly. Blackness stands for a demonic spirit. The shape of the pelvis is a marker for a lower human species. Gobineau introduces the skull icon when he compares the 'yellow' and 'negro' 'species':

> The yellow race is the exact opposite of this [negro] type. The skull points forward, not backward. The forehead is wide and bony, often high and projecting. The shape of the face is triangular, the nose and chin showing none of the coarse protruberances that mark the negro (1967:136).

Gobineau constructs the myth of the inferior negro with the help of two basic mythical components — the symbol of destruction and the icon of ugliness. The color black stands for an encoded innate malice and lack of beauty. The crude bone structure of the head and pelvis, pseudo-anthropological evidence of inferiority, simply complement this basic mythical structure.

The yellow race occupies the intermediate position between two extremes — the barbaric black and civilized white races. The skull of the 'yellow race' represents a mediocre civilization which craves order, peace, and stability, and which lacks progress. In contrast, the white race allegedly stands for superior energy and creativity which none other can match. Despite the fact that the representatives of the yellow race could be the desirable 'backbone of society,' they are allegedly incapable of creating a civilized society; nor could they supply the required 'nerve force or set in motion the springs of beauty and action' (1967:136).

Finally, Gobineau reaches the top of the self-constructed race ladder and crowns the 'white race' with its heroic title of 'civilized.' In Gobineau's view, cultural level and degree of civilization are embodied in this simplistic chromatic triad — white, yellow, black. The chromatic polarity intensifies the cultural gap. The white chroma, the archetypal sign of clarity, light, purity, and strength, becomes for Gobineau the sign of superiority, 'energetic intelligence,' and 'nerve force.' Whiteness in Gobineau's universe is advanced to the level of absolute creativity and wisdom. He exploits the innate human striving for hierarchy and comparison and produces out of it the common myth of the superior 'I.'

In Gobineau's mythical, hierarchical universe, racial or physical natural destiny predetermines cultural, sociopolitical destiny. Thus, the yellow race is doomed to vegetate, the black to be despotically governed, and the white is privileged to govern. The principal motivation for white activity is 'honor,' the same honor which Rosenberg later incorporated into his Nordic religion. The racial ladder constructed by Gobineau would not have been complete without the special function of the Germans within the white superior race:

> The Germanic race was endowed with all the vitality of the Aryan variety and needed it in order to fulfill the role to which it was destined (1967:170).

Nazi-era eugenics would embrace Gobineau's myths and hierarchical division of the species. Advanced technology would merely empower the old myth about the superior 'I.'

VI
The Myth of the Chosen People and the Genetic Fund

Even in the process of debunking and destroying Christianity, Rosenberg could not abandon the seductive myth of the chosen people. It was remarkably related to the myth of the superior race and he skilfully appropriated it for the Nordic myth. First he attempted to turn Christ into a Nordic man and then the chosen people into the superior race. Rosenberg claimed that:

> The Amorites founded Jerusalem, and they established a Nordic strain in late Galilee, i.e. in the nether region from which Jesus was supposed to have come (1970:41).

Following the idea of passing the cultural strain through the genes, Rosenberg needed a proto-matrix: he found it in the myth of the chosen people. This hypothetical mythical route involved turning Christ into a Nordic man and depriving the ancient Hebrews and their future followers of their mythical status. Finally, Rosenberg ended by transferring the myth of the chosen people from the Hebrews to the Germans:

Hebrews	Germans
Nation of Christ	Nation of Christ
Christ = Hebrew	Christ = German
Chosen people	Chosen people
Christianity	Nordic religion

To justify the intolerance of the Germans as they purified their genetic fund, Rosenberg proclaimed that 'the Jew is the teacher of all intolerance, of all fanatical belief, of all that which calls for murder in the name of religion' (1970:183). If the chosen people could murder in the name of their religion, why couldn't the master race representatives do the same in the name of their Nordic religion of honor? Honor presupposes the restoration of a former glory and the Nordic myth claimed to restore the heroic past of the forgotten Nordic man.

Paradoxical as it may seem, the events of the Second World War have reinforced rather than undermined such mythical delusions worldwide. The success of the myth of blood was celebrated, and is still celebrated, long after the destruction of Germany. The creation of the state of Israel actually reinforced the myth of the chosen people in popular global myth-making which perceived the event as the fulfillment of the old prophecies. It also supported the myth of the preserved genetic Jewish fund through the Zionists' efforts. Ultimately, the historic precedent of creating a state on the basis of the mythical narrative provided an excellent source of global mimesis: i.e. global obsession with the preservation of respective unique genetic funds and restoration of particular mythical glories.

Popular historical narratives have traditionally relied on myth as a poetic device and a mode of seducing readers. Raphael Pozner, the author of *Germany*, published in the popular *History of Jewish Civilization* series, reported the events of 1096, the Crusaders' rampage against the Jews, and referred to the Jewish response to the massacre as an example of the 'spiritual strength of a chosen generation of the chosen people.' Allegedly, the myth is reinforced by the fact that the victims preferred to murder their own children rather than allow them to be baptized (1974:5).

A Jewish apologist here has adopted what advocates of the Aryan myth would have considered a model method for collective genetic fund protection. According to Rosenberg, the Germans should have applied the same rigor to guarding their own genetic fund as 'the chosen people' in order to 'repossess a unique status':

Model	**Replica**
Jews	Germans
Genetic fund	Genetic fund
Chosen people	Chosen people

The Zionist movement has consistently relied on the myth of the chosen people and lured many settlers into the mythical promised land of past glory. The myth of the scapegoat and the chosen people have been conveniently combined to summarize two thousand years of existential experience. The events of the Second World War reinforced the myths of the universal scapegoat, the nation-victim, and the chosen people. Consequently, all these myths were instrumental in granting preferential political freedom and sustaining the global mythopoetic cycle.

Both the critics and advocates of Israeli political rights have been engaged in the myth-making process. The myth of the Biblical paradise was transplanted onto the new historical reality of the twentieth century. The mythical land of the chosen people fulfilled the desires of various myth-makers. The guardians of the particular genetic fund of the eternal scapegoat nation were satisfied with the new nation's exclusive citizenship laws and demographic mythopolitics. The global racists were satisfied with the fulfilment of the prophecies by Gobineau and the initial process of the purification of races. World-wide immigration to Israel became the protective genetic fund measure. Israel has become the desired Hitlerian Madagascar where the global undesirables could be dispatched and segrated from the other genetic funds. The 'eternal nomads,' the wandering Jews, could finally be resettled in the segregated promised land.

However, the myth of the chosen people and the Hebrew archetypal man is strikingly similar to Rosenberg's Nordic man. Both defy and ignore the actual practice of a human existence rooted in crossing the boundaries, breaking the mythical taboos, and improving the genetic fund through heterogeneity. Hebrew man and Nordic man are the mythical constructs of deluded myth-makers and guardians of purity, whether established through maternal or paternal lineages. The present Israeli and German citizenship laws equally reflect antiquated notions of belonging and promote the impossible dream of a pure genetic fund. The state of Israel and the global resettlement of population into the promised land of the chosen people actually became the first global endorsement of ethnic cleansing after the Second World War. Radical ultra-nationalist movements in Europe, Asia, and North Africa then embraced the mythology of the chosen people with all its accompanying mythical delusions in order to protect their respective genetic funds.

VII
Motherland and Historical Motherland

The archetypal metaphor 'motherland' encodes both shared biological roots and common sociopolitical and cultural boundaries. Having become a familiar romantic icon in the nineteenth century and the operative mythical tool in creating a common national identify, the motherland-metaphor and motherland-mythology have been perfected in the post-Darwinian and post-Mendelian era. However, 'Motherland,' pure and simple, appeared to be an insufficient rhetorico-poetical device in the nationalist discourse. The idea of the 'proto-motherland' originating in the remote past has become a more seductive mythical construct, since it justifies the future ongoing mythopoesis and the resulting discourse authorizing violence. Dialogues about the land and territorial expansion have been replaced by disputes about the true proto-motherland or 'historical motherland.' The term 'historical motherland' was invented by confused Soviet journalists who were torn between the romantic ideals of the nineteenth century, loyalty to international Communism of the twentieth century, and the rising racism of the post-Second World War era. 'Historical motherland' successfully encoded the direction that the future mythopoesis would take, i.e. from the present reality and fiction to the past and its fictionalized interpretations. The term 'historical motherland' embodied the possibility of rewriting the past and its myth.

The act of creating and justifying a state based on the alleged uninterrupted continuum between the Biblical past and the modern present set the foundation for a semi-fantastic scenario. It created the possibility of staging the old myth, the old drama, and connecting the mythical displacement in time and space with the actual displacement of real people. The force of the mythopoesis actually began to govern reality through ethnopolitics. Consequently, the displaced Palestinians have become the mythical displaced enemies whose expulsion was demanded by the myth of the land and the 'motherland,' which were sacrificed for the sake of the 'historical motherland.' This fictitious pseudo-history has been accepted as real history and served as a foundation for the next mythical layer — the pure genetic fund. This fund could be restored only within the boundaries of the historical motherland and only on the basis of the mythical kingdom of the chosen people.

The Middle Eastern restaging of the biblical drama has contributed to collective global anxiety. Following the Israeli example, prospects for various other historical motherlands became quite real. Having buried the myth of the Nordic and the superior Aryan race, and put aside the myths of the chosen people and the scapegoat, the modern myth-makers could not confine their sign-producing activity to a single historical narrative, to a particular group. The myth required wider dissemination. Thus, the myth of the 'historical motherland,' *the true sign,* provoked a collective global nostalgia. Competition for the heroic title of nation-martyr began. The myths of the unique history and the unique destiny were fused with the myth of the unique blood group, as in case of the Basques. Claims to restore the glorious historical motherland were made amid insistence on a unique psychological makeup, and global flagomania and mythopoesis of distinction began. These processes signified the mythical delusions of many groups, or rather more forcibly, of their most ardent zealots, the popularizers of the popular seductive mythology:

Kurds	Macedonians	Armenians	Serbians . . .
Basques	Greeks	Albanians	Croatians . . .
Volga Germans	Azaries	Chechens	Slovaks . . .

VIII
The Balkans — the Impossible Historical Motherland

Robert Kaplan (1993) of *The New Republic* has described the area of former Yugoslavia as the new Middle East. The Middle East in the Balkans is a post-modern metaphor for the sad, impossible search for the 'historical motherland' which could never be conducted peacefully amid the region's compulsive myth-making and obsession with fantasized pasts and past glories. The Pandora's Box of the eternal mythopoesis has been opened. The underlying argument of Balkan and global myth-making is: 'If it is possible to resurrect the Biblical past why not the Balkan past? Why not the Illyrian, Panonian, and Macedonian, better recorded and more closely situated past?' The epistemology of these temporal leaps has been adopted as a successful tool of turning the myths of the past into present realities. In fact, it is precisely this temporal leap and flight of imagination that makes the ethnomyth possible.

The ethnomyth, the myth of a particular fixed and allegedly stable genetic fund, significantly relies not on existential reality but on flight from the real. It aims at the closure of boundaries and the tyrannical rule of the particular 'I.' The ethnomyth, the myth of the historical motherland, employs temporal displacement and ignores the real practice of being and historical development. The Balkan conflict is the simultaneous restaging of several competing ethnomyths within the same spatial locus where so many particularities are entangled into a single structure. Unlike the historical motherland in the Middle East, the dividing lines in the Balkans are not between the two symbolic myth-making entities but actually involve numerous inhabitants of Europe. To replay the Balkan ethnomyth implies displacing the entire continent of Europe.

Unfortunately, the Balkan mythopoetic drama has not deterred other mythmakers from similar performances in other parts of the world. Such global calamities would not have surprised seventeenth-century thinker Giambattista Vico (1970), who wrote in *The New Science* that a peaceful stage of human development is only a temporary phase in the ongoing production of the heroic myths and glorious tales of distinctiveness. The Neapolitan philosopher had a rather pessimistic vision of the historical process and human development with its attachment to the twin metaphors of heroism and the 'language of the spear.' Contemporary signification and mythmaking have failed to disprove Vico's argument. We can only hope that efforts to deconstruct the mythmaking mechanism may reveal the true signs of humanity, freedom, and civilization, i.e. by signifying the universally flawed heroic mythopoesis of particularities and their respective genetic funds.

Ann Makolkin teaches at the University of Toronto, Center for Russian and East European Studies.

REFERENCES

Aristotle (1984). *Metaphysics* in *Complete Works*, ed. J. Barnes, Princeton: Princeton University Press.

Aaron, R. I. (1952). *The Theory of Universals*. London: Oxford University Press.

Chomsky, Noam (1972). *Language and Mind*. New York: Harcourt, Brace, Jovanovich.

Eco, Umberto (1972). *A Theory of Semiotics*. Bloomington: Indiana University Press.

Dissanayke, Ellen (1992). *Homo Aestheticus*. New York: The Free Press.

Frye, Northrop (1968). *A Study of English Romanticism*. New York: Random House.

Gobineau, Arthur (1967). *The Inequality of Human Races*. New York: H. Fertig. First published 1871.

Jung, Carl (1933). *Modern Man in Search of a Soul*. New York: Harcourt, Brace, Jovanovich.

Kaplan, Robert (1993). 'The Cross and the Crescent' in the *Globe and Mail*, August 7, Toronto.

Lévi-Strauss, Claude (1958). *Anthropologie Structural*. Paris: Gallimard.

Lotman, Yurii (1977). 'Semantika chisla i tip Kul'tury' ('Numerical Semantics and Culture Types') in *Soviet Semiotics*, ed. Daniel Luciel. Baltimore: Johns Hopkins University Press, pp. 227-233.

____. *Universe of the Mind* (1990). Bloomington, Ind.: Indiana University Press.

Makolkin, Anna (1992). *Name, Hero, Icon: Semiotics of Nationalism Through Heroic Biography.* Berlin: Mouton de Gruyter.

____. 'Vico's Firstness, Secondness, and Thirdness: The Common Essence of Nations as a Sign,' in *Vico and Anglo-American Science,* ed. M. Danesi. Berlin: Mouton de Gruyter, 1995, pp. 120-126.

Plato (1972). *Laws.* Moscow: Mysl', Akademiia Nauk.

____. (1974). *Republic.* trans. Grube. Indianapolis: Hackett Publishing Co.

Pozner, Michael (1974). *Germany.* New York: Lion Amiel Publishers.

Proctor, Robert (1988). *Racial Hygiene.* Cambridge: Harvard University Press.

Pyrig, Liubomyr (1993). 'Porozhniy Genofond' ('Empty Genetic Fund'). *Ukraina,* January issue.

Reich, Wilhelm (1970). *The Mass Psychology of Fascism.* New York: Harper and Row.

Rosenberg, Alfred (1970). *Race and Race History.* New York: Harper and Row. Originally published 1933.

Vico, Giambattista (1970). *The New Science.* trans. Bergin and Fisch. Ithaca: Cornell University Press.

Chapter VII

"You Can't Help a Hollerin' and a Shoutin'": The Unconscious World of Antebellum Slaves—A Jungian Perspective

Stephen S. Fitz*

Carl Gustav Jung has influenced the world of modern psychology. His theories suggest that modern man suffers from the predicament of having two personalities — the unconscious and the conscious. Jung believes we all possess an innate unconscious personality due to heredity. He calls it the collective unconscious because it is universal and identical in all individuals.[1] It is the richer and wider realm of our being that appeals directly to feeling and emotion; hence, it is often referred to as our world of instincts. From this unconscious arises many images and associations that are analogous to primitive ideas, myths, and rites. Spirits talk to us. Angels appear before us. We have visions of the future. Jung views such examples as our unconscious awakening. He believes the unconscious personality is the natural, liberated part of our psyche that gives each of us our vivid personality. It adds the necessary spark to our being.

The conscious personality represses and absorbs the spark. It has slowly and laboriously developed apart from the unconscious until finally reaching its present 'civilized' state.[2] During this 'civilizing' process, we have increasingly separated our consciousness from the deeper instinctive strata of the human psyche — the unconscious. This conscious personality is the rational part of our psyche that continually attempts to strip the unconscious of its mystery and numinosity. Our consciousness has gone so far as to ignore or deny the existence of our collective unconscious. Herein lies the predicament for modern man — he is born with an internal battlefield.

Today, modern man turns to science and mathematical equations to put his world in order. He feels secure that technology has freed him from the non-rational world of unconscious superstitions. Jung says, 'Modern man does not understand how much his "rationalism" [which has destroyed his capacity to respond to numinous symbols and ideas] has put him at the mercy of the psychic "underworld." He has freed himself from "superstition" [or so he believes], but in the process he has lost his spiritual values to a positively dangerous degree.'[3]

Anthropologists have often described the effect when modern civilization is exposed to the spiritual life of primitive societies. Primitive people, living close to nature and their own natural psyche, undergo shock when 'progressive' rationalism opposes their foundations of belief. The meaning of their lives is usually lost, their social organization disintegrates, and the people themselves morally decay.[4]

However, the Africans who were brought to America as slaves did not morally decay when faced with modernity. The slaves were able to bridge the gap between the modern and the primitive. Although they lived in a modern world they never denied the existence of the collective unconscious. In fact, they capitalized on its emotional energy. Thus they were able to cope, to adapt, and to transcend their seemingly hopeless situation of bondage.

The slaves rose above their chains of bondage by creating a unique, expressive culture rich with religion, folk songs, folk tales, dances, and magical myths. Historians such as John W. Blassingame, Thomas L. Webber, Kenneth M. Stampp, Leslie Howard Owens, Lawrence W. Levine, and Albert J. Raboteau have shown that the slave's culture, language, customs, and beliefs set him apart from his master. The more the slave's cultural expressions differed from those of his master, the more he was immune to the control of the whites and the more he gained in personal autonomy.

A Jungian perspective on slavery, which I introduce here, has much value. It demonstrates that by tapping the collective unconscious realm of myths, symbols, and dreams, African-Americans created a rich cultural world manifested in religion, folk tales, and song. It was a world that both repelled yet attracted whites, who had been taught to repress their unconscious selves. Requiring rationality and self-control to keep slavery and the civilization dependent upon it in place, the whites' strong empathy for slave culture demonstrates the real presence of the unconscious symbols in the constitution of the human psyche, as described by Jung.

From a semiotic perspective, a Jungian approach to African-American symbolism and the white response to it proves that certain fundamental human symbols possess a validity not tied to any specific culture or language system. They are rooted in human nature itself. To put it bluntly, the

Peirceans and semioticians are right to say that the universe is a profusion of signs. The Saussurian semiologists are wrong to argue that signs are based upon specific linguistic modelling systems. The cross-cultural appeal of slave symbolism even to those who tried to reject it proves the signs, symbols, and psyche of which Jung speaks are really 'there.'[5]

When the Africans arrived in the New World, they were torn away from the political, social, and cultural systems that had ordered their lives. Even worse, they were rarely allowed to preserve family or kinship ties. Nevertheless, African beliefs and customs persisted and were passed on by slaves to their children, despite the fact that slave control was based on the attempted eradication of all forms of African culture. Slaveholders were aware of the unifying aspects of the African culture and thus hoped to destroy it so the slaves would be easier to 'break.' Nevertheless, African folklore, music, language, and religion took root in the New World and was transformed into a distinct Afro-American culture.

Of all the aspects of slave culture, the most durable and adaptable which linked the African past with the American present was religion.[6] Although it had been transformed by the new environment, the slaves' belief systems continued to develop as living traditions, putting down new roots in new soil and 'bearing new fruit as unique hybrids of Afro-American origin.'[7] African styles of worship, forms of ritual, systems of belief, and fundamental perspectives remained vital on this side of the Atlantic. The slaves' natural respect for spiritual power accounted for the openness and adaptability of African religions, which harmonized with other religions such as Christianity. It also accounted for the continuity of a distinctively African religious consciousness.[8]

The Africans believed in pantheons, or group of gods, associated with natural forces and phenomena. The god of thunder, lightning, and rain controlled the sky. The god of the earth governed fertility and punished wickedness by spreading virulent diseases among the people. The water gods dwelt within the lakes, the rivers, and the seas. And still other natural spirits resided in trees, hills, winds, and animals.[9]

Jung says each of us has an emotional 'unconscious identity' with natural phenomena. When this symbolic connection exists, with it brings profound emotional energy.[10] The emotional energy gained from the slaves believing in 'natural' gods enabled them to endure and counteract the emotional oppression of slavery.

The slaves' beliefs were also brought to life by active religious rituals. The ritual experience of the West African people, abundant with vibrant music, dancing, drumming, and singing played a continuous and integral part in the worship of the gods and ancestors. This experience carried over into the New World. Slaves and ex-slaves sought and welcomed the presence of the 'Spirit,' which moved worshippers to shout and dance not only on special occasions, but also during regular religious services. The Africans believed that the worshippers became possessed, that they '[had] been invaded by a supernatural being and [were] thus temporarily beyond self-control, their ego being subordinated to that of the [divine] intruder.'[11]

This mystical participation aided the slave by providing him the means to transcend and forget his sufferings. The unconscious appeal of religion spread throughout the slave quarters. Harry Jarvis, a Virginia-born slave, had the following religious experience:

> I neber had t'ought much about my sins, no way, and I warn't no more ob a sinner dan de mos' o' folks. But I meditated on it a heap, an' I see I war a mighty great siner fo' suah, an' I felt mighty bad about it — couldn't eat nor nuffin' — tell one night de Lord he come an' tell me my sins war all forgibben, an' I got so powerful weak, I could skursely stan'. An' den de glory cam into my soul, an' I sot up a hollrin' an' a shoutin' so's I couldn't stop, an' in de mornin' I went to tell Miss Smith, 'n I couldn't help a hollerin' 'n shoutin'. When you'se got de glory in your soul, you can't help a hollerin' 'n a shoutin![12]

Many other slaves joined Harry Jarvis in his 'shoutin' and a 'hollerin,' especially during the church services.

In the white churches during Sabbath, the slaves, in their segregated galley, would 'break out in a torrent of sacred harmony, enough to bear away the whole congregation to heaven.'[13] The Reverend Lucius Bellinger described a quarterly Methodist meeting during the 1820s in South Carolina: 'The crowd continues to increase, and song after song climbs the hills of heaven. The negroes are out in great crowds, and sing with voices that make the woods ring.'[14]

At a camp meeting in 1838, an observer reported that after the preaching the black participants formed a circle: 'Their shouts and singing was so very boisterous that the singing of the white congregation was often completely drowned in the echoes and reverberations of the colored people's tumultuous strains.'[15] The religious experience for many slaves came from their hearts. A slave would sing from the depths of his soul, while his master, sitting in the next pew, would seem to mouth the words.

The slaves were also noted for having a great collective skill. They could improvise a song and sing it like an old familiar tune. James McKim asked a freeman on the Sea Islands during the Civil War where the slaves got their songs. The answer was simple: 'Dey make 'em, sah.'[16]

Precisely how they made them worried and fascinated Thomas Wentworth Higginson. He became familiar with slave music through the singing of the black Union soldiers in his Civil War regiment. Were the songs, he wondered, a 'conscious and definite' product of some 'leading mind,' or did they grown 'by gradual accretion, in almost an unconscious way?'[17] One of his black men explained how he had a hand in creating a song:

> Once we boys went for some rice and de nigger-driver he keep a-calling on us; and I say, 'O de ole nigger-driver!' Den anudder said, 'Fust ting my mammy tole me was, notin' so bad as nigger-driver.' Den I made a sing, just puttin' a word, and den anudder word. . .[18]

He then began to sing his song:

> O, de ole nigger-driver!
> O, gwine away!
> Fust tine my mammy tole me,
> O, gwine away!
>
> Tell me 'bout de nigger-driver,
> O, gwine away!
> Nigger-driver second devil,
> O, gwine away![19]

Higginson's black soldiers joined in singing as if they had long been familiar with it. 'I saw,' Higginson concluded, 'How easily [a] new "sing" took root among them.'[20]

This spontaneity and sense of instant community was a central element in slave singing. An ex-slave told Jeanette Robinson Murphy how slaves made songs: 'Use us old heads ter make 'em up on de spurn of de moment, . . . notes is good enough for you people, but us likes a mixtry.' He said:

We'd all be at the prayer house de Lord's day, and de white preacher he'd splain de work and read whar Ezekiel done say —

Dry bones gwine ter lib ergin.

And, honey, de lord would come a shinin' thoo dem pages and revive dis ole nigger's heart, and I'd jump up dar and den and holer and shout and sing and pat, and dey would all cotch de words and I'd sing it to some ole shout song I'd heard 'em sing from Africa, and dey'd all take it up and keep at it, and keep a' addn' to it, a den it would be a spiritual.[21]

The experience of this ex-slave testifies to the fact that man possesses religious symbols in the depths of his unconscious mind. Jung believes that among the most important symbols, many are 'not individual but collective in their nature and origin. [They] are chiefly religious images. The believer assumes that they are of divine origin — that they have been revealed to man.'[22]

These religious symbols seem to hold a magical spell over the believer. The energy accompanying the connection between the man and his symbols is fascinating and strange. Jung says this 'religious nature' can be interpreted as a sort of 'mental therapy' for the 'sufferings and anxieties of mankind in general.'[23] The abundance and emotion of the slave religious experience provides compelling evidence for Jung's theories. More compelling though is the effect the slaves' religious experience had on many whites who repressed their spiritual self.

Elizabeth Kilham, a white woman, was affected by the slaves' spiritual power. 'As the slaves stamped, groaned, shouted, clapped, shrieked, and sobbed, their congregation embroidered chorus after chorus of an 'utterly indescribable, almost unearthly spiritual':

Jesus said He wouldn't die no mo',
Said He wouldn't die not mo',
So my dear chillens don' yer fear,
Said he wouldn't die no mo'.

De lord Tole Moses what ter do.
Said he wouldn't die no mo',
Lead the chillen ob Isr'el froo',
Said he wouldn't die no mo'.

'A fog seemed to fill the church.' Miss Kilham writes, '. . . an invisible power seemed to hold us [white people] in its iron grasp; the excitement was working upon us. . . a few moments more, and I think we should have shrieked in unison with the crowd.' Miss Kilham added that she and other whites rushed outside to breathe the air, but the mood was not broken easily: 'More than one of the party leaned against the wall, and burst into hysterical tears; even strong men were shaken, and stood trembling and exhausted.'[24]

Elizabeth Kilham and her friends felt the power of the slaves' religious world. Their emotional religious world appealed to the whites' own instinctive, non-rational, unconscious world. However, because the whites lived in the 'rational' world, the power seemed too much for them to comprehend. They tried to run away from it, as though they were ashamed to express their spiritual being. But, as Martha Colquitt writes, her black grandmother was able to connect with her unconscious power through religion:

> My grandmother was a powerful Christian woman, and she did love to sing and shout. . . . Grandma would git to shouting so loud she would make so much fuss nobody in the church could hear the preacher and she would wander off from the gallery and go try to go down the white folks' aisles to git to the alter where the preacher was, and they was always locking her up for disturbing worship, but they never could break her from dat shoutin and wandering around the meeting after she got old.[25]

Sarah Fitzpatrick, an Alabama house servant, describes a scene all too familiar:

> 'Niggers' commence ta wanna go to church by themselves, even ef dey had 'ta meet in da white church. So white fo'ks have deir servicer in de mornin' an' 'Niggers' have deirs in de evenin'. Ya' see 'Niggers' lack ta shout jes' lack dey want to. My a'nt use ta tare lose in dat white church an' shout, my! she sho' could shout![26]

Often, whites would visit the prayer meetings of the slaves or permit the slaves to express and celebrate the religious tradition of their culture unimpeded.[27] Whites enjoyed watching the prayer meetings of slaves and often found themselves wrapped up in the emotional experience. Despite her criticism that a prayer she heard offered at one meeting was meaningless, Mary Boykin Chesnut admitted she was deeply moved nonetheless:

> Jim Nelson, the driver . . . was asked to lead in prayer. He became wildly excited, on his knees, facing us with his eyes shut. He clapped his hands at the end of every sentence, and his voice rose to the pitch of a shrill shriek, yet was strangely clear and musical, occasionally in a plaintive minor key that went to your heart. Sometimes it rang out like a trumpet. I wept. . .bitterly. . . .The Negroes sobbed and shouted and swayed backward and forward, some with aprons to their eyes, most of them clapping their hands and responding in shrill tones: 'Yes, God!', 'Jesus!', 'Savior!', 'Bless de Lord!', 'Amen!', etc. It was a little too exciting for me and I would very much have liked to shout, too. Jim Nelson when he rose from his knees trembled and shook as one in a palsy, and from his eyes you could see the ecstasy had not left him yet. He could not stand at all, and sank back on his bench.[28]

Whites found this style of worship incomprehensible. Yet their own emotional oppressed unconscious selves compelled them 'to hear the colored ones sing and praise God!'[29]

The white community, in spite of itself, was deeply affected by the prayer meetings of the slaves. This single fact illustrates the power the slaves' world had upon the 'rational' white community. Although the whites lived in more or less a 'repressed unconscious' state, they too were moved by the slaves' religious conviction. A pure 'rational' mind ought to have been repulsed by such frantic behavior. But some whites were even converted to the slaves' religious ceremonies.[30] This single fact bolsters the credibility of Jung's theory, that we all, in the core of our unconscious being, have a haven for religious symbols.

Despite the fact that many slaveholders were deeply moved by the prayer meetings of the slaves, they nevertheless forbade many such religious meetings. One would imagine that the slaveholders would actually empathize and identify with the slaves' spirituality. After all, the slaveholders were Christians and were sharing an 'unconscious energy'. But the whites required rationality and self-control to keep slavery in its place. They feared losing control. So they prohibited prayer meetings and repressed their own unconsciousness in order to maintain control over the slaves.

Furthermore, the whites feared a strong slave identity. Jung wrote: 'There is . . . a strong empirical reason why we should cultivate religious beliefs that can never be proved. It is that they are known to be useful.

Man positively needs general ideas and convictions that will give meaning to his life and enable him to find a place for himself in the universe. He can stand the most incredible hardships when he is convinced that they make sense.'[31] Slaveholders knew that a slave with a positive, meaningful life was more likely to rebel. By denying any prayer meetings, masters believed they could crush a slave's spirit, thereby preventing any type of rebellion.

The consequence of a rebellion was death, and most slaves believed they would return to Africa or go to Heaven when they died. This religious belief had a significant impact on slave life. Frederick Douglass recalled in his narrative that he and a group of slaves believed they would go to Heaven:

> O Canaan, sweet Canaan,
> I am bound for the land of Canaan.[32]

John W. Blassingame recorded that a group of slaves would always sing:

> And it won't be long, And it won't be long
> And it won't be long, Poor sinner suffer here.
> We'll soon be free
> De Lord will call us home
> We'll fight for liberty
> When de Lord will call us home.[33]

Amos Wade, a Virginian slave believed, 'When I die, I go's back to where I b'long — Afrika.'[34]

Slaves, although they did not want to die, generally did not fear death. Their belief in religion endowed their life with meaning and emotion. The slaves would 'experience' church on Sundays. Their masters just 'went' there. This distinction gave whites reason to fear the slaves. The Haitian War of Independence (1791-1804) provided an example of what could occur. Historian Albert Raboteau states:

> Religion played a significant role in the early slave revolts led by Marandal and Biassou. Under one rebel leader, Hyacinthe, fifteen thousand slaves went into battle, supported by the belief that their chief had the power to render bullets harmless, and confident that if they died on the field, they would return to Africa. The revolt led by Boukman in 1791 was inaugurated by an awesome religious ceremony concluded by a bloody pact.[35]

Masters in the southern United States feared exactly this kind of revolt, despite the fact that a white man could normally control a score of blacks. Masters forbade religious meeting because a slave with a strong religious faith could overcome fear of his master.   This strategy of the whites prevented the stirring up of the blacks' unconscious power.[36]

Nevertheless, the slaves held secret prayer meeting. Henry Bibb was threatened with five hundred lashes on his naked back for attending a prayer meeting conducted by slaves on a neighboring plantation.[37] (Incidentally, the master who threatened Bibb was a deacon of the local church.) The slaves were wiling to risk flogging at the hands of their earthly masters to worship their 'Divine Master' as they saw fit because their worship furnished them with a meaningful place in the universe.

The lengths to which slaves went to avoid detection of their secret meetings demonstrate the importance of their religion.   Kalvin Woods remembered preaching, singing, and praying with other slaves while huddled behind quilts and rags which had been sewn together. The rags were hung up 'in the form of a little room . . . to keep the sound of their voices from penetrating the air.'[38]

At other times, slaves preserved their secrecy by turning an iron pot or kettle upside down to catch the sound. The kettle was usually placed in the middle of the cabin floor or at the doorstep, then slightly propped up to hold the sound of the praying and singing from escaping.[39] Lydia Smith recalls, 'When dark came, de men folks would hand up a wash pot, bottom upwards, in de little brush church house us had, so's its would catch de noise and de overseer wouldn't hear us singin' and shoutin'.'[40]

Despite white repression, slaves had little trouble stirring up their unconscious emotions. Even the need to conduct secret meetings did not repress their inner spirits. At one secret meeting a slave preacher forgot about the noise. In his enthusiasm, he jumped and shouted: 'Free indeed, free from death, free from hell, free from work, free from white folks, free from everything.'[41] Peter Randolph, a slave in Virginia, describes a secret prayer meeting:

> Not being allowed to hold meetings on the plantation, the slaves assembled in the swamp, out of reach of the patrols. They have an understanding among themselves as to the time and place of getting together. This is often done by the first one arriving breaking boughs from the trees, and bending them in the direction of the selected spot. Arrangements are then made for conducting the exercises. They first ask each other how they feel, the state of their minds, etc.

The male members then select a certain space, in separate groups, for the division of the meeting. [Then there is] [p]reaching . . . by the brethren, then praying and singing all around, until they generally feel quite happy. The speaker usually commences by calling himself unworthy, and talks very slowly, until feeling the spirit, he grows excited, and in a short time, there fall to the ground twenty or thirty men and women under his influence.[42]

Looking back at these secret religious gatherings, an ex-slave declared, 'Meetings back there meant more than they do now. Then everybody's heart was in tune, and when they called on God they made heaven ring. It was more than just Sunday meeting and then no godliness for a week. They would steal off the fields and in the thickets and there . . . they called on God out of heavy hearts.'[43]

It was this frantic emotion, strong belief, and sense of solidarity that the slaveholders feared. But there was no way a master could forbid a slave to practice a belief that gave meaning to his life. Jung says, 'the Pueblo Indians believe that they are the sons of Father Sun, and this belief endows their life with a perspective [and a goal] that goes far beyond their limited existence. It gives them ample space for the unfolding of a personality and permits them a full life as complete persons.'[44] The slaves, by expressing and holding onto their beliefs, experienced 'full life as complete persons.' If people have a strong 'inner certainty' and conviction, they are able to rise to something greater than their material existence. Arguably, slaves lived in a spiritually free world. In *Man and His Symbols,* Jung writes:

A sense of a wider meaning to one's existence is what raises a man beyond mere getting and spending. If he lacks this sense, he is lost and miserable. Had St. Paul been convinced that he was nothing more than a wandering weaver of carpets, he certainly would not have been the man he was. His real and meaningful life lay in the certainty that he was a messenger of the Lord. One may accuse him of suffering from megalomania, but this opinion pales before the testimony of history and the judgment of subsequent generations. The myth that took possession of him made him something greater than a mere craftsman.[45]

The African-American slave, Nat Turner, was a loner in Virginia, but he become a wise and gifted leader. As a young man, he escaped from his plantation, but returned voluntarily (much to the consternation of the other slaves) to become a religious ascetic.[46] Fasting and praying, he waited for visions of supernatural signs. These signs convinced Turner that he was a person of great ideals and principles. He had come to identify his own freedom with the destruction of whites and liberation for all blacks. He based this belief on his dreams. In his marvelous confessions, he says:

> I was struck with a particular [Bible] passage that said: 'Seek ye the kingdom of Heaven and all things shall be added unto you.' I reflected much on this passage and prayed daily for light on this subject — As I was praying one day at my plough, the spirit spoke to me, saying: Seek ye the kingdom of Heaven and all things shall be added unto you: Question — What do you mean by the Spirit? Answer — The spirit that spoke to the prophets in former days — and I was greatly astonished, and for two years prayed continually, whenever my duty would permit — and then again had the same revelation, which fully confirmed me in the impression that I was ordained for some great purpose in the hands of the Almighty.[47]

Turner found his 'meaning in life' in his undying conviction in God. His apparent ability to speak with spirits, interpret natural signs, and even heal the sick gave him influence over other slaves. These natural gifts affirmed his belief, and that of his African mother, that he was destined for some great purpose:

> I had obtained influence over the minds of my fellow servants (not by means of conjuring and such like tricks), but by the communion of the Spirit whose revelations I often communicated to them, and they believed and said my wisdom come from God . . . I had a vision and I saw white spirits and black spirits engaged in battle, and the sun was darkened — the thunder rolled in the heavens, and blood flowed in streams.[48]

Finally, Turner was shown a pivotal 'sign.' This sign convinced him in 1831 to lead the single most consequential slave uprising in the history of the Unites States:

> And then I found on the leaves in the woods hieroglyphic characters, and numbers, with the forms of men in different attitudes, portrayed in blood, and representing figures I have seen before in the heavens. And now the Holy Ghost had revealed itself to me, and made plain the miracles it had shown me. For as the blood of Christ had been shed on this earth, and had ascended to heaven for the salvation of sinners, and was not returning to earth again and as the leaves on the trees bore the impressions of the figures I had seen in the heavens, it was plain to me that the Savior was about to lay down the yoke he had borne for the sins of men, and the great day of judgment was at hand.[49]

The effect Nat Turner's rebellion had in the South shows the importance of Turner's conviction. He was, just as St. Paul, a 'messenger of the Lord.' The dark spot on the sun that revealed itself in mid-August was the last sign which 'called' Turner to 'arise and prepare myself, and slay my enemies with their own weapons. And immediately on the sign appearing in the heavens, the seal was removed from my lips, and I communicated the great work laid out for me to do.'[50]

As Turner found strength in his faith, Denmark Vesey, another rebel slave, sensitive to the spirit world, relied heavily upon the conjurer Gullah Jack to win the support of his followers.[51] Vesey recognized the slaves' cultural differences from whites and their superior spirituality. He too sought to connect black evangelism to revolution. In an abortive 1822 revolt which was betrayed, Vesey used biblical stories and classical fables to convert reluctant city Negroes in Charleston, South Carolina, while Gullah Jack distributed mystical concoctions of parched corn and ground nuts to Africans working in rice fields.[52] This concoction was said to make the slaves strong and invulnerable, just as Hyacinthe, in the Haitian revolution, was said to have the power to render bullets harmless.

Turner's and Vesey's faith in symbols, in signs, in nature, in religion, and in their dreams proved fruitful. Their beliefs stirred up the emotion needed to not only cope with slavery, but also to rebel against it. Jung's theories may explain the reason for such powerful emotions:

> Archetypes appear in practical experience. They are, at the same time, both images and emotions. One can speak of archetypes only when these two aspects are simultaneous. When there is merely the image, then there is simply a work-picture of little consequence. But by being charged with emotion, the image gains numinosity (or psychic energy); it becomes dynamic, and consequences of some kind must flow from it. Archetypes are pieces of life itself — images that are integrally connected to the living individual by the bridges of emotions. It must be explained in the manner indicated by the whole life-situation of the particular individual to whom it relates.[53]

Jung could argue that Turner's images and dreams were archetypes, for Turner believed that they were integrally connected to his innermost being. The conviction charged Turner with an immeasurable amount of emotion. The symbolic connections Turner made between religion, rebellion, and nature, such as the 'darkened sun,' the 'rolling thunder,' and the 'flowing blood in streams,' illustrate Turner's 'unconscious identity' with natural phenomena which Jung believes gives profound emotional energy. History has shown us the real violent consequences that flowed from Turner's dynamic belief system. Likewise, his fellow rebels are historic examples.

A belief system which acknowledges the power of visions and gods also accepts the reality of dreams. Dreams form a bridge between our conscious and more primitive unconscious expressions which directly appeal to our 'feeling and emotion.'[54] Dreams present images and associations analogous to primitive ideas, myths, and rituals. Jung says these dream images appear everywhere — 'whether the dreamer is educated or illiterate, intelligent or stupid' — and believes that these associations link 'the rational world of consciousness and the world of instinct.' However, because in our civilized life we have stripped so many ideas of their emotional energy, we do not really respond to them anymore. We use such ideas in our speech and we show a conventional reaction when others use them, but they do not make a very deep impression on us.[55] Hence, our 'civilized,' 'rational' life has taken away, or denied one part of our being, whereas the slave found immense psychic energy in his dreams and was often moved to action by them. Steven Ducan, a Louisiana slave, writes:

> On a Sunday night I read the first Chapter of Job, hoping for comfort; went to bed; had a vision. Two men seemed to be after me with a pistol, resolved to kill me. Somehow I overcame them and compelled them to walk before me until I came to a white house. Here I saw a throne. On the throne was Pilate; before him stood the Savior, bound with new grass rope. I said, 'They've crucified my Lord and Master again.' The Savior seemed to speak and ask, 'Are you not a Christian?' I shook my head saying 'No'. The third time of the question and answer, he said, 'Yes you are a Christian; follow me.' He then burst out of his bonds, and walking away from Pilate's judgment-seat, said, 'I've chosen you to preach my word.' I refused. He then seemed to lay a cross on me. My shoes came off my feet and I fell on all fours. Coming to a narrow pass I was barefoot but going on my hands and knees among briers. The merciful Redeemer walked by my side, having a book in his hand, and would say, every now and then. 'I've chosen you as one of my disciples to bear my word to sinners.' Then we came to a river. When I saw it, and that I could not cross it, I said, 'Lord, if you'll jes' take this cross of me, whatever I fin' in you cause to I'll do.' He spoke and the cross vanished. He handed me a book, saying, 'Go preach my word.'[56]

The meaning of this dream could be explored in depth, but it is most important to observe its impact on Ducan. For a time he was a very rational slave who continually experienced but rejected such mystical 'callings.' He recalls living in misery and often falling to the ground bursting into tears 'as if I had murdered somebody.' He was trying in vain to destroy his unconscious, but this dream rejuvenated his strong spirit and inspired him to preach the Gospel:

The mornin' after that dream, I ran home and preached. That night I experienced a great salvation in the chapel. A hymn was sung that I never heard before:

> My God, I know I feel thee mine,
> and will not quit my claim,
> Till all I have is lost in thee,
> and all renewed I am.

The great joy of the blessing came to me here, and ever since my life was full.[57]

Henry Baker, an Alabama slave, also recalls having a dream calling him to spread the Gospel:

> I heered de voice of Heaven sayin', 'Go en take de book out uv de angels' han' an eat hit up, en when you eat up dat book yer belly will be bitter, en yer mouth es sweet es honey. When I took hit on et hit, me belly wuz bitten en me mouth was es sweet es honey and I know'd how tuh go en prophesy to many people.[58]

Jung says the purpose, or general function, of dreams is to 'restore our psychological balance by producing dream material that re-establishes, in a subtle way, the total psychic equilibrium.' Jung calls this the complementary (or compensatory) role of dreams in our psychic make-up.[59] Baker and Ducan were two slaves who initially denied their unconscious identity, their dreams of angels, of crosses, and of Bibles. But both quickly came to realize the power and emotional benefits of their instincts.

Many slaves also placed great significance on their dreams as a window to the future. One slave recalls:

> When I was a small child I used to dream a lot. I remember one night I dreamt that I saw Uncle Link, Uncle Jack and Uncle Peter skinning a cow and cutting her open. A lot of women and children were sitting around and seemed to be crying. I told my mother about it the next morning. She said it was a sign of death to dream about fresh meat. Sure enough that very evening Uncle Peter Price died. I used to dream so much that the old heads got so they took special notice of me and nearly every time it would come true.[60]

The following dream convinced this slave to run away:

> On a Thursday evening, came a trader from the south, named Dr. _____. He looked at Henry, and at a man named George Strawder, and at me, but did not purchase, the price being too high. I dreamed that night that he took us three.

Next morning I told Henry, 'That man is coming to take you and George, and me, just as sure as the world; so Henry, let's you and me make a bargain to try and get away; for I'm never deceived in a dream — if I dreamed master was going to whip me, he surely whip somebody next day.' That's as good a sign in the south as ever was.[61]

These situations illustrate Jung's theories about dreams. He says:

Dreams may sometimes announce certain situations long before they actually happen. This is not necessarily a miracle or form of precognition. Many crises in our history have a long unconscious history. We moved toward them step by step, unaware of the dangers that are accumulating. But what we consciously fail to see is frequently perceived by our unconscious, which can pass the information on through dreams.[62]

Many slaves, too, believed much the same thing as Jung. Jung thought: 'Perhaps God does communicate through dreams. Why would one not believe in the possibility that God speaks through signs and dreams?'[63] Such a belief was common in the Bible. One slave also took hold of this possibility. 'Seldom does anything happen in my family but that I get a warning. God knows what He is about and the best that any of us can do is follow as he directs us through the Spirit':

. . . I's always interest in the working of signs. When I's a little pickaninny, my mammy and other folks used to talk about signs. I hears them talk about what happens to folks used to talk about signs. I hears them talk about what happens to folks 'cause a spell was put on them. The old folks in them days know more about the signs that the Lord uses to reveal His laws than the folks of today. It am also true of the colored folks in Africa, they native land. Some of the folks laugh at their beliefs and says it am superstition, but it am knowing how the Lord reveals His laws.[64]

As dreamers, prophets, and revolutionaries, Turner and Vesey also fit Jung's definition of the hero: 'The hero figure is an archetype, which has existed since time immemorial.' The myth of the hero exists in cultures all over the world: Greek, Far Eastern, Hebrew, Indian, American, and contemporary primitive cultures. Joseph L. Henderson says that '[h]eroes are symbolic representatives of the whole psyche, the larger and more comprehensive identity that supplies the strength that the personal ego lacks.'[65] The slaves had a variety of heroes in their culture who compensated for their own weak egos.

Among southern slaves, a common hero was the conjurer. Because of their belief in witches, voodoo, magic, symbols, and prophets, many of them constructed a psychological defense against their masters by identifying with the conjurer. Slaves admired conjurers and elevated them to hero status. Slaves commonly believed that a conjurer could protect them from their masters' floggings.

The conjurer claimed the ability to prevent all sorts of things. He could make masters kind. He could prevent pain and suffering. He could ensure love and happiness. He could cure illnesses. Because of their extravagant promises, conjurers were very successful in gaining adherents.[66] This was possible because the slaves believed in the value of roots and herbs to cure illnesses, or to protect them from masters.

Frederick Douglass was able to face his heartless master, Covey, due to his belief in a magical root given to him by a conjurer. Douglass remembers:

> I immediately started for home; and upon entering the yard gate, out came Mr. Covey on his way to meeting. He spoke to me very kindly, bade me drive the pigs from a lot near by and passed on towards the church. Now, this singular conduct of Mr. Covey made me think that there was something in the root which Sandy had given me; and had it been on any other day than Sunday, I could have attributed the conduct to no other cause than the influence of that root; and as it was, I was half inclined to think the root to be something more than I at first had taken it be.[67]

Powders and roots given to Henry Bibb also appeared to prevent him from receiving a flogging. Bibb wrote of his

> Great faith in conjuration and witch-craft. I was led to believe that I could do almost as I pleased without being flogged. [After Bibb left the plantation without permission] my master declared that he would punish me for going off; but I did not believe that he could do it, while I had this root and dust; and as he approached me, I commenced talking saucy to him.[68]

William Webb, a Kentucky slave, became so impressed with the conjurer's abilities that he became one himself.[69] Observing the qualities and skill of a conjurer he admired, Webb became the hero of other slaves on his plantation. Noticing that the slaves were disgruntled over their master's cruel treatment, Webb visited their quarters secretly. He prayed for better treatment and had the slaves collect roots. The slaves put the roots in bags, marched around the cabins several times, and pointed the bags toward the master's house every morning. After the master started treating his slaves better (because he had a dream in which the slaves wreaked vengeance on him), the slaves were completely in Webb's power. They regaled him with 'sumptuous meals nightly, and the women were especially attentive.'[70] Incidentally, it is worth noting, that the master was influenced by his own dream.

Folk tales, another cultural aspect of slave life, also fulfilled the essential function of the heroic myth. The myth develops an individual's ego-consciousness and makes him aware of his own strengths and weaknesses. But it does this in a subtle manner.[71] The earliest aspect in the evolution of the hero myth is the trickster, a character common in slave tales.[72]

In the slave trickster tales, a slave, by symbolically identifying with the trickster of the story, could learn the strengths and weaknesses of different types of behavior, other than what his master taught him. The trickster in most stories is the sly, deceitful, cunning figure who can outsmart any of his oppressors. In the slave trickster tales, the trickster was a slave who always outsmarted his master. Trickster stories 'represent our efforts to deal with the problems of growing up, aided by the illusion of an eternal fiction.'[73] For the slaves, the trickster stories represented a world that helped them deal with the oppression of slavery.

The trickster stories show how the slave avoided punishment, while still being able to achieve his mischievous goals. The slaves brought many of the tactics used by the animal trickster or hero into their own lives. Like Brer Rabbit, slaves learned to maneuver as well as they could from their position of weakness. In proverb after proverb this theme was repeated: 'White folks do as they pleases, and the darkies do as they can.' 'It don't make much diffunce whar de rain comes fum, jes' so it hits de gron' in de right place.' 'Juh mought as well die wid de chills ez wid de fever.' 'Better not laugh too quick at de runt pig.' 'Little axe cut down big tree.'[74]

Perhaps the most cunning, deceitful behavior learned from the trickster was the facade of the totally dependent and submissive slave. Slaves learned to act like thoughtless and dependent people because masters regarded such slaves as the best.[75] If looked upon favorably by a master, a slave could reap many rewards. Stanley Elkins writes: 'There were plenty of opportunists among the Negroes who played the role assigned to them, acted the clown, and curried the favor of their master in order to win the maximum rewards within the system.'[76] Henry Bibb wrote: 'I knew then the only alternative left for me to extricate myself was the use of deception, which is the most effective defense a slave can use. I pretend to be satisfied for the purpose of getting an opportunity of giving them the slip.'[77] Frederick Douglass also recalls 'trying to conceal my feelings as much as possible.'[78]

The slaves learned well from their trickster stories. A favorite among their stories was the 'Hog Thrift' tale:

Once an old slave used to make it his practice to steal hogs. The way he would be sure of the animal was he would tie one end of a rope around his prey and the other around himself. The old Negro had been successful for many years in his occupation, but one time when he caught one of his master's hogs he met his equal in strength. He was fixing to have a big time on the next day, which was Sunday. He was thinking about it and had the old hog going along nicely, but at last as he was coming up on the top of a very high hill the hog got unmanageable and broke loose from the old fellow's arms. Still the old man made sure, it was all right because of the rope which tied them together, so he puffed and pulled and scuffed, til the hog got the best of him and started him to going down the steep hill. The hog carried him clear to his master's house, and the master and his family were sitting on the porch. All the Negro could say, as the hog carried him around and around the house by his master, was 'Master, I come to bring you pig home!'[79]

Although the slaves associated themselves with the cunning deceitful hero-trickster, the association, not necessarily the behavior, is significant. 'As a general rule,' says Henderson, 'it can be said that the need for hero symbols arises when the ego needs strengthening — when, that is to say, the conscious mind needs assistance in some task that it cannot accomplish unaided or without drawing on the sources of strength that lie in the unconscious mind.'[80] Hence, hero myths are a way of dipping into the unconscious and freeing its psychic energy.

For the slaves, trickster tales, religious beliefs, dreams, conjurers, magic, spirituals, and other cultural expressions released their inner psychic energy and united them. They had their own distinct world separate from their masters. The slaves allowed the unconscious archetypes repressed in white culture to be expressed in their own. Hence, the energy and spirit in the unconscious realm found a positive outlet in slaves, and enabled them to create an expressive, spiritual world in spite of their oppression.

The power of the unconscious enabled the slaves to endure the most difficult hardships. But such power has also been tapped to bring about catastrophic results, as in Nazi Germany, where the power of the unconscious found its outlet in a devastatingly negative culture. Using rituals, mass demonstrations, and archaic religious ceremonies, Hitler stirred up strong emotional prejudices which eventually led to the Holocaust and Germany's destruction.

These two examples demonstrate the energy and the power which exist in our own minds. Man is the most adaptive and powerful creature on earth because of his mind. Unfortunately, the split between the unconscious and conscious mind is wide. To utilize the power of the mind we must 'heal the split.' Then gods could be invoked to help us in our times of despair, while the Goddess of Reason could further enhance the civilized world. The narrower the gap, the more control people will have over their greatest instrument — the psyche.

A Pueblo chieftain once told Jung: 'We don't understand the whites. They are always wanting something, always restless, always looking for something. What is it? We don't know. We can't understand them. They have such sharp noses, such thin, cruel lips, such lines in their faces. We think they are all crazy.'[81] The slaves have demonstrated that humans are a spiritual people; 'modern man' has demonstrated that we are 'logical.' What we are looking for is a way to accept and harmonize these two worlds. Then we may have a reason to 'A Holler 'n Shout!'.

*Stephen S. Fitz, is an associate at the law offices of Clagett and Gorey, Fairmont, West Virginia. An earlier version of this essay was the author's senior honors thesis in history at Penn State, 1988.

ENDNOTES

1. Joseph Campbell ed., *The Portable Jung* (New York: Viking Press, Inc., 1971), 60.

2. Carl G. Jung, *Modern Man and His Symbols*, ed., M.-L Von Franz (London: Aldus Books Limited, 1964), 43.

3. *Ibid.*, 94.

4. *Ibid.*, 95.

5. For a discussion of this distinction, see John Deely, *Basics of Semiotics* (Bloomington: Indiana University Press, 1991).

6. Albert J. Raboteau, *Slave Religion* (New York: Oxford University Press, 1978), 5.

7. *Ibid.*, 5.

8. *Ibid.*, 7.

9. *Ibid.*, 66.

10. Jung, *Man and His Symbols*, 95.

11. I. M. Lewis, *Ecstatic Religion* (Baltimore: Penguin Books, 1971), 65.

12. John W. Blassingame, ed., *Slave Testimony: Two Centuries of Letters, Speeches, Interviews and Autobiographies* (Baton Rouge: Louisiana State University Press, 1977), 610.

13. Lawrence W. Levine, *Black Culture and Black Consciousness* (New York: Oxford University Press, Inc., 1977), 12.

14. Lucius Bellinger, *Stray Leaves from the Port-folio of a Methodist Local Preacher* (Macon, Ga., 1870), 17.

15. Don Yoder, *Pennsylvania Spirituals* (Lancaster, PA: Pennsylvania Folklife Association, 1961), 24.

16. Levin, *Black Culture and Black Consciousness*, 25.

17. Thomas Wentworth Higginson, *Army Life in a Black Regiment* (1869; Boston: Beacon Press ed., 1962), 218.

18. *Ibid.*, 218.

19. *Ibid.*, 219.

20. *Ibid.*, 219.

21. Jeanette Robinson Murphy, 'The Survival of African Music in America,' *Popular Science Monthly*, 55 (1899), 62.

22. Jung, *Man and His Symbols*, 55.

23. *Ibid.*, 79.

24. Elizabeth Kilham, 'Sketches in Color: Fourth,' *Putnam's Magazine*, 5 (1870), 308-309.

25. Thomas L. Webber, *Deep Like the Rivers* (New York: W.W. Norton and Company, 1978), 125.

26. Blassingame, *Slave Testimony*, 643.

27. Raboteau, *Slave Religion*, 220.

28. *Ibid.*, 221.

29. *Ibid.*, 222.

30. Webber, *Deep Like the Rivers*, 280.

31. Jung, *Man and His Symbols*, 89.

32. Frederick Douglass, *Narrative of the Life of Frederick Douglass, An American Slave*, ed. Houston A. Baker, Jr. (New York: Viking/Penguin, 1982), 120.

33. John W. Blassingame, *The Slave Community: Plantation Life in Antebellum South* (New York: Oxford University Press, 1979), 143.

34. Blassingame, *Slave Testimony*, 212.

35. Raboteau, *Slave Religion*, 26.

36. Blassingame, *The Slave Community*, 147.

37. Gilbert Osofsky, ed., *Puttin' On Ole Massa* (New York: Harper and Row, 1969), 124.

38. Raboteau, *Slave Religion*, 215.

39. Leslie Howard Owens, *This Species of Property* (New York: Oxford University Press, 1976), 157.

40. Blassingame, *Slave Testimony*, 184.

41. Blassingame, *Slave Community*, 137.

42. Peter Randolph, *Sketches of a Slave Life: or Illustrations of the Peculiar Institution* (Boston: 1855), 30-31.

43. Raboteau, *Slave Religion*, 217.

44. Jung, *Man and His Symbols*, 89.

45. *Ibid.*, 90.

46. Michael Mullin, ed., *American Negro Slavery: A Documentary History* (New York: Harper and Row, 1976), 226.

47. Herbert Aptheker, *Nat Turner's Slave Rebellion, Including Nat Turner's Confessions* (New York: Grove Press, 1966), 135.

48. *Ibid.*, 136.

49. *Ibid.*, 137.

50. *Ibid.*, 138.

51. Owens, *This Species of Property*, 158.

52. Mullin, ed., *American Negro Slavery*, 224-225.

53. Jung, *Modern Man and His Symbols*, 96.

54. *Ibid.*, 48-49.

55. *Ibid.*, 49.

56. Blassingame, *Slave Testimony*, 624.

57. *Ibid.*, 625.

58. *Ibid.*, 667.

59. Jung, *Modern Man and His Symbols*, 50.

60. Thomas L. Webber, *Deep Like the Rivers*, 122.

61. *Ibid.*, 124.

62. Jung, *Man and His Symbols*, 51.

63. *Ibid.*, 95.

64. Webber, *Deep Like the Rivers*, 129.

65. Cited in Jung, *Modern Man and His Symbols*, 110.

66. Blassingame, *The Slave Community*, 109.

67. Douglass, *Narrative of Frederick Douglass*, 111.

68. Gilbert Osofsky, ed., 'Narrative of Henry Bibb,' in *Puttin' on Ole Massa*, 42.

69. *Ibid.*, 189.

70. Blassingame, *The Slave Community*, 110.

71. Jung, *Modern Man and His Symbols*, 112.

72. *Ibid.*, 113.

73. *Ibid.*, 114.

74. B. A. Botkin, ed., *Lay My Burden Down: A Folk History of Slavery* (Chicago: University of Chicago Press, 1945), 121.

75. Stanley M. Elkins, *Slavery: A Problem in American Institution and Intellectual Life*, 2nd ed. (Chicago: University of Chicago Press, 1968), 83.

76. *Ibid.*, 111.

77. Osofsky, ed., 'Narrative of Henry Bibb,' in *Puttin' on Ole Massa*, 85.

78. Douglass, *Narrative of the Life of Frederick Douglass*, 69.

79. Randall M. Miller, ed., *The Afro-American Slaves: Community or Chaos?* (Malabar: Robert E. Krieger Publishing Company, 1981), 118.

80. Quoted by Jung, *Modern Man and His Symbols*, 123.

81. Campbell, *The Portable Jung*, 473.

Chapter VIII

Science, Religion, and Feminism:
The Utopian Signs of Céline Renooz, 1840-1928

James Smith Allen*

> Recollection must not be studied by the norms of either empirical precision or deliberate distortion, even error. Rather, memory itself permits elaboration of the self by the redeployment of signs and their meanings.
> — Georges Gusdorf, *Les Ecritures du moi* (1991)[1]

The Western tradition of utopian thought is long and rich.[2] As historians have amply demonstrated, Plato and St. Augustine were certainly neither the last nor the most creative visionaries in Europe, especially in response to the demonstrable failures of individualism and rationalism since the eighteenth century. In the wake of the adverse consequences of the French and Industrial Revolutions, for instance, the romantics and early socialists contributed their conceptions of a better world. The Comte de Saint-Simon, Charles Fourier, and Robert Owen, among others, provided a modern component to this intellectual heritage. Their influence can still be felt in competing ideologies of economic progress and social harmony today. Representations of the future like theirs will continue to appear, thanks in part to the signs derived from these older systems.

The semiotics of utopian thought is less obvious than its history, perhaps because historians have been less self-conscious about signs than have the figures they study.[3] Yet all worldmaking, whether historical or utopian, requires representation in every sense of the word, including selection, illustration, promotion, and expression in particular, since visionary discourse entails a distinct symbolic system.[4] Much more than history, utopia is an autonomous world defined by a discursive resistance to the ordinary and the actual — or at least to the perceptions of them that writers express. Utopian signs have a well-defined structure within an intellectual tradition of their own. Continental European theorists like Michel Foucault and Umberto Eco have long recognized the independent character of such totalizing systems, however inherently historical they are because of their various contexts defined by both the past and the present. Utopias are as indebted to each other as they are to the different milieus in which they are created. A self-contained totality, though never a wholly self-referent one, this species of worldmaking assumes semiotic as well as historical implications.[5]

Clearly significant to the study of signs in utopian thought is the work of an obscure writer in nineteenth-century France: Céline Renooz (1840-1928). All her life Renooz was fascinated by developments in both science and religion, two disparate disciplines that she unified in a feminist cosmology. Her vision of another world was in fact based on a radical critique of positivist thought. This manner of knowing typical of men was so bankrupt, she believed, that only an entirely new epistemology natural to women could establish a truer, more just order in society. Her feminist vision was a function of her reflections not only on natural history and Western religions, but also on their special systems of signs. Once men's semiotic representation of knowledge was reformed in the interest of women, she thought, the world would be a better place for everyone. In Renooz's writing, then, discursive and historical elements are inseparable in ways that are certainly worth scholarly attention.

Renooz's obscurity should pose no obstacle to such a study; the essential details of her life are easily summarized.[6] Born and educated in Liège, she married an engineering student in 1859, and moved with him to Madrid where they had four children. But their marriage was painfully unhappy, so she broke with her husband and moved alone to Paris in 1875 to pursue her interests in natural history, feminist organization, and polemical journalism. Because Parisian publishers cruelly refused to consider her work without subvention, Renooz founded the Société Néosophique in 1897; this small but faithful coterie of friends and disciples raised the money necessary to promote her sometimes paranoid, always controversial views on science and religion. In all Renooz published more than a dozen contentious volumes on evolution, cosmology, and the history of Western religions (see the Appendix). In addition to this work, she sponsored conferences and maintained an extensive correspondence with allies and adversaries alike. After a brief illness Renooz died at age 87, leaving behind her the personal papers that were eventually acquired by Marie Louise Bouglé for her archival collection on the history of the women's movement in France.[7] Thus Renooz's long life of tumultuous intellectual engagement is well documented by her many publications and by even more boxes of letters, newspaper clippings, and manuscripts, including her unfinished memoirs.

Renooz's ideas — her entire raison d'être — progressed across three different but related fields: evolutionary embryology, scientific epistemology, and visionary feminism.   Her earliest interests actually developed in response to Charles Darwin's *The Origin of Species*, translated into French by Clémence Royer in 1862; Renooz's first book, *L'Origine des animaux* (1883), critiqued Darwin's theory of evolution, because she found its method 'irreconciliable with the rigorous demands of science.'[8] Instead of tracing the origins of species by the established conventions of natural history — i.e., Darwin's approach — Renooz proposed examining evolution in light of recent work in embryology.   The results, she felt, were conclusive:

> The structures developed by humans and flying animals at the beginning of their evolution are vegetable structures — forms that are faithfully reproduced in the first phases of present-day embryonic life resembling primitive vegetation. But in its slow replication of evolution, the vegetable world is just the *reverse* of that for present-day animal life. In other words, in the vegetable phase of animal gestation, the cephalic extremity is inverted, while the caudal extremity is on top.[9]

For Renooz nothing could be more obvious: the vital center of life in the plant is located in its lowest extremities, its roots, while the most important extremity of the human being is the head, which appears upside down in the fully formed fetus. Embryologically the head develops in the same relation to the body that roots already have to the plant. And so, Renooz argued, ontogeny recapitulates phylogeny both within and across species: animal evolution occurs only after plants have sufficiently developed structures for animals to imitate in their earliest stages of life.

Much later, in 1908, Renooz succinctly summarized her views on the vegetative origins of animal life in a series of newspaper articles written for the *République sociale* in Montpellier:

> The differences which exist between plants and animals and which serve to characterize the two kingdoms are those which exist between humans today and humans in the embryonic, that is, primitive state. The temporary stages through which the embryo passes in order to reach the features that characterize the new-born animal are those that primitive vegetation traversed in order to resemble the features which characterize present-day animals.[10]

Evidence for this special relationship between plant and animal life, Renooz asserted, can be found everywhere, including the remarkable peace humans feel in the woods, as opposed to the profound anxiety they experience in the ocean. The close ties between flora and fauna were also evident materially: 'protoplasm in animals is the same as that of former vegetable species, because it contains the initial biochemistry of all life.'[11] Consequently, for Renooz, the 'grand problem' of science is to rewrite its account of human evolution based on the 'natural laws' of vegetable life.

One significance of this curious argument, based on creative analogy drawn from biology, is Renooz's rejection of a principal feature of Darwin's theory: the differentiation of species by natural selection. 'The vegetable origin of animal life leads us back to the fixity of species,' she wrote,

> but it [also] leads us to the evolution of each species. It shows us that all of them follow their respective evolution, tranquilly, coexisting without conflict with their neighbors and perpetuating across the ages the special characteristics for each one of them.[12]

In short, her version of evolution was symbiotic and functional rather than competitive and conflictive. Nature for her was not represented by animals fighting for survival but by plants cooperating in harmony. But this quasi-ecological critique of Darwin's struggle for existence had another significance; Renooz's early anti-Darwinism was at the heart of a whole new scientific epistemology.

The failure of Darwinians to recognize the obvious — to acknowledge the utility of embryology to the study of evolution — could be blamed, Renooz felt, on fundamental flaws in the scientific method. Therefore, she argued, the basis of all true scientific knowledge could not be empiricism, the pervasive positivist model for all fields before the Einsteinian revolution. Rather, science as knowledge had to become intuitive; it had to adopt woman's manner of knowing, whose promotion Renooz assumed as a personal responsibility. Hence Renooz's inspiring statement of principles for the journal that she founded in 1888, *La Revue scientifique des femmes:*

> Science must be recast in order to show men who they are and what they ought to be. It is to women that this task is entrusted. With the help of the power that even the most obstinate of men recognize in them — intuition — women can bring to the old world the light that will re-create intellectual life. . . .[13]

Once science was established on these new epistemological foundations, all morality would be logically derived from knowledge and would ensure a more creative and peaceful existence for everyone — thanks to female intuition.

This insight central to her life's work first occurred to Renooz in a flash of intuitive inspiration. On a warm June morning in 1878, she was reading Helvétius's *L'Homme* in the Bibliothèque Nationale in Paris when she fell into a trancelike state that lasted for two full weeks, a critical period during which she outlined the major features of her subsequent scholarship. As she noted later, 'All this came to me instantaneously and with such force and conviction that absolutely no doubt about it was possible.'[14] Nature alone provided, she said, the necessary touchstone for truth in scientific research, but also for all knowledge, in sharp contrast to the unnatural manner of knowing in traditional science and scholarship. But because of the inevitable resistance on the part of men with an institutional stake in established knowledge, Renooz realized that she must assume a lifelong mission to promote her understanding of self-evident truth, and that ultimately her task was for the moral improvement and redemption of humankind:

> It seemed to me that the enormous power of thought, which overwhelmed me and made it possible for me to see all of Nature's mysteries so clearly, was a moral force at whose insistence I felt compelled to save the old world . . . . It seemed to me that my fate from now on was to awaken human intellectual life, to guide it, to correct it, to bring peace to men, to recreate them, so to speak, for a second time by awakening them to a new moral order.[15]

By this logic Renooz made female intuition a profoundly moral, albeit also a deeply personal, crusade to create not just a new vision but also a new world.

Renooz understood that science underlay morality, and so she initially focused her attention on rediscovering the scientific laws of the universe. Physical forces, she explained, were not those studied by men using their fatally flawed empiricism; gravity and electromagnetism were in effect illusions. Rather, by her new method Renooz claimed to have created a truer physics, to have framed

> All natural laws: the causes of electricity and light, the true cause of gravity, ... the essence of the generative principle, its intimate connection with our simplest acts, our most secret thoughts, . . . the origin and development of my

conception of the Divine Principle, . . . [and] the mystery of sexual evolution on which rests *all moral law* . . . .[16]

Behind this elaborate physical and metaphysical system, Renooz argued, lay the true prime mover, the great god oxygen, whose irresistible energy infused all animate and inanimate matter[17]: 'in our solar system oxygen surpasses all other elements; its impact cannot be exaggerated; it is of such force that it determines the entire physical and physiological disposition of our planetary system.'[18] But this fundamental discovery was made possible by the means unique to women whose intuition redefined knowledge of the universe and reestablished its morality. Without women there could be no scientific or moral order.

Perhaps Renooz's most revealing publication about the special epistemological role of women was her brochure, *La Science et l'empiricisme*, published in 1898. Here she reclaimed for science its original meaning as knowledge in general, rather than its modern definition as a discipline in particular. The earlier, more universal notion of science, Renooz wrote, was most appropriate to orderly, unbiased, abstract thought with all the certainty of mathematics, the 'mathèse' of the ancient world, manifested most clearly in the instinctive knowledge of women and children[19]:

> Throughout their life women maintain their childhood instincts. Indeed, throughout their exceptional evolution they continue to see clearly the effects of Nature in the same way children do . . . . Thus like children women can realize spontaneously the truths that they apprehend without even trying.[20]

Although the pamphlet was actually intended as a critique of the positivist bible, Ludwig Büchner's *Kraft und Stoff* [*Force and Matter*, 1855], it forthrightly asserted the place that women should have in science and society because of their intuitive grasp of fundamental truths. These truths represented the spirit of the Société Néosophique, outlined on the inside of the pamphlet's front and back covers, that privileged women's mentality, knowledge, evolution, and morality: 'To be a Néosophe is to be better and more knowledgeable than others; it is thus a matter of possessing the qualities necessary to work for the regeneration of humanity.'[21]

It was a series of small steps in Renooz's thinking, then, that eventually took her all the way from embryology to epistemology to feminism. By 1888, when she published her first article critical of the scientific method,

Renooz was already interested in women's issues, especially in higher education and scholarly research. But she was even more concerned with elaborating her feminist vision of universal harmony through the new cosmology of both physical and spiritual forces that she was to define in *La Nouvelle Science* (1890-1920): 'Let us hope that the coming generation will take the next step that separates the old world from the new one that will be based on the ABSOLUTE TRUTH, a great and simple truth like Nature itself, at the heart of which we were born.'[22] In its turn this utopian conception rested on yet another, much larger project tracing the origins of patriarchy in Western society. The establishment of a new cosmology, Renooz knew, required an understanding of its historical roots reaching back to the ancient world when men had usurped women's naturally superior place in the social order. This insight led her to write a six-volume study of the original role of women and its displacement in religious practice, her magnum opus, *Ere de vérité* (1921-1933).

By this circuitous route, Renooz's interest in science and religion — or more precisely, in signs and history — are linked. Her visionary cosmology is closely tied to a clear conception of the past. Or as she put it,

> for the purpose of creating a NEW WORLD, the inevitable first condition to realize is thus that of regenerating Science in order to give it a new force at the same time that History is being corrected. And that can only be accomplished by the light of female intuition, a power whose source lies uniquely in the absolute.[23]

By reforming the way we know the truth, in and through a woman's intuitive reading of the evidence, we can understand the past and the present in order to create a better future. This radical epistemology was necessary because men had falsified the historical records that had once celebrated the divine roles women played as goddesses and priestesses in the ancient world.[24] And so

> we will apply ourselves especially to showing all men of good will the works made possible by the female mind. We will try to teach them to recognize the *hidden* knowledge contained within the books that were suppressed. We will rescue from oblivion the censored truths, and we will bring to light the fascinating history of the Ancient Mysteries.[25]

Such a project was possible if one had the key to knowledge that enabled Renooz to discern in the Bible, for example, what incredible spiritual power women had before men seized control of religion and altered the sacred texts. But Renooz knew and proved, to her satisfaction anyway, that the most important figures in the Old and New Testaments, including Moses and Jesus, were really women. The new world needed to know this historical 'fact' thanks to a new manner of knowing, i.e., to a whole new system of signs.

In 1908 Renooz outlined her complex history of religion and its basis in feminist epistemology. Her pamphlet, *Evolution de l'idée divine*, likened the historical development of divinity to the organic process of maturation. Before the tenth century BCE, when goddesses and priestesses predominated, 'Theogony was the expresion of youthful sentiments. It suddenly appeared in the early stages of humanity's evolution, because it responded to the need of all men, the need to adore Woman.'[26] But for the next millennium, a struggle erupted between gods and goddesses: 'the second manifestation of the Divine Idea was the source of conflict between men and women, of jealousies, of hatreds that appeared in the adult male in particular.' Ultimately, the gods won and expelled the goddesses from the Judaeo-Christian pantheon as we now know it: 'the third manifestation of the Divine resulted from a benighted mental condition, accompanied by the ardent desire to dominate which in time developed among certain men.' With each phase came dramatic changes in social and political institutions as well as religious life, resulting in the subjugation of women and the rewriting of historical records, including the sacred texts, that documented the former powers of women. 'Since *man changes laws only after having changed gods*,' Renooz concluded, 'social renewal will occur only by reestablishing in the world NATURAL RELIGION, which will re-create the moral life of humanity.'[27] This would begin by restoring women to their rightful role as the divine bearers of truth.

As a consequence of her vision of knowledge and the past, Renooz's passionate commitment to feminist action was naturally complemented by an equally passionate exploration of its radical necessity: to redress the primal injustice done to women's original divinity that she alone had discovered and felt compelled to reestablish. Accordingly, the end of her life was devoted to explaining and promoting woman's special calling:

In order to finish our historical efforts, we have thus written the history of this Renaissance whose . . . first stages have already passed. The last stage alone remains to be realized. It is much awaited, and its animator will be the True Messiah of the new world, the *real teacher* of humanity.[28]

Renooz's ideas during a lifetime of creative work were centered on a particular view of women that now placed them at the center of a new, more harmonious cosmos. Here nature was not a realm of tooth and claw like a wild jungle, but peaceful and interdependent like a well-tended garden. Here knowledge was not mere power, but social morality. Here woman was not a victimized object, but an active agent in an orderly universe ultimately of her own making. That Renooz often confused women's causes with her own is, of course, no reason to dismiss her vision or its semiotic and historical implications.

It took a disaster as monumental as World War I, however, for Renooz to develop a specific utopian vision in keeping with her system. This terrible war, she firmly believed, was the direct result of men having usurped the female prerogative in all fields of knowledge and action. 'Therefore the preconditions of an enduring peace are above all the *reestablishment of moral authority*, which is a corrective for man's brutal instincts . . . : the return of Woman to her natural Authority.'[29] This authority resembled that which mothers have over their sons, a natural force powerful enough to bring about the union of all races, all nationalities, all beliefs, all truths in the world, and thus to create an enduring peace. According to Renooz, 'la Matrise' was most likely in the establishment of a sacred city, an international center where the representatives of the major states would be guided in their collective decisions by the new knowledge that Renooz's work had suggested: 'Creators of the Great Work will erect a Sacred City — which will become an Eternal City — because it will be the City of *Redemption*, that is, one whose science is *remade*.'[30]

In conclusion to this scheme, Renooz proposed a peace treaty and a universal constitution whose implementation she considered 'a return to Nature, a return to Truth, a return to Reason.'[31] The treaty's twelve articles emphasized the need to overcome the causes of war, especially in social, ethnic, and nationalist rivalries, by urging a reorganization of humanity based on the eternal laws of nature, i.e., on the naturally complementary instincts of males and females: women's spiritual force will direct the physical force of men. And so the treaty appended the draft of a universal constitution determined by these principles. Here the welfare of society, the organization of work, the constitution of families, the education of children, and the provision of health care would be structured in the interest of every language, every race, every nationality, based on *la Vérité absolue*. 'L'Esprit féminin' would ensure the order in Renooz's 'Ratiocratie' that marked the practical culmination of her very particular system of signs.

Ultimately, Renooz's system brought together her interests in organicism, mysticism, history, and women, the guiding principles of her vision. In science, biology became the touchstone of truth, by analogy the model for all fields of knowledge: the secret of human evolution, she believed, lay in the example set by embryology and physiology. Similarly, scientific certitude existed in the intuitive faculties instinctive to women and children who apprehended phenomena naturally, without the falsifying methods of empiricism. There was no rational basis to this assertion; Renooz thought it obvious to everyone capable of abstraction, whether or not it could be proven experimentally. Historical examples demonstrated that such proof was itself epistemologically suspect. Once the records were restored to their original forms, women's science, as both knowledge and morality, promised redemption in Renooz's utopian vision, the product of a lifetime of feminist experience and insight.

One source of interest in Renooz's work is, to be sure, its special place in the history of ideas.[32] It owes much to earlier intellectual movements, such as experimental science, messianic romanticism, and especially utopian socialism, even though her writings often disavowed their most obvious influences. The empirical methods of the physiologist Claude Bernard and the anthropologist Paul Broca, for example, loom large in Renooz's commitment to scientific observation and demonstration. Renooz relied on certain authorities in physiology and sought access to laboratory space at the Sorbonne, ironically placing her work squarely in a French positivist tradition. But also like the poet Alphonse de Lamartine and the philosopher Edgar Quinet before her, Renooz developed a prophetic vision of social justice and spiritual renewal. This Rousseaulike conception of a better world returned a benign, in fact beneficent nature to its rightful place in a society that had been corrupted by men. More in tune with the natural, Renooz believed, women will inspire men to achieve true social harmony, just as Prosper Enfantin the Saint-Simonian visionary and organizer had argued they would.

Yet Renooz's work also shares in subsequent challenges to the ideologies of positivism and rationalism.[33] Renooz clearly participated in the fin-desiècle's reassessment of experimental science and political liberalism. For her, progress and materialism were pernicious myths. Not having read either the neo-Kantians like Charles Renouvier, syndicalists like Georges Sorel, or the avant-garde like Alfred Jarry — the French counterparts to Nietzsche, Marx, and Freud — Renooz still recognized the limits to reason in the scientific method and the rational individual, pillars of Western self-confidence and patriarchal hegemony on the eve of the twentieth century. Like the vitalist philosopher Henri Bergson and the mystical nationalist Charles Péguy, Renooz questioned the empirical assumptions of institutional science. In this way Renooz joined many feminist thinkers — Maria Deraismes and Madeleine Pelletier in particular — in anticipating the post-modern critique of phallogocentrism and its intellectual manifestations. The Women's Liberation Movement in France, represented by Hélène Cixous, Julia Kristeva, and Luce Irigaray, owes much to such early feminist thought.[34]

Within this remarkable synthesis of European ideas, Renooz's real interest, however, lies in her complex expression of multiple, often conflicting sign systems. Her uncompleted memoirs offer the best site to overhear this heteroglossia in her work.[35] Despite its forthright chronological organization, 'Prédestinée: L'Autobiographie de la femme cachée' incorporates the features of several different texts — private diary, personal correspondence, scientific scholarship, polemical journalism, utopian vision, and feminist debate — instances of which are even attached to the manuscript where Renooz's retrospective narrative plays off of them. Rusty pins hold in place fragments of her childhood journal, letters she received and copies of those she sent, articles clipped from scholarly reviews and various newspapers, and pages torn from her other writings. This curious collage suggests the contrasting discursive practices at work in Renooz's self-consciously intertextual writing. At one point, citing Albert Kölliker's *Embryologie* (1882), she remarks how 'I had only to add some citations here and there . . . in order to lend more authority to my writing,' even though Renooz had more subversive purposes in mind.[36]

Another instance of Renooz's problematic semiotic deserves attention. It concerns her theory of radiant energy that she felt made climatic conditions at the north and south poles particularly dangerous. In the first volume to *La Nouvelle Science*, Renooz had asserted the primacy of oxygen as a force in the universe. The inordinate consumption of oxygen by the sun made its rays the primary source of physical and spiritual animation on earth. But when the sun's rays hit the planet tangentially, as they do at the poles, the result is a turbulence unmediated by the earth's absorption of their energy. 'The consequences of this are that all unfixed objects on this part of the globe must be caught up by the movement caused by tangential radiation and swept by it into the depths of space.'[37] The extraordinary winds at the poles, Renooz warned, simply preclude any possible exploration there. For this reason, then, Renooz wrote to the editor of the newspaper *Le Matin* explaining the failure of the Andrée expedition by balloon to the North pole in 1896; a similar fate, she felt, awaited this Swede's foolhardy imitators.

In light of Renooz's theories, based as they were on her intuitive epistemology, this warning made perfect sense. Its explanation in the eight newspaper articles she clipped and saved for her memoirs, however, was much less sensible. The published responses to her warning were unequivocally cruel.[38] Several journalists made fun of her, while others like Elysée Réclus flatly contradicted her: 'The frightful storms that Nansen [one of Renooz's sources] discussed are no more frightful than other storms in the tropics.'[39] But Renooz was unmoved. Her original article, she noted in her memoirs, had been travestied by the press; its scientific language had been deliberately reformulated to make her look absurd. As M. Dautherive, the editor of *Le Matin*, admitted in a letter to Renooz, 'It seems impossible to me for a newspaper to clarify such difficult problems. Readers do not possess language as scientific as yours, Madame.'[40] Renooz's counter-discursive practice had to be translated into the dominant system of signs in order to make her views intelligible, despite Renooz's deliberate incorporation of the press's own polemical strategies.

In effect, Renooz's feminist vision is a concatenation of often incomprehensible, nearly always contradictory discourses. She had intended, of course, to define a semiotic system in opposition to the dominant one in both science and religion. And in some ways she succeeded. Her many publications attest to this success. But her patently illogical and selectively informed texts convinced no more than a handful of devoted followers.[41] Whatever persuasive rhetorical strategies she adopted, Renooz failed to reach a larger audience, largely because of her subversive discourse, one whose fundamental dissonance proved to be unintelligible to her contemporaries. Her mixing of voices, mimicking the discursive practices of her intellectual adversaries, only made matters worse; the resulting cacophony was even less convincing. In time, as she came to despair of ever completing her personal crusade, Renooz turned increasingly defensive, self-righteous, and dogmatic, isolating herself from all criticism, striking the pose of a persecuted martyr, and escaping into flights of self-aggrandizement and occasional mysticism.[42] Her language was simply too foreign.

Unfortunately, few of her peers were listening. Like membership in the Société Néosophique, her publications appealed to a very small group; printings rarely exceeded one hundred copies.[43] Even fellow feminists seemed to have ignored her. After publishing a few of her pieces in the most important newspaper to defend women's rights (*La Fronde*), Marguerite Durand returned Renooz's articles on women's issues.[44] As for Clémence Royer, Darwin's first French translator, Renooz was little more than a crackpot — 'that intelligence struck by delusions of grandeur and a mania for pretention,' Royer wrote to Mme. de Ste. Croix in 1897.[45] Renooz's apparent paranoia complicated her efforts to communicate, much less understand why those efforts were unavailing. Eventually she came to blame her frustrations on a single individual, Mathias Duval, professor of physiology in the Faculty of Medicine at the University of Paris, a man who more than once had called Renooz mad — to her face. When he died in March 1907, she devoted five full pages of her memoirs to the disruptive role he had played in her work. 'The antichrist,' she called him in her rage, '*a vandal of scholarship*' — a judgment expressed in Renooz's alternative system of signs.[46]

Renooz's marginal status, socially and intellectually, is typical of utopian thinkers in general but also of feminist visionaries in particular. Like other lone voices in the wilderness, from Old Testament prophets to the leaders of May 1968 events in France — or more tellingly, from the medieval religious writer Hildegard of Bingen to the African-American evangelist Sojourner Truth — Renooz is in very good company historically. All radical voices appear in apparent isolation, because they challenge prevailing assumptions about the world. For example, Renooz's work lends credence to Gerda Lerner's argument in *The Creation of Feminist Consciousness from the Middle Ages to Eighteen-Seventy* (1992). Like the women Lerner studies, Renooz 'transformed the concepts and assumptions of male thought and [not so] subtly subverted male thought so as to incorporate women's cultural knowledge and viewpoint.' Renooz's writings actually mark a culmination in a 'tradition of women's long-range resistance to patriarchy and the factors which have brought about changes in women's consciousness of their own situation.'[47]

Although Lerner emphasizes the explicit manifestations of this consciousness in the West, I want to suggest that Renooz's distinctive contribution to this history lies in her understanding of signs and their power in male hands. She identified men's semiotic control of women everywhere, especially in institutions like the Napoleonic Code, the university, the scientific method, the religious beliefs and practices of Christianity, even the study of history. But her work also goes further in reasserting a belief that women can regain their historical agency through writing itself. As Renooz says at the very beginning of her memoirs:

> I do not want to abandon my personality to the novelistic fantasies of bigots, much less to the slander of the envious. On the other hand, I do want to make known the rather extraordinary circumstances which led me to unprecedented work in the history of scholarship. I will not do myself justice simply to show what I did — I also want to say who I am.[48]

Through their command of signs, Renooz implies here, will come women's identity, their very existence, perhaps even their destiny.

The lesson of Renooz's work is thus semiotic as well as historical. Literary theorists, I think, can recognize in her writing the role played by her context, especially in the dialectic between experience and language. That much is obvious. It underlies her quirky but no less sincere expression of a harmonious world re-created by women. This feminist vision is based not solely in the autonomy of its language, but also on the prolonged and intense personal pain of its author. But even more to the point are the subjectivity and agency of women suggested in the dialectical context that Renooz's thought manifests. Despite her apparent paranoia, perhaps even because of it, Renooz gave voice to her identity in and through her writing, primarily as an act of self-assertion and ultimately of human dignity.[49] In the futility of her efforts, Renooz remains obscure, indeed pathetic, but such a demeaning judgment is unfairly derived from the phallocentric world that she sought to combat. All her life she resisted the objectifying and marginalizing effects of patriarchy, in its institutions and more, in its signs. For this courageous work, as Georges Gusdorf claims for autobiographical memory, Renooz's work deserves sympathetic as well as critical analysis.[50]

James Smith Allen is Professor of History, Southern Illinois University, Carbondale.

APPENDIX
MAJOR WORKS BY CÉLINE RENOOZ, 1883-1933

L'Origine des animaux. Histoire du développement primitif. Nouvelle théorie de l'évolution réfutant par l'anatomie celle de M. Darwin. Vol. 1. Paris: J.B. Baillière et fils, 1883 [subsequent volumes never written]

Editor, *La Revue scientifique des femmes.* May 1888-March 1889

'Prédestinée: L'Autobiographie de la femme cachée' [1890-1913, uncompleted manuscript]. Bibliothèque Historique de la Ville de Paris, Fonds Marie Louise Bouglé, Papiers Céline Renooz, Boxes 16-19

La Nouvelle Science:
Vol. 1: *Les Forces cosmiques. Synthèse des lois de l'univers, l'évolution des astres, Principe d'une nouvelle physique.* 3rd ed. Paris: Librairie Nouvelle, n.d. [originally entitled *La Force*, 1890]
Vol. 2: *Les Facteurs de la vie. Les Eléments de l'univers, les familles solaires, la chimie nouvelle, les stades de l'évolution chimique.* 2d ed. Paris: Editions Rhéa, 1920 [originally entitled *Le Principe générateur de la vie*, 1892]
Vol. 3: *Les Evolutions phylogéniques.* Part I: *L'Origine des animaux* [already published in 1883]; Part II: *L'Evolution de l'homme et des animaux. Histoire positive du développement primitif démontrée par le développement embryonnaire*, premier fascicule. Paris: Vieweg, 1888 [never completed]; Part III: *L'Origine végétale* [never written]
Vol. 4: *La Paléontologie nouvelle* [never written]
Vol. 5: *Le Dualisme physiologique* [never written]
Vol. 6: *La Psychologie comparée de l'homme et de la femme, bases scientifiques de la morale.* 2d ed. Paris: Société d'Editions Scientifiques chez l'auteur, 1901 [originally published in 1898]

Ere de vérité. Histoire de la pensée humaine et de l'évolution morale de l'humanité à travers les âges et chez tous les peuples.
Vol. 1: *Le Monde primitif.* Paris: Marcel Giard, 1921
Vol. 2: *Le Monde ancien.* Paris: Marcel Giard, 1924
Vol. 3: *Le Monde israélite.* Paris: Marcel Giard, 1925
Vol. 4: *Le Monde celtique.* Paris: Marcel Giard, 1926
Vol. 5: *Le Monde chrétien.* Paris: Marcel Giard, 1927
Vol. 6: *Le Monde moderne.* Paris: Marcel Giard, 1933

ENDNOTES

1. Georges Gusdorf, *Lignes de vie*, Vol. 1: *Les Ecritures du moi* (Paris: Editions Odile Jacob, 1991), p. 11. (Note that all translations here from the French are my own.) Cf. discussion of the modern crisis in memory, history, and signs in Richard Terdiman, *Present Past: Modernity and the Memory Crisis* (Ithaca: Cornell University Press, 1993), esp. pp. 3-32.

2. See esp. Frank E. and Fritzie P. Manuel, *Utopian Thought in the Western World* (Cambridge: Harvard University Press, 1979).

3. See Dominick LaCapra, 'Rethinking Intellectual History and Reading Texts,' *Modern European Intellectual History: Reappraisals and New Perspectives*, ed. Dominick LaCapra and Steven L. Kaplan (Ithaca: Cornell University Press, 1982), pp. 47-85; and idem, *Rethinking Intellectual History: Texts, Contexts, Language* (Ithaca: Cornell University Press, 1987).

4. *Caveat lector*: this essay deliberately assumes an equivalence between 'representation,' 'discourse,' and 'sign systems'—despite the important connotative differences that exist among these terms—in order to highlight the intersections between the disciplines that use them, viz., intellectual history, literary theory, and semiotics, respectively. Similarly, this essay also assumes that utopian thought is a type of representation, discourse, or sign system, primarily because visions of alternative worlds generally entail a whole other language, a radically different epistemology even, from prevailing modes of expression and knowledge. Utopias in fact redefine the relationships between sign and referent that underlie the specific manner of knowing at work in normal representational, discursive, and semiotic practices. Such assumptions are not unprecedented: see Michel Foucault, *The Order of Things: An Archeology of the Human Sciences* (New York: Random House-Vintage, 1973); Umberto Eco, *A Theory of Semiotics* (Bloomington: Indiana University Press, 1976); and Jonathan Culler, *The Pursuit of Signs: Semiotics, Literature, Deconstruction* (Ithaca: Cornell University Press, 1981).

5. For useful reflections on sign systems and history, see Fredric Jameson, *The Prison-House of Language: A Critical Account of Structuralism and Russian Formalism* (Princeton: Princeton University Press, 1972); Richard Terdiman, *Discourse/Counter-Discourse: The Theory and Practice of Symbolic Resistance in Nineteenth-Century France* (Ithaca: Cornell University Press, 1985); and James C. Scott, *Domination and the Arts of Resistance: Hidden Transcripts* (New Haven: Yale University Press, 1990).

6. There are no serious studies of Céline Renooz or her work. See Henry Carnoy, *Mme Renooz et son oeuvre* (Paris: Imp. de E. Laton, 1902), a brief but inadequate profile ghost-written by Renooz long before her career had finished (cf. letter from Renooz to Carnoy, 3 December 1901, Bibliothèque Historique de la Ville de Paris (hereafter BHVP) Fonds Marie Louise Bouglé: Papiers Renooz, box 10, d. 1901, no. 5); and the obituary by Louise Chapel in *L'Ere de vérité*, Bulletin mensuel de la Société Néosophique. Vol. 2, No. 2 (April 1928): 1.

Recent histories of the women's movement in France—e.g., Maïté Albistur and Daniel Armogathe, *Histoire du féminisme français du moyen âge à nos jours* (Paris: Editions des Femmes, 1977); Steven C. Hause with Anne R. Kenney, *Women's Suffrage and Social Politics in the Third French Republic* (Princeton: Princeton University Press, 1981); and *Feminisms of the Belle Epoque: A Historical and Literary Anthology*, ed. Jennifer Waelti-Walters and Steven C. Hause (Lincoln: University of Nebraska Press, 1994)—make no mention of her. Cf. Laurence Klejman and Florence Rochefort, *L'Egalité en marche. Le féminisme sous la troisième République* (Paris: Presses de la Fondation Nationale des Sciences Politiques, 1989), pp. 72-74.

The present study of Renooz is part of a larger examination of French women's identity and agency in their autobiographical writings, tentatively entitled *Poignant Relations: The Arts of Feminist Consciousness in Modern France.*

7. See Maïté Albistur, *Catalogue des archives Marie Louise Bouglé* (Paris: Bibliothèque Historique de la Ville de Paris, 1982), photocopied typescript. To avoid unnecessary repetition here, all my references to Renooz's personal papers in the Bouglé archival collection will provide just the box number, the dossier title, and the folio number. I will omit, however, the specific information required on the *bulletins* used to order this material at the BHVP: 'Fonds Bouglé: Papiers Renooz.'

8. Renooz, *L'Origine des animaux. Histoire du développement primitif. Nouvelle théorie de l'évolution réfutant par l'anatomie celle de M. Darwin* (Paris: J.B. Baillière et fils, 1883), I:5. Cf. Renooz on Clémence Royer's commitment to Darwinism, in Renooz to Dr. Verrier, 29 October 1897, BVHP box 10, d. 1897, no. 22: 'Clémence Royer is 40 years behind the times....'

9. Renooz's emphasis. Renooz, 'Une révélation,' *La Religion laïque et universelle* (15 May 1888): 266.

10. Renooz, *Le Grand Problème* (Paris: Publications Néosophiques, [1908]), pp. 61-62.

11. *Ibid.*, p. 7.

12. Renooz, *L'Origine des animaux*, I:6.

13. Renooz's emphasis. Renooz, 'Régénération morale par la science,' *La Revue scientifique des femmes* Vol. 1, No. 2 (June 1888): 49.

14. Renooz, 'Une révélation,' 267.

15. Renooz's emphasis. *Ibid.*

16. Renooz's emphasis. *Ibid.*

17. See the deification of oxygen in Renooz, 'Prédestinée: L'Autobiographie de la femme cachée,' BHVP box 16, d. Retour en France, fol. 39: in 1878 'I spoke for the first time of Oxygen's psychological and physiological role; I asserted my belief in the existence of the God-Oxygen. Naturally I was not understood.'

18. Renooz, *La Nouvelle Science*, Vol. 1: *Les Forces cosmiques. Synthèse des lois de l'univers, l'évolution des astres. Principe d'une nouvelle physique*, 3rd ed. (Paris: Librairie Nationale, n.d.), pp. 127-28.

19. On 'la mathèse,' see Renooz to Hubertine Auclert, 22 August 1897, BHVP box 10, d. 1897, no. 2: 'I use the mathematical method which the ancients called 'mathèse' and which is quite simply the knowledge of order. This order in facts, ideas, and observations permits me to provide solutions [to important problems]....'

20. Renooz, *La Science et l'empiricisme* (Paris: Bibliothèque de la Nouvelle Encyclopédie, 1898), p. 9. Cf. Renooz, 'Prédestinée,' BHVP box 16, d. 'Ma Vocation scientifique,' fol. 4: 'Intuition is the unusual Mental Power that tears away the veil between us and the truth and that opens up to us a new horizon by giving us the sudden, spontaneous knowledge of a certain fact that no other method used by men can discover.'

21. *Ibid.*, inside back cover.

22. Renooz, *La Nouvelle Science*, Vol. 1: *Les Forces cosmiques*, p. 187.

23. Renooz, *Ere de vérité*, Vol. 1: *Le Monde primitif* (Paris: Marcel Giard, 1921), p. 5.

24. Johann Jacob Bachofen, *Das Mutterrecht: Eine Untersuchung über die Gynaikokratie der alten Welt* (Stuttgart: Kraus und Hoffmann, 1861) makes a similar argument that Renooz acknowledges. See Renooz to Edouard Lecoq, May 1908, BHVP box 11, d. 1908, no. 18: 'Mme Fournet had this work's preface and table of contents translated and published...,' even though Bachofen's work had already been translated into French by 1900. Cf. Gerda Lerner, *The Creation of Patriarchy* (New York: Oxford University Press, 1986), pp. 26-27.

25. Renooz, *Ere de vérité*, Vol 1: *Le Monde primitif* (Paris: Marcel Giard, 1924), pp. 13-14.

26. Renooz's emphasis. Renooz, *Evolution de l'idée divine (simple aperçu)* (Paris: V. Giard et E. Brière, 1908), p. 3.

27. Renooz's emphasis. *Ibid.*, p. 55.

28. Renooz, *Ere de vérité*, Vol. 6: *Le Monde moderne* (Paris: Marcel Giard, 1933), p. 738.

29. Renooz's emphases. Renooz, *La Paix glorieuse. Nécessité de l'intervention féminine pour assumer la paix future. Edification du monde nouveau par la ratiocratie universelle. Le nouveau statut des peuples. Dédié à Monsieur Wilson, président des Etats-Unis* (Paris: Publications Néosophiques, 1917), p. 4.

30. Renooz's emphases. *Ibid.*, p. 12.

31. *Ibid.*, p. 15.

32. For Renooz's intellectual context, see esp. Harry W. Paul, *From Knowledge to Power: The Rise of the Science Empire in France, 1860-1939* (Cambridge: Cambridge University Press, 1985); Paul Bénichou, *Le Temps des prophètes. Doctrines de l'âge romantique* (Paris: Gallimard, 1977); and Frank E. Manuel, *The Prophets of Paris* (Cambridge, Mass.: Harvard University Press, 1962).

33. See William Logue, *From Philosophy to Sociology: The Evolution of French Liberalism, 1870-1914* (DeKalb: Northern Illinois University Press, 1983); Roger Shattuck, *The Banquet Years: The Origins of the Avant-Garde in France, 1885 to World War I*, rev. ed. (London: Jonathan Cape, 1969); H. Stuart Hughes, *The Obstructed Path: French Social Thought in the Years of Desperation, 1930-1965* (New York: Harper and Row, 1968); and Claire Goldberg Moses, *Feminist Thought in Nineteenth-Century France* (Albany: State University of New York Press, 1984).

34. See Claire Duchen, *Feminism in France from '68 to Mitterrand* (London: Routledge and Kegan Paul, 1986); *French Feminist Thought: A Reader*, ed. Toril Moi (Oxford: Basil Blackwell, 1987), pp. 1-13, 110-30; and Hélène Cixous, *The Newly Born Woman* (Minneapolis: University of Minnesota Press, 1985).

35. For more on Renooz's memoirs, see James Smith Allen, 'Narrative and Ideology in the Memoirs of Céline Renooz, 1890-1913,' *Modernity and the Spaces of Journalism*, ed. Dean de la Motte and Jeannene Przyblyski (Lincoln: University of Nebraska Press, forthcoming).

36. Renooz, 'Prédestinée,' BHVP box 17, d. 1re étape, fol. 44.

37. Paraphrased in W. de Fouvielle, 'Au Pôle nord. Le Ballon d'Andrée et les courants solaires— La Théorie de Mme. C. Renooz—Une expédition impossible,' *Le Matin* (31 August 1900). Renooz's original article on this subject was never published (see n. 40), but she did outline her position in *La Nouvelle Science*, Vol. 1: *Les Forces cosmiques*, p. 106.

38. See articles in BHVP box 20, d. 1900.

39. Letter from Elysée Réclus to Renooz, 24 March 1898, in 'Prédestinée,' BHVP box 18, d. Ostracisme, fol. 248. Cf. Fridtjof Nansen, *Vers le pôle*, tr. and ed. Charles Robert (Paris: Flammarion, 1897), 2 vols.

40. Letter from Mr. Dautherive to Renooz, 11 September 1900, in BHVP box 3, d. 1900, no. 11.

41. On Renooz's mode of working—without consulting the most relevant authorities in her chosen fields, without correction or revision of her manuscripts—see Renooz to Mme Sales, unknown date in 1897, BHVP box 3, d. 1897, no. 19: 'I have read very few books by men for several reasons—above all, because their ideas shock me. I have never found any logic to them, and I find it tiring to read things that from the start I have considered false. And it is because *I pondered* and I observed Nature *before* studying men's scholarship.... So I cannot quote *my sources*, since I haven't consulted any.... My book [*La Nouvelle Science*] was already fully conceived in my

mind; and when I wrote it, my subject quite simply and all in one gush flowed from my pen.... It did not take me four months to write the book, and I have neither re-read nor corrected my original draft [Renooz's emphases].'

42. Despite her professed skepticism about parascientific phenomena, Renooz dabbled frequently in numerology, took seriously predictions of cataclysmic events, and explained at length the meaning of auspicious signs at the beginning of each new year. E.g., see the graphologist Victor Moussy to Renooz, 11 December 1891, BHVP box 2, d. 1891, no no.

43. See Allen, 'The Intertext of Publication: Céline Renooz and the Société Néosophique, 1897-1928,' paper presented at the annual meeting of the Modern Language Association of America, San Diego, December 27-30, 1994.

44. Renooz, 'Prédestinée,' BHVP box 17, d. Ostracisme, fol. 232. For Renooz's views critical of Marguerite Durand, see Renooz to Unknown, 10 July 1917, Bibliothèque Marguerite Durand, MS. 091 REN No. 2: 'she has been the origin of absurd, really quite in-comprehensible male doctrines....'; and of the suffrage movement generally, see Renooz to Maria Deraismes, 16 February 1889, BHVP box 3, d. 1889, no. 3: 'we are not calling for rights, we are taking them; we are mustering all our energy to show that we can always do as well as men, and quite often, even better than they. We absolutely refuse all help from the present government, finding in scholarship alone the right to govern the world for re-forming social mores and hence the legal system.'

45. Clémence Royer to Mme. de Ste. Croix, June 1897, in Bibliothèque Marguerite Durand, dossier Céline Renooz, no. 6.

46. Renooz, 'Prédestinée,' BHVP box 19, d. 1907, fol. 5.

47. Gerda Lerner, *The Creation of Feminist Consciousness from the Middle Ages to Eighteen-Seventy* (New York: Oxford University Press, 1991), pp. 12, 13.

48. Renooz, 'Prédestinée,' BHVP box 17, d. Souvenirs d'enfance, fols. 1-2. Cf. the theoretical context for such a personal statement of identity sought in and through autobiographical writing: Philippe Lejeune, *On Autobiography*, ed. John Paul Eakin (Minneapolis: University of Minnesota Press, 1989), pp. 3-30, 119-37.

49. This argument is developed at greater length in Allen, 'Variations on the Feminine 'I': Genre and Identity in Women's Letters, Diaries, and Memoirs,' paper presented at the annual meeting of the Midwest Modern Language Association, Chicago, November 9-11, 1994.

50. Cf. the views of other women speaking for themselves, from the eighteenth century onward, in the United States as well as Europe, in *Women, the Family, and Freedom: The Debate in Documents*, ed. Susan Groag Bell and Karen M. Offen (Stanford: Stanford University Press, 1983), 2 vols. Even though Renooz's work is nowhere to be found in this important collection, her ideas are shared by many of her contemporaries in the Western world, most notably Charlotte Perkins Gilman on

motherhood (Vol. 2, pp. 119-23) and Virginia Woolf on women intellectuals (Vol. 2, pp. 359-62). But there are no notable women writers who have treated the same epistemological and semiotic issues that Renooz raises.

Chapter IX

Julia Ward Howe, John Brown's Body, and the Coming of the Lord

Jeffrey J. Polizzotto*

'The Battle Hymn of the Republic' is the most famous poem to emerge from the American Civil War. It transforms the Union war effort from a struggle for national union into a religious crusade for freedom, of cosmic importance in history comparable to the death and resurrection of Jesus Christ. But this powerful text is also about the transfiguration of Julia Ward Howe, the author, from a writer and obscure supporter of reform causes into one of the world's leading advocates of women's rights. Read in the context of its author's life, 'The Battle Hymn' acquires a fascinating subtext that suggests Howe was performing the same task contemporary feminist theorists such as Hélène Cixous and Julia Kristeva have been urging late-twentieth-century women to undertake. Her work and life also point to difficulties and problems with their thought.

Born in 1819 in New York City to one of America's wealthiest families, Julia Ward received a superb education and had written unpublished poetry when in 1843 she was swept off her feet by the forty-two-year-old hero of the Greek Revolution, Samuel Gridley Howe. With his combat days nearly two decades behind him, Howe had turned with equal zeal to ameliorating the lot of prisoners, the insane, and the deaf and blind in the United States. After their marriage, the Howes moved to Dorchester, just south of Boston, where Samuel directed the Perkins Institute for the Blind (Clifford 1979:6-84; Howe 1899:3-150).

The marriage was not happy. Julia felt isolated from the high society life she had enjoyed in New York, and Samuel, while espousing reforms and radical causes such as the abolition of slavery, objected to his wife, a married woman and mother, developing a public persona of her own through publications or political activity. In her letters, Julia described their marriage as 'very unhappy,' termed her husband 'as cold and indifferent to me as a man can well be,' and described her fate in life as a 'living death' (Howe 1854-1865:120-121, 134). They considered separation, but stuck it out. By the mid-1850s, Julia had started to publish — a book of poems, *Passion Flowers*, appeared in 1857 — and make the acquaintance of literary types in Boston. She had also begun to assist her husband in turning out an anti-slavery newspaper entitled *The Commonwealth* (Howe 1899:252-253).

A critical turning point in Julia's life occurred in 1859. Samuel had spoken to her of a man who 'intended to devote his life to the redemption of the colored race from slavery, even as Christ had willingly offered his life for the salvation of mankind.' That man was John Brown: Samuel insisted his wife keep this information secret, for Howe belonged to a group of northerners who were covertly furnishing Brown with arms and money to fight pro-slavery forces in Kansas. Now in 1859 Brown physically appeared at the Howe's residence in Dorchester, shortly before he tried to launch the slave uprising in Virginia which led to his capture at Harper's Ferry and subsequent execution. Samuel Gridley Howe was one of the 'Secret Six' who had financed the expedition. He temporarily fled to Canada to avoid possible punishment for his involvement (Howe 1899:253-256; Pickman 1979:130-134).

For Julia Howe, John Brown was thus both a reality and a symbol — of her own work in the abolitionist cause, but also of the activity her husband undertook apart from her, which excluded her from the public role she craved. Thus it is no wonder John Brown's presence remained in her mind, especially when the Howes moved to Washington with the outbreak of the Civil War — Samuel was to assist with the hygiene of the Union Army — and after Northern soldiers began to sing 'John Brown's body lies a-mouldering in the ground; His soul is marching on.' It was while Julia and some friends had been singing this song 'to beguile a rather tedious drive' that one of them suggested that she 'write some good words for that stirring tune' (Howe 1899:272-274).

The next morning, minor details aside, 'The Battle Hymn of the Republic' as we know it was born. The grim, dirge-like cadence of 'John Brown's Body' at eleven syllables to the line had been transfigured into the fourteen or fifteen of the multi-stanza, upbeat hymn which shifts the emphasis from death to resurrection. As originally sung, there were three lines of John Brown's mouldering body to one of his soul marching on: a variant on the first line, 'We'll hang Jeff Davis to a sour apple tree' is also about death. With the 'Battle Hymn,' John Brown is gone; Jesus Christ stands in his place.

Or does Julia Ward Howe? A careful reading of the poem makes Julia Ward Howe, symbol of the women who took on a more meaningful if by no means equal role in the national life during the Civil War, the real heroine. John Brown, her husband's protege, failed: he was mouldering in the ground. Julia, excluded by Samuel from the public sphere, is at both the Alpha and Omega of her own poem. '*Mine* eyes have seen the glory of the coming of the Lord' translates as follows: Julia Ward Howe, the woman hitherto relegated to the sidelines in her husband's projects and the national civic life, has been vouchsafed the vision and purpose denied to her husband, John Brown, and men. 'As he died to make men holy, let us die to make men free' — the penultimate line of the 'Battle Hymn's' final stanza — incorporates 'us,' men and women together, as participants in the divine struggle. In her published *Reminiscences*, Howe states that it was in fact her musing upon the role of women in the war which led her thoughts in the direction of writing the poem: 'I distinctly remember that a feeling of discouragement came over me. . . . I thought of the women of my acquaintance whose sons or husbands were fighting our great battle; the women themselves serving in the hospitals, or busying themselves with the work of the Sanitary Commission. . . . I could not leave my nursery to follow the march of our armies, neither had I the practical deftness which the preparing and packing of sanitary stores demanded. Something seemed to say to me, "You would be glad to serve, but you cannot help anyone; you have nothing to give, and there is nothing for you to do." Yet, because of my sincere desire, a word was given me to say, which did strengthen the hearts of those who fought in the field and those who languished in prison' (Howe 1899:273-274).

'The Battle Hymn,' in other words, gave the insignificant Julia Ward Howe a purpose. And what a purpose it was — 'Mine eyes have seen the glory of the coming of the Lord!' The stifled housewife had become the definitive interpreter of the intentions of the Almighty. '*I* have seen Him in the watch-fires of a hundred circling camps'; '*I* can read his righteous sentence by the dim and flaring lamps'; '*I* have read a fiery gospel, writ in burnished rows of steel' read following lines. Howe borrows the language of God Himself from Isaiah, chapter 63: 'I have trodden the winepress alone; and of the people there were none with me; for I will tread them in mine anger, and trample them in my fury.' The original words of 'He is trampling out the vintage where the grapes of wrath are stored' were 'He is trampling out the winepress . . .' (Pickman 1979:144-147). As the poem progresses, Howe becomes even more bold. Jesus is referred to as 'the Hero born of woman' who will 'crush the serpent with His heel.' Although she was yet to embrace women's suffrage and equal rights, Howe here adopted, perhaps unconsciously, the rhetoric of the women's movement. She emphasizes that Jesus was born of a woman and was the Son of God. Man had nothing to do with it.

The role of women appears most prominently in the final verse of 'The Battle Hymn.' 'In the beauty of the lilies Christ was born across the sea' creates an image of Jesus being conveyed amidst feminine flowers from the Old World across the Atlantic to the New to fulfill His mission in the American Civil War. 'The beauty of the lilies' or women make this possible. Christ possesses a 'glory in his bosom that transfigures you *and* me' — 'me' being Julia Ward Howe, who has found a purpose apart from a husband whom she once complained 'takes away my voice.' Finally, 'as he died to make men holy, let *us* die to make men free' is an almost blasphemous conclusion. For the first time in the poem, perhaps unintentionally, the pronoun referring to Christ is not capitalized: 'he' is placed on a level with 'us.' And 'us' — men and women, Julia Ward Howe and everyone else participating in this crusade, are improving on the work of God, transfiguring and transcending poor John Brown, who is absent from the hymn.

One may legitimately complain Howe is getting all worked up about very little. *She*, after all, is not dying to make anyone free or even putting herself at minimal risk. Aside from writing poetry, she is rejecting the war effort for the traditional role of mother and homemaker as she sends men off to die. There is a subtext to her subtext: far from opening a new era in history and fulfilling the will of God, her poem can be read as woman performing her traditional Victorian function of providing religious inspiration to men who do the real job.

Howe, of course, did not see it that way. In the *Reminiscences* she published in her eightieth year, she begins by calling attention to the nineteenth century as having 'eminently deserved a record among those which have been great landmarks of human history.' She presents the usual lists of technological and political achievements. But she begins and ends with items that point to her own contribution. The century 'has been the culmination of prophecies' — such as those she made in the 'Battle Hymn.' And it has led to 'the advancement of woman to dignity in the household and efficiency in the state' (Howe 1899:2-3). In the years following the

Civil War, Howe swept aside her aging husband's objections and turned her great energy to the struggle for women's rights. Once again, she fused a political movement which gave her greater personal freedom with a cosmic, transcendent purpose.

'When I turn my face toward the enfranchised women of today, I seem to have an apocalyptic vision of a great multitude, praising God for the new and wonderful revelations of His spirit,' Howe wrote in an essay (Howe 1868-1910:19). Like the Civil War, the American women's movement was nothing less than the opening of a new chapter in God's cosmic blueprint for humanity. Connections between the two crusades appear in the martial metaphors Howe employed to describe women on the march: 'The prophetess of a barbarous age, Deborah, judge of Israel, praised as blessed among women, the wife of the Kenite who slew with her own hand the enemy of her people,' was a model for the 'wives and mothers of America,' who must 'deal with the deadly enemies of the human race' and 'war against vice and frivolity in every shape' (Howe 1868-1910:240).

Ironically, much of Howe's militant prophesying was channeled into a new *peace* movement, the Mothers' Day for Peace, which she publicized all over the western world. A response to the war veterans' Memorial Days springing up after the Civil War, this forerunner of what is now the present commercialized Mothers' Day paralleled the 'Battle Hymn' in that Howe once again attempted to take away the right to interpret the Civil War from the men who fought it. We would commemorate mothers, not veterans; men destroy, women work to realize the millennial dream of peace using their moral influence. 'Arise . . . Christian women of this day. As men have often forsaken the plough and the anvil at the summons of war, let women now leave all that may be left of home for a great and earnest day of counsel' (Howe 1870: 1:302-303).

Women's need to assume roles as political activists and agents of historical change was an important part of Howe's message. Urging suffragists to work as did Jesus for 'the redemption of mankind' — women's moral influence will save men as well as women — Howe preached that 'the weapon of Christian warfare is the ballot. . . . Adopt it, O you women, with clean hands and a pure heart! Verify the best word written by the apostle: "In Christ Jesus there is neither bond nor free, neither male nor female, but a new creature," the harbinger of a new creation!' (Howe 1868-1910:229).

Once again, it is possible to criticize Howe for making much ado about very little, for generalizing her own marginality into overblown visions of transcendental significance. That women are morally better than men and that their entry into politics would purify a corrupt process was an appeal not to women's equality, but to the very stereotype which men used to keep women at home: that women were pure creatures untainted by the evils of society. And while it is possible to point to innumerable reforms generated by the American women's movement for the betterment of society, especially in the fields of health and public welfare, the nation's political life did not appreciably improve once women obtained the right to vote. The decade after the passage of the Women's Suffrage Amendment, the 1920s, was in fact one of the most corrupt and free-wheeling in the nation's history.

The difficulties nineteenth century feminists had in realizing their visions point to a problem at the core of the contemporary feminist enterprise. Modern feminist thinkers such as Hélène Cixous and Julia Kristeva call for women (and men) to undermine patriarchy and the unjust social conditions arising from it. Writing subversive, avant-garde texts is one means of effecting this major change. (Cixous 1986:63, 87). But again, are not marginalized intellectuals straining for significance? At least Julia Ward Howe was a national institution — Cixous and Kristeva may be household words on the Left Bank or Upper West Side, but not in the public imagination. They are undoubtedly aware of their dilemma, and that the challenges they offer to a male-dominated society approximate the image of women as less competitive and corrupt than men which men have invented. For instance, Kristeva's insight that man's realm is symbolic — say, battle, hymn, and republic — and woman's semiotic — the interpreter who must divine meaning — privileges the interpreter over the actor. And her distinction between Oedipal man and motherly woman is one her Victorian predecessors knew well (Kristeva 1986:93, 101). Perhaps it is impossible for feminists to free themselves from thinking with the very categories men have used to dominate them. Julia Ward Howe's efforts to transform herself from passive observer of John Brown's body into Deborah, judge of Israel, and herald of the coming of the Lord should warn contemporary feminists that unless they are extremely careful, they will only reinforce the very authority they seek to undermine.

Dale Carnegie, Inc., Columbia, South Carolina. A version of this paper was prepared for the senior history seminar, Penn State, 1991, and presented at the Semiotics Society of America Annual Meeting, Philadelphia, 1994.

REFERENCES

Cixous, Hélène and Catherine Clement, *The Newly Born Woman* (Manchester: Manchester University Press, 1986). Revised version of *La jeune née* (Paris: Union generale d'études).

Clifford, Deborah Pickman, *Mine Eyes Have Seen the Glory: A Biography of Julia Ward Howe* (Boston: Little, Brown, 1979).

Howe, Julia Ward, 1854-1865, *Letters*. Excerpted in Clifford, *Mine Eyes Have Seen the Glory*.

_____, *Julia Ward Howe and the Woman Suffrage Movement*, 1868-1910 Florence Howe Hall, ed. (Boston: Dana, Estes, 1913).

_____, 'An Appeal to the Women of the World,' 1870, printed in Laura E. Richards and Maud Elliott, *Julia Ward Howe, 1819-1910*. 2 vols. (Boston: Houghton, Mifflin, 1916).

_____, *Reminiscences, 1819-1899*, 1899 (New York: Negro Universities Presses, 1969). Originally published for the author.

Kristeva, Julia, *The Kristeva Reader*. Toril Moi, ed. (Oxford: Basil Blackwell, 1986).

Chapter X

Kant, Goethe, Benjamin, and the Law of Marriage

Thomas O. Beebee*

The title of Michael Makropoulos's study of the thought of Walter Benjamin (1892-1940), *Modernität als ontologischer Ausnahmezustand (Modernity as Ontological 'State of Emergency')*, reveals the extent to which legal theory shaped the thinking of one of Germany's greatest literary critics.[1] Benjamin viewed legal themes as one source of the 'dialectical images' showing the conditions of experience and perception in the early twentieth century. Though without formal training in law or political theory, Benjamin studied under the philosopher Hermann Cohen, whose systematic neo-Kantianism provided a basis for theoretical pronouncements on nearly anything. Furthermore, Benjamin's idea of 'redemptive criticism' caused him to search for ways in which the hidden truth-value of literary works could be pried loose from their subject matter and applied to the critic's present world, Weimar Germany in Benjamin's case.

The procedures of redemptive criticism are admirably demonstrated in Benjamin's reading of the theme of marriage in Goethe's novel *Die Wahlverwandtschaften* (1806; *The Elective Affinities*). Thus, an exploration of the various sources — legal, philosophical, and literary — behind Benjamin's treatment of marriage in his essay on Goethe's novel reveals how his literary criticism functioned as an implicit critique of the political and legal difficulties of the Weimar Republic. Writing in the years 1921 and 1922, Benjamin attempted to accomplish four things simultaneously with his essay on Goethe, according to John McCole: first, Benjamin sought to give a practical demonstration of the idea of immanent criticism which he had elaborated in his dissertation on German Romanticism; secondly, he polemicized against vitalist readings of Goethe's work; thirdly, he set out the categories of a phenomenology of mythic forms; fourthly, he attempted to counter a notion, widely accepted in the critical reception of Goethe's novel, that the *Wahlverwandtschaften*'s main theme of adultery and its consequences upholds the moral conception of marriage as the pillar of civil society.[2] There is a fifth dimension to this essay which McCole does not mention, perhaps because it involves Benjamin's personal life rather than his critical argument: Benjamin's marriage to Dora was collapsing at the time, under some of the same pressures as found in Goethe's novel. Gershom Scholem summarizes both the facts and the analogy succinctly: 'When Ernst Schoen renewed his amicable relationship with Walter and Dora in the winter months of 1921, Dora fell madly in love with him and for a few months was in an altogether euphoric mood. . . . In April . . . Jula Cohn . . . came to Berlin, and Benjamin saw her again for the first time in five years. He developed a passionate attachment to her. . . . There developed a situation which, to the extent that I was able to understand it, corresponded to the one in Goethe's novel *Elective Affinities*.'[3] While Benjamin seemed to have been impelled towards his essay by a feeling of resonance between the dissolution of his own marriage and that described in Goethe's novel, our own use of this personal information must be grounded in the typicality of such situations during the roaring twenties.

I will focus my examination primarily on the third and fourth of Benjamin's objectives, each of which, it turns out, depends upon the other. However, the real 'object' of this essay is not Benjamin's thought, but rather marriage as a complex sign, created anew in literature, philosophy, and politics of the nineteenth and twentieth centuries, which reveals the mutual interdependence of those three realms in German intellectual society. Goethe incorporated varying interpretations of marriage into his texts, and later critics, including Benjamin, have been highly selective in emphasizing the particular legal and social function of marriage which they find best. Prominent divergences concern whether marriage is indissolubile or temporary, whether its purpose lies in propagation or elsewhere, and its relative importance as a form of 'Recht.' German uses the same word, 'Recht,' for both law and for the enablements which English calls 'rights.' As we shall see, a central question raised by Goethe's text is whether marriage is an enabling right or a prohibiting law. In turn, the search for 'Recht' in modern German history has provided political developments which resonate in critics' approaches to the theme of marriage in Goethe's novel.

Spurred on by Goethe's own comments on his work, critics have generally upheld a recuperative reading of *The Elective Affinities*, in which the characters' imaginary adultery is punished by mythic vengeance. In this critical tradition, Goethe's novel simply shows the evil consequences of adultery. So, for example, Oskar Walzel, who finds that the novel 'was written in order to restore honor to the [in the early nineteenth century] profaned marriage institution.'[4] The novel's title, *Elective Affinities*, refers to a chemical process known today as bonding. The married couple Charlotte and Eduard invite, for completely different reasons, two outsiders, the Captain and Ottilie, into their home. Within a few months, the chemical bonding has worked to dissolve the marriage into two adulterous attractions — Eduard for Ottilie, the Charlotte for the Captain — which however are never consummated. Eduard is the most uncontrolled of the actors, passionately pursuing his beloved Ottilie. A child conceived by Eduard and his wife, while each is imagining the features of the extra-marital other, is born with the features not of its biological parents, but of Ottilie and the Captain. Pursued by Eduard, Ottilie withdraws herself from society and dies of a mysterious anorexia, with Eduard following her within a few months. Charlotte and the Captain manage to renounce their passions. If one responds naïvely to Walzel's assertion of Goethe's moral intentions with the naïve question of why Goethe or anyone else should care what happens to the institution of marriage, then the response almost inevitably invokes the political and legal dimensions of marriage: marriage is not a necessary component of individuals' pursuit of happiness; rather, its chief function is the preservation of civil society. Marriage, then, must be preserved as a legal tie, even when its affective bonds have disappeared.

This concern with indissolubility inheres in Immanuel Kant's notion of marriage, as given in his *Metaphysics of Morals*. Kant first defines marriage as the inalienable right of one partner to use the sexual organs of the other: 'Now a natural sexual relationship is either of a merely animal nature, or according to law. The latter is marriage (matrimonium), i.e., the obligation of two persons of different sexes to the life-long mutual possession of each other's sexual characteristics' (§ 24).[5] As Benjamin points out, most commentators have either attributed this definition to the sexually repressed senility of Kant's advanced batchelorhood, or else reckoned it one of those instances in his moral philosophy where logical thinking won out over common sense. Indeed, the definition follows rigorously from a typical Kantian antinomy. Marriage is for Kant the third cornerstone of jurisprudence, dialectically combining the substantial (property as fact) with the causal (contracts as pacts). Marriage appears in the Kantian legal scheme as a contract making each partner the mutual property of the other.

Dialectically, this bondage approaching slavery becomes, due to its mutuality, a foundation of law itself: 'The acquiring of a wife or husband therefore does not occur *de facto* (through consummation) without prior contract, but also not *de pacto* (through a mere marriage contract without subsequent consummation), but rather only *de lege*: i.e., as the legal consequence of the obligation to a sexual relation only by means of the mutual possession of each other' (§ 27, 280).

In its assertion of the mutual rights of both marriage partners, Kant's schema differs drastically from traditional Anglo-Germanic law, in which the woman was legally absorbed into the husband and had no rights over his person. On the other hand, it also departs from Roman law of the empire, which considered marriage a mutual non-possession in which neither partner had substantial rights over the person or property of the other. Reciprocity solves the problem which marriage presents for Kant's legal scheme. On the one hand, the right to possession provides the basis for all right, while on the other hand, since the law is one fulfillment of the categorical imperative, people must always be treated as ends rather than as means — i.e. not as objects of possession.

For Kant, propagation cannot be the purpose of marriage, as it would make both partners mere means to another finality which lies outside their individual wills. Kant rejects this goal as belonging to nature rather than to freedom in a passage quoted by Benjamin: 'The end of begetting children may be an end of nature, to which end it first implanted the inclination of the sexes toward each other; but that the human being who marries must have this end in mind is not to be required for the legality of his union; otherwise, when the begetting of children ended, marriage would also dissolve itself' (§ 24, 277). In other words, marriage is defined through its legal power to regulate sexual relations, rather than through its ability to fulfill any natural needs. In fact, contradicting nearly everyone's experience, Kant makes a world in which marriage's finality is a kind of empowerment — the exercise by both partners of their marriage rights. Marriage becomes people's most direct and long-lasting experience of the legal *per se*.

Benjamin upholds the seeming perverseness of Kant's definition of marriage as a recognition of the gap between facticity and truth which problematizes the critical reception of *The Elective Affinities*. Marriage is the seal (in the sense of a wax seal on a letter) imparted to human relationships:

> Of course, it was [Kant's] greatest mistake when he believed that he could deduce an argument for the moral possibility, indeed the necessity of marriage from such a definition of its nature. From the objective nature of marriage one could obviously only deduce its abjectness — and that is what happens in Kant, against his intentions. But that is exactly the point, that marriage's content [Gehalt] never can be deduced from its subject matter, but rather the content must be conceived as the seal which marriage represents.[6]

Marriage is a seal on human relationships which bears some relationship to their exercise of free will. We will see that Benjamin differs from Kant on the precise relationship which marriage represents. In Kant's system marriage is indissoluble. The sublimation of the subject-object antinomy continues even when the elements themselves have disappeared. As one legal scholar puts it: 'it is admissable to dissolve the pact (the promise of living together), from which follows that the fact of cohabition disappears, but one can never contravene the law, which is independent of the will of the subjects.'[7] Kant's view of marriage could be thought of as a secularization of Christian thought on marriage (officially adopted only after the Council of Trent) which makes it a sacrament and a life-long bond. In sublimating individual desire in the eternity of *lex*, Kant's idea of marriage comes very close to fate, which propels the subjects of Goethe's novel against their will. Thus, readers of *The Elective Affinities* who see the novel as a warning against adultery are blind to the fact that the version of marriage upheld in the novel corresponds to no legal or civil definition of the institution, since the adultery takes place only within the minds of the characters. Fate in this novel is the conflict between legal institution and human desire.

The tragedy of the novel stems not from any moral or legal transgression, but rather from the characters' wandering in limbo between the state of marriage and the state of adultery. Various discourses intervene to show the path not taken. One such speaker is the baron, who is engaged in an adulterous relationship and hoping for divorce from his wife. In a visit to Eduard and Charlotte, he proposes that the law of marriage be constructed so as to encourage dissolubility: 'One of my friends, whose good spirits most often showed themselves in the form of proposals for new laws, used to maintain that every marriage should be contracted for only five years. He would say, "The number five is a beautiful, holy, odd number, and the time period sufficient to get acquainted with each other, to bring up a few children, to separate and, most beautiful of all, to make up again".'[8] (242-3). As Johannes Salzwedel has shown, Goethe derived the baron's friend's position from the actual theories of a famous general of his day, Moritz Graf von Sachsen. Sachsen gives his theory of marriage in a book, *Mes Rêveries*,[9] otherwise devoted to questions of military strategy and the most effective means of killing soldiers. Von Sachsen then states explicitly that he owes the reader a theory of propagation to counterbalance the theories of destruction with which the greater parts of the book are taken up. The idea of the five-year marriage is aimed at increasing the population, as only marriages productive of children would be renewed after five years. Sachsen's is thus a legal theory of marriage, in which the state's intervention stems from its interest in propagation. As we have seen, Kant speaks specifically against this and other views of marriage as necessary to propagation by eliminating children — but not sex — from the legal picture altogether.

Goethe read Kant as well as Sachsen, though no direct influence of Kant's view on marriage has been ascertained in his work.[10] Indeed, Kant's position on marriage may be imputed to Goethe only through irony, by examining the failure of Mittler, who promulgates a view of marriage's indissolubility. In addition, Mittler's name points to his role as mediator, and in fact interpreter, as someone who comes between enunciation and understanding. Mittler upholds the moral ('sittlich') side of marriage. When he arrives at the château and hears that the baron and his lover (both are married to other people) are coming, he immediately departs, flinging out the following as he grabs his hat and cane:

> Whoever attacks the married state for me . . . whoever undermines for me through word or deed this basis of all moral [sittlichen] society, he gets a little taste of my opinion; or if I can't teach him anything, then I will have nothing to do with him. Marriage is the beginning and the height of all culture [Kultur]. It makes the savage gentle, and even the most educated person has no better opportunity to show his humility. It must be indissoluble, for it brings so much happiness, that in contrast each individual unhappiness is hardly worth mentioning. . . . The human condition is so full of suffering and happiness, that one cannot even calculate what spouses owe each other. It is an endless debt, which can only be paid off through eternity. (338)

This view of marriage sounds suspiciously like Christian Fürchtegott Gellert's in the *Moralische Vorlesungen* (*Moral Lectures*), first published in 1770, which Goethe is known to have absorbed. Unlike Kant, Gellert sees marriage, whose basis is love rather than sex, as a means to two ends: 'Geschlechtserhaltung' (propagation), and 'Privatruhe' (domestic peace): 'The main intention of the creator in planting the trait of mutual love can be defined as the preservation of the human species and of domestic peace').[11] The meaning of 'Privatruhe' is dialectical. Its composite form points to a peace and quiet enjoyed in private; yet the term comes to mean for Gellert precisely the opposite, the kind of law and order necessary for the maintenance of the bourgeois public sphere, and which a large number of uncared-for, 'wild' children would threaten — and in fact do threaten in countries with a large number of 'street urchins.' Thus, privacy becomes a public concern, as does marriage itself in this theory. Though the Baron's and Mittler's views seem opposed, they have in common the consideration of marriage as a basis of society in need of regulation so as to preserve other social norms. Both marriage theorists exert absolutely no influence over the events in the novel.

Early nineteenth-century readers of Mittler's words must have noted their ironic inefficacy in a way that later readers have not. The French Revolution had destroyed Gellert's assurances about the integrity of *Privatruhe*. As is well known, one by-product of the anti-clericalism of the revolutionary period had been the freeing of marriage from the domain of canon law and its redefinition as a civil contract between individuals. The same redefinition had become effective in most parts of Germany just before Goethe began his novel, through the 'Reichsdeputationhauptschluß' of 1803. Contemporary thinking tended to link this secularization of the marriage union with a general crisis in the marriage bond and a loosening of sexual mores. It is a historical truism that periods of 'loose morals' occur in the wake of sustained armed conflict, such as the French Revolution and Napoleonic wars had given Europe. Post-war promiscuity, undoubtedly related to Sachsen's thesis on the need for repopulation, in turn causes a rethinking of the marriage institution. (In this sense, Benjamin's essay stands in the same relation to post-World War One Germany as Goethe's novel to post-Napoleonic Germany.) Kant's position on marriage could be seen as a conservative attempt to preserve marriage's indissolubility, introduced by the Catholic church, through the secular means of legal philosophy. If we may judge the views of marriage from other literary productions of the period, as Johannes Salzwedel points out, the concepts of stability and indissolubility had given way to the polar extremes of superficiality and obsession: 'In the period of the *Wahlverwandschaften*, after the French Revolution, the Directory and the dissolution of the Old Reich, more than just the idea of diplomatic balance of power had become yesterday's policy. In addition, the union of reason with conjugal love must have seemed like a dusty, reactionary solution: either Lucinde's liberated attitude or Fidelio's heroism are the new models.'[12]

These examples provide interesting insights into the politics of the erotic in the revolutionary period. The proper contrasting example, of marriage as a union of reason and conjugal love, which Benjamin cites, is that of Mozart and Schikaneder's *Die Zauberflöte* (1791). The trials of fire and water undergone by Pamina and Tamino in that opera provide an allegory of the indissolubility of marriage. As Benjamin points out, Tamino and Pamina undergo their trials not in order to find each other, but in order to stay together forever (129). The setting of *Die Zauberflöte*, Mozart's 'masonic' opera, is a nominally non-Christian Egypt; its marriage ceremony is humanistic rather than legal or religious. Fidelio's loyalty to her husband Florestan in Beethoven's 1805 opera — whose subtitle is 'Die eheliche Liebe' (Married Love) — results from her political loyalty to his cause, which is clearly in sympathy with at least the broad principles of the French Revolution. Marriage is here a means to an end; the ebbing of political engagement would empty the bond of its 'content.' Neither contract nor indissoluble bond, the hero's marriage is instead a form of political engagement. At the opposite pole stands Friedrich Schlegel's *Lucinde* (1799), who seeks her principle of freedom in an amorous bond with Julius which stands outside the legal and customary norms of bourgeois society.

The Elective Affinities upholds neither the sanctity and eternity of marriage, nor its use-value, nor its conventional aspect. Goethe introduced opposing views and conflicting discourses, which prepare a dénouement which accepts none of them. In doing so he foregrounded the ideology of marriage. Goethe had seen, 'that Sachsen's cogent proposal and Gellert's opposing position could provide the horizon for a conversation whose significance far overshadows its actual subject-matter.'[13] The contradiction of the two positions and the inability of either of them to show a way out of the novel's dilemma perhaps reflect Goethe's own highly ambiguous position(s) on marriage, as characterized by Werner Schwan: 'Goethe, before the court of his conscience, indeed was desirous of attributing dignity and authority to marriage and regarded it as a valued institution and a goal worth striving for. At the same time, however, at the level of concrete detail his spirit, which rejected all dogma and every petrified form, was not at all inclined to renounce the principles of liberal permissiveness.'[14] For example, in a conversation with Adam Müller in 1830, Goethe confessed both his admiration for the marriage institution as a 'Kulturerrungenschaft' (cultural achievement) — and his acceptance of its impossibility. As a counselor to his patron, the Duke Karl August of Weimar, who had jurisdiction over all divorce cases in the territory of Weimar, Goethe urged the state to fulfill the desire of the individuals involved, rather than to hold to any rigorous definition of the indissolubility of marriage as an institution, as one finds in Kant. Goethe lived with his lover Christiane Vulpius for many years before he married her. He finally underwent the simple ceremony more out of gratitutude than from any conviction of either the usefulness or inevitability of marriage.

Precisely this historical, ideological component of the conflicting views on marriage in the *Goethezeit* motivates Benjamin's reading in the Weimar period. Not failed marriage as such, Benjamin argues, but rather the main characters' Weimar-like inability to come to the decision to annul the marriage which stands in the way of their inclinations, provides the novel's tragedy and central theme. Benjamin first dismisses the critical oversimplification which identified Goethe's purpose with Mittler's views, and reduced *Die Wahlverwandschaften* to a treatise in defense of marriage: 'Unlike Mittler, Goethe did not wish to justify marriage, but rather to show those forces which arise from marriage in a state of decay. Those forces, however, are obviously the mythical powers of law, and in them marriage is merely the execution of the catastrophe to which it does not itself sentence [verhängt] the characters' 130). The verb 'verhängt' with which Benjamin ends his sentence resonates in a triple register which already projects law as myth. Most immediately, 'verhängen' means to pronounce a sentence, as a judge or jury would do in a criminal case. Secondarily, however, the verb also refers to a declaration of the suspension of normal law and the imposition of a 'state of exception,' to be discussed below. Finally, the verb's nominal form, 'Verhängnis,' refers to an evil or imposing fate to which the characters are subjected. This fate, which Benjamin sees as the subject matter ('Sachgehalt') of Goethe's novel, arises from the 'mythical powers' of law: 'Myth is the subject matter [of the *Elective Affinities*] in the sense that marriage as a juridical institution is subject to mythical law [dem mythischen Recht verhaftet ist], and its decay releases the powers which have always already resided within such law — more or less parallel to what the "state of exception" does for the law of sovereignty').[15] The concept of mythical law — which points not to the phantasmagorical, but to the transcendental — leads us to an earlier (1919) essay by Benjamin, the 'Kritik der Gewalt' ('Critique of Force/Violence/Power').

In fact, the passage of the *Elective Affinities* essay quoted above reads like a 'fill-in-the-blanks' rewrite of the following passage from the earlier essay in legal philosophy: 'Divine power [die göttliche Gewalt] may appear in a true war, or in the divine court [Gottesgericht] of the multitude judging the criminal. All mythical power [mythische Gewalt], from the law-creator [rechtsetzende], which may be called transformational [schaltende], is abject. Also abject is the law-preserver [rechtserhaltende], which may be called the controlled [verwaltete] power. Divine power which is insignia and seal, but never the means of holy punishment, may be called the governing [waltende]'.[16] Benjamin plays in this passage with verbs such as 'walten' and 'verwalten' (both meaning 'to administrate'), in order to accentuate the dialectical relation between law and violence ('Gewalt'). I have groped for English words to distinguish meanings of verbs such as 'schalten' and 'walten' which are largely synonymous, but to which Benjamin capriciously lends distinctive meanings in this passage. Together with 'Recht' and 'Gericht,' the interplay of 'Gewalt' and its variants shows that violation, which should contradict law, also founds it. Law for Benjamin is always, as Günter Figal notes, 'the domain of mediated violence [Gewalt]'.[17] Benjamin also, however, may have considered Kant's own notion of the origin of law as the original taking into possession: 'An object of my will, however, is anything I have the physical capacity to make use of, whose use stands in my power [Macht] (potentia): from which must be differentiated having the same object in my power [Gewalt] (in potestatem meam redactam), which requires not only capacity, but an act of the will as well' (§ 2, 246). In this passage, Kant distinguishes between power as capacity ('Macht') and power as act ('Gewalt'). The latter, an act of the will, becomes, for Benjamin, the foundation of law. Law is thus created out of an originating act of violence. In marriage, this originary violence is the power over the partner's sexual characteristics, so long as this is mutual — marriage is mutual violence.

Benjamin posits an antinomy between positive and natural law, each of which is incomplete, lacking a part held by the other: 'Positive law is blind to the limitlessness of ends [Unbedingtheit der Zwecke] . . . natural law to the limited nature of means [Bedingtheit der Mittel]' (181). These two categories of legal thought represent the poles of the antinomy already encountered between: 'rechterhaltende Gewalt,' the human forces of injunction and punishment which preserve law; and 'rechtsetzende Gewalt,' the mythical forces of conflict which bring about new laws and which is represented in myth. Positivist law is preservative, natural law is mythical. An example of the latter is the revenge of Artemis and Apollo on Niobe. The gods' act of revenge does not punish the infraction of any existing law, but rather creates a new one. Divine power, in establishing a realm of justice, dispenses with the need for law altogether.

For Benjamin, the inescapability of *Gewalt* at the root of all legal systems problematizes the whole notion of contract, including the marriage contract. Benjamin does not hesitate in this essay to confront directly the Kantian notion of justice as the embodiment of the categorical imperative to treat people always as ends rather than as means, 'for positive law, if conscious of its roots, will certainly claim to acknowledge and promote the interest of mankind in the person of each individual. It sees this interest in the representation and preservation of an order imposed by fate' (187). As Richard Wolin notes, the conflict between the two realms is characteristic of the human condition: 'Under mythical justice, which Benjamin contrasts with divine justice, life is governed by a universal network of misfortune and guilt. This is the realm of fate which for Benjamin not only characterizes the pagan religious systems of prehistory, but remains predominant in the modern world under the order of law, where, under the guise of justice, misfortune and guilt are merely rendered abstract and given the personalized form of 'right.'[18]

Such a summary, however, smooths over Benjamin's concern for the antinomies of the two types of law. An example of fate in this essay — to be replaced by marriage in the essay on Goethe — is the death penalty, which in Benjamin's view recreates law each time it is applied: 'More than in any other sentence, law asserts itself above all in its exercise of power [Gewalt] over life and death. At the same time, however, in this power something decadent within the law announces itself most clearly to the finer feelings, because those feelings sense their endless distance from the conditions in which fate in its own majesty would have revealed itself in such a sentence' (188).

In capital punishment, human desire vanishes into the legal aporia it has created, as does morality. These disappear as well, Benjamin argues, into the marriage bond of Eduard and Charlotte, which no longer represents a form of life for these characters, but simply their adherence to fate:

'Marriage is not the object of the *Elective Affinities*. The institution's moral powers are nowhere to be found in the novel. From the beginning they are disappearing like a beach under water at high tide. Marriage is neither a moral nor a social problem here. It is not a bourgeois form of life. In marriage's dissolution, everything human turns to mere appearance; and only the mythic remains as essence' (131). This position on marriage forms the bedrock of Benjamin's seventy-page essay.

The vocabulary of these two readings of Goethe lead to other writings of Benjamin, and through those writings back to the political situation of Weimar Germany. The essay on *Der Ursprung des deutschen Trauerspiels* (1926; *The Origin of German Tragic Drama*) differentiates Baroque *Trauerspiel*, of which Shakespeare's remakes of Seneca provide a good example, from Greek tragedy. For Benjamin, the silent relationship of the tragic hero to his or her fate opposes itself to the volubility of the martyr or tyrant who is the protagonist of *Trauerspiel*. The two dispositions depend upon the very different notions of the world order associated with tragic and Christian thought, respectively. A fallen, 'creaturely' world, a ruined landscape whose redemption is only hinted at through the process of allegory, such are the 'features' which make of *Trauerspiel* a 'mourning-play' rather than a tragedy: 'In the terms of the martyr-drama it is not moral transgression but the very estate of man as creature which provides the reason for the catastrophe. This typical catastrophe, which is so different from the extraordinary catastrophe of the tragic hero, is what the dramatists had in mind when — with a word which is employed more consciously in dramaturgy than in criticism — they described a work as a *Trauerspiel*'.[19] Here, as in his essay on Goethe, Benjamin notes the difference between moral transgression and the mere acting out of the impositions — the 'sentencing' — of fate. *The Elective Affinities* can be seen as a kind of *Trauerspiel*, since other than silent Ottilie the characters emerge from the fallen world of modernity to comment at length about their condition and attempt to circumvent the workings of fate.

The martyr mentioned in the quotation is one possible hero of the *Trauerspiel*, the other one being the tyrant. What unites these two figures, according to Benjamin, are their equal rejection of the common creaturely world and their attempt to bring about, through their suffering and histrionics, the 'Ausnahmezustand,' literally a 'state of exception,' but in the case of the tyrant what we would call a 'state of emergency' or 'state of siege.' Eduard, who abandons his marriage for the battlefield in a search for death, links in his person the sufferings of the martyr with the state of siege. In this point, Benjamin's criticism points unequivocally towards the contemporary politics of Weimar.

In particular, Benjamin's notion of the tyrant derives from the 'decisionist' philosophy found in *Politische Theologie* (1922; *Political Theology*) by the political scientist Carl Schmitt (1888-1985). Schmitt, who made stabs at literary criticism and creative writing, and hesitated in his legal career between criminal law, legal philosophy, and theories of the state before the special circumstances of World War I led him in the latter direction, affected the social world outside of the rather narrow circle of legal theory due to his literary style. Opposed to the cautious reasoning of most legal scholars, Schmitt begins his investigation of sovereignty with a controversial formulation: 'The sovereign is he who decrees the state of emergency [Ausnahmezustand]'.[20] With this sentence Schmitt reverses the normal procedure of scholarly investigation, beginning as it were with his conclusion. However, as scholar Peter Schneider notes, such a sentence fulfills an important function: 'a sentence like this creates suspense. It is striking. It is shocking. One reads the following sentences in order to get over the surprise.'[21] Schmitt's original definition of sovereignty derives from a question all too often asked in the Weimar period: 'Who is in charge . . , when the legal order does not answer the question of jursidiction?').[22] The exception thus illuminates the juridical concept of decision in its purest form.

Schmitt's decisionist philosophy rejects the normativism of Hans Kelsen, whom he saw as the defender of a neo-Kantian conception of law in which exceptions could never be legal; Schmitt equally avoids the positivism of most other Weimar legal theorists. 'Because Schmitt hinges his definition of sovereignty on the sovereign's power to make the decision about whether a state of exception exists, Kelsen is found at the opposite pole, not only avoiding the problem of the exception, but always trying to subject sovereignty to norms.'[23] If we read Schmitt's theory in light of the political developments of his time, it would seem that he saw the only 'remedy' for the political anarchy of Weimar democracy in the creation of an authority empowered to rule by 'state of emergency' declarations.

Those who read Schmitt's work as prophetic or propadeutic to the Nazi *Parteistaat* are not wholly incorrect. Throughout the 1920s, he argued thoroughly and passionately for a broad interpretation of Article 48 of the Weimar constitution, which allowed the president special powers to protect the state, including the power to suspend civil rights.[24] This is of course the 'state of emergency' which Schmitt had seen as crucial to the conception of sovereignty, and yet in his discussions of Article 48 he calls for a limitation of the state of emergency declarations to 'purposeful and temporary single directives and regulations,' ruling out any permanent changes to the constitution brought about by means of the article.[25] Political and legal life in the state of exception is decisionist rather than normative.

Benjamin applies the term 'state of exception' to the status of the protagonists of *Trauerspiel*, who live under the exceptional circumstances of martyrdom or tyranny, and who must continually make decisions, the reasoning for which they share with the audience. Through the concept of 'state of emergency,' we can link the ambiguously heroic status of tyrant and martyr to Benjamin's denunciation of applying any legalistic conception of marriage to Goethe's novel. The elective affinities formed between Eduard and Ottilie, Charlotte and the Captain, create a 'state of exception' within the married state. Marriage norms, such as one finds in Kant and Mittler, can no longer be applied to the characters' situation. Instead, the characters themselves must make decisions. Benjamin intuited an analogy between legal normativism, which was unsuccessfully trying to fill the political vacuum left by the abdication of the Kaiser following Germany's defeat in 1918, and the body of literary criticism on Goethe's *Elective Affinities*, which read the text as upholding norms of marriage. In attacking normative criticism, Benjamin implicitly attacked positivist legal theory.

The Weimar constitution, ratified in 1919, shortly before Benjamin began work on his essay, provided a normative definition of marriage's role in the state (and vice versa) which combined elements of Gellert's, the Baron's, and Kant's conceptions. Article 119 brought marriage under the protection of the constitution: 'As the foundation of family life and of the preservation and increase [Erhaltung und Vermehrung] of the nation, marriage receives the special protection of the constitution'). Propagation, preservation, and a general notion of right all play a role in this definition. The legal historian Willibald Apelt considers this treatment of marriage not as an innovative feature of the new constitution, but rather a constitutional enthronement of contemporary legal conceptions.[26] Interestingly, the West German Grundgesetz of 1949 (as amended 23 August 1976) lopped off a great deal of this language: 'Marriage and family shall enjoy the special protection of the state' (Art. 6, § 1). The East German Constitution, on the other hand, placed 'marriage, family, and motherhood under the special protection of the state. Every citizen of the German Democratic Republic has the right to have his marriage and family respected, protected, and promoted' (Art. 38, § 1).

All of these constitutions explicitly tie the preservation of legal marriage bonds to state interests, so that any attack on marriage becomes a form of 'Verfassungsuntreue' (treason to the constitution). Perhaps Karl von Aretin was thinking of Benjamin when he noted the anti-constitutional tendencies of the period's literature: 'the whole existence of the Weimar Republic was threatened by treason to the constitution. . . . a treason supported during the twenties in literature, in the legal theories of Carl Schmitt, and in a vulgarly social Darwinist pamphlet literature.'[27] Normative law leaves Goethe's text along with mediation — both being represented by the figure of Mittler — in Benjamin's almost unfairly derisive dismissal of the latter's famous speech, already quoted above: 'Such a speech could be drawn out endlessly. It is, to speak in Kant's terms, a 'disgusting mish-mash,' 'cobbled together' out of ungrounded humanitarian maxims and dark, deceptive legal instincts' (130). Benjamin, however, practices some deception himself here, by making Kant appear as a critic of Goethe's novel.

Benjamin not only implicates the contractual basis of marriage as violent, but even begins to draw on the same vocabulary of decay to describe it, and links it to the general situation in Weimar:

> like the outcome, the origin of every contract also points toward violence. It need not be directly present in it as lawmaking violence, but is represented in it insofar as the power that guarantees a legal contract is in turn of violent origin even if violence is not introduced into the contract itself. When the conscious-ness of the latent presence of violence in a legal institution disappears, the institution falls into decay. In our time, parliaments provide an example of this. They lack the sense that a lawmaking violence is represented by themselves; no wonder that they cannot achieve decrees worthy of this violence, but cultivate in compromise a supposedly nonviolent manner of dealing with political affairs.

The marriage of Eduard and Charlotte is, then, a microcosm of the Reichstag of Weimar Germany, their marriage contract a symbol of the Weimar constitution which resulted not from a decision, but a compromise. By bringing Kant's definition of marriage into dialog with Goethe's text, and by citing in 'Goethes *Wahlverwandschaften*' concepts of natural versus positive law developed both in 'Towards a Critique of Force' and also in his treatment of the Baroque tyrant in *Ursprung des deutschen Trauerspiels*,

Benjamin creates a nexus of texts — philosophical, novelistic, and critical — which 'redeem' Goethe's by making it speak about law's relation to the fragile hopes of Germany's political future. The tragedy in Goethe's novel, Benjamin argues, stems not from the failure of marriage, but in the characters' acceptance of the law of marriage as their fate. Their inability to decide matches Germany's own in the fragile and convulsive Weimar years.

Thomas O. Beebee is Associate Professor of Comparative Literature and German, Penn State.

ENDNOTES

1. Michael Makropoulos, *Modernität als ontologischer Ausnahmezustand* (Munich: Wilhelm Fink, 1989). In this essay, quotations will be cited in English only. All translations are by the author.

2. John McCole, *Walter Benjamin and the Antinomies of Tradition* (Ithaca: Cornell University Press, 1993), pp. 117-119.

3. Gershom Scholem, *Walter Benjamin: The Story of a Friendship*, trans. Harry Zohn (New York: Schocken, 1981), p. 94.

4. Oskar Walzel, 'Goethes >Wahlverwandtschaften< im Rahmen ihrer Zeit,' in *Goethes Roman >Die Wahlverwandtschaften<,'* ed. Ewald Rösch (Darmstadt: Wissenschaftliche Buchgesellschaft, 1975), p. 36.

5. Immanuel Kant, *Die Metaphysik der Sitten. Erster Theil. Metaphysische Anfangsgründe der Rechtslehre*, in *Gesammelte Schriften* (Berlin: Reimer, 1914), p. 277.

6. Walter Benjamin, 'Goethes Wahlverwandschaften,' in *Schriften* (Frankfurt am Main: Suhrkamp, 1972), 1.1: 127-8. Further citations in text.

7. Giuseppe de Vitofranceschi, 'L'istituto del matrimonio secondo Emmanuele Kant,' *Sophia* 38.3-4 (1970): 254.

8. Johann Wolfgang von Goethe, *Die Wahlverwandschaften*, ed. Christoph Brecht and Waltraud Wiethölter, in *Sämtliche Werke*, 40 vols. (Frankfurt am Main: Deutscher Klassiker Verlag, 1994), 8: 341. Further citations in text.

9. Moritz Graf von Sachsen, *Mes Rêveries* (The Hague, 1756; Paris, 1757; Berlin, 1758).

10. Cf. Karl Vorländer, *Kant, Schiller, Goethe* (Leipzig: Verlag der Dürr'schen Buchhandlung, 1907); and Gabriele Rabel, *Goethe und Kant*, 2 vols. (Vienna: Selbstverlag, 1927).

11. Christian Fürchtegott Gellert, *Moralische Vorlesungen*, ed. Bernd Witte, in *Gesammelte Schriften*, 6 vols. (Berlin: Walter de Gruyter, 1992), 6: 263.

12. Johannes Salzwedel, 'Gellert und die *Wahlverwandschaften*,' *Euphorion* 83.3 (1989): 302.

13. Salzwedel, 'Gellert und die *Wahlverwandschaften*,' pp. 307-8.

14. Werner Schwan, *Goethes Wahlverwandschaften: Das nicht erreichte Soziale* (Munich: Wilhelm Fink, 1983), p. 102.

15. Burkhardt Lindner, 'Goethes *Wahlverwandtschaften* und die Kritik der mythischen Verfassung der bürgerlichen Gesellschaft,' in *Goethes Walhverwandtschaften: Kritische Modelle und Diskursanalysen zum Mythos Literatur*, ed. Norbert W. Bolz (Hildesheim: Gerstenberg, 1981), p. 37.

16. Walter Benjamin, 'Zur Kritik der Gewalt,' in *Gesammelte Schriften*, ed. Rolf Tiedemann and Hermann Schweppenhäuser, 7 vols. (Frankfurt a. M.: Suhrkamp, 1977), 2.1: 203.

17. Günter Figal, 'Recht und Moral als Handlungsspielräume,' *Zeitschrift für philosophische Forschung* 36.3 (1982): 371.

18. Richard Wolin, *Walter Benjamin: An Aesthetic of Redemption* (New York: Columbia University Press, 1982), p. 51.

19. Walter Benjamin, *Der Ursprung des deutschen Trauerspiels*; in *Gesammelte Schriften*, ed. Rolf Tiedemann, 7 vols. (Frankfurt am Main: Suhrkamp, 1971, p. 268; trans. John Osborne, *The Origin of German Tragic Drama* (London: New Left, 1977), 1.1: p. 89.

20. Carl Schmitt, *Politische Theologie. Vier Kapitel zur Lehre von der Souveränitat* (Berlin: Duncker & Humblot, 1934), p. 1.

21. Peter Schneider, *Ausnahmezustand und Norm. Eine Studie zur Rechtslehre von Carl Schmitt* (Stuttgart: Deutsche Verlags-Anstalt, 1957), p. 20.

22. Carl Schmitt, *Politische Theologie*, pp. 17-18.

23. George Schwab, *The Challenge of the Exception*, 2d ed. (New York: Greenwood Press, 1989), pp. 49-50.

24. Article 48 reads: 'Whenever the public security and order of the German Reich is being substantially disturbed or endangered, the Reichspresident can take necessary measures to restore public security and order, and may intervene with the help of armed forces when this is called for. To this end, he may temporarily suspend, wholly or in part, the basic rights set down in articles 114, 115, 117, 118, 123, 124, und 153.' Schmitt noted that the two sentences of this article had been drafted by two separate committees, and hence did not depend upon each other for their meaning.

25. Heinrich Muth, 'Carl Schmitt in der deutschen Innenpolitikdes Sommers 1932,' *Historische Zeitschrift*, Beiheft 1 (Munich: Oldenbourg, 1971): 88.

26. 'The basic rights section [of the constitution] can be seen as the embodiment of contemporary German legal thought.' Willibalt Apelt, *Geschichte der Weimarer Verfassung*, 2nd ed. (Munich & Berlin: Beck, 1964), p. 349.

27. Karl Otmar Freiherr von Aretin: 'Verfassung und Verfassungsuntreue,' *Frankfurter Hefte* 30.3 (March 1975): 24-5.

Chapter XI

Puritan Constructs and Nineteenth-Century Politics: Allegory, Rhetoric, and Law in Three Hawthorne Tales

Diana Royer*

> Words — so innocent and powerless as they are,
> as standing in a dictionary, how potent for
> good and evil they become, in the hands of one
> who knows how to combine them!
> — Hawthorne, 1847[1]

Lecturing in Salem in 1833 Rufus Choate called for a series of romances akin to Sir Walter Scott's Waverley novels that would supplement American history with valuable detail about 'the state of society,' which Choate delineated as people's customs, domestic life, and relations to each other, 'their opinions, superstitions, morals, jurisprudence and police.'[2] Choate suggested the Puritans as subjects, noting that romance writers could 'display their peculiarities, and decide upon their pretensions,' although to Choate it was 'fit' that 'their tried and strenuous virtues should stand out in such prominence and grandeur' as they did currently.[3] Choate proscribed for fiction the task of contributing to 'moulding and fixing that final, grand, complex result, — the national character.'[4]

Salem was Hawthorne's primary residence at the time of Choate's lecture, and while we can't determine if he was in attendance that evening, it is fair to say that Choate's ideas would not have seemed new to the beginning writer but instead representative of the literary atmosphere in New England as interpreted by those in the legal profession. Daniel Webster, described by Robert Ferguson as 'the most important lawyer-writer of the age,' frequently spoke 'on the duties and place of the man of letters in republican culture.'[5] In Webster's view literature was most important if it 'helped to secure free institutions' and was '"linked to utility and public action"."[6] Such ideas were taken up by most editors, reviewers, and authors in the early nineteenth century, when lawyers and writers were in closer association than they are today. In fact, a great number of writers were professionals, frequently lawyers and government employees, who produced literature in their leisure time.

Hawthorne's situation was a twist on this: among those pioneers who conceived of American letters as a career in and of itself, he found it necessary to supplement his income from writing with various government positions. He took great interest in the machinations of local politics because they affected the offices he and his friends might gain. His correspondence is filled with remarks about needing money and speculations about procuring an office to supply it. 'If any Democratic candidate be elected President,' he wrote his sister Louisa in 1844, 'all will go well enough. I shall be certain of the Post Office, or of something as good.'[7] A letter to Horatio Bridge filled with matters of seeking office for himself and friends observes, 'I have grown considerable of a politician by the experience of the last few months.'[8] Hawthorne was to become disgusted with politics a few years later when new Whig officials dismissed him from his position at the Salem Custom House solely because he was a Democrat. His comments at that time to his friend and personal attorney, George Hillard, reveal that he did not want to be labeled as a politician:

> I do not think that this ought to be done; for I was not appointed to office as a reward for political services, nor have I acted as a politician since. A large portion of the local Democratic party look coldly on me, for not having used the influence of my position to obtain the removal of Whigs — which I might have done, but which I in no case did.

As Hawthorne expressed to Hillard, he viewed himself as 'an inoffensive man of letters,' not as one of the 'thick-skulled and no-hearted ruffians' who made a career of politics.[9]

Yet Hawthorne realized that working the political system could help him advance as a writer. He thought of Choate when ousted from the Custom House, believing the attorney might improve his profile as an author as well as help him retain government office. Choate did write on Hawthorne's behalf after his dismissal, calling him '"a writer of rare beauty, & merit & fame, a person of the purest character, & in politics perfectly quiet and silent".'[10] Surely this response pleased Hawthorne, who had been accused by Whigs of writing political articles for the Democratic Salem *Advertiser*.

Primarily, he wrote reviews that contained, as he put it, 'Never one word of politics. Any one of the articles would have been perfectly proper for a Whig paper. . . .'[11] And although Hawthorne was listed in the *Advertiser* as a delegate to the Democratic State Convention, he declared, 'I do not remember ever being chosen a delegate to that, or any convention, and certainly never was present at one, in my whole life.' Hawthorne was also listed as a member of the Democratic Town Committee, to which he objected, 'I never was otherwise notified of the fact, never attended a meeting, never acted officially, and have no other knowledge of my membership than having seen my name, as aforesaid.'[12]

Hawthorne wished to appear free of party affiliations because neutrality provided wider marketing opportunities for his fiction. Seemingly a political chameleon, Hawthorne published his writing in periodicals aligned with each party, causing both Democrats and Whigs to claim him as one of their own, although he was in fact a Democrat. It was Hawthorne's deliberately general tone of patriotism that led to his being embraced by both parties, and it was primarily due to the personalities of local Whig politicians that his writing for the *Advertiser* was declared overtly Democratic and his removal from the Custom House demanded.

From the outset of his career Hawthorne hoped to succeed at writing without relying on politics for income or publicity. To this end he followed the literary market closely. Many of the tales Hawthorne produced and published in this early phase — 'My Kinsman, Major Molineux' (1832), 'The Gentle Boy' (1832), 'The Gray Champion' (1835), 'The May-Pole of Merry Mount' (1836), 'Endicott and The Red Cross' (1838), and the four Legends of the Province House (1838) — reveal his perception that the market welcomed such patriotic topics and treatments as Choate suggested. Hawthorne would have agreed with semiotician Robert Scholes' view that 'A fictional diegesis draws its nourishment not simply from the words of its text but from its immediate culture and its literary tradition.'[13] In this aspect, Hawthorne provided the market with the general topics readers wanted. His treatment of those topics, however, was not always straightforward.

Choate believed, Brook Thomas points out, that 'preservation of the present order depended upon the public's perception of the past' and 'hoped that through a proper narration of the past a national literature would shape the public's respect for the laws of the present.'[14] Yet, as Thomas' study reveals, writers of the American Renaissance presented a history in their literature that 'often risk[ed] raising the discordant and contradictory emotions Choate wanted to suppress.'[15] Instead of stressing social duty and orderly obedience to law, for example, Hawthorne selectively represented American history and its persecutions in order to question not only that early society, but contemporary society and its laws. Hawthorne found people to be shaped and deeply affected by their society and its laws, requirements, and demands. Often as readers we are asked to sympathize with those characters who come into conflict with society's rules or to judge negatively the actions of characters who stand for the formal legal structures. This is one way Hawthorne questioned the early Puritan and colonial leaders' service to the people they governed. His approach to such fictional topics was guided by his reading and his personal experience.

Marion L. Kesselring has analyzed Hawthorne's borrowing of books from the Salem Athenaeum and discovered that about a quarter of his reading was in history and politics, and another fourteen percent in biography.[16] Perusing the titles entered in the charge-books one sees that early American history was of special interest to Hawthorne: over the years in which he wrote short fiction Hawthorne checked out George Bancroft's *A History of the United States*; Francis Baylies' *An Historical Memoir of the Colony of New Plymouth*; Alden Bradford's *History of Massachusetts* and *Speeches of the Governors of Massachusetts, from 1765 to 1772 . . . And other Public Papers, relating to the Dispute between this Country and Great Britain*; William Douglass' *A Summary, Historical and Political, of the First Planting, Progressive Improvements, and Present State of the British Settlements of North-America*; Joseph Barlow Felt's *The Annals of Salem, from its First Settlement*; Thomas Hutchinson's *The History of Massachusetts*; Daniel Neal's *The History of the Puritans*; Caleb Hopkins Snow's *A History of Boston*; *State Papers and Publick Documents of the United States from the Accession of George Washington to the Presidency*; James Thacher's *History of the Town of Plymouth*; and John Winthrop's *The History of New England from 1630 to 1649*. More specific to the topic of lawmaking, Hawthorne borrowed *A Complete Collection of State-Trials*, published in London; James Grant's *Random Recollections of the House of Commons* and *Random Recollections of the House of Lords*; Ebenezer Hazard's *Historical Collections; consisting of State Papers, and other Authentic Documents. . .*; *Acts and Laws, Of His Majesty's Province of the Massachusetts-Bay in New-England*; *The Proceedings of the Council, and the House of Representatives of the Province of the Massachusetts-Bay*; and numerous publications of the Massachusetts Historical Society. In addition to books, throughout his life Hawthorne was an avid reader of magazines and newspapers, especially those chronicling the punishment of criminals. He followed the murder trial of Captain Joseph White — a legally intricate local case — closely in 1830.[17]

Personal experience enhanced Hawthorne's reading. Two ancestors were directly involved with enforcing American laws: John Hathorne, Hawthorne's great grandfather, was a judge in the Salem witch trials; John's father, William Hathorne, who came to American on the *Arbella*, was a major in the Salem militia, became deputy of the House of Delegates, and reputedly had a burglar's forehead branded with the letter 'B.' That Hawthorne brands a nameless character in 'Endicott and The Red Cross' and later Hester Prynne with a red 'A' reveals his commitment to studying those who made and executed the law of early New England. He was himself a public official three times when the Democrats were in office: from January 1839 to January 1841 he was measurer of salt and coal in the Boston Custom House; from April 1846 to June 1849 he was surveyor in the Salem Custom House; and from August 1853 to October 1857 he was the American consul in Liverpool.

Friends and relations also held political positions. Of Hawthorne's Bowdoin College friends, Jonathan Cilley went on to be a member of Congress, Franklin Pierce became President, and, after a career in the Navy, Horatio Bridge served as Chief of the Bureau of Provisions and Clothing. The great educational reformer Horace Mann, husband of Hawthorne's sister-in-law Mary, was a member of Congress. William Pike, a long-time Salem friend, was Collector of the Port of Salem and active in the Democratic Party. John L. O'Sullivan, godfather to Hawthorne's daughter Una, was elected to the New York legislature. O'Sullivan and Evert A. Duyckinck, both of whom published Hawthorne's work, were quite active in the radical Young America wing of the Democratic party. Hawthorne himself was a more moderate Jacksonian Democrat, but he did praise O'Sullivan's *Democratic Review* in the prefatory paragraphs of 'Rappaccini's Daughter' for having 'led the defence of liberal principles and popular rights.'[18]

Scholarly discussions of nineteenth-century Democratic Party policies have been somewhat vague, primarily because of factions within the party itself. In general, Young Americans based their politics on Jeffersonian democracy, opposing monopolies, among other things, and supporting equal rights, labor unions, and universal education.[19] Hawthorne's brand of democracy was more Jacksonian, affirming individualism, upholding 'personal freedom from artificial social institutions,' and 'arguing for unrestrained self-interest as the surest guarantee of communal growth and virtue.'[20] Before he met O'Sullivan in the late spring of 1837, Hawthorne had published 'Roger Malvin's Burial' (1832), 'My Visit to Niagara' (1835), 'The Great Carbuncle' (1837), and 'The Prophetic Pictures' (1837), all of which exhibit his tendency to question the optimism of Young American thinking, primarily by qualifying the chance for renewal the frontier seemed to offer. The works published after his friendship with O'Sullivan was established continue Hawthorne's scrutiny of political issues — the two did not always see eye to eye, by any means. One piece, 'The Celestial Rail-road' (1843), ridicules the claims of Transcendental reform by rewriting Bunyan's *Pilgrims' Progress*. The narrator, accompanied by Mr. Smooth-it-away, rides the railroad to the Celestial City instead of walking; 'Our enormous burthens,' he tells us, 'instead of being carried on our shoulders, as had been the custom of old, were all snugly deposited in the baggage-car, and, as I was assured, would be delivered to their respective owners, at the journey's end' (810). One character, Giant Transcendentalist, exemplifies Hawthorne's view of the movement: '. . . as to his form, his features, his substance, and his nature generally, it is the chief peculiarity of this huge miscreant, that neither he for himself, nor anybody for him, has ever been able to describe them' (817). Transcendentalism, like the bridge upon which the Celestial Rail-road travels, is of 'elegant' but 'too slight' construction to safely carry people over the polluted bog that represents life's problems (808).

'The New Adam and Eve' (1843) places an innocent pair on earth after its present inhabitants have been exterminated, their observations serving as Hawthorne's judgment on contemporary society and its laws. Portraits appear to the couple 'with features and expression debased, because inherited through ages of moral and physical decay.' The gallows is 'the type of mankind's whole system, in regard to the great difficulties which God had given to be solved — a system of fear and vengeance, never successful, yet followed to the last' (753).

Hawthorne dealt with political content in a good deal of his writing, but usually covertly so as to attain the widest possible reader appeal. His criticism of Puritan and colonial leaders spans most of his career, from the publication of 'Sir William Phips' in 1830 through his writing of *The House of the Seven Gables* in 1851. These fictional treatments of early America exemplify a belief Larzer Ziff ascribes to Hawthorne, 'that the essence of democracy was the feelings and prejudices of the people, which did not need guidance or refinement from leaders but required heartfelt embodiment in public life.'[21] Hawthorne felt it important that governing institutions in America be connected with and sensitive to those they governed because they were supposed to be serving the people, not the reverse as had been the tradition in Europe.

Richard H. Millington sees Hawthorne using narrative authority to 'replicate or parody the operations of cultural authority,' enabling him 'to translate his diagnoses of the ills of character and culture into a narrative practice that makes interpretation curative.'[22] By helping readers revise their relation to the community and to authority, Hawthorne is able to 'intervene in the process by which culture makes us ourselves.'[23] In this fashion literature assists readers in assembling new constructs of society and its laws under which they live, and this, in turn, will help them articulate their protest, desire, or satisfaction.

Hawthorne wanted readers to consider who was making and enforcing law. Do these leaders fairly represent the desires of those they govern? Do they have the best interests of the greatest number of people in mind? Hawthorne's fiction questions the opposing oversimplifications of what various groups thought was good for people. Puritanism, for example, was a dogmatism which oversimplified complex experience. In some ways early Puritan government tended to stultify, or, as Michael Davitt Bell describes it, to 'formalize and repress life by allegorizing it, by subordinating it to abstract conceptions such as "good," "evil," or "Adulteress".'[24] The Puritans' errand to the new world had a typological basis: they compared themselves to the Israelites, seeing themselves as chosen people who had received the promise of a new land. Seeking ways to affirm their experience in New England, they put a typological interpretation on everything they did or thought about doing. Accordingly, they developed a self-sufficient reality-concept: cutting themselves off from European history, they constructed a new community that would serve as a model by which tainted Europe could renew itself. Not to be held accountable to corrupt European religious and social systems, the New England Puritans founded their own law on allegory. But while law can construct a people's reality, it can also distort it, as Hawthorne's fiction suggests. To gain reader complicity, Hawthorne experiments with an allegory that parallels the allegorically-based law of the

Puritans. He develops his fictive world using the law/allegory structured world-system of the Puritans as a foundation. This fictive world is a kind of corrosive pocket inside the Puritan construct which allows him to raise questions about whether the Puritans lived up to their ideals in their development and execution of their law.

Concomitantly, Hawthorne compels the reader performing an analysis of Puritan law to perform an analysis of contemporary law by revealing the distrust of, yet need for, authority as an ongoing tension that Hawthorne's contemporaries shared with the Puritans. Believing that any religious institution is but temporal, the Puritans claimed one's primary allegiance should be to God. Ideally, members of the congregation would voluntarily support the Puritan mission in the New World. But humans are imperfect, and authority was necessary to ensure success of the Puritan endeavor. How much and what sort of authority is what Hawthorne explores, presenting that exploration as a useful method for questioning nineteenth-century politics, since Puritanism had influenced the present structure of American society. The Enlightenment had continued the Puritans' idea that citizens who weren't guided by their reason needed political control, while maintaining that citizens were justified in overthrowing any government which turned tyrannical. Jacksonian democracy furthered the concept of citizen participation in government yet at the same time tried to reduce fears of the masses having greater say in the law. Thus law in Hawthorne's time was subject to the same scrutiny earlier Puritan authority had been: who should make laws and to what degree should law control the American citizen?

To convey the complexity of these issues, Hawthorne infuses his work with ambiguity. Puritan and colonial leaders are not without virtue; their constituents are not without defects. The symbols societies use to define themselves contain ambiguity. Reality, shifting, complex, and indefinable, is inevitably oversimplified by those who make its laws, and, unavoidably, these laws fail to meet human and social needs. Illustrations of this theme lie in Hawthorne's analyses of Puritan and colonial leaders: often those who acted with what they claimed to be divine sanction were blind to the needs of those they governed, considering submission to legal and religious authority — inseparable at that time — of utmost importance.

The theme of a harshly insensitive authority Hawthorne dealt with at length in *The Scarlet Letter*. This point has been competently discussed by so many Hawthorne scholars that analysis here would be redundant. Of preliminary interest to the legal themes which pervade *The Scarlet Letter* are

Hawthorne's Puritan tales. A semiotic analysis of 'The May-Pole of Merry Mount,' 'Endicott and The Red Cross,' and 'The Gray Champion' reveals techniques and themes found in his longer romance. The first piece explores Puritan leaders' use of allegory to polarize complex issues in their effort to control the residents of Merry Mount, revelers who themselves simplify life's issues. 'Endicott and The Red Cross' explores how a political rhetoric that acts on the emotions persuades people to sanction the law without understanding it. Reductive symbols gain the endorsement of a populace that wants a strong leader at any cost. In 'The Gray Champion,' a tale concerning British oppression under the rule of James II after the revocation of the colonies' charters, Hawthorne relies on the connotations of nouns and adjectives to create a discourse which forces the reader to evaluate the efficacy of *both* British and Puritan rule.

The conflict between Puritan religious law and those who 'worship' nature which appears in 'The May-Pole of Merry Mount' has been written about numerous times. Several critics have pointed out Hawthorne's use of words connoting light and dark, the first being applied to the Merry Mounters and the second to the Puritans, to convey his theme that 'Jollity and gloom were contending for an empire' in New England (360). Likewise scholars have connected both parties with beasts; the Merry Mounters, after all, wear animal heads and keep a bear as a pet, and the Puritans act in a 'beastly' manner — that is, they use military force to break up the Merry Mount community. Ostensibly, the tale is about the formation of early American character and the temperament of our nation, how jolly and in tune with our animalistic natures we could be, how gloomy and repressive by force we are. Hawthorne fashions an allegory in response to a Puritan world view that would reduce such a complex issue as the formation of individual and national character to an either/or situation. Likewise he scrutinizes the frivolous attitude of the revelers who simplify life's issues so as to avoid dealing with them. Edith and Edgar, a young couple caught between the two world views of 'jollity' and 'gloom,' afford Hawthorne the means by which he explores the concomitant issues of law and human need.

Hawthorne's allegory of Puritan allegory is parodic, for he aims to create 'a philosophic romance' yet ends up with a 'slight sketch' whose 'facts,' once Hawthorne removes them from 'the grave pages of our New England annalists,' have 'wrought themselves, almost spontaneously, into a sort of allegory' (360). Puritan annalists like Cotton Mather wrote histories as lessons and models of proper conduct, employing allegory in their renditions. For example, in his *Magnalia Christi Americana* Mather offers the lives of William Bradford and John Winthrop not only as testiment to their individual piety but as allegory of the potential American saint, associating Bradford with Moses and Winthrop with Nehemiah. History may be rewritten, Hawthorne is telling us, but the Puritan use of allegory cannot be separated from the past it describes — Hawthorne's way of emphasizing that allegory is inseparable from the methods of thinking behind the Puritan law he wants readers to scrutinize. And so his description is meant to be taken as allegory, allegory as conceived by the Puritans who interpreted the events of Merry Mount.

To convey the reductionist view Puritans took of 'Merry' Mount Wollaston, Hawthorne exaggerates his description of the 'gay colony' which adopts the Maypole as its 'banner-staff' (360). The Maypole is personified: it exhibits May's 'mirthful spirit,' has 'the slender grace of youth,' and is 'dressed' with ribbons and flowers that 'laughed gladly' (360). Hawthorne's description of those who gather around the Maypole, when read closely, indicates the animal nature the Puritans felt humans should repress. Truly the revelers seem grotesque, 'Gothic monsters' half human and half beast, and their dancing with a captive bear hints at bestiality (361). These 'brutes . . . midway between man and beast' (362) signify human nature when control is reduced and primal instincts predominate — something the Puritans were forever on guard against and which they felt had a greater risk of happening in that heathen territory of the wilderness. Hawthorne notes that the Puritans, upon seeing the revelers, 'compared the masques to those devils and ruined souls, with whom their superstition peopled the black wilderness' (362), 'superstition' and 'black' denoting the Puritan interpretation of the wilderness.

The Merry Mounters have 'lightsome hearts' (360) and 'gleesome spirits' (361), which Hawthorne suggests may not be completely admirable: in speaking of the bear that danced with the revelers, he narrates that the beast's 'inferior nature rose half-way, to meet his companions as they stooped' (361). The gaily decorated priest who acts as spokesperson for the community's values urges the crowd to dance in order to show Edith and Edgar '". . . what life is made of, and how airily they should go through it"' (362). In his treatment of the young couple Hawthorne extends his commentary on the Merry Mount outlook on life as well as the Puritan one.

With Edith and Edgar Hawthorne exposes the reductive method of Puritan allegory and the escapist attitude of Merry Mount, for the couple's nature is complex, like that of real humans. Though Lord and Lady of May only for the one day the tale concerns, they 'were really and truly to be partners for the dance of life' (363), a phrase reflecting what their marriage would entail: a combination of seriousness ('really and truly') and enjoyment ('dance of life'). By this phrasing Hawthorne suggests that a merging of the two world views presented in the tale should be explored.

Hawthorne indicates Edith and Edgar are not the typical inhabitants of Merry Mount because they have decided to make a commitment. In a community 'where jest and delusion, trick and fantasy, kept up a continued carnival' (362) these two have planned a future together. Their devotion evolves out of a human need for love that surpasses the frivolous encounters of Merry Mount but that precedes the social constructs the Puritans will put on their relationship. To convey the idea that love is a complex of emotions which cannot be reduced, as the Puritans would have it, to either pagan jollity or religious sobriety, Hawthorne points out,

> No sooner had their hearts glowed with real passion, than they were sensible of something vague and unsubstantial in their former pleasures, and felt a dreary presentiment of inevitable change. From the moment that they truly loved, they had subjected themselves to earth's doom of care, and sorrow, and troubled joy, and had no more a home at Merry Mount. (363)

Hawthorne indicates that real passion brings on troubles in his use of phrases such as 'vague and unsubstantial,' 'former pleasures' (indicating there will be no more), 'dreary presentiment,' 'inevitable change' (for the worse), 'doom of care, and sorrow, and troubled joy.' While this is a severe contrast to the jollity of the Merry Mount community, Hawthorne does not intend to put a damper on lifelong commitments between lovers, but to strike at the demanding nature of human love.

Edith's commentary displays the couple's anti-allegorical world view: '". . . I struggle as with a dream, and fancy that these shapes of our jovial friends are visionary, and their mirth unreal, and that we are no true Lord and Lady of the May"' (363). Critics have pointed out that one can read all the occurrences at Merry Mount as if they are a dream, an illusion, to which the Puritans put an end with their intrusion, awakening Edith and Edgar to the difficulties of life. But this rhetoric of dream and shadow that Hawthorne uses to describe the atmosphere of Merry Mount also underscores Edith's recognition of the unsustainable and insubstantial emotions of the community. Although the couple emblemizes youth and fertility, since roses spring up at their feet, these roses which were to be a 'symbol of their flowery union' wither as soon as Edith makes this recognition (363). Seeing this, the couple still marries, which reinforces an interpretation of their having free will and choosing the real world and responsibility over Merry Mount.

To direct the reader's evaluation of Puritan law, Hawthorne introduces the Puritans with the word 'unfortunately' and employs stereotypical descriptions evoking negative sentiment toward Puritan efforts to subdue and destroy nature: they have a 'sterner faith' that makes the 'dismal wretches' work all day between prayer times, they have weapons 'always at hand' to kill 'the straggling savage,' and they meet only for prayer or 'to proclaim bounties on the heads of wolves and the scalps of Indians' (365). This last has deep connotations since the Merry Mounters dress in wolf skins and welcome Indians into their community. The Puritans' 'festivals were fast-days,' not feast-days; they only sing psalms; and they never dance — any who even thinks of dancing is punished by dancing 'round the whipping-post, which might be termed the Puritan May-Pole' (365). Hawthorne has the Maypole and its converse serve as the two most important symbols of the tale, exemplary of the two colliding world views.

In accord with these two symbols, and showing a need for balance, Hawthorne sets up a dichotomy between the two communities' attitudes toward law. In Merry Mount the 'whole colony were playing at blindman's bluff, magistrates and all with their eyes bandaged, except a single scape-goat, whom the blinded sinners pursued by the tinkling of the bells at his garments' (366). While this game evokes the classic image of blind justice, the symbol of the bell-bedecked scape-goat offers a playful approach to law that contrasts with the Puritans, each of whom approaches Merry Mount to execute their law clad in 'a horse-load of iron armor' (366). Hawthorne puts light and dark symbolism into use to indicate the Puritans are no more just in their legal actions than are the Merry Mounters. The sun has set and the Puritans approach Merry Mount like evil fiends: '. . . some of these black shadows have rushed forth in human shape' (367). Mixing among the reveling Merry Mounters, the Puritans become the 'waking thoughts' that 'start up amid the scattered fantasies of a dream' (367). The party of Puritans is 'hostile' and 'stern,' so much so that 'the whole man, visage, frame, and soul, seemed wrought of iron, gifted with life and thought, yet all of one substance with his head-piece and breast-plate' (367), indicating Puritan reductionism as well as representing their reliance on military strength to oppress those who will not adhere to their laws. Their leader, 'the Puritan of Puritans,' is Endicott, and he enacts their laws with divine sanction: '"But now shall it be seen that the Lord hath sanctified this wilderness for his peculiar people. Woe unto them that would defile it!"' (367). Hawthorne's choice of 'peculiar' to indicate particular is a humorous jab at the Puritans' character and foreshadows Endicott's allegory of the Maypole.

Instead of a tribute to nature, Endicott interprets the Maypole as a '"flower-decked abomination"' (367) whose fall '"shadow[s] forth the fate of light and idle mirth-makers, amongst us and our posterity. Amen, saith John Endicott!"' (368). Endicott's seal on his action of chopping down the Maypole accentuates the connection of religion to law in the Puritan community, a law that will suppress mirth forever. Endicott regrets cutting down the Maypole only because he could have turned it into a whipping-post first, inverting the ideals upon which Merry Mount was founded and transforming the symbol to accord with the Puritan interpretation of law. Exemplifying the severe and animalistic nature of their law, Endicott orders some members of the community to be whipped '"as earnest of our future justice"' and others put in stocks when returned to the Puritans' '"well-ordered settlements",' closing with the warning that '"Further penalties, such as branding and cropping of ears, shall be thought of hereafter"' (368).

Endicott reveals the close ties of Puritan law to religion again when dealing with the priest of Merry Mount: '"It must be for the Great and General Court to determine, whether stripes and long imprisonment, and other grievous penalty, may atone for his transgressions. Let him look to himself! For such as violate our civil order, it may be permitted us to show mercy. But woe to the wretch that troubleth our religion!"' (368). This is a deception on Endicott's part, for civil order and religion are entwined and punishment is unavoidable on any and all counts. For example, the bear is shot because Endicott says he suspects him of witchcraft, but this claim is to mask the real reason for the animal's slaughter: Puritan law required that the animals involved in bestiality be killed. A reader of Puritan histories, Hawthorne knew this law and uses it here to expose Endicott's deceptive rhetoric.

When Endicott comes upon Edith and Edgar, he observes their commitment to one another, and Hawthorne allegorizes the scene with Endicott-like tropes:

> There they stood, in the first hour of wedlock, while the idle pleasures, of
> which their companions were the emblems, had given place to the sternest cares
> of life, personified by the dark Puritans. (369)

In its function as Puritan rhetoric the passage notes not a tempering of
Merry Mount values but a total displacement of them by Puritan mores.
Accordingly, while he perceives that the two differ from their companions
at Merry Mount, Endicott intends to punish them — give them '"a token to
remember [their] wedding-day"' (369) — and refuses Edgar's plea that Edith
be spared. Often critics see Endicott's next reaction as indicative of his
humanity: '. . .the iron man was softened; he smiled, at the fair spectacle
of early love; he almost sighed, for the inevitable blight of early hopes'
(370). These are generally interpreted as a gentle smile and a wistful sigh,
but Hawthorne's earlier portrait of the militant Puritan and his reference
here to the twilight that covers Endicott's face direct us to interpret these as
an ironic smile and a sigh of anticipation for the couple's hopes being
blighted. Endicott, after all, is the one who will thwart Edith and Edgar's
prospects, and his decree, '"We will see how they comport themselves
under their present trials, ere we burthen them with greater"' (370), is full
of malicious hypocrisy. Instead of relinquishing punishment, as this would
seem to indicate, the couple are immediately burdened with more trials:
their gay clothes — interpreted as 'glistening vanities' by Endicott — are
exchanged for the 'decent fashion' of Puritan garb and Edgar's 'love-lock
and long glossy curls' are cut '"in the true pumpkin-shell fashion"' (370).
While Endicott says to bring the couple along '"more gently than their
fellows",' this is not out of special favor to spare the couple, for he goes on
to declare, '"There be qualities in the youth, which may make him valiant
to fight, and sober to toil, and pious to pray; and in the maiden, that may
fit her to become a mother in our Israel, bringing up babes in better nurture
than her own hath been"' (370). Endicott has plans for Edith and Edgar,
who will be forced to live the Puritan life and to declare they enjoy it, for
Endicott orders, '"Nor think ye, young ones, that they are the happiest,
even in our lifetime of a moment, who misspend it in dancing round a May-
Pole!"' (370).

The closing paragraph signifies both the negative aspects of Puritan law
and the impracticality of Merry Mount, suggesting too with what outlook
laws should be conceived:

> And Endicott, the severest Puritan of all who laid the rock-foundation of New England, lifted the wreath of roses from the ruin of the May-Pole, and threw it, with his own gauntleted hand, over the heads of the Lord and Lady of the May. It was a deed of prophecy. As the moral gloom of the world overpowers all systematic gaiety, even so was their home of wild mirth made desolate amid the sad forest. They returned to it no more. But, as their flowery garland was wreathed of the brightest roses that had grown there, so, in the tie that united them, were intertwined all the purest and best of their early joys. They went heavenward, supporting each other along the difficult path which it was their lot to tread, and never wasted one regretful thought on the vanities of Merry Mount. (370)

At one extreme, the 'severest Puritan,' Endicott, bestows his blessing ironically on the marriage of Edith and Edgar, for with his gauntleted hand he expects to militantly crush their joy. At the other end of the spectrum is Merry Mount, whose 'systematic gaiety' and 'wild mirth' are unsustainable when touched by 'the moral gloom of the world.' Hawthorne's hope lies with Edith and Edgar, who are headed in the right direction — heavenward — and realistically accept life as their 'difficult path.' They have put the 'vanities' of Merry Mount behind them, yet they retain, through the symbol of the wreath of roses, 'all the purest and best' joys. Hawthorne's notation that 'the moral gloom of the world overpowers all *systematic* gaiety' (emphasis mine) suggests there is still opportunity for spontaneous joy. Edith and Edgar's outlook, which balances seriousness with happiness, emerges as the best world view under which to conceive a law in sympathy with human needs.

But perhaps the grim figure of Endicott stands broader in Hawthorne's imagination, for the writer invoked the Puritan leader again in 'Endicott and the Red Cross.' The tale displays how people sanction the law without understanding it because they are confronted with political rhetoric that plays on their emotions. The language of the opening paragraph emphasizes Britain's tyranny and the colonies' struggle for rights, a struggle which would lead eventually to the Revolutionary War. Hawthorne seems to be setting Endicott up as early evidence of this patriotic spirit, at least in the first and final paragraphs of the piece. In the opening, aspects of British rule are described with the terms 'tyrannically violent,' 'bigoted and haughty primate,' 'utter ruin,' and 'giant strength' (542). In the closing paragraph Endicott is elevated to heroic status for organizing against such oppression via the words and phrases 'cry of triumph,' 'gave their sanction,' 'boldest exploits,' 'ever honored,' and 'deliverance' (548). Yet the language of the tale framed by these two paragraphs subverts Endicott's heroic status and questions the morality of his legally enforced actions: unconcerned with the views of his people or those of his superiors, Endicott feels his interpretation of the situation is accurate. Hawthorne exhibits the rhetoric of this Puritan leader to be as oppressive as the military force it accompanies and Endicott himself potentially as tyrannical as the British.

Over the ten years preceding the writing of this tale Hawthorne read works by historians such as John Winthrop and Cotton Mather. Thus his playing with the actual facts in this bit of Puritan history is deliberate: Endicott himself may not have been the one to deface the flag; Thomas Dudley, not John Winthrop, was governor in the time period the tale concerns; and Endicott was removed from office for a year for this episode.[25] Hawthorne's omission of this legal repercussion allows the reader who knows this bit of history — and many of Hawthorne's contemporaries would — to question the Puritan leader's legal sanction for his actions. Should one not be aware of history, Hawthorne encourages criticism of Endicott's actions by exhibiting the signs of Puritan culture that have distorted traditional Christian symbols. These Puritan signs signifying strength, brute force, and the military are echoed in Endicott's speech to the community and are closely associated with the law. The community's endorsement of such symbols dovetails into an unexamined ratification of laws.

The church, devoid of steeple and bell, has instead 'a token of the perils of the wilderness' (542): a wolf's head is nailed to the porch, its blood 'still plashing on the door-step' (543). Certainly a wolf symbolizes the wilderness the Puritans sought to conquer, as in 'The May-Pole of Merry Mount,' but as a replacement for the lamb of God it also signifies the brutishness of zealous Puritan leaders like Endicott. Further, all who enter this house of prayer would literally have to step in blood, which evokes anointment with holy water and the hymnal phrase 'washed in the blood of the lamb' and then perverts it. To show the connection between Puritan religion and law, the church is surrounded by the apparatus for inflicting punishment on transgressors. Very close to the church is a whipping post, at one corner of the building is a pillory, and at another corner are stocks. The captive in the pillory is a suspected Catholic; in the stocks stands a supporter of the king. These prisoners signify a strong connection of Church and state, the punishment of different political and religious affiliations. Others chastised on the steps of the house of worship include a man who interpreted the gospel in a manner 'unsanctioned by the infallible judgment of the civil and religious rulers' (543). Hawthorne's choice of 'rulers' rather than leaders reinforces the enjoinment of church and state and underscores his ironic use of 'unsanctioned' and 'infallible.' These prisoners are to endure one hour's punishment for their offenses, but Hawthorne goes on to describe the more enduring punishments inflicted by Puritan law.

Some in the crowd had ears 'cropt, like those of puppy-dogs' (543), which signifies the law's belittling of citizenry. The tone in the descriptions of punishments seems to make light of them, as if the Puritan punishments had no real effect upon those punished. Hawthorne emphasizes the matter-of-factness with which such tyrannical punishments were rendered and accepted: some had cheeks 'branded with the initials of their misdemeanors,' one wore a halter, of which the narrative voice says, 'methinks he must have been grievously tempted to affix the other end of the rope to some convenient beam or bough,' and one woman's 'doom . . . was to wear the letter A on the breast of her gown' (543). The use of 'misdemeanors' and 'doom' and the whimsical tone of the second description would make light of these punishments, yet they are horrid in their reality — physical deformation, manacling, and public emblemization of crimes, all of which would, the Puritan leaders hoped, cause humility in the sufferers. Since punishment was enforced abnegation, not arrived at by introspection and true penance, the law here has replaced personal choice in the matter of repentance. Hawthorne underscores the ineffectiveness of such legally enforced religious humility in the paragraph before when the narrator remarks that the gospeller and woman who spoke against the church elders would no doubt commit their crimes again. Hawthorne wants the reader to consider the nature of the punishments this legal system inflicts; amidst the foregoing text is the harsh image of one whose nostrils have been 'slit and seared' (543).

All these images of punishment come to us reflected in Endicott's breastplate, indicating how legal punishments are grotesquely distorted by a religion using martial methods. Hawthorne invites his contemporary reader to compare this system to the law of the Nineteenth Century:

> Let not the reader argue, from any of these evidences of iniquity, that the times of the Puritans were more vicious than our own, when, as we pass along the very street of this sketch, we discern no badge of infamy on man or woman. It was the policy of our ancestors to search out even the most secret sins, and

> expose them to shame, without fear or favor, in the broadest light of the
> noonday sun. Were such the custom now, perchance we might find materials for
> a no less piquant sketch than the above. (544)

Hawthorne saw the contemporary legal system as having the potential to inflict equally horrible punishments 'without fear or favor' should that system lose touch with the people. How far, he asks the reader, should a democratic law seek out one's 'most secret sins, and expose them to shame'?

Hawthorne warns against emphasizing martial law, which he depicts as encouraging leaders to become separate from and repressive of those they are supposed to be representing. This is suggested by the description of Endicott and his Puritan followers. The entire male population gives Endicott military support. Even the 'savages,' the Indians, are left helpless to '[stand] gazing at the spectacle' (544), their bows and arrows 'but childish weapons' that 'would have rattled harmlessly against the steel caps and hammered iron breastplates, which enclosed each soldier in an individual fortress' (544). Here is the danger of a legal system cut off from the populace and enforced by leaders working in isolation from each other, impenetrable and unreachable, unassailable. Endicott sanctions this: 'The valiant John Endicott glanced with an eye of pride at his sturdy followers, and prepared to renew the martial toils of the day' (544). The word 'valiant' is undercut by Endicott's pride in *followers* — there is room for only one leader here.

To emphasize Endicott's uncompromising nature when it comes to law, Hawthorne plays with history again. Endicott and Roger Williams were of like mind regarding signs of Catholicism like the cross on the flag,[26] yet Hawthorne depicts Williams as attempting to defuse Endicott's wrath. Williams is not 'iron-breasted' (544) like the others but carries a staff 'which seemed to have been recently cut in the forest, and his shoes were bemired, as if he had been travelling on foot through the swamps of the wilderness' (545). In Hawthorne's time, communion with nature was thought to purify, and so it is fitting that Williams has 'apostolic dignity' (545). Before drinking at a natural fountain — importantly placed 'a score of yards from the corner of the meetinghouse' and thus at a distance from the icons of Puritan law and religion — Williams 'turned his face heavenward in thankfulness' (545).

Williams' character is a foil for Endicott's militancy. The news from Winthrop that Williams brings Endicott offers Hawthorne a chance to further exemplify Endicott's war-like nature. Upon reading Winthrop's letter 'a wrathful change came over [Endicott's] manly countenance' (545), indicating any humanity he might retain at this point is being submerged by anger. Indeed, 'blood glowed through [his face], till it seemed to be kindling with an internal heat; nor was it unnatural to suppose that his breastplate would likewise become red-hot, with the angry fire of the bosom which it covered' (545). Endicott's personal anger inflames his rhetoric. He shakes the letter 'so that it rustled as loud as the flag above his head' (545), which shows that his angry interpretation of Winthrop's decree will lead to his taking his own legal action, action fueled by indignation and enacted martially.

Although Winthrop has asked Williams to warn Endicott not to reveal the news which his letter contains, Endicott, declaring Winthrop to be '"wise"' but '"meek and moderate",' says he will '"do according to [his] own best judgment"' (546). He will disobey what he sees as weak law to enact his own. Calling for the silence of his followers by 'a few taps of the drum' — a rapping for military obedience — Endicott meaningfully addresses the crowd as '"Fellow-soldiers, — fellow-exiles",' emphasizing might above religion. Endicott employs a rhetoric designed to scare and incite his listeners, allegorizing issues of authority. He reminds them of their typologically-based mission to New England and asks them why they left their '"native country"' and '"fertile fields"' to come '"to set up our own tombstones in a . . . howling wilderness"' where the '"wolf and the bear"' and '"savage lieth in wait for us in the dismal shadow of the woods",' where '"stubborn roots of the trees break our ploughshares"' and '"our children cry for bread"' (546). All this pain, Endicott reminds them, was '"for the enjoyment of our civil rights"' and the '"liberty to worship God according to our conscience"' (546); again Endicott puts law before religion. To advise the reader of Endicott's rhetorical manipulation of his followers, Hawthorne interrupts the speech with a word from the wanton gospeller, who says '"Call you this liberty of conscience?"' (546). Williams agrees with this man, a 'sad and quiet smile' crossing his 'mild visage' (546). Endicott, however, 'shook his sword wrathfully at the culprit,' which Hawthorne notes is 'an ominous gesture from a man like him' (546), ordering, '"Break not in upon my speech; or I will lay thee neck and heels till this time to-morrow!"' (547).

When Williams attempts to stay Endicott's wrath against the British leaders Endicott declares 'imperiously,' '"My spirit is wiser than thine, for the business now in hand"' (547), and again threatens the people with persecution by the British. He declares they will send '"a governor-general, in whose breast shall be deposited all the law and equity of the land"' (547). What is worse, this man shall inflict British religion upon them. Endicott's rhetoric has the effect he desires on the people; 'a sound of wrath, as well as fear and sorrow' comes forth from them (547). Calling his listeners '"brethren",' Endicott, with 'increasing energy,' threatens they will soon have

> '. . . a cross on the spire of this tabernacle which we have builded, and a high altar within its walls, with wax tapers burning round it at noonday. We shall hear the sacring-bell, and the voices of the Romish priests saying the mass. But think ye, Christian men, that these abominations may be suffered without a sword drawn? without a shot fired? without blood spilt, yea, on the very stairs of the pulpit?' (547)

Endicott connects religion with warfare, thus sanctioning military law. He tells his listeners to be '"strong of hand, and stout of heart"' in fighting for their property:

> 'Here we stand on our own soil, which we have bought with our goods, which we have won with our swords, which we have cleared with our axes, which we have tilled with the sweat of our brows, which we have sanctified with our prayers to the God that brought us hither! Who shall enslave us here? What have we to do with this mitred prelate, — with this crowned king? What have we to do with England?'
>
> Endicott gazed round at the excited countenances of the people, now full of his own spirit. . . . (547-48)

Endicott's speech piles phrase upon phrase to overwhelm his listeners. Secure in having coerced his followers into approving of insurrection, Endicott cuts the cross out of their flag, whereupon he is accused by the Catholic in the pillory of being a '"Sacrilegious wretch"' who '"hast rejected the symbol of our holy religion"' and by the king's supporter in the stocks of '"treason"' (548). Endicott's rhetorical question to the crowd, 'Who shall enslave us here?' is answered by his own actions and words, the removal of the symbol of Christianity, and his declaration: '"Beat a flourish, drummer! — shout, soldiers and people! — in honor of the ensign of New England. Neither Pope nor Tyrant hath part in it now!"' (548). This is ironic given Endicott's dictatorial airs, and the first sentence of Hawthorne's closing paragraph — 'With a cry of triumph, the people gave their sanction to one of the boldest exploits which our history records' (548) — exhibits not only the kind of inflated language Endicott employed, but shows that the populace supports a government of military oppression and intolerance because they do not realize they have been seduced by its allegorizing rhetoric. They have not triumphed yet; a long battle has just begun.

'The Gray Champion' extends Hawthorne's criticism of the Puritan tendency to simplify the complex issue of authority. Both Puritan descendants and the British come under close scrutiny in this tale, set after James II's annulment of the colonies' charters and relating the confrontation between Governor Sir Edmund Andros' soldiers and the colonists, with the mysterious figure of the Gray Champion taking up the cause of the latter. The piece opens with a derogatory picture of the British, which Hawthorne achieves by piling up negative words in the first paragraph: 'groaned,' 'under,' 'pressure,' 'heavier wrongs,' 'threatened,' 'bigoted,' 'annulled,' 'harsh,' 'unprincipled,' 'endanger,' 'tyranny,' 'violated,' 'void,' 'complaint,' 'stifled,' 'restrictions,' 'disaffection,' 'mercenary,' 'sullen submission,' 'evil,' and 'nominal' all describe the British and the colonies under their laws (236). In the midst of this negative volley Hawthorne injects his view of the law's connection to citizenry, noting that the problem with this phase of British government is that Sir Edmund Andros passed laws and applied taxes 'without concurrence of the people, immediate or by their representation' (236).

To reveal the complexity of a government's relation to its constituents, Hawthorne moves next into a commingling of positive and negative adjectives to describe both the colonial descendants of Puritans and the British occupiers against whom they are attempting to rebel. The undercutting and ambiguity begin in the title 'The Gray Champion' and continue in a general narration that includes words with positive and negative connotations. Such a technique makes every element of the tale ambiguous in nature, by which Hawthorne conveys the complexity of all matters dealing with law and rights.

To sketch the colonists' reaction when a possible plan for overthrowing the British is made known to them, Hawthorne speaks of 'doubtful whisper,' 'might be false,' 'smiled mysteriously,' 'subdued and silent agitation,' and 'rouse . . . from its sluggish despondency' (236). In the first instance, the utterance is not based on firm knowledge but it is an utterance all the same. To use the positive word 'might' in connection with 'false' causes a tension in the phrase. A smile is generally a positive facial expression but to attribute mysteriousness to it makes its nature ambiguous. Calling an agitation 'subdued and silent' is somewhat oxymoronic. And to 'rouse,' a verb describing action, from 'sluggish despondency,' an inactive and negative mode, also creates tension.

Describing the British in the same scene, Hawthorne uses 'danger . . . avert it' and 'confirm their despotism' (236), following a negative with a positive idea and then a positive verb with a negative attribute; the opposition within and between phrases further builds tension. Here and throughout the tale Hawthorne uses this tension resulting from linguistic opposition to undermine any reader preconceptions of either the British or the colonists by disallowing a clearly positive or negative interpretation of both groups. Accordingly, the depiction of the British marching into town to confront the descendants of the Puritans is equally weighted with positive and negative words. Hawthorne employs the words 'unquiet crisis,' 'martial music,' and 'disturbing . . . peace' (237). To say a crisis is unquiet is of course to say it is restive, but the very appearance of 'quiet' as the root is allusive enough to cast the phrase in conflict with itself. 'Martial' and 'music' do not accord, while 'disturbing' and 'peace' are opposites.

To describe the colonists Hawthorne applies 'stern emergency . . . happier occasions,' 'gloomy but undismayed,' 'old spirit . . . extinct,' 'worshipped . . . exiles,' 'smiling grimly,' and 'pious fierceness' (237). The first juxtaposes two conditions, one negative and one positive; the second works in the same order, negative first and positive second (although the second term has a negative as its root). The last four reverse this order: their 'spirit' (positive) had become 'extinct' (negative); the Puritans had 'worshipped,' but became 'exiles' for it; they smile but it is a smile colored by unhappiness; and they are religious and warlike at the same time. Moving from such phrases that contain ambiguity within themselves, Hawthorne draws on stereotypical Puritan descriptions to continue to evoke qualified reader response to their characters. '[S]ober garb,' 'severity of mein,' 'scriptural forms of speech,' 'confidence in Heaven's blessing on a righteous cause,' and 'threatened by some peril of the wilderness' (237) are phrases which even the nineteenth century recognized as dubious attributes, not unquestionably admirable. Building on them Hawthorne mentions the contrast of 'veterans of King Philip's War, who had burnt villages and slaughtered young and old . . . while the godly souls throughout the land were helping them with prayer' (237) to raise the question of divine sanction: how justified were the Puritans in their aggression and oppression, and just how different in deed from the British are they?

To animate the comparison of Puritan leaders and British rulers in the reader's mind, the entire tale is constructed not only of conflicting descriptions, but of balanced sentences revealing off-balance meanings. Hawthorne uses an either/or construction ('either . . . or,' 'whether . . . or,' 'neither . . . nor') six times in the piece; 'double' or 'doubly' three times; and 'one side . . . the other' or 'opposite' three times. Hawthorne hints to the reader why he sets up the confrontation between soldiers and citizenry: 'The whole scene was a picture of the condition of New-England, and its moral, the deformity of any government that does not grow out of the nature of things and the character of the people' (239). The next sentence shows what the rift between the conflicting sides lies in: 'religious multitude' and 'despotic rulers' (239). Neither extreme is good, and Hawthorne, who often seeks balance in his characters, here reveals that the mix can be flawed too. The 'despotic rulers' have a 'high churchman' with them, several wear crosses, and they are drunk and 'proud of unjust authority, and scoffing at the universal groan' (239). For such rulers 'obedience' has to be 'secured' since it is not given willingly by the people (239). The Puritans too are guilty of mixing church and state to negative ends, as the earlier quoted 'pious fierceness' and the prayers for successful murder indicate.

As the tale progresses so do the contrasts. On the British side Sir Edmund Andros is 'moving slowly' and is 'elderly, but erect and soldier-like'; he is accompanied by 'the bitterest foes of New-England,' one of whom is Edward Randolph, who 'achieved the downfall' of the colonies' government and thus received a 'sensible curse'; an Episcopal clergyman appears as 'the fitting representative of prelacy and persecution' (239). The contradictions are obvious; except for the second one, they all work in a positive-negative order. On the colonists' part things are 'loudly uttered' (239), the champion makes a sign both of 'encouragement and warning' (240), the 'gray patriarch' is contrasted with the 'young men' of the crowd (240), and the phrase 'unbroken dignity' (240) appears, with the root 'broken' coloring 'dignity.' The confrontation between the British and the colonists elaborates the contrasts: 'on one side . . . on the other' (241), 'solemn, yet warlike' (241), 'the roll of the drum was hushed' (241), 'the advancing line stood still' (241), 'tremulous enthusiasm' (241), 'combining the leader and the saint' (241), 'neither friend nor foe' (242). Verbs are qualified: 'dimly seen' (241), '"respect"' . . . laughing' (241), '"power is ended",' (242), 'to kindle or to quench' (242), 'stood obscurely in an open space' (242), 'uttered no word' (242), and 'soberly affirmed' (242). The conclusion regarding the Gray Champion, whom Hawthorne pointedly calls 'the type of New-England's hereditary spirit' (243), continues the ambiguous mixture: 'in sunshine and in twilight' (243), 'its humbling lesson to the monarch and its high example to the subject' (243), 'twilight of an April morning' (243), and 'stood . . . fallen' (243).

By casting terms in conflict with themselves and balancing sentences with opposing elements, Hawthorne builds an unavoidable tension in the text that casts ambiguity on the nature of both British and colonial rule. The reader is pushed to weigh all aspects of the nouns so modified, and by extension to judge them. Whereas in 'The May-Pole of Merry Mount' he suggested that Puritan severity and Merry Mount frivolity be blended to formulate a proper atmosphere for the dispensation of authority, Hawthorne's rhetorical method in 'The Gray Champion' and the historical moment of a colony in transition reveal the complexity of the issue of what kind of authority is 'best.'

Hawthorne meant readers to apply his studies of Puritan and colonial law to mid-nineteenth century politics. As a Jacksonian Democrat, he feared the government would grow increasingly estranged from its people and thus that its laws would not be in the best interests of its citizens. By writing allegory that depicted the allegorical world view of the Puritans, Hawthorne created a fictive world that allowed him to raise questions about the Puritan development and execution of law and about the British authority of the time. Semiotic analysis of Hawthorne's Puritan tales reveals reality as complex and ambiguous, sending conflicting signs that Puritan law, which simplified fundamental issues through allegory, was not designed to interpret and resolve. As the population in the colonies grew and diversified, the Puritan community fragmented, and with it the typological view of its mission in New England.

Hawthorne worried that nineteenth-century America too could disintegrate under a political system that had ceased to see the support and nurture of its citizens as its priority and that devalued their input. Unlike optimistic Young Americans, Hawthorne was not pacified by

Transcendentalism or reform movements. A journal entry from 1835 conveys his life-long attitude toward such idealism:

A sketch to be given of a modern reformer — a type of the extreme doctrines on the subject of shaves, cold-water, and all that. He goes about the streets haranguing most eloquently, and is on the point of making many converts, when his labors are suddenly interrupted by the appearance of a keeper of a mad-house, whence he has escaped.

At a later date Hawthorne returned to this entry and added, 'Much may be made of this idea.'[27]

Hawthorne was not alone in his questioning of ideologies or in encountering difficulties while attempting to define and portray the American democratic world. In 1827 Catharine Maria Sedgwick published *Hope Leslie; or Early Times in the Massachusetts*, a study of the collision of the Puritan world view with that of Native Americans. Although Sedgwick seems to favor Native American spirituality and the sense of obeying one's conscience, her novel ultimately proposes a blending of these with the Puritan emphasis on conduct and adherence to the letter of the law. Yet the alternative worlds she creates to portray this mixture keep getting destroyed. William Fletcher's homestead in New Bethel, to which he had retreated when Winthrop's settlement 'perverted [power] to purposes of oppression and personal aggrandizement'[28] is raided by Native Americans in retaliation for outrages other whites perpetrated. Fletcher's wife and baby are killed while his son and an adopted daughter are taken captive. Sedgwick employs numerous plot twists and character doublings in her attempt to define a character suitable to the conditions in Colonial America but is ultimately unsuccessful: Hope Leslie, the most promising character as her name indicates, marries conventionally at the end of the novel. While the household she proposes to set up initially seems slightly unorthodox because she will be caring for her former instructor, this elderly schoolteacher is so childlike he clearly stands as her surrogate child.

Herman Melville was another nineteenth-century writer who found he could not settle on what kind of authority or society was best. In 'The Piazza,' Melville portrays a narrator whose desire for a pleasant world affects the accuracy of his vision. From ignoring the bugs that infest his plants to putting mythic constructs on his excursion into the woods, this narrator has a skewed outlook. When he meets the inhabitant of a cottage he had viewed from his piazza, a cottage he had convinced himself must be inhabited by a fairy being, he discovers the woman who lives there has suffered many hardships and leads a lonely, work-filled existence. His illusion pierced, depression follows and the narrator finds it difficult to maintain his ennobling view of the world — although he does not give up trying.

'Benito Cereno' is Melville's more extensive study of projecting one's world view onto another reality. The naive American captain Amasa Delano boards a ship transporting slaves and ignores all signs of danger he encounters. Delano believes no human is capable of evil action, and thus slaves sharpening axes and the ship's captain, Benito Cereno, fainting at the words of his servant Babo are peculiarities Delano sees as resulting from Cereno's weak leadership. In actuality the slaves have revolted, have murdered Cereno's partner, and are holding Cereno and his crew hostage while forcing them to pretend to the visiting Delano that all is well. Melville studies not only the difficulty of achieving accurate perception, but the responsibility that comes with such vision, for while he criticizes Delano's optimism he suggests that had Delano realized and acknowledged the slave revolt immediately, Delano, his crew, and Cereno's crew would probably have been killed. Melville does, however, end the tale with a condemnation of Delano's wilfully deluding outlook: this eternal optimist refuses to admit Babo's evil nature and thus cannot grasp Cereno's inability to forget the events he has witnessed. Delano retains a limited, naive view of the world. Such a construct of reality may not preserve his life the next time evil arises.

As did Hawthorne, Melville found the optimistic, transcendental world view limited. He satirizes the philosophy in 'Cock-A-Doodle-Doo!', a comic piece akin to Hawthorne's 'The Celestial Rail-Road.' A depressed Thoreauvian narrator wanders through a bleak landscape lamenting the existence of locomotives which bring death with their convenience. When he hears a cock crowing lustily, his miserable mood begins to fade; after hearing the cock several times he views a passing train with gaiety instead of trepidation. The narrator feels 'as though [he] could meet Death, and invite him to dinner, and toast the Catacombs with him, in pure overflow of self-reliance and a sense of universal security.'[29] Seeking the cock, the narrator discovers he is owned by Merrymusk, a poor man who lives with an invalid wife and four sickly children in a shanty by the railroad. Merrymusk will not sell the narrator the cock at any price because the animal cheers his family. Melville exposes the hollowness of such optimism by having the narrator visit the family some time later only to find them on their deathbeds — yet declaring they are well because the cock's crowing inspires them. The cock crows as Merrymusk, his wife, and children, all with radiant expressions, die in turn. Flying to the roof of the house, the cock crows and then drops dead at the narrator's feet. Despite witnessing this scene and having to bury the entire family, the narrator declares he has been cheerful ever since and crows a good bit himself.

The Civil War pointed up the absurdity of optimistic philosophies and politics, as far as Hawthorne was concerned. He seemed even to lose faith both in his ability to craft fiction that criticized society and in the possibility that fiction could correct society. Physically ill and discouraged over the war, he became obsessed with the themes of immortality and ancestral ties to England — a country he had criticized in earlier writings. The unfinished romances, 'The Ancestral Footstep,' 'Dr. Grimshaw's Secret,' and 'Septimius Felton,' were at once fictional returns to British roots and attempts to create a world apart from the American world Hawthorne saw disintegrating. In the 1863 preface to *Our Old Home*, a collection of short pieces on England dedicated to former President Pierce, Hawthorne distanced himself from contemporary politics via allegory:

> The Present, the Immediate, the Actual, has proved too potent for me. It takes away not only my scanty faculty, but even my desire for imaginative composition, and leaves me sadly content to scatter a thousand peaceful fantasies upon the hurricane that is sweeping us all along with it, possibly, into a Limbo where our nation and its polity may be as literally the fragments of a shattered dream as my unwritten Romance.[30]

As Puritan and colonial law had failed to meet human needs, so it appeared contemporary law might fall short. Hawthorne tried, in his fiction, to work out the problems associated with governing America. In 'The May-Pole of Merry Mount' he offered the optimistic suggestion that a sober consideration of responsibilities be balanced with a joyful embracing of life, that the law be humane by considering human needs and nature. In 'Endicott and the Red Cross' he criticized the manipulative use of political symbols and deceptive rhetoric — a practice on the rise in pre-Civil War America and the very sort of empty patriotism on which modern politicians rely. Hawthorne raises questions about authority in this tale that he cannot answer: Why is a violent leader seen as most desirable? Why are temperate leaders like Williams swept aside? Why does a populace seeking freedom from oppression sanction a new government that oppresses them?

The questions increase in 'The Gray Champion,' and the text nearly deconstructs under their weight. Hawthorne warns that a government should have the support of its constituents, that it must grow out of the character of its people, but the pervasive rhetorical opposition and contradiction in the tale make obvious that what this character is remains undefinable, shifting, perhaps even illusory. Hawthorne had followed Rufus Choate's suggestion in examining Puritan society as a way to define the current 'national character,' but his exploration unearthed complexities he, as democracy's artist of *aristocratic* conscience, could not bear to gloss over. The writer found it increasingly difficult to create a world within a democracy that was unmoved by the conflict of the individual and the law.

Diana Royer is Assistant Professor of English, Miami University, Hamilton Campus.

ENDNOTES

1. Nathaniel Hawthorne, *The American Notebooks*, ed. Claude M. Simpson (Columbus: Ohio State University Press, 1972), 280.

2. Rufus Choate, 'The Importance of Illustrating New-England History by a Series of Romances like the Waverley Novels,' *The Works of Rufus Choate*, ed. Samuel Gilman Brown, 2 vols. (Boston: Little, Brown and Company, 1862), 1:322.

3. *Ibid.*, 335.

4. *Ibid.*, 344.

5. Robert A. Ferguson, *Law and Letters in American Culture* (Cambridge: Harvard University Press, 1984), 208, 236.

6. Ferguson, 236.

7. Nathaniel Hawthorne to Louisa Hathorne, 15 March 1844, *The Letters, 1843-1853*, ed. Thomas Woodson, L. Neal Smith, and Norman Holmes Pearson (Columbus: Ohio State University Press, 1985), 21.

8. Nathaniel Hawthorne to Horatio Bridge, 1 March 1846, *ibid.*, 148.

9. Nathaniel Hawthorne to George Hillard, 5 March 1849, *ibid.*, 263.

10. Note 5 to Nathaniel Hawthorne to George Hillard, 5 March 1849, *ibid.*, 265.

11. Nathaniel Hawthorne to George Hillard, 12 June 1849, *ibid.*, 277.

12. Nathaniel Hawthorne to George Hillard, 18 June 1849, *ibid.*, 280-81.

13. Robert Scholes, *Semiotics and Interpretation* (New Haven: Yale University Press, 1982), 112.

14. Brook Thomas, *Cross-examinations of Law and Literature* (Cambridge: Cambridge University Press, 1987), 3.

15. *Ibid.*, 3.

16. Marion L. Kesselring, *Hawthorne's Reading, 1828-1850* (New York: The New York Public Library, 1949), 8.

17. Thomas discusses the case as a basis for *The House of The Seven Gables*: *Cross-examinations*, 57-9.

18. Nathaniel Hawthorne, 'Rappaccini's Daughter,' *Tales and Sketches* (New York: Viking Press, 1982), 976. This edition prints the texts from the Centenary Edition. Further references are to this edition and appear in the text.

19. John Stafford, *The Literary Criticism of 'Young America'* (Berkeley: University of California Press, 1952), 4.

20. Ferguson, *Law and Letters*, 202.

21. Larzer Ziff, *Literary Democracy* (New York: Viking Press, 1981), 118.

22. Richard H. Millington, *Practicing Romance* (Princeton: Princeton University Press, 1992), 7.

23. Millington, 9.

24. Michael Davitt Bell, *The Development of American Romance* (Chicago: University of Chicago Press, 1980), 174.

25. Frederick Newberry, *Hawthorne's Divided Loyalties: England and America in His Works* (Rutherford: Fairleigh Dickinson University Press, 1987), 34.

26. Lawrence Shaw Mayo, *John Endecott* (Cambridge: Harvard University Press, 1936), 84.

27. *Hawthorne's Lost Notebook*, 1835-1841, ed. Barbara S. Mouffe (The Pennsylvania State University Press, 1978), 12.

28. Catharine Maria Sedgwick, *Hope Leslie* (New Brunswick: Rutgers University Press, 1991), 16.

29. Herman Melville, 'Cock-A-Doodle-Doo!,' *The Piazza Tales and Other Prose Pieces, 1839-1860*, ed. Harrison Hayford, et. al. (Evanston: Northwestern University Press, 1987), 274.

30. Nathaniel Hawthorne, *Our Old Home*, ed. William Charvat, et al. (Columbus: Ohio State University Press, 1970), 4.

Chapter XII

Natural Society: The World of Federalism

Virginia Black*

> The difficulty is that we do not make a world of our own but fall into institutions already made and have to accommodate ourselves to them to be useful at all. And this accommodation is, I say, a loss of so much integrity and of course of so much power. But how shall the droning world get on if all its *beaux esprits* recalcitrate upon its approved forms and accepted institutions and quit them in order to be single minded?
> —Ralph Waldo Emerson

This essay depicts a broad understanding of autonomous, or semi-autonomous, 'worlds.' Worlds are characterized as having networks of internal relations that function in logically and causally interconnected ways. Identifying worlds works through endogeny: what is proper and necessary to constitute a world? As applied to the world of social and political federation, such an analysis yields insights into how best to distinguish the rightful tasks and jurisdictions of the parts (the states and smaller communities) and of the Nation.

What is needed is a reliable methodology: What federative principles underlie and support stable, civilized social orders? A hermeneutic is proposed. Then human trust and good faith are discovered to underlie the federal conversation.

I
Worlds

Worlds are of many kinds. They admit of many origins, features, and paths. Their structures are distinct, and their internally facing constituents, functions, and relationships are different from those of other worlds. Coloration, tone, atmosphere, spirit — these ineffables are different too, if only by subtle discernment. Institutions are one kind of world (schools, business enterprises, the national treasury, the Common Market). Culture is another kind of world: the norms and mores of an ethnic group, or of a language, demarcate a world. Objects can also furnish worlds (the Ionic column, the human anatomy, a road with a terminus). Modalities are worlds (logic, the moral order). There is the world of sports. And there is the computer world.

Music constitutes a world. So do medicine and science. There is the painful world of insanity. And there is the joyful world which I call 'my garden.' Shangri-La is a world. Museums are worlds. The *polis* was a world. The scholarly academy is a world. A holiday and even a contest is a world. A diocese or a university is a world. Heaven and Hell are worlds apart. The underground called the Warsaw Ghetto was a world. The Bronx Zoo is a separate world, a 'concrete particular.' And on a more general plane of discourse, so are wolf packs and termite swarms, constituting 'sets' with members. The ecosystem is a very big world indeed. And who has not heard of the Underworld?

But all worlds, however substantively distinct, general or particular, have something in common. That is their separateness, or they would not be *a* world, or *this* world, or *that* world. This is a conceptual remark. There are worlds and worlds. To be world A is not to be world B; and so worlds, in having identities, necessarily present the limits of division. When these divisions are indistinct, then we have to decide whether to call them ones or pluralities, units or aggregates. Our purposes often help us to make this decision.

But we do not decide upon unities that prevail in nature. Rather, we discern, then denote them. A dog is a natural unity with many parts that cohere one with another. Flocks of migrating geese are natural unities, too, though we are unsure whether to count the stray who lags behind as belonging to the flock. The English language is a unity — but should we count *de facto* and other terms that stray in from foreign tongues but keep their original orthography?

Some worlds are general, abstract: the world of all red things, the animal kingdom, genera and species, like the *arachnida*. Some are concrete: my lovable dog Fido is a world unto himself. As persons, each of us is a world.

Some worlds are social: democracies, families, tribes, cantons, dioceses, states, communities, federative orders. Playgrounds are worlds whose territorial edges can be blurred. Social worlds need have no physical geography as part of their definition; administered territories have no necessary contiguity within the Nation, and geography is legally inapropos. Social worlds are conceptual entities. But because social worlds normally occur *somewhere* and because man has his feet on the ground, often territory denotes contingencies of place. Some interests are regionally correlated too, like agriculture. Although exogenous to the social world, territory is fought over mightily by sovereign states as if their internal existence depended on it; and when a territory is won, it is inhaled like an intoxicant.

Heraclitus' *kosmos* was one organized, philosophical world. Academics live and breathe in the world of their disciplines.

Endogeny. Worlds have a second feature in common, not conceptual but causal: what naturally belongs. Endogeny. Some of their parts work inwardly, one with another. They 'hang together,' seeming, to our perception, to constitute a single, indivisible whole. Sometimes we have to help manufacture this whole because not all worlds are fully natural units. We unify them for our purposes (machines that we invent; institutions that are the products of our volition and strenuous, ongoing development). But still, if we develop them rightly, they hang together and function well-oiled.

When it comes to identifying their substance, what is distinctive about these worlds is that decisive segments of them interact as composites and fold their parts inward together, in harmony with each other like the cogs of a gear in motion. Certain strategic parts influence each other; they communicate. Their interior is organized, formatted.

This inward-looking integration of parts helps to characterize them as each a world with an identity distinct from a different world. To confirm this identity, we look to see whether the interactions visible within a world are internal, or endogenous: whether their coordinations depend on each other in that they *have* to stand in some relationship to each other such that, were a part or a function to be removed, the world would limp or topple. Otherwise, a coherence and consistency hang on, resisting, at least when healthy, error and dissipation.

A single machine is one whole, one interactive world, even when its parts are rusty and loose. Worlds can often be repaired. We are familiar with societies or neighborhoods rejuvenating themselves, getting a new lease on their identity. Things external to worlds, such as objects or causes, can injure them (oxygen can injure iron), or, conversely, they can nestle in cooperatively, as a gear operates within the semi-autonomous order of a larger machine. But a component that enters a world whose parts are already in endogenous union may not be internal to this world, or the world may reject it — an accident, an unnecessary or exogenous part — unless, as in manufactory or invention, we make it so. While the unity that is a world may not survive without some externalities, its selfhood is, by them, unaffected. (Now and again a world requires some support from the outside, as a ball cannot rest or roll except on a floor. Nevertheless it is not a ball *because* it depends upon the floor; the floor is external to the ball's description).

Trust within the social world. The interior dialogue of social worlds, the conversation that binds them together, depends on trust. For X to make a contract of sale with Y, something reciprocal passes between them. Y knows that X's promise is secure. X believes that Y will respond as anticipated. Influence passes through human worlds, like the world of a mother and child, by way of implicit trust. The federal conversation, as we shall see, is composed of sovereign and subordinates whose influences, ascending and descending, rest on trust. Trust passes horizontally between equals as well. Trust is a syntax that makes federal sentences hang together.

Federations are worlds that we depend upon. This is as it should be. For it is not a coincidence that 'federal' derives from Latin, *foedus,* which means faith, covenant, pact, consent, agreement, and therefore the trust that makes agreements work.

Denoting identity. Big and small, superior or subordinate, in major or minor scale, all worlds have an acknowledged independent or semi-autonomous unity in that their growth or construction, discovery or conception, once in place, usually requires internal coordinates for a world's existence and identity. But in order to know that we confront a world which we have partially constructed, and to speak about it, a semiotic of naming, of referring, is necessary for this world to be perceived as a whole. Its interior parts link reciprocal meanings into a coherent unity; but however this operation makes these parts appear coordinate as one — the many and the one — unless they are given one name — 'this is Emerson School'; or 'we call these numbers fractions'— they, in time, conceptually disintegrate. Their permanence is subject to the logic of denoting, or else no longer are they understood as the unifying individual with a single referent that sustains our knowledge of them.

The parts of a world of course last longer if endogenous relations, functionally intertwined with one another, can be located and we have the desire and integrity to hold them, if necessary, together. But discovering and precising such relations, as we shall see, are not certainties in the world of social institutions. The Common Market is no longer an institutional world if we no longer determine to supply it with a referent and a name.

Recently my district neighborhood formed a civic association, but no one, even our assemblyman, knew exactly the territorial boundaries of this semi-autonomous locale. In distributing leaflets for a call-to-meeting, our members had to decide where to discontinue the distribution. Because the range of distribution was so unclear as to be meaningless, errors were not possible. But even if errors were possible, it did not matter because, given the nature of our project, no one could be outside a district whose territorial limits were not known. In defining a world, the purpose often matters most: what, and why, does one want to know? But naming matters too. Where shall 'Homecrest' begin and end? The name promotes the search; resolving the search requires a name.

Limits. Worlds have boundaries, and so they have limits. To identify a world is to stand ready to define its properties and divisions. To declare that a world has thus-and-so qualities is to declare that it does not have contradictory qualities that destroy its unity and coherence. Limitation is the other side of the coin of identifying a world. Later we shall see how important are these divisions, these limits, to the world of federation. For example, cities normally separate counties into parts. Republics and bills of rights limit what administrative officials are permitted to do.

Worlds have outer boundaries, some impervious, others nebulous and penetrable. But the logic of their form remains intact in that all worlds have a unity independent of the unity of another, some sphere of distinct properties and features. Accordingly, to be a world is to exist with a discernible, even if somewhat indeterminable, identity. Federal worlds are orders with discernible identities and the limits which the boundaries of their systems, QED, entail.

Jurisdictions nicely mark social worlds that constitute themselves as legal. But this can beg the question: what we want to know are what limitations *warrant* legitimate jurisdiction? As United States Founding Father James Madison put the question: What are the 'proper lines of partition' between the authority of two governments? When we already know the lower body's liberties, procedures, rules of order, and what it counts as its law, these mark out the boundaries of its jurisdiction. But this convenience presupposes and depends upon the fact that the social body's limits and identity have at least provisionally been settled and that experience already suggests its appropriate divisions.

The graphics of the federal world depict a kind of set-theory icon — a 'virtual set'— a Venn diagram with members of different sizes (subsets and individuals) taking their places within a circle. The federal world is an armillary of universal, endogenous intersections, generally functionally organized and reflecting logic and causation. But it also includes, we shall later note, a pervasive, ineliminable deontology of natural and chosen trustworthy relations.

II
The One and the Many:
The Federal Logos

e pluribus unum

The primary characteristic of every federal system is a specified division of sovereignty between the local governments establishing the federation and the general government established thereby.   —Felix Morley

The logic. There has never been a season or a snowflake like any other (the many). But the seasons cycle in dependable orders, and the snowflakes always have six sides (the One). Federations are worlds that rest upon a metaphysical base: the One and the Many. In logic and metaphysics, the One is a general concept, or a genus; the many are its representations — its subordinate parts, species, sub-classes, and importantly, its individual members reflected in the 'particulars' or 'determinations' found in the empirical world: in unique objects, events, judgments, images, persons. Individual members of the federal union have special bonds, 'dyadic associations' that are the smallest and initiating connecting units without which there could be no federation.

In esthetic worlds, the One is what the parts have in common, what imparts symmetry and uniformity to their order (a stand of twelve Ionic columns of a Pantheon); the many are the diversities that impart interest, idiosyncracy, expression to the whole (each distinctive caryatid, each goddess, bearing up a portion of a frieze).

In federative worlds, the One is a sovereign legal unit (though limited in power); the many are its subordinate localities: the neighborhood, village, town, guild, city. The sixteenth-century political philosopher Johannes Althusius described federalism in the Medieval world as a 'government with estates' (*Ständestaat*).[1] As rule, not exception, primary sovereignty accrues to the estates. In a different federative world, say, that of the Papacy, a sovereignty mediating a single, unitary God stands atop the order. Authority descends. The many expressions of its unity are its dioceses, convents, monasteries, bishoprics, its prelates and mothers superior, each with administrative discretions, semi-autonomies, of its own.

The natural social unit. Federations proper are legal and political worlds. Politics define their boundaries; law defines their working parts. But they begin, in their anterior logic and presumption, as social units like families or fraternal brotherhoods, since legal units logically depend upon non-legal units, and larger combinations logically depend upon smaller. The people's natural bonds of love and trust, and their civic sense, comprise the incipient and valid legal community.

Without primary associations (*Gemeinschaft*), legal organization (*Gesellschaft*) would have no meaning. This is something that the philosopher Thomas Hobbes forgot when he set up a political sovereignty over an abstract 'law of nature.' He forgot that society — virtue, duty, sympathy, emotion, trust, *les corps intermédiares* — dwells in the million interludes between the individual and the State.

We shall see the legal commonwealth is hard enough to hold together; for we are as disposed to separate as to bind. China believes it possesses an ancient claim on Tibet. The Tibetans believe otherwise.

But separation need not be ill-willed; it has a good side, for when a commonwealth loses harmonious order among its branches and becomes dysfunctional or degenerates as a whole, division and decentralization are the natural route to prefer. For in associations that are close or local, as in separating from what we tend to avoid, we more happily live our lives.

Federations already established maintain their existence as political/legal bodies, their 'estates,' with a unitary identity as One, which we may call a State or a Nation, and hence also with the essential limitations that prescribe the boundaries of their capacity, jurisdiction, authority, and responsibility.

One and many: federation as inevitable

> Ours is a system of governments, compounded of the separate governments of
> the several States composing the Union and of one common government of all
> its members, called the Government of the United States.   —John C. Calhoun

Federative orders are nesting boxes: they are internally working social
units that include as their most important components other unitary and
internally working social units of lesser magnitude and jurisdiction, subject
somewhat, and in degrees, to a supervenient order — a central or sovereign
political administration.   Montesquieu called the federation a 'society of
societies.'

The nesting boxes can go on and on, worlds within worlds.   The
smallest grouping is often a family; but often also it is a simple dyad, two
bonded individuals that if referred to as a single union can be understood as
a whole that is part of a larger whole.   A political federation is One — a
kind of wide-striding giant surveying the landscape of his domain and what
is internal to it.   Its parts are many — small, energetic steps toward
improvement of its endless remedies and projects. Remote and abstract, the
giant, the central overseer, is not always sure that it knows what it ought to
do — its windows are dark. Its minor modules, its parts, see also through
a glass darkly. But outlines of its projects begin more clearly to display their
specifications, feeding back on their initiating agents and communal busy-
bodies the joys of effective efforts toward their ends.   The unity of the
corporate One, the Nation, is abstract, intangible, constructed, but because
it is choice-inclusive[2] it may also be principled.   The separateness of its
parts are particular, diverse, and varied, visibly empirical aggregates — but
they have a close, less erring awareness of how principles ought to be
applied.

One and many — Union and members — necessarily belong together.
We cannot imagine a battle without a leader to direct and govern the
battalions. From the One come the primary rules. From the many come
the discretions that select the details under the rules.

In identifying something as a federative order, the abstract unity of the
supervenient Whole depends upon its parts (no Canadian provinces, no
Confederation). Contrariwise, its parts do not depend upon a superior unity
for their identification as self-contained unities with semi-autonomous and
endogenous relations of their own. (In the American Federation, the local

governments *created* the Union. This is the norm, since we live day-by-day in local habitats). Without variations, there is no significant One whenever 'one' designates the unity of a numerically disparate aggregate. There is no Columbia River without the continuous flowing of many source waters. There is no forest without many trees. As the nesting boxes get smaller, so the details of their reality burgeon: It is the difference between my real dog Fido and the choice-inclusive unity of 'the animal kingdom.'

Nature. Federative orders are natural. (1) Their form is logically natural; for as a meaning postulate, there can be no One without the many. (2) They are organically natural in that having parts is internal to being federated (although no particular part is internal to being federated). (3) They are consensually natural in that their substance and their many voices are combined through choice and pact (*foedus*, covenant, trust).

The family is organic through natural affiliation, affinity, and affection. But ideologies, passions, and interests also generate groups (political parties, unions, corporations, professional associations) whose members discover and influence each other, and sometimes combine by virtue of a 'social contract' *(foedus)*. In 1935, my father-in-law helped to found the Montefiore Protective and Mutual Benefit Association of Montreal. One can scarcely imagine its maintenance without the trust and good will that the association presupposed.

(4) Federative orders are natural in another way. It is logically impossible to imagine a federative union whose lower units determine the relationships between sovereign units (as if a canton settled and declared the boundary conditions between Switzerland and Austria). Suppose a federative Union, two of whose member localities are contending over the terms of commerce on a shared river — what if one of the quarreling vicinities is allowed unilaterally to mandate the terms? We can hardly imagine otherwise than that *natural justice* requires a neutral third party to resolve the situation. The principles of justice and fairness belong to the One when it has to adjudicate conflicts between the many that are its members.

(5) The several States, wrote John C. Calhoun, 'preceded the [Union], which was created by their agency.'[3] The small units naturally combine to form and legitimate the Whole. Where a Whole already exists, dividing it normally results from dispute or decision. (6) It is natural for people to learn and to develop themselves. Because our development occurs within institutional structures like the familial community, the school, and the

neighborhood, the conditions for natural development are federated composites, pluralities of semi-autonomous 'estates.' Sometimes we determine the formation of an institution, or we construct its unity by naming it. When we have done so, we have constructed the orders that comprise our personal world. Transmission of culture between parents and offspring is natural pedagogy. Where this bond is broken or absent, and familial learning is disrupted, the primary federal bond is weakened at its source.

The roots of the federative principle cannot decay because they grow out of nature and logic. Nothing in human nature disrupts the inclination to associate. Nor does anything in human nature silence for long the intrinsic satisfaction, for the joy of the effort, of choosing. Thus is federating as natural as birth.

Communication. In federation proper, the parts and the Whole are reciprocally in touch with one another. Individuals communicate with each other. Groups communicate with groups, groups with individuals. The Union — let us call it a Nation or Republic — communicates with its members, factions, regions, combinations — and vice-versa, they communicate with it. The Union communicates with the individuals who aggregate and consolidate, forming the systems that comprise the smaller sectors. But not only do parties and individuals communicate. The unspoken voices of influence, as we shall see, communicate as well.

This communication network is the federal conversation. While there can be no conversation without a dyad, or no vocabulary without a society to have developed and formed it, there is nothing to pass between the members unless meanings develop in the form of influence undergirded by trust. In government, some great portion of these meanings must be explicit. Shortly we shall see how significantly the implicit voices of the federal conversation and its manifold influences shape the character and the legitimacy of its divisions.

Context and conflict. Federating is not a one-way process. Separation is as common as unification. Serious conflicts of loyalty pull former unities apart, or, foreseen, obstruct divisions ever joining together. Perils of one sort or another — natural disasters, war, deep, prejudicial histories — trace out transition periods that defy efficacious union. Some bondings, weak or uncertain to begin with, grow tiresome. Even when small obstinacies like retaining the traditional currency intrude into grander designs (Great Britain with respect to the world of the Common Market), no enthusiasm seems sufficient to raise up a zealotry for cooperative reunion. Failures set in, expulsions become the rule, or history teaches a region a different message: 'go it alone.' Athens and Sparta preferred to remain enemies. The American South almost seceded from the North. New York State quarreled with Vermont over possessing its magnificent green hills. Threats of Scottish devolution dent the shape and unity of the British Isles. Israelis and Palestinians differ so deeply on religion, history, and strategies for co-existence that they will never combine. All the European nations are dissatisfied with details of the proposals for economic and political union.[4] The Confederation of Independent States that was formerly the Soviet Union scarcely hangs together; Chechnya wants separation from its vaster sovereignty. Quebec pulls for freedom from greater Canada. Chiapas wants the same; it claims that the central government of Mexico has forgotten it. The Roman Empire shattered into regional fragments, chaotic over long centuries until their jurisdictions were settled for a time. The suzerainty of the Ottoman Empire watched while one religious or ethnic section after another struggled, then won partial autonomy. (Artificial union by outsider mandate or force is always precarious. The wars in Yugoslavia today are a breakdown partition of peoples that probably never should have been joined).

Contexts and history condition these transitions into and out of unity, situational remnants lingering even when federation is established — or terminated. Sometimes separate unities become aware that solidification is essential for their survival: the loose federation of Hebrew tribes in the land of Canaan solidified under kingship when the domination of the Philistines grew more dangerous. Sentiments grow for autonomy, splitting longtime unions. Histories of pain and victimization by conquest leave trails of suffering that will not be overcome until separation and new reunion soothe the wrongs, helping them pass out of memory. Long, successful separation breeds a kind of covenantal loyalty within a people who have, in excluding themselves, fashioned a new externality — until a catastrophe shakes the domicile that everyone thought was eternal.

However natural the orders of the federative principle, nonetheless their circumstances, particularities, histories, and perversities determine, finally, their ease or difficulty of arrangement, or whether they arrange themselves at all. But always present is some federal organization: The pattern of groups within groups, lastingly being created, always reappears. For no sooner does one system devolve than, like a kaleidoscope, the smaller pieces that never dissolved, or that find an organizational realignment, drift into patterns that vindicate their search for a renewed, unifying whole.

Divisiveness invades a lobby, and the dissenting members, walking out, form a new union. Cliques, factions, guilds, trade societies, boards, workshops, clubs, and corporations resurge with hope. Ideologues find each other in exercising their zealous rhetoric. Villages extend into townships. Financial institutions buy each other out. Lobbies consolidate their interests in order to monopolize. Hitherto forbidden societies, churches, religious orders congeal their doctrinal obsessions.

Even if inventive new institutions do not emerge, marriages continue, sexual friendships bond, and parturition creates new dyads: mother and child. Natural, inescapable social monads furnish the search for comfortable spheres of order and security. There can be no separation without unification. *To separate is to separate into a different whole*, a whole that is *other than* the whole that went before. 'The way up and the way back are the same.' In the eighteenth century, an altogether new type of federation appeared. This was the factory. Omni-management — businessman, investor, owner, inventor, entrepreneur, all in one — had, or borrowed, investment capital. Brand new societies with distinctive, interior-grounded interrelationships arose. The factory town came into existence, bearing with it an endogenous self-sufficiency that changed the face of the modern world. The Great Discontinuity was a new federal phenomena.

III

The Federal Conversation: Unspoken Voices

Communication. Nothing of magnitude or importance hangs together unless communication influences its inner parts. Feedback mechanisms tell each other when to turn off or on. Animal kingdoms in characteristic ways posture and resonate: wolf packs, bat colonies, and flocks of birds share voices, radar systems, body language. Nobody communicates more gladly than news reporters, more theatrically than politicians!

So also does human association generate intricate idioms, syntax, and vocabularies that make knowledge, directions, persuasion, and influence causally effective. The federal conversation describes a dialogue of continuity and change between the One and the many. Its end is secure maintenance of respective spheres of autonomy. But it is also good in itself. Good influence and good education are the pedagogical product of truthful, trustworthy communication. *Bona fides* (*foedus*, covenant) builds the nation.

The federal association requires that its collections and compounds speak to each other.

A benchmark of federal communication, once its identity is established, is compulsory jurisdiction. Jurisdiction is eminently fitted to aid in the identification of otherwise contestable boundaries or limits of authority. Within its designated precincts, single jurisdiction fosters one public law and one public legal administration, enforcement, judgement, and sanction.

With this explicit and shared vocabulary, pertinent facts are reported and spread; and common histories, traditions, mores, and opinions begin to weld and test their strength. Institutional structures of all sizes and purposes consolidate as unitary processes, and may come to be seen as belonging both to the larger and to the lesser domains. As what is familiar grows disvalued by some sectors of a federated public, insofar as their interests no longer are served, dissent may set in: the interior language becomes a melee of voices — critical, disgruntled, naively honest or ulteriorly meretricious — in all shades from apathy to vigor. And so federations develop communicational differences seldom in isolation from one another. For it is a belief of free societies that truth, knowledge, and morality arise from the foundations of civil humaneness and civil dissent introverted through a pervasive, underwritten trust. Even if for no practical reason at all, the federal conversation, by which districts or interests come to reliable conciliations regarding their self-identities, properties, and claims, is a great and intrinsic good. Human nature revels in the passage of messages that connect one human being, or one human conglomerate, with another. The globalization of the computer reminds us of our intrinsic fascination with interlocking voices.

Exogenous? Endogenous? It would be illuminating, convenient, and probably conflict-thwarting if we could legitimate the conceptual boundaries of the federal structure, assigning to each municipality, each *arrondissement*, each nation/state, its proper and necessary domain of sovereign authority, autonomy, and responsibility. What is internal and what is external to the federal structure and its sub-divisions are rational questions that must admit of answers. From these answers, appropriate legalities bearing immorality-avoiding norms may follow. In recent days, the quest for political legitimacy has been ridiculed in the literature as old-fashioned and futile. But a consensus of living communities gives the lie to this myth: Every association whatsoever with any consciousness of its mission believes that its legitimacy — its right to exist on its own terms and for its own purposes — is established, or should be established.

We are looking for a hermeneutic, a methodology, of the federal principle, for standards or firm rules of thumb to define and interpret matters that common sense does not adequately locate on the jurisdictional map of federation. Granted the overlap, intersection, and passing back and forth of permissions, prohibitions, and necessities, and of the rights and duties denoting legitimacy and power, what exactly belongs where? What procedures, decisions, measures, interactions, implementations, and to what extent, rightly sustain either centrality or decentrality — a scattering to its parts — of good governance? We know that national efforts defend the Whole, and that nations make treaties with each other. We know that pervasive or serious issues of justice relevant to federal property in the broadest sense belong to the Nation. Looking inward toward their primary parts (provinces, states, counties, and the like), matters pertaining to these primary part/whole junctions properly also belong to nations.

Justice requires a neutral third party to adjudicate from a higher-order perspective the actionable disputes between these largest but subordinate parts. If they look to themselves as judges in their own cause, the canons of natural justice are violated. And so, national justice requires a Supreme Court to transcend first-party contention. In the United States, the trade routes, overlands, waterways, 'post Offices and post Roads,' and all the manufactured infrastructures of human intercourse (canals and bridges and roads) — all that pertains to freedom of economic access (the 'interstate commerce clause') — were appropriately declared a *national* prerogative. Was it luck, prescience, or hindsight wisdom that recognized prosperity, peace, liberty, fairness, and the common good come together when trade is broad and free?

Accordingly, federation requires a constitutional language to set out the limits of autonomy and authority, and a concomitant Supreme Court to adjudicate discourses of disagreement. These higher systems can belong only to the supremacy. Their definition and function fix their properties. In so doing, they also fix their moral and legal limits.

But these institutions only beg the question regarding matters that are not intuitively clear to common sense, expedience, and everyday morality; for what we want to know is in what federalized region these other matters *ought* to be placed. We need close observation and the hindsight of experience to verify our judgments. Unless we can discover what is endogenous to federated departments, even if only by exclusion from what is not, federations, however unavoidable in form, remain *ad hoc* and accidental in their contents. It is like searching for the *meum* and *teum* of the meaning of justice. What are the boundaries of just property? We take up this vital question after we have looked at the pros and cons of nation vs. its departments.

Subsidiarity. Given our desire for economies of time and substance — the most return for the least investment and risk — and for the avoidance of moral wrongs, one exceedingly meritorious principle has long been understood and seldom rejected: the principle of subsidiarity. Subsidiarity is the overarching, *prima facie* rule that things should be done, all else being equal, at the smallest possible level of effectiveness.

A keyword here is experiential knowledge. Only where one knows the factors that are closely involved can one anticipate that the wanted consequence will reasonably conform to the actions carrying out their intentions, and indeed which intentions are reasonable in the first place. The facts and reasons that constitute knowledge interpret our experience; our experience, in turn, tests our claims to know. Hence, experience is the middle term that links what is to be done with the level at which it is best to be done. Subsidiarity has no point unless we believe that the alderman is closer to the needs of the people than the government of the province, and so, all else being equal, contacting the alderman carries advantages with it.

We cannot imagine a mailman's daily route through a tortuous neighborhood being decided at the national level! Nor a national government requiring some costly project of its poorer constituencies while giving them no funds to pay for it, a project that could be done well on a smaller, more convenient scale. In the near past, in America, a state, in order to exonerate itself from administrative decrees coming from on high, had to show that if applied, a decree would work an immorality. But a new ruling has followed a more sensible path: Now a state may also show that the political command works havoc with the local conditions, or they with it. That is, if applied, the national policy will be ineffectual or counterproductive. To simplify: A city planning board ought not to have to create a drug rehabilitation center when the public interest is better served by a fire station.

Appropriate and lasting remedies rest not only on the broad realities of sound principle, but on sentiment and information as well. Since these are optimally available *in situ,* prevailing circumstances rightly determine which decisions and which details will likely yield the desired results, and so, which decisions and details should be implemented. Subsidiarity, reason, and morality dictate why Israeli Arabs, consonant with the safety of all, are given full control over their mosques and other holy places in Jerusalem.

James Madison's 37th. The framer of the American Constitution James Madison gave us clues to an astute hermeneutic in *The Federalist*. His voice cautioned care in the language of politics and union. Madison believed the conceptual boundaries and distinctions we need to know in guiding federal philosophy are unknowable with any precision. In his famous *Federalist Paper 37,* he embarks on a brief, relevant, and perceptive excursion into epistemology and the semiotics of language. 'Faculties of the mind' and our uncertainties about nature and human nature generate inherent obscurities in our knowledge; for as thinking and knowing beings, we are partial and imperfect. Especially do our social institutions as objects fall under the imperfections of man's 'eye . . . in survey[ing] the works of nature.'[5]

Madison cites three general difficulties in the federal conversation. (1) Social terms are abstract, and hence their 'proper lines of partition' are equally vague. (2) We are always uncertain about the facts that would help to mark out the lines between central and decentralized power. (3) Our use of words reveals that 'complex ideas' may have no sign; nor do words unequivocally designate. Though God's voice to us is luminous, our human language, he wrote, is 'dim and doubtful.'

The acute warnings of Madison's insights into the discourse of federalism and his appropriate SOS — integrated within the most efficable document of political philosophy ever composed — give us heart when we observe federative squabbling. We come to learn that this squabbling is inherent — tensions invariably exist between districts, special interests, and centralized power. But political dissent under a frame of toleration and right is a far better alternative than violence. If these stumbling blocks are internal to the political semiotic, is it small wonder that the troublesome semiotic suffers least, on balance, when its interpretive dialogue is kept open, local, and trustworthy?

I think, nevertheless, it makes sense to ferret out what elements are proper (endogenous) to the sub-divisions of a federal order and what are not. Insights may arise through a hard look at some of the disadvantages and advantages of political federation: the One and the many in interaction. So let us ask first: What undesirable limitations does devolution to the states or to communities impose? Because they causally connect, these limitations may overlap in function, a sign of their internal, reciprocal accord. But it is necessary to denote them separately.

Disadvantages of home rule. An empire or large sovereign body already recognized to be in place must look upon federation as a kind of unfortunate severance. Empowerment at the top seldom welcomes its own diminution. (Those who governed the former Soviet Union did not prefer to break it up into unruly segments.) In fact, decentralization looks futile, formidable, and dangerous if it connotes a breaking up of uniformities previously perceived as working well. Even the new South Africa whose parliamentary majority, in early 1995, is 62 percent, warns against 'a dangerous drift toward federalism.' Having legally, but with pain and fear, only very recently resolved its racial separateness, such a drift must be interpreted as yet another round of pernicious, dangerous divisiveness. We can surely understand this misgiving. And again, a patriotic Frenchman was heard recently to utter: 'We want Europe with national states, not a federation.' This gentleman opined that the Western nations, already self-identified, patriotic, proud, jealous, and legitimate, should be kept intact; if joined, then only with thin lines of essential, commercial, working ties that can be gained in no other way.

The term decentralization would be meaningless, though, if the *derivation* of unitary power were acknowledged, namely, that superseding unitary power normally derives from the sectors combining toward more general association when they see benefits in doing so. When local purposes are already set, it may be prudent to unify under higher dominions to protect these purposes, as the Hebrews empowered Saul to reign when foreign invaders with an iron armory threatened their tribes. When the delegation of authority ascends from bottom to top, and the voluntary 'middle institutions' are executing their functions, no such conception as 'decentralizing' makes sense; for the people are already divided into parts. As Samuel presciently warned the Hebrews when he anointed and solemnized the kingship of Saul, it is the potentates at the top who are dangerous.

What, then, are disadvantages of allowing autonomy to the sections of a national Whole?

(1) When larger coordinations are necessary, perspective is limited. When the general stands too long among the troops, he sees only the present situation, never the overall strategy. (2) If a program must prevail nationally, state implementation may be bogged down by adverse

circumstances. These can turn into self-defeating excuses. What the federal government mandates, or pays for, it should also have a voice in administering, at least in seeing that its general guidelines are conformed to. (3) The common good of the national society (protection, for example, of its shores) may be neglected or obstructed if the shorter-range focus is pervasively dwelled upon. Special interests (for example, keeping an army base open at excessive cost to the nation, even where the base generates local employment and revenue for a community) can sacrifice a larger good so fully that it is hard to restore even its conceptualization. (National farm subsidies are one such special interest, for which the public pays billions of inessential dollars.)

(4) Where a national goal or its steps toward maintenance must be coordinated, fragmentations at subordinate levels may block the efforts toward the goal. There are cases, for instance, where compliance with federal environmental standards is neglected or poorly done by the several states. (5) Legalisms in local bureaucracies can thwart larger measures for larger and nobler national purposes.

> . . . the preservation of a multiplicity of relatively powerful local governments, within the union, creates a complicated and legalistic system. It makes the conduct of foreign policy, necessarily entrusted to the central government, unusually difficult for a true federation, since actions taken in regard to other sovereign powers are always likely to react on the domestic balance.
> — Felix Morley

'. . .local government,' wrote Clint Bolick, 'in its various permutations and combinations is all too often cumbersome, expensive, inefficient, uncontrollable, and oppressive.'[6] In the Oakland Hills of California in 1991, calamitous fires destroyed thousands of homes. Those who tried to rebuild their homes encountered 'nine separate agencies and eleven different reviews . . . before gaining [community] approval.'[7]

(6) Ethnic or religious homogeneity can stultify. New ideas, inventiveness, and creativity originate in the diversities that large, modern nations attract. (7) Madison wrote that '. . .independent neighbors are natural enemies.' Of course, they are not. Madison's vision when he wrote was turned in the direction of remedying by federative unions the glaring disputations between the states. Nevertheless, as the post-Civil War Constitutional Amendments in America and the 'Reconstruction Congress' tended to confirm, sectional constituencies are prone to self-preoccupation

and provincialism; and they can perpetrate injustice and oppress the rights of minorities under their sanction. It is a law of logic that the inclusion of some implies the exclusion of others. Like-minded prejudice breeds the demagogue.

Sometimes even large evils invade the regional mentality. If the scope and protocols of regional autonomies are too strong or vast, or if the Central Order from which outside criticism can arise is not at least partially in charge, these evils have no check. Municipal powers can threaten too. Grassroots movements can tyrannize. Too local can be too ignorant. Hill country mentality is often not a pretty sight.

But are the forgoing disadvantages unique to the substrata, and are they irremediable? When we study the disadvantages often imputed to counties or communities, to see whether these shortcomings might also pervade the texture of nations, perhaps on an even larger scale, we observe that the particularities in concrete situations tend mostly to augment and exacerbate whatever self-interest and aggrandizements lodge in our human nature. Size plays a part in this; for painful regional histories and prejudiced opinions can exactly map themselves upon the scope of nations. Nations, by logic, are larger than their constituent communities. But in absolute terms, communities can be as large as nations. In America, the babble of cultures can be healthy.[8] In tiny Israel, diversities can disrupt the most ordinary of ongoing affairs.

To show that a secondary sector like a city can, or does, act in disvalued ways is not to show that it must. Nor is it to show that the Whole of which it is a part does not also so act. Nor is it to show that only in town and village do certain disadvantages prevail. Situations at small and large range are seldom comparable. But whenever they are, investigation of their differences helps to reveal their most strategic causes. When these causes are unfavorable, we must try to avoid reinstituting them.

Adversities confined to time or place can often be remedied. We have learned that the common good is as neglected and obscured by large-scale, democratic representation weak in the face of special interests as by community self-interest. And serious harms that surge up in prejudiced localities can, in these days of global communication, be checked by watchdog competition, whistle blowing, excoriation by public press, the voices of university and church.

If these fail, we have to use the solution heretofore discovered: The Nation must exercise its rightful sovereignty and prohibit the evils by laws and sanctions. But it equally goes the other way. We can say that in the 30's and 40's of this century, it was the German nation that was evil. In this vast, terrifying armageddon, goodness, resistance, and succor yet lodged in the hearts of individuals.

Benefits of home rule. We have examined shortcomings and impossibilities when local fibers weave the cloth of social life. Now, what strengths reside in government when home rule prevails? It seems that allocation to subordinate sectors allows us to enjoy a range of values that may otherwise attenuate or be lost.

The human inclination to associate generates the rights of groups to compose their preoccupations and to exercise autonomy over their separate character and over their chosen actions, including the action to join up with other groups if the latter consent. If, without violating the rule of law, or the common good and the proscription against serious harms and atrocities, we could learn what these smaller modules are most gifted in bringing about, perhaps we could formulate guidelines that distribute rights and duties to the several parts of the federative system. Analyzing the advantages and disadvantages of parts and whole may be the route whereby to discover what part of social life is appropriate to each, or where common problems are best solved. It would seem without question, for instance, that a disabled veteran who has given his life to his nation in its time of danger deserves that the nation ease the misfortunes resulting from his disablement. It seems more questionable, though, that a vicinity suffering a natural emergency has a right to national disaster relief at any cost. For the latter, at least, there are reasons pro and con — not so for the former situation.

(1) In taking matters into our own hands, we can better discern efficiencies of scale. Forming firm associations with community-wide goals, we are thereby enabled to discern that our goals are best left unfinished, or contrariwise are completed and need no further enhancement, no further funds, empowerments, management. On these closer scales, we can see and measure consequences faster and more accurately: '. . .those closest to the matters to be dealt with best [know] what ought to be done.'[9] Certain dimensions of social problems become more salient in the restricted environment. What is easier to perceive is easier to remedy. We generally wait less long for the assemblyman to act than for officials attached to a national bureau.[10]

The 'concrete particular' is *prima facie* more compelling than the common, the near and personal than the remote and abstract. We feel undermined by not being in control. We *know* what we need. Here in this vast array of efficiencies and evaluations, the federal principle leans in the direction of the local. It is the Center that requires defending.

(2) In self-rule resides the ideal expression of small-scale democracy. With self-rule citizen involvement is fostered. So, too, the loyalties that reinforce our desire to take part become real and living. And vice-versa, in taking part, to which we are more disposed when we believe the problems and solutions are nearby, our loyalties toward that in which we participate are sharpened into trust.

(3) The strongest force for rule, argued David Hume, is public opinion. Smaller and proximate governments tend to homogeneity of culture and opinion. To be like-minded is to be more readily effective when setting out a project or policy. In the municipality, public opinion congeals into a more decisive directive. Importantly, when we are like-minded on an issue, we compromise with greater good will. In contrast, dissent and faction breed hostilities, and compromise is confusing when we are uncertain about what the group will consent to.

(4) Successful experimentation has always been recognized as a prerogative of neighborhood, town, school, and village. Madison spoke of the 'federative' system that 'admits local experiments of every sort which, if failing, are but a partial and temporary evil; if successful, may become a common and lasting improvement.'[11] In El Paso, Texas, bilingual education has been interpreted to mean that children, together, share a classroom in which two languages, Spanish and English, are taught at the same time. Language-immersion is no longer the model. The new practice has been adjudged successful, both in terms of learning and in terms of cementing friendships between children of quite different cultures and expectations. The new bilingual experiment will soon be tested for its possible 'nationalization.' If the El Paso experiment had been a disaster, its costs would have been minimal and its scale of damage small.

(5) Under our natural human habitat in the family, in the neighborhood, and at the corner grocery, we discover our common passions and interests that can soften conflict or hasten its remediation; while priority values, those we can agree to face-to-face, come to the surface. Extreme positions tend to diminish as fewer tendentious conflicts fester into fanaticism. (6) Knowledge, information, influence, and adaptation are made possible where

they reside closer to problems and the conditions that generate them. Out of these come the trust and security that inform us our problems are resolvable, our social order is stable. In educational institutions, for example, and in schooling generally, information about present situations allows us to know what children need, what standards we can set, how better to reach them, what we can afford.

(7) Where the scope of the public good is smaller, the public good is more readily reached, or re-thought. The general interest is best served when power monopolies — what James Madison called 'national assumptions of power' — are very cautiously measured to suit their national purpose. That a small nucleus of persons, a leadership, will invariably influence the flow of institutions ('Michels' Law'), and that this leadership will be accountable to those whom it serves, help to assure that these institutions will fulfill their purposes.

(8) It is, by and large, the central administrations of towering governments that perpetrate fraud and theft of the public purse — that squander, deceive, and embezzle in ways that are difficult to correct and debilitating for the overall populace to deal with. (9) Importantly, town-and-village controls lessen the most intractable coercion by keeping excesses in the public eye. Statism, history informs us, tends to the destruction of liberty; the thrill of power and control is overwhelming. Institutions of freedom, such as divisions of power, the rule of law, bills of rights, checks and balances, Montesquieu's *les corps intermédiaires*, make coercion from the Center much less necessary. But even where coercion is necessary and proper, these institutes of freedom are also much more necessary and proper.

Effective home governance helps to close options where they first arise. To close options is to define, and thus to limit power more exactly to those dimensions essential to its exercise.

> The great overriding advantage of the federal system is that it operates to avert the dangers inherent in government by remote control. The essence of federalism is reservation of control over local affairs to the localities themselves, the argument for which becomes stronger if the federation embraces a large area, with strong climatic or cultural differences among the various states therein. One justifying assumption for such a loose-knit system is that citizens as a body are both interested in, and for the most part competent to handle, local problems. When that assumption is valid there is little doubt that

federalism . . . serves admirably to foster freedom without the sacrifice of order.   — Felix Morley

There is a kind of blind tendency to view omnicompetent government, perhaps because its center is remote, as a 'utopian citadel.'[12] Utopian visions gone awry, as they must, lead to disappointment, then to despair and anger — then to the turbulent rage and violence typical of unwarranted revolution.

(10) The overriding value of federative relations played out in the secondary sectors, is, in my judgment, trust between persons and trust in social and political institutions. We most trust what we know. And we know best what occupies our precincts because it is concrete, present, influential. We can check out its credentials. When people feel coerced but believe the source is illegitimate, the essential social trust that is strengthened by the knowledge that secures personal control begins to disintegrate. 'Peace in our times' sounds good — who could reject it? But when its legitimacy broke trust, its author was held as perpetrating treason. Even when coercion is most destructive, trust, though tarnished, normally continues; for trust occupies the simplest relationship, that of two persons out of which our social world is born. Under extreme conditions, even family trust can be destroyed, as Adolf Hitler demonstrated when his regime spread hatred into the smallest crannies of people's associative interactions.

We saw that the word 'federal' derives from *foedus* (covenant, promise, faithfulness — trust). It is not difficult, then, to understand its permeation of the social world through the most minute of its federative fibers. Makers of political policies at all levels build on this trust in courting public confidence in the wisdom and lastingness of their proposals.

The advantages of keeping functions of social life at the local level can scarcely be overemphasized; for most of the functions we have examined, or their product, are not well done by nations.

A hermeneutic of federal justification. Remembering Madison's reminder of our uncertainty about facts that would help us separate what is best done centrally from what is best done on home ground, is there, nevertheless, a general, instructive hermeneutic resident in the pros and cons of practices allocated respectively to national, state, and community structures? Are these actual allocations wise and valid? Are certain purposes owned by the subordinates that the Nation dare not trespass; vice-versa, is the Nation privy to purposes that the nature of national life reliably vindicates? In our assessment, above, of state, community, and nation, certain advantages seem to put both large and small inventories in their principled places. We are looking for what is right and fitting in dividing social worlds into sections that can most harmonize their interiors while also harmonizing their connections with worlds external to them. Here below, we begin this search.

(1) The proper jurisdictional location for some practices can be read off directly from clear statements of what these practices are, and whether or not they are construed as advantageous primarily, or only, at the level at which they are exercised. For example, where a larger perspective is absolutely essential, it *logically* follows that the nation must oversee. The same is true of 'the higher law': only a national constitution and a national court can tend to matters where, say, fairness among states is involved.

Safety from threats external to the entire Whole and its parts, commerce between the states, and matters of foreign affairs can only be secured from the Center. All this is derivable as soon as we understand the meaning of the federal One-and-many and its nesting box analogy.

(2) Some ideals are universal (natural justice, legal equity, certain civil liberties, the responsibility entailed by personal autonomy). Fidelity to these ideals leaves their *location* decidable in that they can be enjoyed at many levels of life; but their meanings admit of little situational variation. Economic freedom is a similar matter but different in one respect: the theory is invariant and universal, but its exercise may admit of more expediencies thrown up by local conditions. For example, to aid victims of a flood, the market rate for loans at interest may, at discretion, be overridden and lowered.

(3) A number of what we may call mid-level rules, or procedural legal postulates, admit of light maneuvering at the administrative end, provided their basic meanings are not distorted. Checks and balances, the rule of law, division of powers, republican government — all pertain both to nation and state; but their jurisdictional plane of action, their 'operational definition,' determines, to an extent, how severely or how liberally they may be exercised. The integrity of conceptual divisions must be added here to the integrity of jurisdiction. Loose interpretations of these safeguards of liberty destroy them more surely than neglecting their application in an instance or two.

(4) The Constitution of the United States declares that the powers of the central government shall not exceed those powers that are necessary and

proper. No one can disagree. But 'necessary and proper' needs interpretation. I would like to suggest some *prima facie* clues to their meaning:

All else being equal, subsidiarity should prevail. Accordingly, the municipal branches should determine their own autonomies in those cases where —

(a) knowledge of immediate conditions is a foremost consideration; or there is reason to believe that situational changes can be imminent, critical, and unforeseeable except by close observation and foresight;

(b) personal involvement, self-rule, referenda, direct representation, consensus are foremost factors in the success of an endeavor;

(c) close evaluation or periodic assessment is essential before knowing whether to sustain a practice or to alter it;

(d) no obvious associative links with higher orders qualify the here-and-now business of the community;

(e) endogeny — causal or logical integration between parts — is strong, dependable, organized, and vital for the identification of an endeavor, such that its disruption would cause grave harm;

(f) a powerful governing Center looms dangerously or destructively over the existence, well-being, or viability of the subordinate parts.

Where damage to national unity and safety, necessary authority (as with treaties or foreign alliances), pervasive social morality, justice, and the common good are not compromised, all else belongs to the subordinate parts.

A theory of transition from state to nation or back to the states has not, so far as I know, been worked through. Painful stumbling over major changes in jurisdiction, such as is happening now in the former Soviet Union, can spoil any theory of what belongs where. Transition theory must be developed that is as conceptually sturdy as the theory of federation itself.

The federal semiotic. The following broad analogy may prove fruitful when arguing that a given function rightly belongs to state or nation. If we do not push the analogy strenuously or too much in detail, it may enlarge our understanding to compare the three branches of federative systems — judicial, executive, legislative — with the three theories of truth that philosophers have developed — coherence, correspondence, pragmatic. And again, three levels of textual interpretation (semiotics) also appear to correlate with the three branches of federative systems.

(1) The *judicial* arm of federation can be seen as representing *coherence* among statements alleged to be true. A jurisdictional dispute demands a logically coherent reconciliation of statements both normative (rule-guided) and factual. Also the requisite continuities of legal meaning over a period of time, and the justice and fairness consonant with these continuities, are provided by the consistency of drawing upon precedent and established curial practices. To bring a problem to legal judgment is to examine these logical connections. We can call these connections a kind of judicial *syntax*.

(2) The *executive* arm of federation can be seen as representing the *pragmatic* elements in joining principles or rules to the definite decisions of officials who apply or administer these rules. Administrative federalism enforces the law; but before it does so, its discretions stand as an interpretation of the law: What are its implications for day-to-day operations? To administer the law is to connect the sender of the law with the receiver of the law. This is like the semiotic level of communicating the text that we call *pragmatics*.

(3) The *legislative* arm of federation can be seen as bringing public interests into *correspondence* with laws that represent or voice these public interests with maximum integrity. Proper law denotes reference to the relevant facts of the social life of the people. It corresponds to these facts. Accordingly, legislation is a legal *semantic:* it welds the signature of the law-making text with the social reality that requires guidance or governance.

These analogies can be guidelines for thinking about and sorting out the categories of activities that political bodies engage in. Curial judging, for example, needs to reflect logical consistency as well as fairness, or after a time its imperatives will not be listened to. Administrative directives need to attach themselves intimately to those who will be affected by them, or after a time the decisions will be ridiculed and abandoned. The obligation to obey the law cannot endure where these fundamentals are ignored.

IV
Whispered Voices: The Assumptions of Federation

Influence as initiative. Federalism is meaningless unless its several parts communicate with one another. What is the point of whole-and-part unless each has something to contribute? We as participants confronting each other — deliberating, justifying — seeing now this perspective, now that, criticizing and absorbing the reciprocal criticism of 'the other' — fulfill in so doing an inherent, abiding sociality in our nature, while the federal exchange, if worthily done, collectively improves our lot.

We are not only reasoning beings. Emotions lie deeper than the curiosities and surveys of the mind. There are things we cannot, or would not, or should not, say; and seldom do we even formulate them to ourselves. Behind the overt encounters and contestations of the federal conversation, whispered voices are often stronger. For they motivate the undercurrents that make federal ties living adjustments to our needs, and living influences upon our aspirations as groups and individuals.

However, this implicit knowledge that lodges in our whole self, while denoting real emotions, requires an explicit language in order to communicate. Hence no complete fidelity to the text can be expected; for as Madison reminds us, complex (and, we have to add, subtle) ideas may have no sign; nor do words unequivocally designate. Sign and object are different; but the sign is all that we can use to talk when we awaken the federal conversation. We are fortunate, at least, to be able to share language in common.

Federation as a pedagogy of trust. What do these whispered voices — this implicit conversation — say? Why are they important? They almost defy interpretation, for they are the reality itself that joins person to person in the primordial federal dyad. Trustworthy influences are often nonverbal.

The whispered voices in the contexts of federation reveal what we identify with, what persons and qualities, sentiments, values, and trusts are intimate and close. Without identification with what we believe we belong to — what group, what characteristics, reflect our affiliation and loyalty, even if these are only remembered, imagined, tenuous, silly, implausible, or in danger of loss — there is nothing to initiate the voluntary grouping that defines the lowest common denominator of federal union. Affection and love — organic union — may inspire pairing, extending itself to offspring. But for rational purposes, for what we see as necessities protective of survival (we agree to build a well in our arid fields), we make contracts, we agree, and we promise (*foedus*, trust). (Thus do those worlds we call 'species' persist: flocks of birds group in formation to escape danger; herds of elk flee in unison to avoid predation.) But beyond these rudimentary choices, inclination drives us toward identifying with others, yearning to be counted a member of their combination.

Such inclinations — 'This is what I am' — and what they lead to are to be counted as *educative*. *They are a form of instruction*. The identifications that constitute our selfhood are primary influences under our volition that enact our autonomous wills, changing what we are into what we become. The influence of others clothing themselves in features that we approve and come to cherish — ethnicity, religion, ancestry and heritage, regionality, family, culture, language, sentiment, race, tradition — is the matrix, the whispered influence of the federal conversation. This influence is the whispered school of federal interaction. 'This is our ancestral place.' 'History won this for us.' 'We have practiced this tradition for 2000 years.' 'You are like me.' 'Now we are free — we can speak as we wish.' 'That makes us second cousins.' 'We are both descendants of the Scots!' 'Let's get together.' To understand these scarcely articulate identities that school us in association and compose our selfhood is to understand the dynamic influences that make part-and-whole work as federation. After these passionate sentiments, and secondary in substantiality and value, come the mental things: opinions, like-mindedness, shared interests and goals, ideals and ideologies. We cannot imagine these interpersonal relations, generated out of seeing ourselves as similar to some selected others whom we admire, without imagining that trust, the analogue for 'federation' *(foedus)*, is the silent language that identifies our existence with that of others whom we join, in open or in secret.

It is a harsh but logical truth that to be included in a group is to be excluded from another group. This is why virtue has so often to be taught: It does not easily occur to us that our group prejudicially defines what we love only at the expense of ignoring the identities of others who are not part of us. We have to learn the equalities that make sentience and sensitivity a common property to be shared. But it is good to remember that to model oneself after the traits one identifies with is not the same as to be included in a group even of one's own kind: Identification is a conceptual activity, whereas group affiliation is actual membership. Some groups are exclusive but benign. And we can take our models from a plurality of influences so diverse as to make it impossible to know which loyalty excludes which others, or which loyalty is highest in our ranking.

Without *bona fides,* no conscious interaction or union prevails whatsoever; for lies and misrepresentations, irregularities, infidelities, and unreliability cannot be preferred by our nature, and soon destroy our deepest instincts. Since good will between persons and associated entities is elemental and ubiquitous, it comprehends our material life and our spiritual life. As we come to depend upon it, it measures out our duties and responsibilities. In time, it sums up our *anlage* with other persons in our world. Resolutions, contracts, settlements, understandings and agreements, delegations of power, promises, stabilities, limitations, anticipations — because we take these federated relationships for granted as reliable, we scarcely need say them. If we discover we relied upon them and they do not pertain, we cry out, and one more federal bond is broken. When trust is betrayed, federation cannot even begin. Integrity defining the many faces of *bona fides* keeps federation together in a healthy, compound Whole.

The civic humanism that steadies urban civilizations in the modern world cannot survive without positive modalities of trust between its human members. In the end, the smallest parts of federation are citizens as individuals who impart and receive influences. And the personal dignity of individuals can have no meaning apart from the good will composing the federal armillary.

Virginia Black is Associate Professor of Philosophy, Pace University.

ENDNOTES

1. Friedrich, Carl Joachim, *The Philosophy of Law in Historical Perspective* (2nd ed.), Chicago: University of Chicago Press, 1973 (VIII, 'Statutory Law against Natural Law'; 'The Doctrine of Sovereignty in Bodin, Althusius, and Grotius,' pp. 57-66).

2. 'Choice-inclusive' is John Lachs's useful term which I first came across in his 'Human Nature' (Fourth Annual Patrick Romanell Lecture delivered at the American Philosophical Association Eastern Division meeting on Dec. 29, 1989, Atlanta). The term is a convenient alternative to the overused 'contestable' and 'indeterminate,' while describing exactly how these terms are created.

3. Calhoun, John C., *A Disquisition on Government and Selections from the Discourse* (introd. and ed. C. Gordon Post), NY: Macmillan, 1988, p. 85.

4. 'Summer of Discontent,' *U.S. News & World Report*, June 6, 1994, pp. 48-50.

5. Madison, Hamilton, Jay, *The Federalist Papers*, NY: New American Library, 1961, No. 37: Madison.

6. *Grassroots Tyranny: The Limits of Federalism* (review), *The Federalist Paper*, October 1993.

7. (untitled article), *Reason*, January 1992, pp. 36-41.

8. Black, Percy, 1995, 'Babble of Cultures: Challenge to Law in the 1990's and Beyond.' Submitted for publication.

9. Beloff, Max, *The American Federal Government* (2nd ed.), NY: Oxford University Press, 1969, p. 11.

10. The subject is treated in Black, Virginia, 'The Methodology of Confirming the Effectiveness of Public Policy,' *The Monist*, Vol. 56, No. 1, Jan, 1972.

11. Goodman, Paul (ed.), *The Federalists vs. The Jeffersonian Republicans*, NY: Holt, Rinehart and Winston, 1967, (in Adrienne Koch, 'James Madison and the Politics of Republicanism,' pp. 75-76).

12. *Ibid.* p. 73.

REFERENCES

Barnett, Randy E. (ed), *The Rights Retained by the People,* Fairfax, VA: George Mason University Press, 1989.

Beloff, Max, *The American Federal Government* (2nd ed.), NY: Oxford University Press, 1969.

Calhoun, John C., *A Disquisition on Government and Selections from the Discourse* (intro. and ed. C. Gordon Post), NY: Macmillan, 1988.

Dauer, Manning J., *The Adams Federalists*, Baltimore: The Johns Hopkins University Press, 1968.

Dicey, A.V., *An Introduction to the Study of the Law of the Constitution* (8th ed.), London: The Macmillan Press Ltd., 1975.

Elazar, Daniel J., *Federalism as Grand Design, Political Philosophers and the Federal Principle,* Lanham, Md: University Press of America, 1987.

Epstein, David F., *The Political Theory of the Federalist,* Chicago: University of Chicago Press, 1986.

Friedrich, Carl Joachim, *The Philosophy of Law in Historical Perspective* (2nd ed.), Chicago: University of Chicago Press, 1973.

Goodman, Paul (ed.), *The Federalists vs. The Jeffersonian Republicans*, NY: Holt, Rinehart and Winston, 1967.

Madison, Hamilton, Jay, *The Federalist Papers*, NY: New American Library, 1961.

Morley, Felix, *Freedom and Federalism,* Indianapolis: Liberty Press, 1981.

Strauss, Leo and Cropsey, Joseph (eds.), *History of Political Philosophy* (2nd ed.), Chicago: Rand McNally & Co., 1972 (Martin Diamond, 'The Federalist,' pp. 631-651).

Chapter XIII

Two World-Views: Corn Law Protest in *The Sheffield Independent*, 1825-1835

Angela Michele Leonard*

This paper takes as its primary text a relatively undistinguished South Yorkshire local — selected because of its association with Ebenezer Elliott, the 'Corn Law Rhymer' — to example how semiotic analysis of a popular cultural artifact, i.e. the local press, can contribute to a historical understanding of socio-economic realities. Between 1825 and 1835, the city of Sheffield (in South Yorkshire), England, consisted mostly of mechanics in cutlery trades, artisans, and other skilled industrial laborers. However, for these members of the country's working and lower-middle classes as well as some merchants and manufacturers, the 1815 Corn Laws were seriously hurting their livelihoods. To this one measure was attributed reduction in journeymen's wages, joblessness among industrial and agricultural laborers, over-cultivation and devastation of soil, as well as soaring food prices. Lord Milton (one of few *landed* MPs who abandoned the protectionist argument) remarked that the Corn Laws created an 'artificial scarcity' by halting the importation of foreign wheat, literally closing the ports, until the nation's own crop averaged 80*s*. [shillings] a quarter.[1] Typical British free traders, like Sheffield's 'industrious masses,' complained that this tariff reduced the country's wheat supply at a time when the local product failed to satisfy the population's demands.[2]

In March 1828, the Duke of Wellington, as the Prime Minister and positively disposed towards the 1815 Corn Laws, introduced a sliding scale, modelled after the bill proposed by George Canning in the previous session.[3] Sixty-six shillings would be the pivot point, and as the domestic price rose, the duty would decline. For every shilling decline in the domestic price below 66*s*., the duty would increase by 1*s*. So when the domestic price reached 73*s*. a quarter, only a nominal 1*s*. duty remained. The bill passed in June 1828, and served as the basic Corn Law until its repeal in 1846.[4]

But prior to 1846, the 1815 Corn Laws spawned a reformist and agitational mood in Sheffield which the *Sheffield Independent* earnestly reported.[5] The *Independent* opposed the Corn Laws, and repeatedly affirmed its intention to use fully the 'power of the press' to achieve repeal. Borrowing protest strategies of the British antislavery movement, the *Sheffield Independent*, on February 4, 1826, pledged to defeat the Corn Bills which it accused the landed gentry of misrepresenting:

> {L}et every periodical which is not bribed, or brought up, put forth all its strength to set the true state of affairs before the public, and boldly combat the accumulated falsehoods of the farmers' Journals, and such like abominable, lying, and time-serving, publications. Let there be meetings called in every town and borough, to draw up, and forward petitions to his Majesty's Government against that root of all evils, that prime bulwark of an unbearable tyranny, the Corn Laws.[6]

This essay will semiotically document the *Independent*'s commitment to the abolition of the Corn Laws. It is based on codification and analysis of all the 'newstexts' — editorials, minutes of town meetings, Parliamentary speeches, public letters (even from the middling sort), and excerpts from polemical pamphlets — in the *Sheffield Independent* for the period 1825-35 that even slightly discuss Corn Laws.[7] Protest against Britain's 1815 Corn Law has been documented in numerous quantitative and narrative studies, which usually put in chronological order the causes and consequences of this protectionist legislation.[8] What has not been analyzed, however, are the characteristics of the discursive protest against the law.

As a semiotic analysis of the *Sheffield Independent*, this essay will demonstrate that coincident with the construction of a dialectic about the 1815 Corn Law is the employment of an arsenal of linguistic devices (especially metaphor, repetition, alliteration, figures of speech, and substitution) which challenge and subvert the hegemonic power of the 'landed interest.' Anti-Corn Law newstexts in the *Sheffield Independent*, collectively, construct a system of polysemic signs — a discourse — that paints two socio-economically polarized realities: the 'landed interest' opposing 'all the consumers' — from merchants to labourers — over the corn bills. Other contributions to this discourse formation are signifiers from many different fields of knowledge — rural economy, sports (e.g. foxhunting), Scripture, biology, etc. — which strengthen distinctions made between the two attitudinally different worlds, thereby boldly outlining the sides of a debate. Yet, as the polysemic signs help distinguish the contesting sides of the Corn Law debate, they also reverse the position of hegemony held by the two groups. Therefore, in the aggregate and axiomatically, the anti-Corn Law discourse in the *Sheffield Independent* ultimately transforms 'landlords' into 'jolter-headed foxhunters,' while the 'industrious' masses — those having physically invested the most into the country's economic base — are portrayed as humanists and as the legitimate heirs of the soil and all of its means.

I have borrowed the term 'newstexts' from Teun Van Dijk, who explains that it fuses two concepts — news and text: by 'news' he means 'a text or discourse on radio, on TV, or in the newspaper, in which new information is given about recent events'; 'text' refers to the *content or meaning* of the factual information, but the 'newstext does not include advertisments, weather reports or comics.'[9] The scope of this paper has been deliberately narrowed to a ten-year period for two additional reasons: one, manageability; and two, in 1835, Parliament decided to suspend discussion of the Corn Laws for at least one year.

I

Portraying nineteenth-century Britain as a country of two worlds was common in literary annals, as documented in Asa Briggs's seminal essay on the nomenclature of 'class.' And in 1805, forty years before Friedrich Engels wrote his famous work, *The Condition of the Working Class in England*, Charles Hall wrote: 'The people in a civilised state may be divided into many different orders; but, for the purpose of investigating the manner in which they enjoy or are deprived of the requisites to support the health of their bodies and minds, they need only be divided into two classes, viz., the rich and the poor. . .' Socialist reformer Robert Owen, who usually spoke in terms of a conventional three-class society (upper, middle, and lower), occasionally also envisioned society as bi-polar: 'There will be . . . at no distant period, a union of the government, aristocracy, and non-producers on the one part and the Industrious Classes, the body of people generally, on the other part; and the most formidable power for good or evil are thus forming.' Within the *Independent*'s newstexts, the binary tendency continues, for two groups emerge which establish the opposing sides in the Corn Law debate[10]: 'Landlords' or the 'landed interest' always constitute one full side of the question. And the bulk of the population, often referred to as the 'industrious classes' or 'working classes,' constitutes the other side.

First, some words about the 'landed interest' (or 'landlords'). The phrase 'landed interest' appears frequently as interchangeable with 'agricultural interest.' Actually, the *Independent* often groups all persons associated with the soil (farmers, tenants, toilers, landlords, etc.) under a single rubric, like the label 'agriculturists.' But it will be shown later how other issues differentiate farmers from landlords, and how the word 'interest' signifies an association of the 'landed' with 'agriculture.' In his study of 'class' mentioned previously, historian Asa Briggs traces the use of the word 'interest,' and he concludes that it served 'to direct attention to particular economic groupings.'[11] But in the *Independent*, the word 'interest' appears occasionally in different referent combinations — such as 'agricultural interest,' 'mutual interest,' and even 'all interest' — yet it still only applies to and identifies two large socio-economic groupings — the landed proprietors, or the 'agricultural interest,' with everyone and anyone else falling into 'all interest' or 'mutual interest' groups. The term 'interest' in the *Independent* also figures synonomously with 'class' or 'section,' as used in Lord Milton's treatise against the Corn Laws. In his pamphlet, Milton entreats his fellow landowners to reconsider the societal repercussions of the 1815 Corn Laws 'upon every class of society, upon every interest, upon every section of the community.'[12]

The *Independent* is relentless in its resolve to depict the 'landed interest' as the evil force behind the Corn Laws. It assaults landed magnates by injecting familial signifiers ('brothers and sisters') to attack primogeniture as part of its polemic, as well as to resurrect a vision of wholeness or national unity that at one time was observed and enjoyed by all. The press charges 'the landed' with making

> beggars of his brothers and sisters, by absorbing the whole of the property, to himself, which to be allowed to retain, he compromises with the Government, by the invention of every abuse, in numberless and nameless pensions, and sinecure places, in Bishoprics, Rectorships, and so on, and in a large standing Army and Navy, the officers of which fall little short of the number of Common men.[13]

The *Independent* theorizes that before the practice of primogeniture — which dictated that real estate of a person dying intestate pass exclusively to the eldest son or eldest male heir — the land 'belonged to the people; the people settled it; the people defended it' (4 Feb. 1826, p. 1, col. 6). At that time the 'people' constituted a nation of culturally and/or biologically related 'brothers and sisters.' The press uses rhetoric that resembles the language of Biblical parables, for it makes an uncanny link here between the historical record and the story of Joseph in Egypt, sold into slavery by his siblings. Jealousy, greed, and theft caused splits in Joseph's father's house, and these same vices have polarized England.

The parasitic description of the ruling class as 'absorbing the whole of the property, to [itself]' conjures up a vision of sedentary or sessile aquatic animals with numerous pores remarkable for sucking up water or other substances. This language of dietetics, and of the land as digestible, by implication characterizes the ruling hegemony of Britain as 'leeches'[14] or absorbers. We also learn that these elites gain rights to the land through acts of collusion with the Government, Bishops, Rectors, military personnel, and so on. Their conniving and theft is ongoing since land ownership is essential to their very existence.

Lumped in with the 'whole of the property' fall 'tenant rents.' After the Napoleonic Wars, the *Independent* relates, landlords 'fearing nothing as much as the reduction of their rents, raised a plan for protection saying it was impossible for taxed English agriculturists to compete with Continental growers.'[15] But the Corn Laws of 1815 'conspired against the people' — for 'the farmers believing that the prices thus fixed [wheat at 80*s*. a quarter] would be realized [and] readily took land at exorbitant rents. Between the enactment of this law and 1822, the fluctuations in the price of wheat were 112 shillings a quarter to 38 shillings. The effect of this was tremendously injurious to the farmers, and many of them were ruined.'[16] So, the *Independent* resounds, 'the Corn Laws were passed to make the breadeaters pay, besides their own share of taxation, the share of the farmers too, and this out of no compassion for the farmers, but solely to fill the pockets of the landlords.'[17] The 'landlords' are, therefore, justifiably described as 'a selfish and ambitious class of men whose sole object in continuing the present system of Corn monopoly is to keep up their rents. They know full well that this cannot be done unless high prices be secured to the produce of the land.'[18] Yet they refused to reduce the rents.[19]

Like editorials, minutes of town meetings contributed to the formation of the *Independent*'s anti-Corn Law discourse by exposing further the greed of propertied capitalists. For example, at a 'Public Meeting: On the Subject of the Corn Laws,' a Sheffield mechanic surnamed Hill reasoned that a 'regular importation of grain would keep prices steady' and provide the farmer with a system to better judge what rents he 'could afford to give for any land he might be induced to take.' But as he continues, Hill's remarks disclose his burdensome knowledge of a cruel and unjust reality where parsimonious 'landholders' perniciously manage to retain control and the tenant famer remains dispossessed and powerless with or without tenancy reform:

> [S]upposing a farmer's lease [expired] when the price of grain was high; he applies to his landlord to have it renewed; the landlord says, the price of Grain is now so and so, I cannot renew your lease without you [giving] me an advanced rent. Well, the farmer is obliged to submit[.] Now, there is [sic] some phenomena in nature [which] takes place . . . the Ports of these Realms open for the admission of Foreign Grain; . . . a great quantity is imported which lowers the price to a considerable amount. Now, the farmer, who is possessed of no capital, is compelled to sell at market price, to enable him to pay his rent. What is the consequence of this? Why, if he does not live under some benevolent landlord, he is racked up stick and stone, or otherwise it keeps him very poor, perhaps, as long as as he lives, having the old rent keeping him down.[20]

This hypothesized scenario indicates the ripple effect of the Corn Laws. Their immediate implementation after revision in 1815 resulted in the construction of a 'vexaciously oppressive' system tantamount to 'wage slavery' — a system that locked tenant farmers into set rents ('old rents') regardless of seasonal changes in grain production or market values.[21]

As mentioned earlier, the *Independent* frequently refers to all parties with a vested interest in the land as 'agriculturists,' but it distinguishes between the 'farmer' and the 'landlord.' Both Hill's dialogue as well as that of the *Independent*'s editorials implicitly and categorically separate farmers from landlords. Strategically, anti-Corn Law publicists tried to convince tenant farmers that they were merely rural equivalents of industrial laborers. This technique was intended to divide the 'landed interest.'[22] So the term 'agriculturists' appears frequently in the *Independent*, but its intended referent is 'landlords' just as that of 'farmers' is the 'toiler' or 'agricultural labourer.'

Historical circumstances may explain the *Independent*'s differentiation between 'tillers of the soil' and 'agriculturists,' since by 1815, falling on the heels of the enclosure movement, 'agricultural society consisted of three principal groups,' according to Donald G. Barnes: 'the landlord, the larger farmer, and the rural labourer who was subsisting in part on poor rates.'[23] On one occasion the *Independent* inadvertently admits that agriculturists normatively consisted of more than just two groups. In its remarks on the Report of the Committee on Agriculture (1833) the *Independent* mentions that tenancy rents for agricultural laborers are 'a vast deal higher than [those of] industrious and intelligent tenants, possessing the advantages of capital and experience.'[24] Yet strategically, the *Independent* would typically group farmers together, and then situate them with the 'industrious classes.' Notably, when the substantive issue of 'rent' surfaces, an 'agriculturist' becomes known strictly as a 'farmer.' Hence, the concept 'rent' introduces the idea of an existing hierarchial socio-economic structure.[25]

It is very important to highlight how all of these signifiers — farmer, 'labourer,' toiler, agriculturist, landlord — which are similar generically, acquire new signifieds when re-constituted in anti-Corn Law discourse. This phenomenon demonstrates the potential power possessed by words of any discourse when they are taken out of their familiar domain. Returning to the situation with farmers, though, although there were attempts to enlist them in the anti-Corn Law campaign, historians remind us that

> the farmer remained for the most part protectionist; working to small margins, he was 'terrified at what might be the result if repeal were passed.' Moreover, landlords expected their tenants to share their political commitments; there was always the threat of eviction or the refusal to renew a lease, and in the years after the Reform Act [1832] it was still not uncommon for tenants to receive written advice from the landlord's agent at election time naming the candidate who ought to be supported.[26]

Nevertheless, to Corn Law protestors, the farmer represented just another disenfranchised constituent functioning at the lowest level of society; hence, the farmer resembled all other 'industrious masses' who witnessed themselves fighting daily against slippery forces that landed them in desperate states of homelessness, starvation, and joblessness — as statistics from Lord Milton's reprint will later illustrate and confirm. But more about 'landlords.'

Any newstext with the signifier 'landlords' or syntagmatically related terms also takes the form of an arsenal of name-calling.[27] In fact, if all the lexicals to describe 'landlords' were arranged in a paradigmatic axis, they would unsettle the position of power the graphematic 'landlords' signifies or denotes.[28]

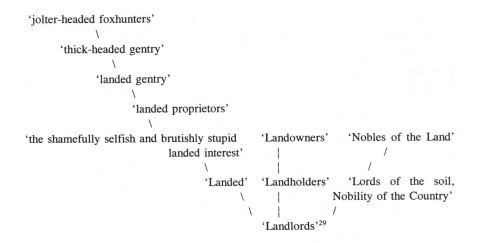

'jolter-headed foxhunters'
  \
  'thick-headed gentry'
    \
    'landed gentry'
      \
      'landed proprietors'
        \
'the shamefully selfish and brutishly stupid   'Landowners'   'Nobles of the Land'
          landed interest' | /
            \ | /
            'Landed' 'Landholders' 'Lords of the soil,
              \ | Nobility of the Country'
              \ | /
              'Landlords'[29]

Arranged upward or 'headward' rather than downward (which seems logical given the inherent nature of images), the axes depict landlords as spatially gravitating further and further away from the ground: 'the shamefully, selfish and brutishly stupid landed interest,' 'thick-headed gentry,' and 'jolter-headed foxhunters.' For all their political, social, and economic position, these 'nobles' are depicted as mindless, thoughtless, and rootless. They live off (and above) the land but not on it. The *Independent* demystified those who comprised the country's hegemony — 'the landed interest' — by attacking their mental faculties.

Highly significant in this axis of descriptors is the signifer 'foxhunters.'[30] The compound 'foxhunters' stimulates discussion about its social connotations, its zoological referent, and its allusion to sport. Like the carnivorous creatures they chased for sport, the 'foxhunters' — i.e. landlords — by denying workers (whom we can liken to a lower species: insects, rodents, etc., which foxes consume) unconditional access to daily bread, indirectly prey on the flesh of the masses. 'A rapacious oligarchy,'[31] as they are also known, socially endowed with elements of power, force and cunning — akin to a 'fox' — threatens the very survival of the propertyless. Indeed, most of Britain is defenseless and cannibalistically 'hunted' out for every shilling it earns. Landlords seem passionately driven to possess all in their sight.[32]

An even more glaring vision of how the landed abuse British laborers materializes when they engage in the sport of foxhunting. Shooting, unlike hunting, was legally restricted to a privileged group. As 'leisure activity' (as opposed to 'labourers' work'), it was 'a birthright' of the aristocracy.[33] Britain's history of foxhunting contains countless bloodstained narratives of the 'great masters of the hounds' who blatantly trampled over the 'lower orders' (their tenants or local laborers) who interfered in any way (from being physically in attendance at a hunt, or agitating the hounds, or practicing vulpicide) with the 'conventions' created for their national sport. In fact, their cannibalistic tendency had been developed into a maxim by the end of the century: 'Better kill a man than a fox.'[34] In his brief sketches of early master huntsmen, Raymond Carr tells us that not one 'MFH' did not harbor an acute disdain for the 'lower classes.' John Chaworth Musters, known as Jack Musters (1777-1849), physically assaulted all members of the 'lower orders' who offended him. Squire Osbaldeston (1781-1866), considered one of the 'greatest' masters of hounds, paid the local village inns two pounds to distribute drinks to all local stocking makers who stayed home during hunting festivities.[35]

Biographies of wealthly landed huntsmen typically characterize this class as permanently 'rooted' in the ruling structure of the country. Yet the allusion to 'fox' in the *Independent*'s newstexts adds to the ironic depiction of landowners as groundless and powerless. Most varieties of vulpes possess very short legs, lie low, run at great speeds, leap fences at least two meters high, swim well, but are basically terrestial animals moving by walk or trot.[36] One could reason, then, that any spatial elevation of such a creature would render him harmless, immobile, and out-of-sorts. In fact, when one recalls the earlier vision of the landed as parasitic and aquatic animals, we might conclude that any spatial verticality would be life-threatening for them.

Clearly, in this context the factually-constructed image of the fox as a mortally treacherous animal changes into myth. In this new mythical context, this zoological signifier also functions as a subversive tool for the *Independent* by debunking the perception of landlords as omnipotent. This semiotic interpretation of the fox suggests that legitimate political power comes not through hereditary succession (i.e. the divine right of kings or by the law of primogeniture) but derives from and must be sustained by a democratic polity, which believes in the 'natural rights of man.' Echoing Thomas Paine in this respect, the *Independent* appears positively disposed toward the lower classes, suggesting that those closer to the 'soil' are not only more powerful than the monarchical elites — although their power is latent — but also they come by their power 'naturally' and, hence, legitimately.[37]

In the 1830s, John Stuart Mill acknowledged that the 'English government is an oligarchy of landholders' [whose] 'fancies go before all other people's most substantial interest.' But Mill believed a formidable group of land reformers could change this reality. He looked somewhat to the working class for support but principally to the middle classes — that group whose 'most essential interests are made to give way to the idlest fears, the most silly prejudices of the landowners.'[38] It is to the worker and the middle classes that we now turn.

II

The *Sheffield Independent*'s anti-Corn Law newstexts semantically identify and contextualize the 'other Britain' as the world of 'industrious classes': farmers, factory hands, mechanics/artisans, as well as upper-middle-class merchants and manufacturers.[39] Because salaries and export ventures were market-driven productions dependent on the system of free trade, the *Independent* portrays Britain's laborers and merchants as those most adversely affected, directly, by the precarious and erratic scale of duty imposed on foreign products. In its February 4, 1826 issue, the editor wrote 'I know, what every man in business knows, and what they [workers] know very well themselves, that the wages by a great part of the working population are not, nor have not been this long time, sufficient to purchase even the necessaries of life' (4 Feb. 1826, p. 1, col. 6).

Anti-Corn Law newstexts highlighting the 'working classes' were meant to silence 'the most insufferable cant' by speaking the truth. Whereas newstexts featuring landlords rhetorically invoked metaphors such as 'fox hunters' and resorted to name-calling, the news extracts about the 'working population' delineated tangible facts and figures. These statistical reports centered on such issues as low wages, fluctuations in the duty on wheat, acceleration of technological development abroad, loss of a national pool of skilled labor, and free trade.[40]

Anti-Corn Law writers promoted a spirit of solidarity among the industrious. In fact, the *Independent* exposes and supports this 'interest' bonding by quoting viable reforms proposed by members of one group (e.g. Sheffield mechanics) to resolve the economic dilemmas of another (e.g. tenant farmers), as in the case of Sheffielder Hill, mentioned earlier.[41] However, the *Independent* also identifies these groups as separate, which in reality, they were. Consider again Hill's speech at the 'Public Meeting,' reported in the November 25, 1826 issue of the *Independent*, which inadvertently broaches the issue of diversity in the 'industrious classes.' Hill, like Ebenezer Elliott, an urban agitator against corn legislation, hypothesizes a scenario which he believes depicts the tenant farmers' subjugation. By feigning knowledge of an oppressive rural lifestyle, he assumes the social identity of a member of this 'interest' group. But the mere fact that the situation is imaginary (as the word 'supposing' denotes) betrays Hill's superficial familiarity with farmers, and indicates distance, instead, between the speaker and his subject. Hill must force identification with farmers because he comes from a different social sphere. Because Hill's language is in conflict with his ulterior motive, his 'text' presents an illusion of 'class' unity. Hill generalizes about 'the farmer' entrapped economically by high rents instead of referencing particular individuals. His actual acquaintance with a tiller of the soil, therefore, is as elusive as his description of 'some benevolent landlord.' (The chasm manufacturers and merchants created between themselves and freemen will be discussed later.)

Extracts which the *Independent* published from Lord Milton's pamphlet on the Corn Laws reveal a correlation between region and income of agricultural workers. Although dubbed a pamphlet, Milton's 'letter' (generically speaking) to landowners shows that agricultural workers in partly manufacturing districts could bargain for higher wages. Milton's document details wage differences between agricultural workers in occupationally distinct regions, as well as those between men and women. The highest wages given to a farmer between 1809-1814, who resided in partly manufacturing country, were

> 15*s*. a week (in 1813); and the lowest 11*s*. a week. From 1814 to 1824 they were generally 13*s*. or 14*s*., and occasionally 15*s*., never falling below 13*s*. Since 1824, they have been at 14*s*. and 15*s*. In another district, (purely agricultural) the wages of farming labourers, from 1809 to 1815, were 12*s*. a week, and those of women, 5*s*.; in 1830, they were 12*s*. and those of women, 4*s*. 6*d*. In a third, purely agricultural district, the highest wages given in the month of May, since the commencement of the war in 1803, were 14*s*. a week (in 1812, 1813, and 1814) and the lowest, 9*s*. (in 1823.) The highest average price of wheat in the same period was in 1812; the lowest in 1822.[42]

These figures gain meaning when weighed against the average price per quarter loaf or pound of bread. Between 1819 and 1828 it was 1*s*. 6*d*. and between 1829 to 1835 it was almost 2*s*.[43] In 1826, wheat sold for £3,5*s*. (exclusive of duty) per quart; in 1827 and 1828, it sold for £3,2*s*.; in 1829, it rose to £4,6*s*.; in 1830 and 1832 it dropped to £3,10*s*.; in 1831, it was £3,18*s*.; but in 1833 it dropped a whole pound.[44] And with the tariff assessment, wheat was definitely priced above an affordable limit. Because wages were so low laborers budgeted money only for food.

Lord Milton's additional figures attest that agricultural workers with more disposal income were still too improvished to purchase 'the necessaries of life' even during the boom periods (particularly from 1800-1812) because of the exorbitant price of wheat:

> The weekly consumption of wheat in a labourer's family, consisting of himself, his wife, and three children, may be stated at about two-thirds of a bushel; the amount of their enjoyments will therefore depend, [*ceteris paribus*], upon the excess of the weekly wages above the price of two-thirds of a bushel of wheat . . . . it appears, that in the first period of five years ending with 1807, the average excess of the weekly wages above the price of two-thirds of a bushel of wheat, amounted to 4*s*. 1*d*.; in the second period, ending with 1812, it was 2*s*. 10*d*.; in the third, ending with 1817, it was 5*s*. 8*d*.; in the fourth, ending with 1822, it was 5*s*. 10*d*.; and in the last, ending with 1827, it was 5*s*. 4*d*. It necessarily follows from this statement, that the period which is uniformly cited as the greatest of agricultural prosperity was precisely that in which the surplus income of the labourer was the smallest. . .

In the *Independent* anti-Corn Law newstexts, the 'industrious classes' also included the 'mechanics.' But when discussion centers around this group, the newstexts expose a chasm which manufacturers and merchants created between themselves and less economically well-off freemen.[45] By 'mechanic' we mean both semi-solitary workers, assistants hired by master cutlers, as well as small ironmongers.[46] Like farmers, mechanics recognized the controlling factors which separated them from the commodities they produced. As the voice for all exploited groups, the *Independent* claims mechanics lost income because manufacturers set prices on their products.[47] Moreover, the *Independent*'s editorial of February 4, 1826 asserts that manufacturers drained the already depressed economy by pricing non-agricultural necessaries without thought or sensitivity to the working consumer's average weekly earnings. According to the *Independent*, manufacturers were preventing 'the industrious mechanic from selling his labour at the highest prices and at the same time made him pay two or three prices for everything he consumes.' One must conclude, then, that power and position kept the 'working population' socially stratified and, semantically, a diverse body.

As in the case of the farmers, semi-independent cutlers' earnings were disproportionate to the costs of necessaries (*Independent*, 4 Feb. 1826, p. 1, col. 6.).[48] Although craftsmen's average weekly wages were slightly higher than that of rural workers, Lloyd asserts that 'the average standard earnings [were] low in relation to the degree of skilled workmanship involved.'[49] In terms of mechanics' wages, other variables affected their actual earnings. They suffered deductions for tools and materials essential to their trade,[50] and had to pay out the traditional monthly contractual agreements: rent of workplace and equipment (e.g. the forger for his hearth, the grinder for his trough, the cutler for his side, etc.), as well as the cost of power, and the engagement of assistant workers. Many skilled craftsmen also had a short life expectancy due to the environmental and occupational hazards of their trade. Charles Turner Thackrah documented as early as the first quarter of the nineteenth century that cutlers were generally intemperate and short-lived. John Tatham reaffirmed Thackrah's research later in the century.[51] While grinders made the highest salaries in the cutlery industry, as Lloyd's and Bowley's data show, they also contracted the most serious diseases (lung, pulmonary, tuberculosis, eye injuries, etc.) and, accordingly, had the shortest life expectancy of all occupations.[52] In his study of *The Cutlery Trade*, Lloyd found that from 1830 to 1840, at least four-fifths of the deaths among steel-fork grinders occurred while they were between the ages of twenty and thirty-nine; but for the population as a whole, less than one-third died during these ages of their lives.[53]

Sheffield artisans, actually, lived comfortably when compared with those in other manufacturing districts. During hard times, many became 'penny capitalists' and advanced into 'master cutlers.' Because of their entrepenurial distinction and skilled labor they were categorized as members of the middle class, though 'hardly raised above the lowest,' as Ebenezer Elliott qualifies.[54] Many small ironmongers like Elliott felt the pains of penury familiar to other members of the working classes, recounts Arthur L. Bowley in his classic work *Wages in the United Kingdom in the Nineteenth Century*: 'Influenced by a marked extent by commercial depressions and inflations,' iron tradesmen's earnings were 'actually regulated by the market price of iron and steel.' While wages were often determined by a number of shillings 'to each £1. in the selling price per ton' of iron, actual weekly earnings for the bar iron merchant were not 'directly proportionate to the piece-rates; for in times of inflation a man earns just what he pleases; in times of depression he can scarely make a living.' In fact, 'iron fell faster than most other commodities owing to improvements in the method of smelting in the blast furnace.'[55]

Lower middle-class mechanics like Elliott, Hill, Wright, Sheldon, Eyre, Cullock, and Bradshaw, voiced their economic aspirations but remained acutely self-conscious of their social place, a place undoubtedly beneath that of manufacturers. And the *Independent*'s reporting reinforced this stratification by occupationally identifying individual speakers at public gatherings as 'Mr. Bishop, another mechanic,' or 'Mr. G. Knowles (a working man),' or 'Mr. Morton (another workman) . . . having a numerous family of small children,' for example. While such class typing may have been unconscious, the *Independent*'s Corn Law newstexts document how psychologically entrenched class consciousness was in this society. As suggested earlier, industrial elites maintained control over working freemen comparable to the power landlords wielded over their tenants. Though the lower classes respectfully recognized the authority wielded by the ruling class, they were not deferential nor voiceless, as Hill's testimony at the Sheffield assembly of November 25, 1826 demonstrates: 'I sincerely hope, Mr. Chairman, that though the mechanics of this country have long been ignobly termed the "swinish multitude," they would now be found qualified both to think and speak upon even such subjects as the Corn Laws.'[56]

Just as other industrialists tried to align themselves politically with agricultural laborers and factory hands, this middling section of local townsmen — which R. S. Neale paradigms as neither working nor middle class — forged a more plausible identification with manufacturers and merchants through the pronouns 'we' and 'ours.'[57] In his remarks before fellow 'working men,' Hill states:

> [T]he landowner is protected by a number of Restrictive Laws, all of which have a tendency to make provisions dear; such, for instance, as the tax upon butter, cheese, eggs, apples, poultry, etc. . .; these taxes are all for the protection of the landowner, whilst the manufacturer has to contend in the same market with the foreigner, whose provisions are much cheaper than ours; consequently they can perform labour at a much lower rate than we can.

Similar to other newstexts, the above passage highlights the two adversaries of the corn debate. Hill's speech distinguishes the 'landowner' and 'they' from the 'manufacturer,' 'ours,' and 'we.' An even closer syntactic examination of the quote reveals Hill's cognitive association of landowners with the law. Each clause with the signifier 'landowner' also contains a derivative of 'protect': for example, 'the landowner is protected . . .' or 'for the protection of the landowner.' Whereas the landowner is blanketed from economic collapse, the manufacturer is vulnerable in the face of a competitive and 'foreign' (or unknown) market. Not only does the manufacturer face possible financial disaster but even his physical survival is unsecured, for he, too, partakes of 'provisions' which are 'dear' and which are for him also 'taxed.' Industrious classes paid 'dearly' not only for bread and other necessaries, but also they paid taxes on the very materials out of which their own products derived. '[T]he iron, the steel, the wood, the bones, in fact the whole almost of the raw material that he makes use of is taxed, which the foreigner knows nothing of,' charged Sheffield lower-middle-class citizen Hill.[58] Unhampered by excessive taxes or tariffs, cheaply made foreign cutlery easily competed in the home market, and threatened the viability of Britain's own cutlery industry. The *Independent* editorialized that 'Manufacturers would as little relish the untaxed admission of cutlery . . . as the farmers would the unrestricted importation of grain.'[59]

Even though the lower-middle-class mechanics crafted their Corn Law protest to present themselves as representative of middle-class industrialists as well, the *Independent*'s editorials suggest that manufacturers and merchants perceived themselves as the most victimized by protectionism. Lending substance to the manufacturers' contention, the *Independent*'s editorial of October 25, 1834 accused the landed interest of crippling the nation for its own personal, immediate monetary gain:

> At the end of the war, our manufacturers were fifty years a-head of all others; and had they been allowed fair play, we should necessarily have attained such a degree of national prosperity, and universal comfort as it is difficult to conceive. But we were ruled by landlords, . . . fearing nothing as much as the reduction of their rents. . .[60]

Manufacturers joined their economic status and progressivism with that of the entire nation to dramatize their economic suffering as always exponentially greater than that of the others. They reasoned that the Corn Laws retarded Britain's growth as an industrial nation, subverted her commerical supremacy in the world community, and fostered the emigration of skilled labor.

But according to both the mechanic and manufacturing 'industrious classes,' countries dependent upon Britain's importation of their foreign grain responded to the restrictions by refusing to accept Britain's manufactured exports. So the Corn Laws' immediate retaliatory and long-term repercussions dealt a death blow to Britain's merchants and manufacturers. In their Parliamentary petition on the subject of the Corn Laws, the mechanics of Sheffield resolved that restrictions on exported manufactured goods equally affected their capacity to obtain adequate incomes, as well as that of the 'master' and large-scale merchant. Trade prohibitions engendered 'an unfriendly jealous feeling and disposition towards this country,' remarked Hill, 'calculated to drive [others] to manufacture for themselves those articles this nation has for centuries supplied them with and will ultimately cause them to become nations of manufacturers and artizans to the utter and inevitable ruin of this kingdom.'[61]

Though a diverse body, each middle-class constitutent was ideologically wed to the other in the Corn Law debate, because each subgroup felt robbed of its competitive edge in foreign trade. Rather than wait for England to lift protectionist measures, foreign markets either located cheaper resources or established their own factories to manufacture products previously imported. These new industries, ironically, were often sustained by the technological aid of British immigrants. Hill noted, 'I am credibly informed, that one of the largest steam engines ever erected, is in a state of forwardness for the purpose of manufacturing against us in Germany.'[62] Supporting the complaints of this constituency is an editorial reprinted from the *Bath Journal* that states, 'by prohibiting the introduction of corn from those countries whose staple is corn, we provoke hostility; and that, as a retaliative measure, those countries prohibit our manufacturers in return . . . .' The editor adds 'can we blame the conduct of the government of the United States of America, who have prohibited nearly the whole of our manufacture of goods, avowedly in consequence of our having prohibited their corn and flour?'[63]

III

In conclusion, the *Sheffield Independent* serves as a 'cultural artifact' consisting of linguistic variables that inform our understanding of the reality from which its newstexts came. The *Independent*'s Corn Law newstexts constructed a discourse that presented two contesting social realities. Because of its political strategies and language: 'meetings called in every town and borough, to draw up and forward petitions to his Majesty's Government against that root of all evils', Richard Cobden would describe the *Independent* as a 'middle class agitator' using 'working class rhetoric.'[64] Yet similar to William Howitt (Quaker journalist who also bashed aristocratic privilege under the pseudonym John Hampden, Junior),[65] the *Independent* borrowed working class rhetoric (e.g. vivid exaggerations of oppressive forces, the 'root of all evils, that prime bulwark of an unbearable tyranny') to denounce the Corn Laws and its advocates. To its credit, the *Independent*'s Corn Law discourse acknowledges all affected parties. Corn Law protest brought together a broad spectrum of commited individuals: some concerned about their profits, others about their earnings. The *Independent*, inadvertently, exposed its own ideological bias with its description of Corn Law protest as a struggle between 'the consumer and the aristocracy' rather than 'labor versus capital,' as the familiar chant of the day called it.[66] Popular rhetoric indicted merchants and manufacturers along with the 'landed interest' because they contributed to the artisans' precarious economic welfare. The *Independent*, on the other hand, linked the upper-middle class with the struggling 'free traders.'

Because of its ideologically coded newstexts, the *Independent* functioned as a platform for Corn Law protest. As a staunch advocate of 'free trade,' the paper resoundingly proposed a single solution to the economic problems attributed to the Corn Laws: 'repeal.' In the March 15, 1834 issue, it unflinchingly reaffirmed its discursive commitment toward the ultimate defeat of the measure:

> Let none be discouraged by doubts and alarms. Everything can be accomplished by the use of means. The experience of the last ten years affords the most satisfactory evidence of the efficacy of perservering discussion and activity. . . The more this subject [Corn Laws] is discussed, the sooner it will be brought to a successful issue.[67]

* *Angela M. Leonard is Visiting Assistant Professor of History at Bucknell University.*

ENDNOTES

1. 'Lord Milton and the Corn Laws,' *The Sheffield Independent*, 13 Oct. 1832, p. 4, col. 1; reprinted from *The Sun*. Lord Milton, son of the fourth Earl Fitzwilliam, closely collaborated with the manufacturing classes of the West Riding between 1800 and 1830. On their behalf he championed several reforms. See David Spring, 'Earl Fitzwilliam and the Corn Laws,' *American Historical Review* 59 (1954): 287-304; and E. A. Smith, *Whig Principles and Party Politics: Earl Fitzwilliam and the Whig Party, 1748-1833* (Totowa, New Jersey: Rowman and Littlefield, 1975). Anthony Wood summarizes that 'the Corn Law [of 1815] was worked out on the assumption that eighty shillings a quarter [£4] was the lowest selling price that would give the producer a reasonable remuneration.' When the price dropped, no importation of any foreign corn was permitted; but when it rose above eighty shillings, the ports would reopen to duty-free importation. 'Thus the law would bring in no revenue. The ports would simply be open or shut for three-monthly periods according to the average selling price in the preceding six weeks' (Wood, *Nineteenth-Century Britain 1815-1914*, 2nd ed. [Essex, England: Longman, 1982], 61-62).

2. With protectionism, farmers 'exhausted' the soil. Retrospectively, the *Sheffield Independent* remarked that this agricultural system 'by which rich harvests are made ruinous to the tiller of the soil, has worked to perfection. An unexampled succession of fertile years has brought many of them to ruin' (25 Oct. 1834, p. 2, col. 4).

3. As early as 1826, *The Sheffield Independent* had anticipated the problems with the 1815 legislation. The sliding scale, the press claimed, was manipulable and, therefore, problematic. Recorded transactions of quarterly averages were not all *bona fide*: 'if a large corn merchant wished to depress the average, he would induce a friend to purchase inferior corn, by which a low average would be obtained; or if he was desirous to raise the average, he would sell the higher priced corn, which, of course, would effect his purpose' (28 Oct. 1826, p. 2, col. 5). Also, *The Sheffield Independent* stated, Lord Goderich showed Parliament the defects of the 1815 statute which allowed for extremes, manipulation, and overall instability in the market, moving from 'total prohibition of imports to unbounded admission of grain' when ports overflowed and stored imports were nearing spoilage. He proposed (on Lord Liverpool's behalf) that with a sliding scale the duty would fall as the home price of corn rose.

4. This was the Corn Law in effect when Ebenezer Elliott (the 'Corn Law Rhymer') published his first edition of *Corn Law Rhymes* in 1830, and the same measure operating when Richard Cobden established the Anti-Corn League in 1838. This

legislation also addressed other types of grain, each with their pivot points — barley at 33*s.*, oats at 25*s.*, and so on. In 1842, Sir Robert Peel revised the scale and it provided less protection than the 1828 Act.

5. Hereafter, the abbreviated title *Independent* refers to citations from *The Sheffield Independent*.

6. *Independent*, 4 Feb. 1826, p. 1, col. 6.

7. The newstexts studied in this essay are drawn directly from *The Sheffield Independent*, which is only available in the United Kingdom. Concurrent with *The Sheffield Independent* was another local, *The Sheffield Iris* (1794-1848), started by the local poet, James Montgomery. This was the only Sheffield paper in existence at the start of the nineteenth century, but by the late 1820s, the *Iris* could be best described as 'liberal conservative.' Because of the *Iris*'s ideological bent, which resulted in the imprisonment of James Montgomery in 1795 and 1796 on charges of political libel, the area reformers became less tolerant of the *Iris* and moved to establish their own paper to voice with vigor reform opinion, ergo *The Sheffield Independent*. See Donald Read, *Press and People 1790-1850: Opinion in Three English Cities* (Westport, CT: Greenwood Press, 1975), 73, 91.

8. Donald Grove Barnes, in *A History of the English Corn Laws from 1660-1846* (New York: F. S. Crofts and Co., 1930), gives a 'continuous narrative' of the Corn Laws from before 1660 to their repeal in 1846. This is not a history of the corn trade; instead, it emphasizes public opinion: 'An attempt is made in the case of each law passed and of each measure agitated to determine what social forces and classes favoured or opposed the proposal.' Barnes realizes that the best known Corn Laws are those of the nineteenth century, 'yet in the period down to 1660 importation was of less significance than the internal trade and exportation' (preface; 1). C. R. Fay chronicles that only after the 1660s did the legislation contribute to the formulation of 'a deliberate national policy.' The Corn Law of 1815 evolved in response to the agricultural depression of that year. By then, agriculturists and the landed interest had suffered tremendous fluctuations in their fortunes. An abundance of wheat in 1813 forced them to lower the market costs of their commodity (and this drop in corn prices would continue until 1835). But in 1814, a harvest of poor quality led to the admission of foreign corn (Charles R. Fay, *Life and Labour in the Nineteenth Century* [Cambridge, Eng.: Cambridge University Press, 1945], 137.

9. Van Dijk, *News as Discourse* (Hillsdale, New Jersey: Lawrence Erlbaum Associates, Publishers, 1986), 2-4.

10. Briggs, 'The Language of 'Class' in Early Nineteenth Century England' in *The Collected Essays of Asa Briggs, vol. 1: Words, Numbers, Places, People* (Urbana:

University of Illinois Press, 1985), 3-33. Hall, *The Effects of Civilisation on the People in European States* (London: By the Author, 1805), 3-4. Hall's divisions, however, are based on one's economic posture.   The 'rich' includes all those propertied: 'people in the same circumstances as to property enjoy the same advantages in those respects, whether the means of placing them in those circumstances are derived from landed estates, benefices of the church, the practice of the laws, or any other profession or trade' (4).   Hence, Hall criticizes equally manufacturers and merchants for depriving the poor of 'basic necessaries of life' (77-89).   Owens, 'Address to the Sovereign,' *The Crisis*, 4 August 1832; also in Briggs, 7.

11. Briggs, 3.

12. *Independent*, 21 Oct. 1826, p. 3, col. 3; and 7 Aug. 1830, p. 1, cols. 3-5; 13 Oct. 1832, p. 4, col 2.   Also review Lord Morpeth's words about the Corn Laws as favoring the 'landed interest' or 'one class,' 7 Aug. 1830, p. 1, col. 4.

13. *Ibid.*, 4 Feb. 1826, p. 1, col. 6.

14. *Ibid.*, 26 Oct. 1833, p. 2, col. 4.

15. *Ibid.*, 25 Oct. 1834, p. 2, col. 4.

16. *Ibid.*, 26 Oct. 1833, p. 2, col. 4.

17. *Ibid.*, 25 Oct. 1834, p. 2, col. 4.

18. *Ibid.*, 15 March 1834, p. 2, col. 5.

19. *Ibid.*, 25 Oct. 1834, p. 2, col. 4.

20. Report of a 'Public Meeting: On the Subject of the Corn Laws,' *ibid.*, 25 Nov. 1826, p. 1, col. 5.

21. Thomas Tooke outlines seasonal conditions from September 1792 to September 1856 in 'Appendix VI: Chronological Statement in a Summary Form of the Character of each of the Seasons in this Country, from 1792-1856,' in *The History of Prices, and the State of the Circulation from 1793 to 1837; Preceded by a Brief Sketch of the State of Corn Trade in the Last Two Centuries* (1838-57; reprint, New York: Johnson Reprint Corp., 1972), 6:470-88. See also, Barnes's *History of the English Corn Laws from 1660-1846*, and Fay, *Life and Labour in the Nineteenth Century*.

22. Briggs, 'The Language of 'Class''; David Martin, 'Land Reform,' in *Pressure from Without in Early Victorian England*, edited by Patricia Hollis (New York: St. Martin's Press, 1974), 144.

23. Barnes, 114.

24. *Independent*, 19 Oct. 1833, p. 4, col 1.

25. Consider T. Perronet Thompson's *Catechism on the Corn Laws*, 3rd ed. (London, 1826). He claims that the matter of 'rent' polarized 'landlords' and the rest of the nation. He defined rent as 'the superfluidity of price, or that part of it which is not necessary to pay for the production without a living profit.'

26. Martin, 144; G. Kitson Clark, *The Making of Victorian England* (Cambridge: Harvard University Press, 1962), 8; Norman Gash, *Politics in the Age of Peel: A Study in the Technique of Parliamentary Representation, 1830-1850* (London: Longman Press, 1953), 181. The personnel of agricultural Britain was far more complicated than indicated. For instance, some peasant entreprenuers owned small tracts of land which their entire family managed. Too, some estate tenant farmers were men 'of substantial means whose enterprise depended on hired labourers; many such farmers did little or no manual work. . .' (Dennis Mills, *Lord and Peasant in Nineteenth Century Britain*, (Totowa, NJ: Rowman & Littlefield, 1980), 28.

27. Secondary sources confirm that the related signifiers reflected the widely held attitudes toward landowners.

28. Saussure contends that language has two axes: the syntagmatic or horizontal axis and the paradigmatic or vertical axis. The syntagmatic axis can form a complete sentence, while the paradigmatic axis can delineate word substitutions for the completed thought or words in the syntagmatic axis. Anthony Easthope provides an illustration of this:

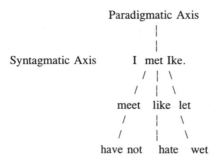

Ferdinand de Saussure, *Course in General Linguistics*; translated by Roy Harris (La Salle, IL: Open Court, 1972), 121-25; Easthope, *Poetry as Discourse* (London: Methuen, 1983), 36.

29. Most of these descriptors are scattered throughout the *Independent*, 4 Feb. 1826, 6 May 1826, 28 Oct. 1826, 23 June 1827, etc.

30. In her article, 'The Unspeakable in Pursuit of the Uneatable: Some Comments on Fox-Hunting,' *Folklore* 94 (1983): 86-90 (like the epigrammatic title she took from Oscar Wilde), Venetia Newall links fox hunting to the English country gentleman. Given the principal geographic site in this study, it is quite significant that the first sign of the modern hunting sport — of what evolved into the 'classic fusion of a great landed aristocrat and his tenant farmer in a common enthusiasm for foxhunting' — appeared in Yorkshire (a region of the country that includes Sheffield) once the Duke of Buckingham retired from the court of Charles II and committed himself almost full-time to the sport. See Raymond Carr, *English Fox Hunting: A History* (London: Weidenfeld & Nicolson, 1976), 28.   From the Saxon times onward, hunting was a favorite pastime for British upper classes, and hunting of foxes regularly dates back to the end of the seventeenth century. Poet John Masefield once noted, 'a man wanting to set down a picture of the society of England will find his models at the games'; see his 'Introduction' in *Reynard the Fox* (New York: The Macmillan Company, 1920), v.

31. *Independent*, 15 March 1834, p.2, col 5.

32. Twenty years after the *Independent*'s articles, the 'fox' was still depicted in literature as malevolent and callous. Hablot Knight Browne's (Phiz) monthly cover designs for Charles Dickens's *Bleak House* (1852-53) include a 'fox' weathervane. And on the book's cover, the weathervane is directed againt the wind, symbolically resisting the forces of social turmoil; the presence of the 'fox' in the illustration might signify the privileged class's apathy toward the helpless nineteenth-century British poor.

33. See William Baker's article, 'The Leisure Revolution in Victorian England: A Review of Recent Literature,' *Journal of Sport History* 6 (Winter 1979): 76-87.

34. Clarence Dalrymple Bruce, *The Essex Foxhounds: 1895-1926 and Adjacent Hunts* (London: Vinton and Company, n.d.), 166.

35. Carr, chapter six, 90-105. James Farquharson, anointed the 'Meynell of the West' (after the revered father of the modern sport, Hugo Meynell), was a staunch supporter of the Corn Laws, and preached to his tenants that without this legislation they would fall to the 'degrading level of those [labourers] on the continent.' As founder and president of the Blandford Agricultural Show, Farquharson established a prize for those laborers who reared the most children without parochial assistance. Given the fact that local proprietors were responsible for contributing substantially to poor relief, the latter attitude is very significant, because it also provides a sense of the parsimoniousness of the landed. An additional source on Farquharson is Alexander Henry Higginson, *The Meynell of the West* (London: Collins, 1936). Carr notes that vulpicide was an established 'sin' in the nineteenth century. In some communities 'landlords would have soon got rid of a tenant with notorious vulpicidal tendencies and many great hunting landlords made sure that their leases included a clause prohibiting the destruction of foxes,' 113. See also Newall, 87.

36. *The Larousse Encyclopedia of Animal Life* (New York: McGraw-Hill Book Co., 1967), 553-55; Ronald M. Nowak and John L. Paradiso, *Walker's Mammals of the World*, vol. 2, 4th ed. (Baltimore: Johns Hopkins University Press, 1983), 933-34, 959-60.

37. This notion finds support in other contemporaneous literature. Consider the description of the 'industrious orders' in *The Extraordinary Black Book: An Exposition of Abuses in Church and State, Courts of Law, Representation, Municipal and Corporate Bodies*: 'The industrious orders may be compared to the soil, out of which everything is evolved and produced; the other classes to the trees, tares, weeds and vegetables, drawing their nutriment, supported and maintained on its surface . . .' (London: Effingham Wilson, 1832 ed.), 217-18.

38. John Stuart Mill, 'Reorganization of the Reform Party,' *Westminister Review,* 32 (1839): 479, 485.

39. As with the word 'interest,' Asa Briggs contends that the phrase 'industrious classes' also communicated a sense of shared economic intentions among these sub-groups. He states the literature presents 'an influential social cross-current which directed attention not to the contrasting fortunes and purposes of 'middle classes' and 'working classes' but to a different division in industrial society, that between the industrial classes and the rest. Those writers who were more impressed by the

productive possibilities of a large-scale industry than afraid of social 'disintegration' dwelt on this second division' (Briggs, 7).

40. *The Independent* was relatively accurate in its depiction of Britain's economic landscape, for one can reference several government documents that validate these newstexts as an excellent source for locating legitimate protest against the 1815 and 1828 corn duty.

41. Also see the pamphlet 'Cheap Corn best for the Farmers proved in a Letter to George Hulme Sumner, Esq. M.P. for the County of Surrey,' *Independent*, 11 March 1826, p. 4, col. 2.

42. 'Lord Milton and the Corn Laws,' *Independent*, 13 Oct. 1832, p.4, col. 1.; reprinted from the *Sun*.

43. See also 'Average Prices of Bread in London 1545-1925' in *Abstract of British Historical Statistics*, compiled by B. R. Mitchell and Phyllis Deane (Cambridge, Eng.: Cambridge University Press, 1962), 497-98.

44. 'Appendix No. 8' in the 'Report from Select Committee on Agriculture' (1833) *British Parliamentary Papers, Agriculture*, 2: 633.

45. Engaged in an industry dating back to 1161, most of Sheffield's laborers or 'mechanics' (as they were called) worked in the cutlery trades. Several histories recount the development of the iron and steel industry in Sheffield. To begin see: Mary Walton, *Sheffield: Its Region and Its Achievements*, 5th ed. (Otley, West Yorkshire, Eng.: Amethyst Press Limited, 1984); Robert Eadon Leader, *History of the Cutler's Company in Hallamshire, in the County of York*, 2 vols. (Sheffield, Eng.: Pawson and Brailsford, 1905); *Sheffield and its Region: A Scientific and Historical Survey*, ed. by David L. Linton (Sheffield, Eng.: The British Association for the Advancement of Science, 1956); Thomas Baines, *Yorkshire: Past and Present*, 2 vols. (London: William Mackenzie, [1873]).

46. In 1824, 8,549 were employed in the cutlery trades of Sheffield; in 1830, 10,369; in 1833, 10,757; and in 1841, 13,237. The second largest parliamentary and municipal borough of Yorkshire, Sheffield parish boasted a population in 1831 of 92,000; by in 1841, it rose to 111,000. G. I. H. Lloyd maintains that the population expansion in Sheffield 'serves as an index of the growth of the cutlery industry down to the middle of the nineteenth century.' He also states that a typical cutler survived as an 'out-worker'; he was frequently employed by several firms simultaneously, and that he did 'piece work' (*The Cutlery Trades; An Historical Essay in the Economics of Small Scale Production* [1913; London: Frank Cass & Co., Ltd., 1968], 152, 209-210). In 1841, Sheffield Township had 68,186 residents.

See Great Britain, Census Office, *Abstract of the Answers and Returns. Age Abstracts 1841* (London: W. Clowes & Sons, 1843). *Sheffield Local Register*, 1 May, 1824; *Sheffield Local Register*, 1830; House of Commons Select Committee on Commerce, 1833; Census. These figures are also available in Lloyd, 445-46, 158, 447.

47. According to the *Independent*, the 'landed interest' prevented 'the industrious mechanic from selling his labour at the highest prices and at the same time made him pay two or three prices for everything he consumes' (*Independent*, 4 Feb. 1826, p. 1, col. 6). Historian G. Lloyd confirms that cutlers could request 'a high scale of piece-work prices' when the trade activity boomed but they quickly lost it when normalcy or depressed conditions returned. At those times, they were compelled 'to concede discounts from what they naturally enough regarded as the proper standard of payment,' 210. Unfortunately, many artisans experienced fewer good times than bad. The journeymen mechanics also suffered wage losses for imperfections. Manufacturers typically counted thirteen to fifteen items to a dozen to compensate themselves for possible imperfect articles. To secure the maximum discount from artisans they pitted workers against each other (Lloyd, 212).

48. Manufacturers as master cutlers even discriminated and held leverage over semi-solitary artisans within their trade society. Historically, the Company of Cutlers was a manufacturers' society. Even after Act 54 of 1814, which drastically curtailed the Company's control over its trade, this group refused to relinquish any of its offices to freemen (lower-tier members of the guild aspiring to become 'masters'), who had always comprised nine-tenths of the Company, or to permit them to use the Cutler's Hall (Leader, 1:94-100).

49. Lloyd, 210. Lloyd also provides tables which detail wage differentials among cutlers with different skills.

50. This deduction from a worker's wages was called the 'truck' or 'stuffing' system, which was outlawed in 1831 (Lloyd, 217).

51. Tatham found that, comparatively speaking, the mortality figure for cutlers, generally, between ages twenty-five and sixty-five was 59 per cent higher than that for other occupations, and that mortality among cutlers beyond age thirty-five exceeded the standard among employed males by 64 to 72 per cent. Royal Commission on Depression of Trade, 2nd Report, Part I, Qu. 1168; Lloyd, 210, 213, 217, 211. According to Thackrah, the grinding and filing created serious medical problems; drilling disfigured the chest; iron particles from grindstones clogged respiratory passages; and the noise from the machinery impaired hearing; see A. Meiklejohn, *Charles Turner Thackrah: The Effects of Arts, Trade, and Professions on Health and Longevity; The Life, Work and Times of Charles Turner Thackrah*, 2nd ed. (London: Longman, Rees, Orme, Brown, Green & Longman,

1832; reprint, Edinburgh: Livingstone, 1957), 89. John Tatham, 'Dust Producing Occupations' in *Dangerous Trades; The Historical, Social, and Legal Aspects of Industrial Occupations As Affecting Health, By a Number of Experts*, edited by Thomas Oliver (New York: E. P. Dutton & Co., 1902), 137-39.

52. Shear-grinders rarely reached life expectancy for the average male. For more details on health conditions among cutlers, see the following: Sinclair White, 'Steel Grinding,' *Dangerous Trades*, 408-16; Thomas Oliver, 'Iron and Steel Industries,' *ibid.*, 756-60; Simeon Snell, 'Eye Diseases and Eye Accidents in Relation to Industrial Occupations,' *ibid.*, 761-87. Although most statistics in *Dangerous Trades* are based on findings in the last quarter of the nineteenth century, Thackrah's discoveries establish continuity, citing conditions that resemble those the cutlers experienced at the beginning of the century.

53. Lloyd, 231.

54. For more on the concept 'penny capitalists,' see John Benson, *The Penny Capitalists: A Study of Nineteenth-Century Working-Class Entrepreneurs* (New Brunswick, New Jersey: Rutgers University Press, 1983). Before the end of the eighteenth century, the development of the cutlery industry contributed to expansion of the merchant and manufacturer class, or 'master cutlers' (Lloyd, 236). While pondering the favorable reception of his political poetry, Ebenezer Elliott describes himself indirectly as a literary 'mechanic' — 'a man of the middle class — hardly raised above the lowest,' 'Preface' to the *Corn Law Rhymes*, 2nd edition.

55. Bowley, 120-21. 'The chief charge during the period was the invention of the hot blast by Neilson in 1828, which reduced the coal consumption per ton of iron at the Clyde ironworks from 8 tons 1 1/4cwts. in 1829 to 5 tons 3 1/2cwts. in 1830.' Walter Thomas Layton and Geoffrey Crowther, *An Introduction to the Study of Prices* (London: The Macmillan Press, 1938; reprint, New York: Garland Publishing, 1983), 65.

56. Only surnames are cited in the press. See *Independent*, 25 Nov. 1826, p. 1.

57. See R. S. Neale's 'Class and Class-Consciousness in Early Nineteenth-Century England: Three Classes or Five?' *Victorian Studies* 12 (Sept. 1968): 4-32. This group was not comprised of property owners, but of artisans in small workshops and shopkeepers with professional and educational aspirations. They knew that only through radical change would they share in the privileges and authority of the upper classes. Therefore, they wanted these class barriers shattered. Neale also states that lower working and upper middle classes were especially deferential to those stratas above them. See also E. P. Thompson, *The Making of the English Working Class* (New York: Penguin, 1968); and Arno J. Mayer, 'The Lower Middle Classes as a

Historical Problem,' *Journal of Modern History* 47 (Sept. 1975): 409-36. Mayer notes, too, that the lower middle class 'both aspires [to] and resents' the upper (423).

58. *Independent*, 25 Nov. 1826, p. 1, col. 4.

59. *Ibid.*, 10 March 1827, p. 3, col. 2.

60. *Ibid.*, 25 Oct. 1834, p. 2, col. 4.

61. *Ibid.*, 25 Nov. 1826, p. 1, col. 4.

62. *Ibid.*, p. 1, col. 5.

63. *Ibid.*, 24 Feb. 1827, p.4, col. 3.

64. Indeed, the *Independent* resembles the Anti-Corn Law League which Cobden founded. About the League he wrote, it was carried on 'by those means by which the middle class carries on its movements. We have had our meetings of dissenting ministers; we have obtained the co-operation of the ladies; we have resorted to tea-parties, and taken those pacific means for carrying out our views, which mark us rather as a middle class set of agitators' (John Morley, *The Life of Richard Cobden* [2 vols., London: Chapman & Hull, 1896 ed.] 1:249).

65. [William Howitt], *The Aristocracy of England: A History for the People* by John Hampden Junior, 2nd ed. (London: E. Wilson, 1846).

66. See Alan Fox, *History and Heritage: The Social Origins of the Industrial Relations System* (London: George Allen & Unwin, 1985), 96.

67. *Independent*, 15 March 1834, p. 2, col.4.

Chapter XIV

'The Red Specter' and the
Coup d'état of 1851

Natalie Isser*

The Second Empire, created by the power of the ballot box and by bayonets, lacked legitimacy in the same fashion as preceding regimes. Its establishment was the result of the Revolution of 1848 that inspired conservative fears of social upheaval and the radical reorientation of French institutions. The Revolution of 1848 also reflected the economic developments of the nineteenth century and the changes it had wrought. The economic upheavals had led to a migration from the countryside to the cities, and a migration of foreign workers seeking employment.[1] The changes both in the cities and the countryside created new political and social cleavages that were punctuated by sporadic episodes of violence. The events of the Revolution of 1848 also had rekindled the old fears and memories of the Revolution of 1789. The Terror and the violence of the past was recalled by the violence of 1848. Riotous behavior had become more pronounced as the economic recession increased the suffering of the poor.

Government bureaucrats (the prefects, the sousprefects, the procureurs, and the gendarmie) concentrated on keeping peace, maintaining order, and above all protecting private property. Procureurs and prefects performed their duties during a period of political turmoil and change, and were probably overzealous in their accounts, as they, too, feared, revolutionary consequences. They were highly educated members of middle-class families who frequented the company of the local notables and reflected the prejudices of the upper bourgeoisie. Nevertheless, while their reports frequently revealed sophisticated insights into contemporary local social and economic problems, they also reflected the prevailing prejudices of their class and the local notables.[2]

The heady atmosphere of political change unleashed by the Revolution also led to an enormous outpouring of newspapers, brochures, and other propaganda. Each emerging group vied for adherents to its party as the Revolution developed. The demand for universal male suffrage made the media's impact more urgent. However, the tools employed by the journalists were traditional, and familiar, based upon past historical and literary memory.

The Revolution of 1848 also aroused feelings of hope as well as fear, and many saw an opportunity to redress existing distress and past social grievances. Many workers felt the Revolution provided an occasion for them to protest, demonstrate, and strike. This seemed the only way to achieve both dignity and opportunity. However, others saw the Revolution as the means to complete the unfulfilled agenda of 1789. The new regime, thus, was divided by diverse social and political aspirations. The leadership, men of talent and good will, contained many who had been deputies and bureaucrats during the July Monarchy, and who were anxious to preserve social harmony. As a result, early policies responded to progressive demands: universal male suffrage, the right to work, freedom of press and association, the elimination of slavery in the colonies, and other major reforms. But ideological rifts also divided the government into those who favored economic laissez-faire and liberty (liberalism) and those who supported government economic planning and equality (radical democrats and socialists). These arguments were made more strident by the economic decline and suffering throughout the countryside. The political dialogue that ensued was a cacophony of name-calling, anger, demands, and threats from various groups. Pushed by radicals, the government leaders asked socialist Louis Blanc to participate, but they reluctantly supported his ameliorative policies such as the National Workshops.

In the towns and the cities economic problems, exacerbated by the Revolution, were reflected in the continuity of high prices, unemployment, and dislocations caused by the early disruption of modernization. The intensity of economic deprivation varied from province to province and from commune to commune. Political activity was affected by these anxieties, and as in the Revolution of 1789, a variety of political clubs' rhetoric reflected the despair of various constituencies. Many of these clubs had continued to exist, though remaining underground, throughout the 1830s and 1840s. They were mostly republican, socialist, or anarchist. The number of clubs mushroomed under the freedom of the republic, and included all political opinions ranging from women's emancipation, occupational groups, and émigré workers to those advocating a new society. Dues were collected to spread political propaganda (circulars, caricatures, and pamphlets) which were distributed all over Paris and the provinces.[3] Sometimes the radical clubs sent delegates to the provinces to spread republican ideas or to found branches of their Paris clubs.[4] These activities were kept under suspicious surveillance by government officials.[5]

Songs, political caricatures, and placards were frequently used to indoctrinate a population that was still largely semi-literate. All political groups used these semiotic devices to gain adherents. The unlettered could learn the proper messages from the songs as these titles demonstrate: 'The Marseillaise of the Workers Union,' the 'The French People for Louis Napoleon,' and the 'Universal Male Vote.'[6]

Even more effective methods for spreading political messages were the placards pasted on the walls of the town or neighborhood. They had a short simple message usually accompanied by a picture or caricature. Local speakers could gather a crowd, read the inscriptions, and then draw a lesson from the poster. Newspapers and brochures were another important source of information, but they had not become a mass medium in 1848; they were financed by either mail subscription or some form of government subvention. Brochures, too, cost many centimes, and like the journals were aimed at an educated, literate reading public. Posters tended to represent left-wing ideas, while a large part of the press, dependent upon the middle class, expressed their views. Each party had a paper which advocated a distinct point of view and many were polemical and strident. In the freedom of 1848, the number of newspapers exploded, but most, especially the democratic republican and Bonapartist papers, were ephemeral and many disappeared after a few issues.[7] While clerical and conservative papers could rely upon subscriptions and the loyalty of their readers, the democratic papers supported by mail tried to expand their influence by having journalists and other club partisans read their columns to the crowds gathered in the public squares or in the cafes.

To counter both the clubs and conservative criticism, the republican government created its own forms of propaganda in order to elicit support and enthusiasm for the new regime. Based upon traditions of the earlier revolutions and past administrations, the government used ceremony, ritual, and symbol. Planting of liberty trees was one of these civic occasions. The local priest was recruited to provide a blessing, and other fetes and parades were arranged around these new saplings. Parades with fireworks sometimes enhanced the excitement of the festivities. Public demonstrations and speeches were held around these tiny trees.[8]

French public opinion was assailed by a wide variety of politically encoded messages in both literary and symbolic images. Hence it was alerted to the fissures in French society that subsequent developments would bring. The need to pay for welfare and 'make work' policies caused the republican government to levy a forty-five centime tax upon the land. The tax imposed the greatest burden upon the small or marginal peasant proprietor. Throughout France, especially in the poorer regions, resistance was strident, bitter, and violent. Riots, demonstrations, and threats were the norm, and often tax collectors were assaulted.[9] One observer reported: 'The reception of taxes has resulted in a lively resistance in several departments. It should be noted that it is the result of instigation whose only aim is to create obstacles to the orderly development of republican institutions.'[10] Because the Revolution of 1789 had challenged the traditional legitimate political base of the state, all subsequent regimes were declared illegitimate by some part of the population. Therefore, they were politically fragile. Political opposition came to be perceived as a part of a conspiratorial tactic, justified or not, for the forcible destruction of the existing administration. All officials' description and analysis of every regime was laced with this dialogue. The descriptions of violence used by both republican and Bonaparte supporters in this period contained the same imagery which would appear later in government propaganda. One sousprefect wrote that the 'forty-five centimes tax resistance is used and exploited by malcontents for furtherance of their hate and their own ambition.'[11] Others noted that grave disorders necessitated the need to call upon the gendarmie to combat the 'menace,' and the sousprefect was nervous about the loyalty of the National Guard — whose officers were often the leaders of the 'outrages.'[12] The peasants hurled threats of pillage and assassination at the large proprietors, artisans, and other bourgeois if they paid their taxes.[13] Such resistance intensified existing suspicions of the lower classes and fears of the authorities over communal stability and governance.

Continual violence was also apparent in the political debates themselves, especially among the club members who congregated in bistros and cafes, where they imbibed too much wine and ideology. The local cafe served an important communal social function, providing shelter and relaxation for the local populace. They were places to conduct business and hire workers;

they could be a meeting place for mutual aid societies and other clubs. Above all they were the locations in which to party: drink, dance, sing, and express opinions. Drinking was not only acceptable but the major form of relaxation: and too much drinking always led to noisy quarrels and fighting; sometimes that violence spilled out into the streets.[14] Such disturbances annoyed the local officials who feared the divisive consequences of such arguments, and who felt the efficacy of their administration was reduced. Their irritation was increased by the prejudicial attitudes felt toward the lower classes by the bourgeois. One explanation characteristic of these feelings was expressed by one observer:

> The civilization [culture] in this third arrondissement of the Bouche-du-Rhône is extremely barbaric; great ignorance is widespread and the customs are coarse. The people here are half-savage, therefore, political dissensions are expressed with a brutal violence. As in all imperfect societies, there is a continual recourse to force.[15]

Procureurs and prefects declared that the activities of both the urban and rural masses were unruly, conspiratorial, barbaric, and uncivilized. These feelings would be expressed in more elegant language in later propaganda. Philosophically, though, apprehensions were also based on what liberals and conservatives perceived were the 'excesses of the revolutionary activity' that was expressed in the oratory of democratic citizens.[16]

Officials distrusted many republicans whom they suspected were too 'fanatical' or left wing.[17]   Many supposed republicans were considered secret socialists with hidden agendas.[18]   Clubs assumed an influential political role in many urban locales, and their leaders seeking support and attention, combined ideology and anger that evoked strikes, riots, and the smashing of machinery.[19]   In response, prefects warned that 'no disorders on their part will be tolerated.'[20]   Club members spoke of their need to preserve liberty saying: 'We have blood in our veins and the courage of martyrdom, we are an important presence and we are inspired by conscience and instinct for order; we are directed by liberty and God.'[21]

The propaganda of the Society for the Rights of Man and the Club of the Incorruptible contained similar themes, but one of the delegates spoke passionately of the oppression of the workers and their desperate condition that required immediate change.[22]   Others declared that the republican government was doomed, and when it fell their leadership would implement their radical social changes.   One observer wrote: 'This conviction is so bold that it will result in many provocations and will create a fire that must be stamped out.'[23] One worker, accused of violent behavior, explained his actions at his trial with the following words:

> We must preserve this club as the example and symbol of worker democracy, that has had to submit to a series of changes because of an election that has not responded to the popular will. Today as a result we organize into tirailleurs [riflemen] and I hope that those who answered the appeal of the 28 February will not stand aside. It is important that we remain united in order to defend our rights if they are scorned. [24]

The news of the Revolution, as it spread throughout the countryside, was generally accepted without much opposition. However, many peasants, though unaffected by the rhetoric of the clubs, hoped that their economic grievances would be assuaged. The forests in the southern departments of Var, Basses-Alpes, and Bouches-de-Rhône were either owned by the government or leased to the larger local landlords who used the timber for ship building, or other commercial purposes. These lands were no longer available to the small proprietors and tenant farmers. The loss was hard to bear, and the peasants frequently expressed their resentment against the forest rangers and the landlords in an effort to retrieve the customary use of the woods.[25] In towns like Entrescasteaux, they indulged in aimless rioting, vandalism, arson, and wanton destruction. In some areas the landlords permitted the peasants to use the forest and the common in order to keep the peace and preserve their property. One landlord who refused to bow to violence was harassed so badly by the mobs that he was forced to leave town. Others found their homes pillaged, livestock slaughtered, and their grape-arbors and fruit trees uprooted. In Draguignan, peasants entered the city hall and burned the public records.[26]

The public prosecutors found that public opinion in the rural communes solidly supported the peasants.[27] Though committed to upholding public order, the prosecutors made little attempt to punish the offenders, and in the few cases where the ringleaders were arrested the sentences meted out by the courts were extremely mild — usually three or six month imprisonment. The procureur-general recommended such a policy because he claimed:

> These outbreaks are not political in nature. They are the explosion of old hates, or old grudges over the refusal of the granting of the customary rights in the forest. The cause is not political. In every revolution and fall of a government

the people of our country-side believe that the laws which hamper them have fallen, and with it their legal obligations. Thus the crowd erroneously guided by its own interests thinks it has legitimate grievance.[28]

The peasants' behavior, though viewed with disfavor by officials, did not carry the same onus as those in the urban clubs. What was absent in these instances was the rhetoric, and the verbal imagery that threatened existing interests. The propertied classes, though upset by this kind of peasant unrest, never viewed it with the same anger as the city rebellions. The absence of radical speeches and the apolitical nature of the uprisings, while hardly acceptable, never appeared as threatening as those of the workers who peppered their appeals with inflammatory propaganda. Moreover, peasants were more interested in local issues than national causes and ideologies. Peasants in many cases remained loyal to the church and were influenced more often by their priests and the local notables than by the radical rhetoric of the towns. However, peasant violence that emerged from radical instigation of the local village clubs frightened proprietors with their allusions to class resentment.[29]

It was in the urban centers where worker dissatisfaction was the strongest that the animus against it was also strongest. In Paris, crowds of workmen, carrying rakes and the tricolor, milled about the government offices demanding more aid. 'These claims of the workers,' commented the procureur, 'especially at Paris, cause immense difficulty. The question of organization of work appears to me the most pressing of our problems. God willing that the Republic find a solution.'[30]

In early April, 1848 about six hundred workers marched to the Prefecture in Marseilles to demand an increase in salary. The prefect M. Ollivier attempted to persuade the demonstrators to leave. When they did not disperse quickly enough, the National Guard was called to 'assure civil order.' The authorities noted prophetically, 'Agitation lies dormant in the working classes and grows each day — God willing, the question of work needs to be solved before more irritation and impatience gains among a large number of workers.'[31] In Limoges, the unemployed vented their frustration by occupying the City Hall for several days.[32] Lyons was the scene of Luddite-like destruction of factory machinery.[33] Foreign unskilled workers, Belgians in the north and Italians in south, were attacked by French laborers as rivals for the few jobs available.[34]

Elections held in April confirmed the conservative climate of the nation despite the sound and fury within the cities. The legislators were conservative republicans, suspicious of welfare, of high taxes, and of too much government. They implemented their beliefs by abrogating the National Workshops and relief projects.

In June, 1848 the workers responded with urban insurrections in Paris and in Marseilles. The uprising was suppressed with fury. The June Days led to the beginning of repression — a repression directed by republicans against their fellow citizens. Unlike past monarchs, the middle classes used the army led by the Republican General Cavaignac to destroy the barricades and punish the rebels. The paradox was heightened because the peasants, who had fought tax collectors and had indulged in aimless violence, now in turn supported the army and the ruthless suppression of working-class opposition to the Republic.

Six hundred insurgents were arrested in Paris and all members of the club of the Society of the Rights of Men were immediately incarcerated.[35] Clubs were banned and their leaders arrested or discredited. Republican and leftist newspapers were heavily censored. Police surveillance prevented the open articulation of left-wing political views. The procureurs, already preoccupied with the maintenance of public order, querulously complained that the authorities were not firm enough.[36] In Toulon, all migratory workers, suspected of disturbing the peace, were banned. The government of Piedmont-Sardinia also forbade them to cross the frontier.[37] The insurrections of June had exacerbated the existing suspicions of conspiracy and fear of the another Terror.[38]

Meanwhile, Louis Napoleon, the nephew of the Emperor had been on the political sidelines awaiting his opportunity. He had run for a seat in the provisional legislature in a by-election on 4 June 1848, which he won, but it was the political apprehensions and the heritage of his name that led to his final triumph in the presidential elections of 1849. The Napoleonic Legend had become part of the political mythology of the Restoration and Orléanist Monarchy. The image of Napoleon Bonaparte as a military genius, powerful ruler, and heir of the Revolution had been established by the writings of the Emperor himself. He characterized himself as a military genius; he doctored his political record so that he would appear the heir of the best of the French Revolution. After his fall he posed as the chained Prometheus of St. Helena. His portrayal of himself as a nationalist revolutionary hero was also perpetuated by the veterans of the army, by poets (Delavigne and Hugo), by song-writers like Béranger, by lithographers, painters, and popular writers. The Napoleonic pretender had remained aloof during the writing of a conservative presidential constitution, but once that document was ratified, he ran for presidency of the Second Republic. He posed as the protector of the poor citing his own book *The Extinction of Pauperism;* he also claimed to be the champion of law, order, and tradition. Further, he had assumed the aura of the Napoleonic imagery of national glory.

In 1849, a massive electoral win by Louis Napoleon created the Napoleonic Republic. The conservative presidential constitution was based upon the principle of separation of powers, which immediately led to gridlock in the new National Assembly over electoral and constitutional reforms, especially the clause that forbade the re-election of the president. The Bonapartists immediately began to argue for revision of the constitution in order to gain more power for the executive and a new provision for the re-election of Louis Napoleon. Despite concerted efforts of government officials and Bonapartist propaganda, these efforts failed. The Bonapartist newspaper *Dix Décembre, Journal de L'Ordre* was one of the most vociferous voices that called for change. Repeating the arguments of that newspaper, the case for revision was stated brilliantly in an anonymous pamphlet entitled *La Révision de la Constitution* in 1851. It was the prevalent belief that Granier de Cassagnac, an ardent Bonapartist journalist, was its true author and many thought that Louis Napoleon helped in its composition.[39]

The brochure declared that the Constitution of 1848 was hastily conceived, written in a period of perilous turmoil. The result was a series of grave weaknesses that needed change. The constitution was never ratified by the people and therefore did not reflect their true desires. Further, the constitution was undemocratic because it placed the president (elected by universal male suffrage) in a subordinate position, thus thwarting the function of popular democracy. These reasons gave the constitution a 'transitory and accidental character.'[40] Moreover, the separation of powers led to ineffectual arguments and discussions which prevented any political decisions.

The most inflammatory and the most Bonapartist of arguments, however, were directed against parliamentary government itself. The author noted that from Louis VI to the Committee of Public Safety French tradition had endorsed the centralization of the French government and its institutions.

Parliamentary government suited the English temperament and custom, but in France it could not work. The old aristocracy had been driven from power by the Revolution of 1789, leaving the country divided into many coteries, bitter rivalries, disparate ambitions, and personal desires for power. Under these circumstances, France required the unity of a national party that would reconcile these diverse groups. Only Louis Napoleon Bonaparte could unite all classes and parties.[41]

This brochure was good Bonapartist propaganda, and although the author was biting and polemical in the treatment of his political enemies, he did not, in spite of his emphasis upon the need of a national party, successfully convert the conservative opposition to the Prince-President. His rhetoric was too partisan, but some of his ideas about the inefficient National Assembly would be repeated in later works.

The opportunity to end the Republic was seized by the Prince President after a plebiscite that permitted him to rule for ten years. Placards and banners peppered Paris claiming only a coup could save the state and universal male suffrage. There was little reaction in Paris when the coup d'état succeeded in December 1851. But if Paris was passive in the face of the coup d'état the rest of France was not. Popular unrest was evident in the armed insurrections around Montarges (in Loiret), Clamecy (in Nièvre), Poligny (in Jura), La Palisse (Allier), Figeac (Lot), Digne (Haut-Provence), Nîmes (Gard), Capestang (l'Hérault), l'Arriège (Villeneuve-sur-Lot), and Marmonde (Lot-et Garonne).

Under these emotional circumstances, a propaganda pamphlet appeared written by Auguste Romieu. Entitled *Le Spectre Rouge de 1852*, the brochure created a sensation. It enjoyed a wide circulation and favorable comment in the conservative press. In a period of intense political discourse this pamphlet stood apart. Its popularity was aided by the severe repression of left-wing activity and press censorship, and by the armed violent opposition to the coup d'état. But the major reason for the brochure's success rested on its clever use of semiotic allusions and the author's sensitivity to the anxieties and concerns of the middle class. He, unlike Granier de Cassagnac, couched his arguments in less partisan language, and spoke to the common interests of all conservative parties.

Romieu had been a prefect in Dordogne during the regime of Louis Philippe. After the Revolution, he had been elected to serve the Republic and had been sent as Commissioner extraordinary to serve in Haut and Bas

Rhin. After the June Days, he served the Bonapartist cause and became an important official within the Ministry of the Interior.[42]

The author opened his pamphlet with a striking and dramatic warning: 'A Red Specter that many did not wish to recognize has emerged and each day and each hour its menacing proportions are growing; it is not only civil war that awaits: it is the Jacquerie.'[43] Jacquerie was a term that Romieu and his contemporaries constantly used. Jacquerie, the name given to peasant riots in the thirteenth century, invoked images of anarchy, senseless cruelty, and unbridled violence. The term 'Red Specter' was even more effective semiologically because it connoted the worst fears of the middle classes. 'Red Specter' became a catchword and a durable symbol that became a part of the subsequent political vocabulary during the Second Empire.

Romieu used metaphors and political and historical analogies to explain his vision of the Red Menace. He noted that agitation had manifested itself throughout the country, and claimed that France was a powder keg, ready to be ignited at the first signal. He claimed that the revolutionaries had directed a campaign of hate against the rich, against the petit bourgeois, and against the farmers (8). He instigated inter-class dissension by complaining that the poor were envious of the propertied.

In the pamphlet, Romieu asserted that General Cavaignac had saved French civilization in 1848 after a bloody victory in the June Days, but that subsequent parliaments were ineffectual debating societies that inevitably would bring about total conquest by the proletarians. Romieu made an analogy to the situation in classical Rome by alluding to Julius Caesar's ultimatum to a quarrelsome and ineffective Senate, thereby justifying his seizure of power. Romieu used this analogy to justify both Napoleon's coup in 1799 and Louis Napoleon's coup d'état in 1851. Romieu created a romantic portrait of dynamic military leaders who embody the will of the people, and out of sympathy for their plight, act on their behalf.[44]

Romieu complained that the preoccupation with liberal ideology so often expressed by ineffective legislators bore no relationship to the reality of existing society. According to these well-meaning individuals 'it would be better to concern ourselves sooner with the welfare of the masses, and to quickly assuaged their needs in order to make them more content.' Romieu applauded these sentiments, but argued that they were naive because it would take twenty years before the results of such efforts could be felt among the poor. In the meantime, however, Romieu pointed out France could not afford to wait for such reforms to emerge eventually from philanthropic projects (20). Continuing to utilize classical analogies, he buttressed his arguments by quoting Tacitus, who had declared that the 'mob is a terrible monster, ungrateful, perfidious, seeking constant gratification, cruel, vindictive, impatient, and habituated to all kinds of vices' (24). Romieu rejected the notion that the crowds revolted in order to obtain economic justice. He argued that the government had already responded to their needs. What the crowds' violence generated instead was confusion, disorder, disdain for morality, and the mockery of religion and family (25). He likened the mob to schoolchildren who engaged in rebellious acts of vandalism in the schoolroom as a protest against all authority.

Romieu's attack was part of an on-going cultural struggle between liberals and conservatives. Seeking the support of the conservative Catholics, he became a passionate advocate of traditional morality. He asserted that although technical scientific progress was exciting and limitless, bringing great gifts to humanity, it could not replace the moral order. Romieu argued that the worship of Reason had led men astray, caused false pride, and resulted in erroneous presumptions of human infallibility.

History, as interpreted by Romieu, revealed that Charlemagne had stopped the march of the barbarians by supporting the spread of Christianity. The social contract, in Charlemagne's time, was one of duty not rights, and the world he founded was based upon faith not reason. The feudal Europe that emerged — a Europe that Romieu looked back upon fondly — was predicated upon an unwritten agreement between actual parties, rather than upon a rational principal evolving from the imagination of a 'sophist from Geneva' (i.e. Rousseau) (32).

The decline of this system was precipitated by the creation of representative governments with legislators who were primarily lawyers. Subsequently, liberals in their debates, questions, arguments, amendments, and abstract discussions, substituted abstract philosophical formulas for religious values. Romieu averred that the greatest mistake of the nineteenth century was the secularization of French society. The Guizot Law of 1833 reduced religious influence in the public schools and weakened Christian values (56).

The author then focused upon the underlying fears of social upheaval and of violence. A major force contributing to the disintegration of society was the prevalence of the popular media — newspapers and other literature that delivered messages of hate and envy to millions of peasants who were then prompted to act upon their envy towards the middle classes. Romieu believed that the French nation had degenerated into antagonistic and apprehensive classes: the rich and greedy poor. The envious poor were driven by hate, and by a thirst for pillage: 'all that holds them in check is the army' (47).

He continued: 'O, bourgeois as the hour of danger approaches who will save you? The government of the division of powers is impotent: stalemated.' He then alluded to a powerful and fearful historical memory. The bourgeois republic was stained with blood. Robespierre and Danton taught the people how to murder, and their successors learned their lessons well. The people (the tyranny of the majority) will murder lawlessly so that inevitably conflict must appear between the furious, delirious masses and the disciplined vigorous army. 'Your books, your debates, your constitutions, your principles must disappear—vanished in the conflagration of the great conflict. The duel is between order and chaos' (68). In order to enjoy safety, law and order, and security the bourgeois will have to relinquish their love of codes and acquiesce to real authority that provides order—the army. While some hope that revision of the constitution or a change in voting laws can bring amelioration, it will be of no avail. Only the army can save us in 1852. 'The existing regime based on liberal idealism has been unable to cope either with crime or other excesses' (99). Concluding his long essay, Romieu urged the return of a dictator in the tradition of Louis XIV or Napoleon who would head the government — and provide a brilliant, glorious, glittering administration, for the French people love light splendor, military glory, and fetes.[45]

By invoking Rousseau and Danton, Romieu underscored the evils of the revolution and illustrated the dangers of the tyranny of the majority. His second recurring theme was the emphasis on the ineptitude and weakness of parliamentary institutions. Third was the constant criticism of the secularization of French life, and the weakening of tradition and morality. Without that glue the poor lower classes were unmanageable. Romieu constantly used the words materialism, greed, avarice, and jacquerie as descriptive adjectives. But these terms were not just propaganda or even vile exaggerations. Rather they reflected — even if it was erroneous — perceptions of the lower classes and their behavior that had permeated official rhetoric and reports during the Revolution of 1848, especially after June Days. The pamphlet, by its allusions and language, reflected and enlarged upon existing prejudices, fears, and apprehensions of the middle classes, the propertied, the religious, and the bureaucrats.

Finally, Romieu had achieved a notable aim in the publication of his views. He had incorporated existing prejudices and clothed them in allegorical and classical imagery that provided a vivid and viable shorthand for the readers of 1851. In 1851 the vast majority of the French were not interested in creating an egalitarian society, and were not yet sympathetic to the plight of the poor. 'Red Specter' became the symbol of all that they most feared.

The code words Jacquerie and Red Specter, created by Romieu, became shorthand terminology that enabled people of various persuasions to encode political debate. For many Catholics, the Red Specter meant a threat to the Church and their visions of a traditional, culturally conservative society. For some peasants, the Red Specter meant the threat to peace and the need for public order. For many of the middle classes, Romieu's notions of the threat to property was the most dangerous element. To others, especially Legitimists and Orléanists, the major goal was to preserve a society that provided economic liberty, but which was not egalitarian. The use of political codes, therefore, enabled the participants to bring their own perceptions to the interpretation of the metaphors. It helped to perpetuate stereotypes, prejudice, and social antagonisms. As the government repression and returning prosperity eliminated unrest and reduced violence, the usage of the term Jacquerie diminished. However, Red Specter was continually unleashed by conservatives during the debates over the liberalization the Empire and over the important Roman Question, which was a acrimonious debate over the extent of the Pope's temporal power. As in 1852, the term continued to convey for each group their own particular menace.

There is a need in political discourse for the use of symbols and verbal imagery to enable readers and listeners to reduce complex issues and problems to simpler explanations or arguments. As the process of political participation became more widespread, and public opinion became more influential, mass communication required new elements in the civil discourse. Cartoons, ceremony, slogans, symbols, and verbal imagery gained more significance. Just as in our own age of television short-spot commercials and analysis provide effective symbolism, as evidenced by the infamous Willie Horton advertisement in the Dukakis-Bush presidential campaign in the United States in 1988, and the Harry and Louise television announcements critical of Clinton's medical insurance reforms, Romieu's pamphlet presented semiotic rationalization for the Coup d'état of 1851.

Moreover, despite exaggeration and verbal excesses, the Romieu pamphlet gave some indication of the direction that the conservative regime was to follow once it had assumed power. Louis Napoleon's government, at least for the first ten years, did follow a program that embraced some of the conservative values enunciated in the Romieu brochure. The Bonapartists did form a tenuous alliance with the Party of Order (Legitimists and Orléanists). It supported the Catholic Church by permitting expansion of religious orders and schools. A harsher repression of the left, republicans, socialists, and anarchists, was continued which successfully drove the opposition underground.[46] Cabaret violence was attacked and subdued rather easily. During the 1850s imperial decrees strictly regulated cafes and closed them if there was rowdy behavior or public riots. By the 1870s, both as a result of the government's action and a change in the workplace, cafes altered their recreational patterns.[47] Prosperity raised the standard of living even for the poor which led them to spend money on other forms of recreation. Local theatres, circuses, marionette shows and the development of the cafe concert became more popular.[48] Press and theatre censorship established in the first ten of years of the Empire was relaxed after 1860, but restrictions on the sale of the popular literature, and supervision of the book sellers never eased. The quest for public order never abated.

The use of codes in political discourse, therefore, has been a part of mass communications long before the era of the video and radio media. Furthermore, exaggeration, prejudice, and stereotypes also existed as part of ongoing debates. It reflected not only arguments but also the programs of the protagonists. The media is not the culprit, rather it is the human propensity for distortion. Just as the term Red Specter so brilliantly enunciated by Romieu appealed to the political sensibilities of the conservatives and the propertied, the opposing arguments of the Republican-Socialists contained threatening and angry denunciations of the wealthy, and expressed the frustrations of the poor in language that greatly exaggerated the goals the left. Yet despite the misperceptions and prejudices of both sides, the political shorthand of each reflected the ongoing political culture, attitudes, and most significantly the apprehensions of both sides. 'Red Specter' by Auguste Romieu represented the most cogent example of the attitude of many conservatives who were not Bonapartists, who indeed disliked Louis Napoleon, but who preferred him rather than the barricades manned by republicans.[49]   Despite their misgivings, as Romieu had predicted, they reluctantly supported the army and the coup d'état, in order to preserve the *status quo*.

The term 'Red Specter' continued to evoke fear of social upheaval long past the coup d'état, but the semiotic interpretations of what that threat was changed as the political, historical, and cultural events altered French political dialogue.   The defeat of France in the Franco-Prussian War, the fall of the Second Empire, the suppression of the Paris Commune (a proletarian urban uprising), and the establishment of the Third Republic created new divisions and different debates.   The image that Romieu created and the political shorthand of the words remained but readers attached another interpretation to the phrase created in 1851.

Romieu had visualized the Red Specter as the coalition of democratic republicans and socialists.   He probably had not read Karl Marx's *Communist Manifesto* which was not widely known in France.   In that notable pamphlet Marx, too, had written of a Red Specter that originated in the oppressed working classes and which possessed revolutionary potential. The emergence of the Third Republic and its success in defusing the social question and the relegating of monarchists and Bonapartists to the political sidelines brought stability. The establishment of the Republican regime was challenged in a variety of political crises (May 1877, the Panama Affair, the Boulanger Affair, and the Dreyfus Affair) that obscured the problems and suffering of the poor and the underclass.   The Third Republic, however, achieved a solid legitimacy which permitted the government to support the concept of a loyal opposition and civil liberties.   Even the cultural debates over the role of religion in the state and schools were finally defused in the passage of a series laws in 1905, that led to the separation of church and state in France.

However, social and economic problems caused by rapid industrialization did not receive the same attention.   The working classes were alienated from mainstream political activity.   Unions formed, accompanied by some violent strikes.   The socialist movement also grew, but was disunited.   Its various ideologies included Syndicalism, Marxism, and Anarchism, while terrorism plagued French politics at the end of the nineteenth century.   Marxism gradually became predominant in the socialist movement. The Marxist vision of the 'Red Specter' became the prevailing one by the end of the century. Romieu's definition was relegated to the scrapheap of history, replaced by Marxian rhetoric.

In its turn, Marx's definition of the Red Specter was replaced in the latter half of the twentieth century by the fear of Soviet-styled Communism created by the success of Bolshevik Revolution, and its spread by the 'Evil Empire' (a phrase enunciated by President Reagan to characterize the former Soviet Union). The term Red Specter illustrates how political shorthand, a phrase or metaphor, can be as effective as any visual propaganda. It also reveals that the meanings attributed to language is dependent not only on the writer's intentions, but also upon the environment that ultimately shapes the reader's interpretation.

Natalie Isser is Professor Emerita of History, Pennsylvania State University, Ogontz Campus.

ENDNOTES

1. Archives Nationales, MSS, Paris, Ministry of Justice, BB 30, 358, Aix (hereafter referred to as AN, carton no.) Acte d'Accusation. In the trial of revolutionary participants of June 1848, the pre-trial interrogations revealed that a very large number of insurgents were born in the countryside and had migrated to Marseilles in the 1830s and 1840s. This was true of other cities.

2. Bernard Le Clère and Vincent Wright, *Les Préfets du Second Empire* (Paris: Colin, 1973); c.f. Lynn M. Case, 'New Sources For the Study of French Opinion during the Second Empire,' *Southwestern Social Science Quarterly* 18 (1937): 161-170.

3. Natalie Isser, *The Second Empire and the Press* (Hague: Nijhoff, 1974), 11; AN, C933 contains the records of club minutes, C934 the police reports of club activities; cf. Alphonse Lucas, *Les Clubs et Les Clubistes* (Paris, 1851).

4. Lucas, 1-20.

5. Charles Moulin, 'Les clubs et le presse,' in *1848, Le Livre de Centenaire* (Paris, 1948), 140-143; AN, C939, Reports from the Committee of Club delegates; C940, Club recommendations to department delegates.

6. Jules L. Puech, 'Chansons sur les hommes de 1848,' *La Révolution de 1848,* 33 (1936): 82-97; Pierre Barbier and France Vernillat, *Histoire de France par les Chansons* VII, *La République de 1848 et le Second Empire* (Paris: M. Fourny, 1959).

7. Isser, ix-xii, analyzed the development of the Bonapartist press.

8. *Ibid.,* 10-12.

9. AN, BB30, 358, Aix, Procureur Reports, 1, 2, 3, 4, 8, 11 March; 17, 19, 21 April, 4; 6, 7, 11, 18, 19 June; BB30, 365, Procureur Reports, Toulouse, 23 March 1848; BB30, 360, Grenoble, 19, 21 March 1848; Albert Soboul, 'La question paysanne en 1848,' *Pensée,* 18-19 (1948): 55-66, 19-37; Maurice Agulhon, *The Republican Experiment 1848-1852,* translated by Janet Lloyd (Cambridge, London: Cambridge University Press, 1983); Peter Amann, 'Changing of Outlines of 1848,' *American Historical Review,* 68 (July 1963): 938-953.

10. AN, C932A, Report to the Minister of the Interior, 5 June 1848.

11. *Ibid.,* Lot, 5 June 1848; Haute Garonne, 10 June 1848.

12. AN, C932A, Gers, Sous-prefect to Minister of Interior, 5 June 1848.

13. Ibid., Charente, Tarn, Sous-prefect Reports, 5 June 1848; Puy de Dôme, 8, 10 June; Creuse, 9 June 1848.

14. Anne Parella, 'Industrialization and Murder 1815-1904,' *Journal of Interdisciplinary History,* 22, (Spring 1992), 641.

15. AN, BB30, 358, Aix, Procureur report, 14 March 1848.

16. *Ibid.* Aix, 4, 6, 111 March; 17, 19, 21 April; 4, 6, 7, 11, 17, 19 June 1848; Archives Departmentales, MSS, Marseilles, (hereafter referred to as AD), carton no., Police Reports, M6, Lambesc, 3 March 1848.

17. AN, C939, Report of Commune de Montrouge, 7 April 1848.

18. AN, C940, Club reports, 14 April 1848.

19. AN, BB30, 358, Aix, 30 August 1848. The campaign slogan of the left wing clubs during the municipal elections in Curban was 'The rich have ruled long enough!' Peasants also broke into the rooms of the city hall where votes were being counted to try and break up the elections. Aix, 7, 8 February, 14 March, 10, 17 July, 31 August 1849; Arles 29 January, 7 November 1849; AD, M6 (29), Arles 16 June 1849. In Barbantane there was a fracas between the moderate republicans and the legitimists, 14 May 1849.

20. AN, C939. These words were underlined in the report.

21. AN, C933, Petition to the National Assembly, 24 June 1848.

22. AN, C941 'Citizen Thoré to the people of Paris'; cf. C934, contains police reports of club activities.

23. AN C932A, Sûreté-General to the Minister of Interior, Melun, 19 May 1848.

24. AN, BB30, Grenoble, Court of Appeal, 20 February 1850.

25. AN, BB30, 358, Minister of Finance to Minister of Justice, Paris, 13 April 1848.

26. *Ibid.*, Aix, 4, 6, 11 March; 17, 19, 21 April; 4, 6, 7, 11, 17, 18, 19 June 1848; AD, police reports M6 (26), Lambesc, 3 March 1848;

27. AN, BB30, 358, Aix, 19 April, 6 May 1848,   A petition from a neighboring commune was reported, begging that the prosecution be dropped.

28. *Ibid.*, Aix, 17 April 1848.

29. Eugen Weber, 'The Second Republic, Politics, and the Peasant,' *French Historical Studies* 11 (Fall 1980): 521-50 is a very cogent analysis of the various theories of peasant political involvement during the Revolution of 1848-50.

30. AN, BB30, 358, Aix, 11, 21 March, 5 April 1848; Paris, Minister of Finance to Minister of Justice, 13 April 1848.

31. *Ibid.*, Marseilles, 11 March 1848; AD, M6(26).   This file is full of letters and petitions to the prefect seeking economic amelioration or complaining of bad conditions.

32. AN, BB30, 358 Aix, 11 March, 11 April 1848.

33. AN, BB30, 361, Cour d'Assises de Vienne, Affaire de Limoges, 30 April 1848.

34. AD, M6, Police Reports, 3, 30 March; 6 April 1848; AN, BB30, 361 Procureur Reports, St. Étienne, 30 March 1848, Roanne, 8, 10 March; Lyons, 17, 21 April; 19 May , 6 June 1848.

35. AN, C933, Paris, Police Report 24 June 1849.

36. AN, BB30, 358, Procureur reports, Aix, 3 July 1848; c.f. Howard Payne, *The Police State of Louis Napoleon Bonaparte* (Seattle: University of Washington Press, 1966), 11-26.

37. *Ibid.*

38. AN, BB30 358, Grenoble, Court of Appeal, 20 February 1850. The authorities were convinced that the uprisings in Paris and Marseilles were coordinated planned rebellions to destroy the Republic. Ollivier in written testimony presented to the court (25 June 1848) also held this opinion. However, the Minister of War did not agree. Paris, Minister of War to Minister of Justice, 12 September 1850.

39. Adrian Dansette, *Louis-Napoléon à la Conquête du Pouvoir* (Paris: Hachette, c 1961), 328.   Granier du Cassagnac was a journalist on the newspaper *Le Constitutionnel*. A series of articles attributed to him in that paper, appeared from 4 April to 9 May 1849.   These articles attacked the stalemate in the National Assembly, the republicans' "odious" ideology, the Legitimists' archaic notions, and the Orleanists' timid materialistic goals. cf. Frederic Bluche, *Le Bonapartisme* (Paris: Presses universitaires de France, 1981), 317.

40. *La Révision de la Constitution* (Paris, 1851), 6.

41. *Ibid.*

42. London *Times,* 5 November 1851.

43. Auguste Romieu, *Le Spectre Rouge* (Paris, 1851), 5. The page references in the text are to the pamphlet.

44. Louis Napoleon used the example and image of Julius Caesar as the populist military leader throughout his political career. In 1861 he published a biography of Julius Caesar with the help of the historian Victor Duruy. This was the most durable of the analogies that he sought to create about himself and his regime.

45. Romeiu, *Le Spectre rouge.*

46. Thomas R. Forstenzer, *French Provincial Police and the Fall of the Second Republic, Social Fear and Counterrevolution* (Princeton, New Jersey: Princeton Unversity Press, 1981); cf. Payne, *The Police State of Louis Napoleon Bonaparte.*

47. Charles Rearick, *Pleasures of the Belle Epoque. Entertainment and Festivity in Turn of the Century France* (New Haven and London: Yale University Press, 1985), 96.

48. Cafe-concerts had a large mass following by the 1870s. The producers were forbidden to use costumes, prose dialogue, mime or dance. However, cafe entrepreneurs eluded government regulations by producing an 'illusion' of costumes and sets. These programs in cafes were cheaper than in the theatres and became very popular among the workers and petit bourgeois. Albert Delpit, 'La liberté des théâtres et les cafe-concerts,' *Revue des Deux Mondes* (1 February 1878): 623.

49. Robert R. Locke and Ray E. Cubberly, 'A New Mémoire on the French Coup d'État of December 2, 1851,' *French Historical Studies,* 12 (Fall 1982): 564-88.

Chapter XV

Soviet Historiography and
the Problem of Myth

George Enteen*

One of the striking features of the collapse of communism and the demise of the Soviet Union was how swiftly it occurred and how closely it coincided with the weakening of the Communist Party's controls over intellectual life. The recovery of genuine historical investigation seemed to open a door to common sense, and the disabling of ideologically determined language created a space for public discussion. This essay suggests that the return of common sense and ordinary language fatally wounded Soviet mythic discourse. It asks whether the concept of myth can be employed to clarify the history of Soviet historical scholarship, especially the writing of the history of the Communist Party.

I contend that Soviet historiography underwent two closely related but distinguishable processes between 1917 and 1938. The first may be designated, for want of a better word, as ideologization. The second process was mythologization. With respect to ideology, I have two meanings in mind. The first is the marshalling of thought to defend and advance the interest of a specific group. Marxism-Leninism, as the presumed ideology of the working class, is an example of this meaning. Stalin's specific interpretation of Marxism-Leninism, fashioned to overcome his rivals for power, is another example. The second meaning of ideology refers to a broad perspective or a field of axioms and postulates that constitute a foundation of a political system. Liberalism constitutes an example, as again does Marxism-Leninism.[1]

Both of these meanings of ideology found expression in Soviet historiography. From the time of the Russian Revolution into the early 1930s, world history, including Russian history and the history of the Soviet Communist Party, was refashioned to conform to canons of Marxism-Leninism. That is to say, the results of historical research were encoded in the terms and categories of Marxism-Leninism. This was achieved by a rather large apparatus of scholar-propagandists that was called into being for just this purpose. First, the categories of class conflict and economic determinism were intruded on a large scale. Then world history was depicted as a unilinear march of mankind from primitive communism through the agonies of slave-holding society, then feudalism and capitalism to the October Revolution, which opened the door to the radiant future of communism. These distinctive modes of production or types of societies were called socio-economic formations.

These socio-economic formations, in their totality, constituted a periodization of history. Soviet historians were preoccupied with periodization, raising it, in some respects, to a fine art. To discern stages in the past is a requirement for any historian. Anyone who has devised a syllabus for a history course and earmarked assignments into separate categories has performed an exercise in periodization. It is implicit in any construction of events that goes beyond mere chronology and assumes narrative form. To know that the past differs from the present is the beginning of historical consciousness; to perceive that one historical age differs from another constitutes a further refinement and represents an achievement that has not been attained in all cultures. Such consciousness grows out of the discovery that human experience deposits traces more durable than 'the pattern of last year's wind on the surface of a lake. . . .'[2] The historian seeking to depict the past construes reality 'under the modality of a "pastness" both distinct from and continuous with the present.'[3]

In effect the doctrine of socio-economic formations constitutes a master narrative that turns history into a process and governs its meaning. Periodization provides the framework of meaning for party historiography, an infrastructure of control, and a scaffolding for the regime's mythology. As a mode of designating the field of historical discourse, periodization assigns explicit meaning to long stretches of time and implicit meaning to the specific events that take place within them. Periodization determines the structure of the specific narratives that describe wars, revolutions, party congresses, etc. It prejudges whether a specific act is progressive or regressive with respect to history's goal of communism. The master narrative defines what is a historical fact, what and who is incidental and accidental, what is foreground, and what is background.[4]

I

In the early 1930s, when the process of ideologization neared completion, a shift of emphasis occurred. Narrative moved to the foreground; individuals became larger than life as they were transformed into symbols. That is to say, a mythology was contrived. Of course, ideology was not abandoned, just as mythology was not entirely absent during the process of ideologization.

In the period of transition between the processes of ideologization and mythologizing, in 1930 to be precise, a young but prominent Party historian, D. Ia. Kin formulated a construct that would serve as a foundation for mythological narratives. He used the materials at hand in political and historical polemics, while he kept his ear cocked for suggestions and hints that could be found in the pronouncements of Stalin. I call this construct the Stalinist conception of Party history, though the Stalinist historians, at their leader's behest, usually presented it as the Leninist conception. This mode of naming was part of the process of mythologization.

Kin forged his model of Party history in the course of a polemic against V.G. Iudovskii, an Old Bolshevik, with a distinguished Civil War record, who finally perished during the anti-cosmopolitan campaign of Stalin's final years. Iudovskii produced a model of Party history that differed from Kin's and may be deemed a rival interpretation of Leninism. For Iudovskii, the Party members themselves devised the goals and worked out the means of their realization. For Kin, history itself posited the goals, which gave them an objective existence.

The stated goals of the Party constituted, in Iudovskii's understanding, the point of departure for both the definition of the discipline and for the analysis of events. He stated that it is 'completely necessary' to evaluate Party activity 'from the angle of vision of those goals which the Party sets for itself.' In order to delimit Party history from history in general, the 'only possibility is that we construe the Party in the capacity of an active subject in specific objective conditions.'[5] When the Party changes its goals, it necessarily modifies all its activities, including its mode of organization. Goal shifts form the basis for periodization. Party members must be judged by their success in advancing the Party goals in a specific period.

The concept of Party goals constituted the point of departure for Kin's model also. Kin asserted that a happy coincidence prevailed between the goals of history itself and those of the Bolshevik Party. The objective course of history coincided with the subjective intention of the Party to create a communist society. Kin demarcated the Party from the working class, on the one hand, and from the revolutionary movement, on the other. The internal history of the Party consists of overcoming factions; the task is 'to discern the revolutionary currents.' The Party does so 'by overcoming bourgeois muddle.' The method of struggle is to assert the Leninist tendency in the face of 'unleninist, anti-Bolshevik tendencies.' Thus for Kin, the emergence of factions was inherent in Party life. Wrong opinion is not an individual failure but has a class basis. The historian must show that the Leninist line was worked out precisely through the overcoming of factions. It is this process that propels the Party and history forward.

Kin used the term self-propulsion (*samodvizhenie*) to describe the mechanism of change, but the term is a misnomer. Movement originates outside the Party; immature workers enter the Party from the ranks of the proletariat, and unstable elements of the intelligentsia infiltrate as well.[6] The actions and beliefs of the intruders produce a crisis. The Party's action propels history forward in that it changes the original setting, producing arrangements a step closer to history's final goal, but not changing it sufficiently to forestall the further intrusion of alien class elements. This passive, reactive stance is surprising in the Party of such a pro-active leader as Lenin, who always sought the initiative. It is, however, analogous to Marx's depiction of the proletariat: as heroic as it is, it is responding to capitalist exploitation.

Kin's teleological assumption about the goals of history may be deemed the core statement of the Stalinist conception. Upon it rests the epistemological assumption of a single truth, a single true reading of historical evidence that points in the direction of the objective goals. This position includes the corollary that truth must be substituted for error. One does not argue with false opinion, one unmasks and annihilates it. Without these assumptions none of the assertions of Marxism-Leninism about class, faction, and historical action could be made to cohere.

Kin's model provides a framework to accommodate all the events of Party history. It supplies a fixed context for all Party conflicts, assigns identical motives to all of the participants, and assures a constant outcome. In this sense the model may be deemed a quasi-narrative. It functions as a paradigm dictating the form, structure, and meaning of actual events. Stalin's triumph became paradigmatic of all events of Party history and as such functioned as a master narrative. This aspect of the model provides the primary link with mythology.[7]

II

To seek a definition of myth is to enter a thicket of ideologies. Ivan Stenskii thinks that there is no referent for the term[8]; Joseph Kocklemans laments that each scholarly discipline defines myth from its own unique perspective.[9] My only hope of avoiding an extended discussion is to cite the two definitions that make most sense for my purposes. The first of them derives from the structuralism of Lévi-Strauss, which in turn derives in large measure from the work of the Russian folklorist, Vladimir Propp. A myth is a narrative that expresses in concrete terms abstract forces, such as life and death, nature and culture. These stand in opposition to each other but are mediated in the course of the telling so as to produce a sense of reconciliation. Lévi-Strauss has in mind the narratives of pre-literate societies. I am asking whether significant traces of this structure can be found in works that have clothed themselves in the fabric of empirical investigation. I am looking for points of reference between the conception of binary oppositions and Mircea Eliade's distinction between *sacrum* and *profanum*.

The second definition I have in mind sees myth as the product of a specific state of mind or mode of consciousness. Alternatively, it views myth as a specific use of language. Here I am drawing on the work of Ernst Cassirer and also on the writings of the Soviet semiotician, Yuri Lotman. It posits a mode of thinking, a modality of symbolization, if you wish, that was universal before the emergence of theology and the appearance of the discursive reason associated with scientific investigation. The mode of thought expresses itself in concrete narratives; it possesses its own wisdom but is guided by rules that appear absurd in the light of discursive reason. In Lotman's words:

> This powerful identification which lies at the basis of this type of consciousness entails seeing in different phenomena of the real world the signs of a *single* phenomenon, and in all the diversity of objects of one class to identify the *single object*.[10]

All things are perceived as standing in homeomorphous relationships with each other.

Lotman disagrees with Cassirer in his understanding of how this mentality appears and operates in history. For Cassirer mythic consciousness and narrative consciousness (discursive reason, in Cassirer's terms) are sequential. The latter replaces the former as civilization triumphs over barbarism. Cassirer, however, was among the first to note a reversal of what had seemed to him a natural process. He sounded an alarm about the revival of an archaic mentality (Nazism). For Lotman, both forms of consciousness exist simultaneously in all cultures.[11]

One meaning of myth is excluded from the present discussion — the abuse of sources for the conscious end of misrepresenting social reality. Stalinist historiography is replete with falsification; it can probably claim the greatest number of masterpieces in this field. As a source, it is a seam of gold inlaid with fabulous jewels, but it is not a concern of this essay except insofar as the apparatus of falsification is implicated in the attempt to control language.

Stalinist historiography found its highest embodiment in a textbook entitled, *History of the All-Union Communist Party (Bolshevik). Short Course.* It is usually referred to as the *Short Course.* Its publication in 1938 was accompanied by a decree of the Communist Party's Central Committee which affirmed the official character of the textbook and the purpose of bringing to an end the multiplicity of interpretations that could (allegedly) still be found in the literature. Before its appearance as a book it was published serially in the party newspaper, *Pravda.* By 1953, the year of Stalin's death, it was published 301 times, in over 42 million copies in 67 languages.[12] The work was composed by a commission of three historians, who labored under the closest supervision of Stalin. The book may legitimately be attributed to him.

The special role of party textbooks in the Soviet Union warrants mention. In most societies research sets the pace for discourse. The findings of investigators make their way into popular works, including textbooks. This was reversed in the Soviet Union: textbooks on Party history set the pace and provided the point of orientation for researchers. They marked the boundaries of the permissible.

III

We have noted the paradigmatic character of Kin's model, its capacity to give events an identical structure and meaning. This apprehension of events as structurally uniform itself betokens mythology. Stalin's triumph over his rivals for Party leadership forms the basic paradigm. The October Revolution itself, the charter myth of Soviet society, acquires the same dualistic structure. Before the bourgeoisie could be defeated, the bourgeois agents within the Party had to be overcome. In the *Short Course*, Trotsky is presented as the main obstacle to proletarian success. The need to defeat him mobilized the working class. In the same way, pre-revolutionary Party rivals had to be overcome, — Populism, then Economism, then Menshevism. In each case the Party grew in strength through smashing its enemies.

The meaning Stalin gave to his success over his Party rivals was retrojected into the past and became the pervasive meaning of all the events that constitute Party history. Each episode bore the meaning of the whole.[13] Stalin's defeat of his rivals stood outside of ordinary time. It was to be reenacted in all future and past events of Party history. The pattern itself, in the fashion of myth, is timeless. In this system of repetitions, however, one can detect the emergence of a cyclical sense of time which works against the Marxist sense of linear time. This marks a step in the direction of classical paganism where history was viewed as a series of cycles of decline and regeneration.

Such structural identity, *i.e.*, the pattern of repetitions, helps to accommodate still other mythic constructs, to wit: the fusion of Lenin and Stalin into a single symbol, Lenin/Stalin, and its elevation to a timeless meaning. It acquires its significance from the rival symbol, Trotsky, and Trotsky himself was enlarged and besotted with Bukharin-like elements through the figure of the double-dealer (*dvurushnik*). This phoenix-like creature could be discredited and defeated endlessly but never destroyed. Constant vigilance and the leadership of Lenin/Stalin were required to keep it at bay. This example also points to a revival of a cyclical sense of time, still within a unilinear framework of Marxism.

In the light of these symbols, history ceases to be human history and comes to resemble the stories of geologists and geo-physicists who write about the transformations of earth forms and galaxies. The English philosopher, R.G. Collingwood, introduced a distinction between external and internal history. External history, devoid of consciousness, is akin to historical geology — the rise and decline of earth forms, the birth and death of stars. Inner history consists of motives and other such meanings which men and women create and to which they respond.[14] Human beings with (sometimes) discernable motives, who face (at least apparent) alternatives disappear from the pages of Party history. Lenin, Stalin, and Trotsky are transformed into natural forces, and god-like struggles between good and evil ensue. Trotsky does not act on the basis of a specific motive nor as the result of a (potentially fallible) decision that he made. He breeds evil because that is his nature; he relates to the proletariat in much the same way that the ocean relates to a coastline or a lion to a morsel of its dinner.

Gnostic assumptions and Manichean-like themes[15] found in Marxism resonate deeply in the narratives built on Kin's model. Even more than in Marx's writings, history is transformed into a sacred tale. What seems on the surface to be a mean or mundane event, such as building a dam, holding a meeting, or personal aggrandizement through the removal of a foe, becomes an action of transcendent and universal significance in the march toward the shining future. Nothing is narrated merely because it happened and had meaning for the actors. The pronounced dualism imparts a sacred character to the story. It demands choice and inculcates loyalties.

In Party histories, events ceased to be mere events that pointed to the past. More and more events pointed inward to the world of human emotions and upward to a world of symbols that provided identity, meaning, and normative orientation. Increasingly they acquired meaning by linking the sacred and the profane. To understand this process, we can again use some of the distinctions drawn by the Russian School of Semiotics. According to Yuri Lotman, 'one of the possible classifications of culture is its articulation according to the type of relation it has to the sign.' For instance, the culture of the eighteenth-century 'Enlightenment' strips away transcendent meaning from natural objects and processes; it tends to denude the world of meaning. 'The world of objects is real. . . . Only that exists that is itself; all that 'represents' something else is a fiction.' The 'medieval' type of culture, in contrast, possesses a 'high semiocity,' which means 'that everything is significant.'[16]

The *Short Course* is a sign of reversion to the medieval type of culture. The world again becomes rich in omens and portents. In this universe, causal analysis exists on the surface, but in a less obvious way events and persons are metaphoric, and values align hierarchically. Wisdom consists of discerning the transcendent in the commonplace. This can be seen most clearly in the treatment of Trotsky. The book not only blackened him but in the very naming of him as 'Judas Trotsky' elevated him beyond his mere person. He had joined the Bolshevik Party 'to disrupt and destroy it from within.' The October Revolution triumphed despite him and in a sense over him. He became a metaphor for the bourgeoisie.[17] This same tendency can be seen at the sociological level, in the depiction of the working class. At the outbreak of the World War, 'a certain section of the workers' were 'infected' by 'bourgeois jingoism.' These workers 'naturally did not, and could not, reflect the sentiments of the working class.'[18] In this light, the position of the working class, including its sentiments, was something objective, residing apart from and above actual workers.

A second example of Soviet mythic thinking — the myth of the kulak — differs from the cult of Stalin in that it is less clearly derived from the narrative character of the Kin model. It differs also in that it is a spontaneous construction, not contrived and managed like the others. It entrapped and blinded its creators. In this sense, it is a form of 'word magic' that may be viewed as a pathology.[19] The 'myth of the kulak'[20] represents an inability or unwillingness to differentiate between the word and the objects it refers to. Anyone who is designated by the word 'kulak' bears all the characteristics of the group. If one is covered by the word 'kulak,' he is necessarily greedy, cunning, exploitative, and implicated in conspiracy against Soviet power. He is, moreover, fated for extinction by the laws of history. He has no right to exist.

The word 'socialism' constitutes another example of 'word magic.' One judges the worth of a society and the policies of its government, not on the basis of observable characteristics, but with respect to an essence, or inner character, which is discernable from its name. Any society possessing highly developed market relations is classified as capitalist and is assumed to be one of diminishing freedom; a society that liquidates such relationships in the course of revolution is deemed socialist and is, by definition, one of growing freedom. Property relations — the absence or presence of private property — is the sole variable determining whether a society is moving toward or away from freedom. Historical traditions, political institutions, the presence or absence of law, and even economic performance have only remote bearing on such judgments.[21]

IV

What sort of world was conjured up by this increasingly sacred tale? What was the emotional burden of these signs and symbols? One side of it was consoling and comforting, a familiar story in which destruction and resurrection are linked. Its world was not one of facts but of 'evocation and identification' that aimed at a 'fusion of past and present.' It was mythic in that it sought a 'history that lay beyond history.'[22]

This is not the entire world conjured up in Stalinist myths. The many faces of the *dvurushnik* compel one to constant vigilance. Enemies, who are immensely powerful, are on every side and never sleep. This is a world, in Hannah Arendt's words, of 'ice cold logicality.'[23] The Kin model results in part from a mentality that conceives politics in entirely conspiratorial terms. Conspiracy theory is prone to stereotypes that demonize historical actors and transform events into symbols. Behavior and observation give way to moot premises and unbending categories. All meanings derive from ideological postulates; all actions are explicable with reference to the category in which the actor is placed. Such a world is notable for its sterility.

This ice-cold world manifests itself not only in the figure of the *dvurushnik* who epitomizes conspiracy. It shows up also in Kin's account of ideas. Ideas that have not found sanction in Party resolutions, i.e., ideas that are not official, have no legitimacy. They penetrate the Party boundaries in secret, contained in the baggage of members who pass themselves off as genuinely proletarian. Only when they seek to divert the Party from the true path is their nature revealed.

Stalinist mythology shows still another face. Owing to the great emphasis placed on consciousness, belief, and knowledge, there is a resemblance to the vision of Russia as the Third Rome. God's plan for the redemption of mankind is contingent upon the strength of the faithful not to fall into heresy, as was the case with the first two Romes. The heretics are clever enough to devise needed technology, but they work against God and Russia. Adherents of the faith have a great responsibility for all of mankind. Stalinist historiography teaches that the triumph of false opinion results in the frustration of the proletariat and jeopardizes mankind's passage to communism.

V

In conclusion, I would like to suggest, that although the *Short Course* retains the essential features of Marx's manichean vision of history as a dualist struggle between progressive and reactionary forces, it contains a subtle shift. Labor has been displaced as the central concept. It is the Party itself that mediates between what is natural and what is cultural, between the past and the future, between the proletariat and the bourgeoisie, progress and reaction, freedom and exploitation, light and darkness.

Is it possible that a body of historiography deemed a classic of falsification can have truth value? I think the answer is yes. The *Short Course* reflects and reinforces the basic political and social realities of Soviet history — the destruction of Russian civil society that began with the outbreak of the First World War and culminated in the mass terror launched in 1936. In the *Short Course*, conspiracy was the dominant, if not exclusive, mode of politics. The postulates of Leninism as well as the style and strategy of Stalin had made conspiracy the actual mode of politics. Looked at in a certain light, politics mirrored historiography.

Second, the *Short Course* conveys a specific image of the Soviet social structure. It is composed of the working class, its ally the peasantry, plus the leading stratum of the working class, the intelligentsia, which, in turn, includes the Party. And finally there are the remnants of the exploiting classes. The drama performed on the historical stage excludes the workers themselves. The struggle is played out between Lenin/Stalin, on the one hand, and the *dvurushnik*, in his various guises, on the other. The workers and peasants bear witness; they laud the victorious Party; they demonstrate support, but they do not participate. They are not invited to think about the goals of society, to voice an opinion about how to achieve them, nor to participate in the allocation of resources. Their thinking, hence their citizenship, is confined to the workplace — how best to fulfill the tasks assigned to them. They must ever be on guard against an unthinking gesture that could identify them as a remnant of the exploiting classes.

I have tried pose the question of the relationship between myth and history in Stalinist historiography. I have implicitly asked to what degree was this process of mythopoesis a spontaneous reversion to archaic mental forms and to what degree was it a contrivance and conscious manipulation. Some of the myths clearly were contrived. The elevation of Stalin and the fusion of his name with Lenin's is the best example of a 'rationally managed' myth. Others were spontaneous, engendered by ideology and by the circumstances in which the Party leaders found themselves. The myth of the kulak is an example of a non-contrived myth, a manifestation of the word magic bred by a mythic mentality. Other myths are a mixture of contrivance and spontaneity. How they combine is a question for separate investigations.

One must avoid the temptation of identifying mythopoesis with the entire product of Soviet historiography. How, when, and where myth intruded requires further study. Party historiography acted as a polar star on all fields of scholarship but exerted greater force on some than on others. Even in the heyday of Stalinism, historians made brilliant advances. Achievements in archeology, furthest removed from Party history, are the first to come to mind.[24] Progress was made in the editing and publishing of source materials as well. One should take note also of successes in related fields, such as semiotics. The Tartu school, guided by Yuri Lotman, somehow avoided the vicissitudes of myth even as it provided tools for laying them bare. These achievements reflect the final glow of the silver age of Russian culture. Calling attention to the intrusion of myth reveals not only the disaster that befell Soviet historians. It also underlines the courage of those who triumphed over those circumstances and kept alive traditions of European culture.

I am not proposing that the patterns of myth I have found in Stalinist historiography are the only ones present, nor that they can be found only in Soviet scholarship. My findings are tentative and leave a residue of questions. If Soviet historiography, especially in its embodiment in the *Short Course*, signifies a mythic mentality, whose mentality does it represent? Was it Stalin's alone? What about the reading public? Did the *Short Course* reflect the mentality of the populace? Did it effectively shape its mentality? Was Stalinist mythology received differentially within Soviet society and in the communist world outside the Soviet Union? Can we find ways to investigate this differentiated response?

A final word about the substance and power of the mythic elements indicated in this essay. An impression rather than a conclusion is in order. These myths definitely moved some of the people in many societies for some of the time. They, nevertheless, possess little substance and power. They imitate religious mythology; even their associated rituals mimic religious antecedents. There is no evidence that they uplift and transform, nor frighten in the manner of traditional religions. They are pale indeed in the light of national myths, despite Stalin's limited success in incorporating Russian national symbols into his compound. Clearly, they lack the authority of ancestral voices. These matters should be kept in mind in all discussions of the collapse of communism.

George Enteen is Professor of Russian History at Penn State.

ENDNOTES

1. This corresponds roughly to the distinction made by Karl Mannheim, *Ideology and Utopia: an Introduction to the Sociology of Knowledge,* trans. by Louis Wirth and Edward Shils (New York, 1936), pp.64-70.

2. Herbert Butterfield, *The Origins of History* (New York, 1981), p.17.

3. Hayden White, *The Content of Form: Narrative Form and Historical Representation* (Baltimore and London, 1987), pp. 88-89.

4. These thoughts about periodization are taken largely from my article, 'Problems of CPSU Historiography,' *Problems of Communism* 38, September-October, 1989, pp. 72-80.

5. *Voprosy prepodavaniia Leninizma, istorii VKP(b) i kominterna* (Moscow, 1930), p.169.

6. *Ibid.*, pp. 147-148.

7. I have adapted these thoughts about the Kin model from my article, 'The Stalinist Conception of Communist Party History,' *Studies in Soviet Thought*, 37, 1989, pp. 259-274.

8. *Four Theories of Myth in the Twentieth Century: Cassirer, Eliade, Levi-Strauss and Malinowski* (Iowa City, 1987), p. 1.

9. 'Ideas for a Hermeneutic Phenomenology of the Natural Sciences,' in *Phenomemology and the Natural Sciences: Essays and Translations* (Evanston, 1970), pp. 150-169.

10. Quoted in Ann Shukman, 'Dialectic of Change: Culture, Codes, and the Individual,' *Linguistic and Literary Studies in Eastern Europe*, vol. 5, *Semiotics and Dialectics*, ed. by Peter V. Zina (Amsterdam, n.d.), p. 322.

11. Ernst Cassirer, *The Myth of the State* (New York, 1955), especially part 2; Yuri M. Lotman, *Universe of the Mind: A Semiotic Theory of Culture*, trans. by Ann Shukman (Bloomington and Indianapolis, 1990).

12. Seen N.N. Maslov, '*Short Course of the History of the All-Russian Communist Party (Bolshevik) — an Encyclopedia of Stalin's Personality Cult,*' *Soviet Studies in History*, Winter 1989-1990, pp. 41-61, a translation of '"Kratkii kurs istorii VKP(b)" — Entsiklopediia kul'ta lichnosti Stalina,' *Voprosy istorii KPSS*, 1988, no. 11, pp. 51-57.

13. This pattern was first perceived by M. Ia. Gefter; see the first edition of Roy Medvedev, *Let History Judge: The Origins and Consequences of Stalinism*, trans. by Colleen Taylor (New York, 1972), pp. 516-18.

14. R.G. Collingwood in *The Idea of History* (Oxford, 1947), pp. 210-214.

15. See Alain Besancon, *The Rise of the Gulag: Intellectual Origins of Leninism*, trans. by Sarah Mathews (New York, 1981).

16. Problems in the Typology of Culture, in Daniel P. Lucid, ed., *Soviet Semiotics: An Anthology* (Baltimore and London, 1977), pp. 216-219.

17. *Short Course*, pp. 327, 199, 205, 207.

18. *Ibid.*, p. 163.

19. See Charles Morris, *Foundations of the Theory of Signs* (Chicago, 1938), p. 42.

20. The Russian word kulak literally means fist but also designates the wealthier peasants. It is problematic whether this group survived the Russian Revolution. Nevertheless, the collectivization of agriculture that began in 1929 was conducted under the slogan of 'eliminating the kulaks as a class.'

21. George M. Enteen, Cheryl Kern-Simirenko, and Tatiana Gorn, *Soviet Historians and the Study of Russian Imperialism* (University Park, 1979).

22. I have borrowed some of the formulations that Yehuda Yerushalmy stated in a different context, *Zokhar: Jewish History and Jewish Memory*, p.23, 44, 74. This is akin to Mircea Eliade's notion of the creation of a world that frees one from the 'terror of history'; see David Carracco and Jane Swanberg, *Waiting for Dawn: Mircea Eliade in Perspective* (Boulder, 1985), p. 137.

23. *The Origins of Totalitarianism* (New York, 1951), p. 254.

24. A. L. Mongait, *Archaeology in the U.S.S.R.,* trans. by David Skvirskii (Moscow, 1959).

Chapter XVI

Ghosts in Utopia: Semiotics of the Post-Historical World

William Pencak*

> It may be that someone in the year 2240 will discover my name, and tell the world that in this distant past there was at least one man less limited than the mass of his contemporaries who had pushed fatuity to the point of believing that they had reached the apogee of civilization.
>
> Prince Klemens von Metternich

Hegel and his disciple Alexandre Kojève have told us history came to an end when Napoleon won the Battle of Jena in 1806, 'the moment when the difference, the opposition, between Master and Slave disappears.' The triumph of 'the universal revolutionary power actualized in France by Robespierre-Napoleon' led to the 'annihilation of Man properly so called or of the free, historical Individual.' History was closed: since then 'the two world wars with their train of minor and major revolutions have merely brought the backward civilizations of outlying provinces into line with Europe's (actual or potential) historical positions.' We are thus living in the post-historic age. Liberty, equality, and fraternity, the enthronement of the free individual as the bulwark of state and society, ironically terminates freedom to alter the course of history in a meaningful way. As Kojève put it, freedom equals death.[1]

In our own time, the march of technology has joined the march of Napoleon in predetermining the future. 'The machine is accelerating the emergence of organization in every phase and turn of life,' wrote Roderick Seidenberg in his 1950 book *Post-Historic Man*, perhaps the first work explicitly to articulate this concept. 'History may be looked upon as a highly charged transitional phase in man's development; and its span, coincident with the ultimate and final organization of his activities, may conceivably taper off into an unchanging condition of perfect adjustment.'[2] In *The End of History and the Last Man* (1992), Francis Fukuyama argues that nations have no choice but to embrace the liberal-capitalist order underlying the prosperity of the advanced countries. All must join the international network of economic and technological transfers or be relegated to poverty and insignificance.[3]

The only problem with post-historicism is that the battle and the date are off by almost 2,500 years. In *The Histories*, where Herodotus has a lot of fun deconstructing oracles that are either ambiguous or dead wrong, he nevertheless places absolute credence in one prophecy alone: when the Persians should 'span the sea with ships . . . wild with hope at the ruin of shining Athens, then shall bright Justice quench Excess, the child of Pride . . . and gracious Victory shall bring to Greece the day of freedom.'[4] History came to an end on the plains of Marathon, when the survival of Athens ensured that freedom, justice, and reason would never be extinguished by brute force. We can then adopt Kojève's perspective, and say that subsequent history has simply brought the rest of the world into line with Athens.

Of course this is nonsense; we could just as easily argue science and intelligence would inevitably triumph once Og made fire or Ug made the first wheel. Except for those who confuse God and Geist with Rube Goldberg, there is enough unpredictability in history to satisfy anyone. Immanuel Kant's prediction that republican governments would bring the world 'perpetual peace' — rulers could be warmongers but peoples had no quarrels with each other — is a prime example how even the greatest of minds cannot forecast the course of history.[5] Herodotus himself went out of his way to leave the future open: freedom and tyranny both were possibilities everywhere. Liberty spread from Egypt to Greece and was briefly enjoyed by Persia, but the barbarian Scythians were the most steadfast defenders of their homeland. Herodotus closed *The Histories* with a retrospective anecdote: King Cyrus of Persia chose liberty for his people — they should remain poor rather than subjugate others, for he knew imperialism and luxury brought slavery to the conquerors as well as the conquered. But Cyrus changed his mind, and was killed by the Massegetae. Many Greeks were also tempted by tyranny, and others betrayed their land and worked with the Persians.[6] For the Father of History, unlike his patricidal heirs, history was a never-ending struggle between precarious freedom and threatening power.

As we examine the twentieth century, we can only marvel at the arrogance of those who announce the end of history in an age that has arguably changed its course more than any other. The world wars ended the European balance of power which had dominated the world since the sixteenth century. In their wake followed the rise and fall of Communism and Fascism, decolonization, and the emergence of the United States and Japan as world powers. Today, the nation-state is challenged both by a multi-national economic order and micro-nationalisms uneasily contained in multi-ethnic states. Demographic, nuclear, and ecological catastrophe have yet to occur but cannot be ruled out. The 'end of history"? Or the desperate effort of statesmen and intellectuals to deny that the world is rapidly changing, and to ignore threats to the pleasant life of the upper bourgeoisie to which they belong?

Post-historicism has semiotic value, however worthless it is as philosophy or history. Insanity and crime teach us much about personality and social order; intellectual absurdities likewise have meaning for the historian of ideas. Rather than analyzing the contemporary world from a post-historical perspective, I propose to examine post-historicism itself as a sign, its adherents not as a community of interpreters but as signifiers themselves. My guides will be Charles Peirce, Thorstein Veblen, Carl Becker, Eric Voegelin, Michel Foucault, Eugen Rosenstock-Huessy, and Walter Benjamin.[7]

Writing in the late nineteenth century, philosopher Charles S. Peirce (1839-1914) took issue with the Social Darwinism of his age. It was an optimistic world-view remarkably similar to the late-twentieth-century idea that liberal capitalism is the final step of historical evolution. Peirce disagreed, remarking based on case studies in the history of science that Darwinism 'has made no figure at all, except in a retrograde motion.' Peirce argued that history did not evolve: it erupted in cataclysms, where a habit of thought which ceased to work was overthrown by another, 'sure to be widely disparate from the first, and as often as not its contrary.'[8] Ruled by the 'Gospel of Greed,' the so-called 'progress' of the 'economical' nineteenth century was but the self-congratulation of an unjust world signifying 'comfort for the greedy master of intelligence.'[9] Peirce correctly predicted that 'the twentieth century . . . shall surely see the deluge-tempest burst upon the social order — to clean up a world as deep in ruin as that greed-philosophy has long plunged it into guilt.'[10]

Underlying Peirce's critique is an argument from the sociology of knowledge. Evolution's celebrants were 'a large class of academic professors who are provided with good incomes and looked up to as gentlemen.' Under that circumstance, 'scientific inquiry must languish,' Peirce asserted. True knowledge must be pursued *against* the 'moral weight of the community . . . because science implies a desire to learn, and a desire to learn implies dissatisfaction with current opinions.'[11] Peirce is saying that he who pays the piper calls the tune, and whether our musician is a Hegel employed by the Prussian state, a William Graham Sumner teaching at Yale University, a Kojève working for the Common Market, or a Fukuyama consulting for the RAND corporation, the intellectual rewarded with tenure, prestige, royalties, and speaking engagements is unlikely to bite the hand that feeds him. In the twentieth century, the life of the mind, like the 'serious' art and music establishment, has been institutionalized and subsidized in ivory towers, estranged from the community support which had previously required artists and thinkers to be at least minimally responsive to a non-specialist audience. Esoteric styles and languages develop to restrict rather than enhance communication: the inaccessible elite of intellect reflects the equally remote aristocracy of money, and reinforces it by serving as gatekeeper (through the educational system) to the realm of wealth and power.

Thorstein Veblen (1857-1929), another outsider who never fit into the turn-of-the-century academic establishment, developed a critique similar to Peirce's at much greater length in his book *The Higher Learning in America*. This might whimsically be entitled 'The Leisure of the Theoried Class' to complement Veblen's more famous *The Theory of the Leisure Class*. The university itself was a sign of capitalism's 'conspicuous waste' of resources better spent securing adequate livings for workers. Privately endowed schools also signified the 'pecuniary emulation' of men who competed with each other to build universities much like villas at Newport.[12] The professor, despite his pretensions of gentility, is a laborer paid to turn out a product — teach so many students, publish so much material, attend so many ceremonies. Placed in a secure situation as long as he produces adequately and does not become overly rambunctious — Herbert Marcuse has shown that inconsequential dissent can be turned against itself as the badge of a free society[13] — the professor lives in a post-historic — that is post-tenured — Utopia (or dystopia) for most his career. Without material anxiety, yet without the power to which he thinks his intellectual accomplishments entitle him, the post-historicist universalizes his privileged position in an unmatched feat of hubris: if I can't make a difference, nothing or nobody can.

Examples of post-historical mingling of material ease with spiritual malaise abound. Comparing late-twentieth-century bourgeois man to the pathetic 'last man' imagined by Nietzsche in *Thus Spake Zarathustra*, Francis Fukuyama laments that 'satisfaction, as opposed to physical security and material plenty' arises 'not from the goal itself, but from struggle and work.' He predicts 'boredom' will spur 'rebellions against that middle-class civilization with its security, prosperity, and lack of challenge.'[14] An alternative scenario, sketched by Vincent Descombes, is simply to wallow in pleasure: 'As the threshold of post-historicism is crossed, humanity disappears while at the same time the reign of frivolity begins, the reign of play, or derision (for henceforth nothing that might be done would have the slightest meaning).'[15] Thus, we have Lyotard's 'libidinal economy,' Lacan's 'jouissance,' Bataille's 'excesses,' Baudrillard's 'seductions,' and Foucault's 'heterotopias' as escape hatches from our well-furnished prison.[16] What could be more a sign of the flagrant self-indulgence of late-twentieth-century capitalism, of the *Circus of Ambition* as John Taylor has dubbed the Reagan years, or of the way of life Tom Wolfe has satirized in *The Bonfire of the Vanities*,[17] than philosophers urging even greater doses of narcissism? Such pronouncements must ring hollow indeed to the world's majority, which would be delighted to have a bit of leisure and affluence to discover their true selves, or to the numerous intellectuals and citizens who still work hard for worthy causes. Even if we may uncritically swallow the establishment line that Socialism and Communism are dead, and therefore serious attempts to make capitalism socially responsible are absurd efforts to revive a failed system, we surely have a more useful role than to shout Hallelujah to the as yet unrealized possibilities of technology.

Carl Becker (1873-1945) taught us that 'Everyman [Is] His Own Historian.' We do not discover 'the truth' about the past, but write narratives that accord with our own needs. Sensitive to the world-views of ages past, we are frequently uncritical of our own 'magic words . . . with uncertain meanings that are permitted to slip off the tongue without fear and without research; words which, having from constant repetition lost their metaphysical significance, are unconsciously mistaken for objective realities.'[18] How does this apply to post-historic intellectuals? They confuse their privileged yet irrelevant situation in the academic world with the lot of humanity as a whole by writing a history to match their own situation. Trained to think of their activities as worthwhile, but aware that they are not making real history, post-historical thinkers project their own superfluousness onto history itself, now and forever more. History is henceforth meaningless, but this then gives the post-historicist meaning. Only detached, privileged intellectuals — like the audience of ghosts in the opera *The Ghosts of Versailles* — can really interpret the world as they alone 'deconstruct' the dogmatic illusions held by those poor fools who think life has a greater meaning. From utter insignificance the intellectual has soared to unprecedented heights as the only legitimate interpreter of human existence. So he thinks, but of course he is really deconstructing himself by unthinkingly presenting his work as a sign of the institutionalization of the intellectual into irrelevancy. 'End of history' talk may hold water on the Left Bank or the Upper West Side, but Vaclav Havel, Fidel Castro, Alexander Solzhenitzyn, and the late Pablo Neruda have looked at history and their role in it differently.

Eric Voegelin (1901-1985) was a political theorist much influenced by Peirce and William James.[19] He elucidated the symbolisms different civilizations developed to express fundamental human experiences of nature (interpreted through science and technology), the soul, the social order (developed through government), and the transcendent. He regarded these as the basic constituents of humanity, and maintained that adequate symbolizations or philosophies interpreting human existence had to take them all into account. Man could not just be economic, biological, or political man; he had to have a soul and a relationship with a God or gods, because this was historically the case. Nor could a thinker legitimately freeze man's historic quest for meaning in dogmatic formulations about the perfect social order, the perfect race, or what the true nature of God must be.[20] Voegelin's thought may therefore be regarded as the monumental demonstration that humanity as a whole represents the community of inquirers defined by Peirce, testing hypotheses concerning 'what is good, true, just, beautiful, etc.' throughout history, which of course precludes any definitive answers.

Voegelin was especially critical of intellectuals who created 'dream worlds' or perfect societies removed from the practical symbolizations through which peoples have defined themselves.[21] Extending this analysis to the post-historicists, they too have created a dream world based upon their own world of academe. While enamored of technology and wallowing in efforts to attain psychic happiness, the post-historicist seriously shortchanges the political and religious problems still taken quite seriously by most of the human race. But then polite professors do not ask each other questions about politics or religion in a dream world where they are permitted endless introspection — indeed, the nature of academic research requires an individual to spend a good deal of his life alone — thanks to technological abundance. By way of contrast, the symbolisms of Eastern European and Latin American liberation movements amply demonstrate the relevance and interconnectedness of traditional Christianity and the quest for social justice in our own time.[22]

Michel Foucault (1926-1984) shared with the post-historicists the notion that the world of liberal capitalism has not brought freedom but new forms of enslavement. He tried to demonstrate that modern institutions control people more effectively by obtaining their mental assent than traditional societies had through physical force.[23] Foucault's work can therefore be used to show how the academic institutions which house the post-historical intellectual insidiously control him and shape his work. 'The medium is the message,' as Harold Innis and Marshall McLuhan have taught us,[24] the medium in this case being the university, the message that the minds of both professors and students must be regulated and disciplined to support the bourgeois order.

It was when Foucault left academe to protest social injustice that he illustrated the possibility of the 'heterotopias' about which he theorized. These were 'spaces' that lay outside of disciplinary control, where alternative ways of living could be tested.[25] By his political actions, Foucault fulfilled the historic function of the intellectual exemplified by the Hebrew prophets and Socrates down to Havel and Neruda in our own time. Myths of objectivity and detachment, like the myth that knowledge is a seamless web or society evolves smoothly over time, are part of the disciplinary mechanism which paralyzes intellectuals while less reflective people shape history. Like Peirce, Foucault stressed discontinuity and rupture in history. Societies can be characterized by 'discourses' which, if examined decades or centuries later, have changed drastically, reflecting the new ways in which they control their populations.[26]

Eugen Rosenstock-Huessy (1888-1976) adopted the motto '*Respondeo etsi mutabor*' — I respond although I will be changed — as more useful to the modern world than the Cartesian '*Cogito ergo sum*' — I think therefore I am. What people *must* respond to, like it or not, are the great revolutions which have and continue to sweep humankind. 'The things created by genuine revolutions are all immortal,' he wrote in his masterpiece *Out of Revolution: Autobiography of Western Man*. 'The Great Revolutions are eccentric, they exaggerate, they are brutal and cruel. But the life of the rest of the world is regenerated by their outbreak.' Germany of the Reformation gave the world secular, monarchical government; England of the Civil Wars parliamentary rule of the gentry; France of the Revolution democratic individualism; Bolshevik Russia economic planning. Each thus developed a partial aspect of human experience and elevated it into an ultimate end, thereby introducing it into the course of history which 'others can use as a thing of relative importance.' With each revolutionary advance came a set of myths, institutions, personality types, ideas, ceremonies, and a new calendar and pantheon of heroes — and villains. 'Each partial choice of man for one or the other eternal value is a decision made by inspired people in an hour of danger and despair,' but 'reality is bigger than any one of them.' If people in a revolutionary or personal crisis cannot help but be advocates for their sacred cause, in calmer moments scholars and nations should follow the path of the great medieval thinker Abelard who 'urged upon men's thought the conception of totality, completeness. He refused to listen to any single authority, any arbitrary voice of the past.' Juxtaposing alternative solutions to profound questions in the famous *Sic et Non*, 'he asked for the authorities' togetherness, [for] their simultaneous representation,' showed that they contradicted each other, and therefore left the way open for people 'to criticize and use their own judgment freely.' By remaining open to an open history, recognizing the contributions of different societies while spurning their mutually exclusive totalitarian pretensions — including that of hegemonic bourgeois liberalism — Rosenstock-Huessy hoped through his writings to shape a future which avoided the perils of stagnation and cataclysm.[27]

If I save Walter Benjamin (1892-1940) for last among the critics of post-historicism, it is because he warns us so eloquently that the temporarily victorious do not only attempt to control the present but also distort the past. History is forever in peril of 'becoming a tool of the ruling classes. In every era the attempt must be made anew to wrest tradition away from a conformism that is about to overpower it,' he wrote in the brief 'Theses on the Philosophy of History.' Correctly written history must stress that history happens, as 'the tradition of the oppressed teaches us . . . in a "state of emergency".' We are only aware of a historical event when we 'seize hold of a memory as it flashes up at a moment of danger.'[28] For historians uninvolved in a dangerous world and the struggles of the oppressed for justice, history can indeed become a bland reflection of experience which culminates in genteel people enjoying the good life — perpetually, intone our post-historicists. But such experience and interpretation of history is so exceptional, not to say arrogant and trivial, as to be beneath contempt.

For all its philosophical insignificance, however, post-historicism has been the underlying assumption of the governing classes of the modern 'democratic' nations at least since the late nineteenth century. Oblivious of the internal and external proletariats and ecological destruction underwriting their historical moment of happiness, they have blithely held themselves up as models to the peoples they exploit — 'The White Man's Burden,' 'The New World Order.' The smug post-historicist intellectual thus explicitly articulates the ideology of the master. Benjamin recognized, as with any form of historical determinism, post-historicism is both a system of theology and a system of mirrors creating an illusion, a chess automaton which has to win.[29] If only history would play by its rules and concede that the best and brightest have won!

As alternatives to serving as court poets and stenographers in the interest of power, we may follow in the path of Foucault's activism. We may also contemplate Max Weber's brilliant essay 'Politics as a Vocation' which demands that the intellectual search out the limitations and contexts of his plans before acting, but that he nevertheless act in a reasoned manner and take moral responsibility for the consequences of his deeds.[30] Or we may follow Walter Benjamin and publicize the 'counter-tradition' of rebels and voices crying in the wilderness to oppose the official stories that have suppressed it.[31]

In his important work *Posthistoire*, Lutz Niethammer has written the collective biography of some of its practitioners — Antoine Cournot, Arnold Gehlen, Kojève, Ernst Jünger, Martin Heidegger, Carl Schmitt, Hendrik de Man, Bertrand de Jouvenel, Jean Baudrillard, and Peter Brückner. In contrast to 'revolutionary intellectuals who dedicated themselves for a long period to political organization,' who 'lead the alliance between bourgeois intellect and the masses,' the post-historicists became 'the ornamentation on an alliance between power and the masses.'[32] Withdrawing from 'the space of history,' they linked their careers and staked the course of history itself on particular regimes — Heidegger's espousal of Nazism being the most notorious — rather than adhering to a principled critique and struggle for justice. To put it bluntly, they sold out, and the modern world has made selling out easier than at any time in history. Foucault's insistence that the intellectual protest injustice but grant absolute allegiance to no creed is one way to guard against this snare.

Post-historicism is the ideology of the tool of power, either disillusioned or still active. Forget it, nothing you can do matters, unless you want to mess up the best, or the only, of all possible worlds. Since all *I* can do is jump on the bandwagon, the post-historicist implies, that is all anyone else should do either. Wallowing in his detached irrelevance, the post-historicist is the model citizen for a state that relies for legitimacy on silent acquiescence and occasional cheerleading rather than informed, critical participation.

In the long run, post-historicists will be little more than a curiosity of intellectual history, like the Alchemists or the Sophists. They have exposed themselves as uncritical signifiers of an immoral world which has created unprecedented problems threatening life on earth while celebrating its squandering of lives and resources as the pinnacle of history. By neglecting questions of class, race, gender, and ecology which have made the lives of a vast majority of the planet's population miserable, the post-historicists have performed the task of diverting First World attention from addressing real problems to celebrating technology and achieving psychological liberation. They thereby contribute, from the ruling elite's perspective, to the denigration of non-technologically-oriented learning and trivialization of criticism in the eyes of the masses. At any rate, they need not fear they will be forgotten. As unfolding events belie his prediction that history has come to an end, the estranged, institutionalized, pampered post-historical thinker will some day acquire true significance as a historical artifact.

* * * * *

Artistic artifacts will accompany intellectual ones. A prominent example of contemporary post-historic consciousness is the opera *The Ghosts of Versailles*. It beautifully mixes the paradoxical traits of arrogance and *weltschmertz* characteristic of this mode of thought: the late twentieth-century west is the apex of material history, but must shamelessly raid its past to obtain spiritual sustenance.

Two centuries after their deaths, Marie Antoinette, Louis XVI, and other 'ghosts of Versailles' are moping around in limbo longing for the good old days before the French Revolution. The playwright Beaumarchais informs them he can change history. He will prevent their executions and spirit them away to America by sending them back in time, to interact with the characters from *The Marriage of Figaro* and *The Barber of Seville*, whom he can miraculously bring to life. What's in it for Beaumarchais is he loves Marie Antoinette and plans to take her away from Louis XVI. She turns out to be the eighteenth century's Marilyn Monroe — a bored, frightened, sensitive victim of a glitzy world long on style and short on substance rather than the Nancy Reagan of the ancien regime. Three universes — Beaumarchais and his fictional characters, the French Revolution, and the returning ghosts — get all mixed up. At the end, Marie Antoinette nobly decides to die rather than flee. She thereby saves Beaumarchais' soul, which he has risked by altering history, and expiates her own sins and those of her people by submitting to her execution.

In a nutshell, that's what *The Ghosts of Versailles*, 'grand opera buffa,' music by John Corigliano, libretto by William T. Hoffman which premiered at New York's Metropolitan Opera on December 19, 1991, is about.[33] It is like no other opera of which I know. Instead of asking the audience to be interested in the fate of characters that are supposed to represent real people experiencing love, anger, death, etc. in a fairly straightforward way, the observer needs to keep three universes in mind as the characters and musical styles of Beaumarchais' plays, the French Revolution, and the ghosts interact. There is also a fourth world — the librettist's and composer's — which intermittently appears when the characters step out of their roles to comment on the opera itself.

These asides usually occur right after an especially moving or dramatic scene. They consciously intend to provoke laughter: following Marie Antoinette's powerful opening number in which she relives her life and execution, her husband turns to the audience and comments, 'My wife was always hard to please.' This sarcastic remark undercuts the fact that soprano Teresa Stratas has brought to vivid life a horrible imprisonment and death which would have made Joan of Arc cringe. As Marie Antoinette later dreams of a new life with Beaumarchais, the cynical Louis gets chuckles with the observation: 'Excessive in life, excessive in death.' And after Louis is finally sufficiently aroused to duel with Beaumarchais to keep his spouse, and the author is 'killed,' he then pulls out the sword as all the ghosts giggle uproariously as they remember they are already dead. Except perhaps in the final two scenes, every time we get close to the characters words and music pull us away, remind us we are only watching ghosts, and in effect deconstruct the opera as it is being presented. The audience, like the opera, stands simultaneously at the end of the story and at the end of history. We are thus invited to be post-historical theorists as we *participate in* this remarkable work of art.

What is interesting is why anyone would want to write an opera which discourages, rather than invites, identification with the fate of the characters. It is therefore important to examine *The Ghosts of Versailles* from a semiotic perspective: the context in which it was written, the musical and theatrical codes or conventions it uses and tries to undermine simultaneously, and the audience which participates in the experience as it laughs and applauds at certain junctures to comment on the production. For *Ghosts* is a semiotic opera, which tells several stories pertaining to different yet intertwined sets of characters, theatrically existing at different times in history and even different realms of being — figures in a play, historical characters from the French Revolution, 'ghosts' observing themselves two hundred years in the past, and a real life audience, which reacts to the whole experience while becoming part of it.

The Ghosts of Versailles is not a great opera, although there is a lot of wonderful music in it. The Met did itself proud by putting on a show that could hold its own with the contemporaneous extravaganzas of Andrew Lloyd Webber — *Les Misérables* and *The Phantom of the Opera* — also evocative of the peculiar mixture of aristocratic culture and egalitarian idealism which ensures that France and the French will always be interesting if not attractive. The reason *Ghosts* is musically problematic is that it would make a marvelous final exam for students in an opera history class: the best tunes are variations on Mozart and Rossini, the rest being standard spooky music for the ghosts, predictable *sprechstimme* to forward the plot — that is, words intoned at specified pitches, volumes, and durations — and fortissimo chaos for the Revolution. Rossini, if legend is to be trusted, passed the perfect critical judgment on such an opera over a century ago in one of his famous *bon mots*: 'Your opera is both original and good; but what is good is not original, and what is original is not good.'

Yet *Ghosts* is immensely interesting, not only as musical theater but as a meditation on musical and political history. It is a fascinating symbol of the predicament of musical composition and social aimlessness in the 'post-modern' age. What is Corigliano's and Hoffman's view of history? The Old Regime was a bore: Marie Antoinette was lonely and homesick at court. She compares herself to the bird in the gilded cage: 'I never saw the world outside, I never knew the world of pain.' Louis XVI is a philistine whose most-repeated phrase is a mechanical 'don't . . . care.' The world of Versailles is a scene of corruption, vanity, stupidity, and evil where true love is thwarted behind a facade of pretentious elegance. The aristocrats in Beaumarchais' play need Figaro and Susanna to solve their problems, keep their lives interesting, and lend a dose of sanity and intelligence to a bunch of walking Goya portraits. Similarly, Beaumarchais himself plays Figaro to Marie Antoinette's Countess, with Louis standing in for Almaviva.

But the Revolution is even worse. It is led by Begearss, a sadistic megalomaniac whose aria — 'Long live the worm!' — is a *tour de force* for Graham Clark, who acrobatically impersonates a worm as the creature which triumphs over man and beast by devouring them in death. He whips up the crowd into a frenzy against a nobility which finally lives up to its name by bravely facing its doom. The only people who actually suffer in this opera are high-minded aristocrats courageously facing their deaths while plebeian monsters curse them and parade around with heads on poles. As Alex Ross pointedly wrote in *The New Republic*, Simon Schama's *Citizens*, a contemporaneous book which condemns the French Revolution for its irrational destruction of a progressive monarchy, 'is, by comparison, a Marxist tract.'[34]

So where do authenticity and justice reside? Why, in America, of course, and New York in particular. Beaumarchais is planning to spirit the royal family away to the land of the free, a journey in fact made by many refugees from the Revolution, among them Talleyrand and the future King Louis Philippe. Two possible destinations are mentioned: New York, which Louis hears is a 'lively town,' and Philadelphia. When Marie Antoinette mentions the possibility of living in the latter city — the port of choice for most French exiles — Louis responds, 'If you call that living,' and a ghost chimes in, 'I thank God I'm dead,' which gets the expected laugh from the New York audience. These throwaway lines and the reaction to them signify America, New York, and the world of the Metropolitan Opera itself as paradise found, the best of all possible worlds.

But Marie Antoinette turns it down. Like Wayne and Garth, she is not worthy, and resolves to die to expiate her past aristocratic indifference and pardon her enemies, as 'forgiveness is the only way to freedom.' Such a message is especially ironic at one of the world's most expensive theatres: one can doubt if the patrons spend more on charity than they do on $100 opera tickets preceded by $100 dinners and followed by $100 hotel rooms. Few in the happy auditorium are probably aware that their *prima donna* is assisting them in deconstructing themselves: Teresa Stratas, a singer of great beauty, subtlety, and intensity — she was the first to sing all of Alban Berg's *Lulu*, perhaps the greatest modern opera of all, written in the 1930s — was in fact born in abject poverty and spends a great deal of time and money helping the poor.

The *Ghosts of Versailles* therefore performs two parallel tasks. It renders contemporary opera palatable to an audience that just wants to hear the same old operas, for to a large extent it is a composite of two of the most-performed works in the repertoire, and it rewrites history so that prosperous folks rejoicing in the end of Communism can dump all revolution in the trashbin — librettist Hoffman did so in an interview — and identify with the enterprising barber, the resourceful intellectual Beaumarchais, and the romantic, self-sacrificing queen.[35]

The stereotypes in this opera would make even Rossini blush, not to mention Mozart, who with the help of Lorenzo da Ponte — who in fact would up in New York and introduced their operas there — created such three-dimensional characters as Don Giovanni and Leporello, Despina and Don Alfonso, and virtually everyone in *Figaro*. In *Ghosts*, middle-class men are the activists and thinkers, except for the scene where middle-class Susanna takes charge of the incompetent noblewomen. Aristocrats and revolutionaries are lecherous slime (Almaviva, Begearss) or dolts (Louis XVI). Women are ruled by their hearts and sacrifice themselves. The conventional stereotypes of class, race, and gender are so blatant that one starts to wonder whether the opera is parodying itself.

The appearance of the non-Western 'Other' through a 'Turkish' entertainment is perhaps the most insulting stereotype of all; it goes so far it may even be parodying the very caricatures it presents. Supposedly based on the rage for things Turkish in Mozart's day — exemplified in his opera *The Abduction from the Seraglio* — the music and some of the words are in fact Arabic. After all, it's all east of Suez. Accompanied by music that makes 'The Dance of the Seven Veils' sound like the Ninth Symphony, Marilyn Horne sings about a woman whose house contains a cesspool, whose husband beats her, and who has no 'he-camel or she-camel,' thereby setting a record for the number of anti-Arab stereotypes presented in the shortest possible time. Huge figures of Middle Eastern warriors and a sultan are in fact cardboard and comic, much like Saddam Hussein and his SCUDS which were duds in the war of the previous year. If ever Arab terrorism had a legitimate target, this scene would be it!

The libretto would be another candidate for destruction. Much of it is the pseudo-sensitive drivel which made the film *Last Year at Marienbad* such a hit among those trying to appear profound and tasteful without any idea of how to carry it off. What can be done with an opera that opens: 'My charger is out of breath. Alas! How weary is my heart. I wandered from field to field at the whim of my steed, without page or squire, close by a fountain?' People think they are funny for being 'bored as a rug, . . . egg . . . [or] potato.' Is Figaro's soliloquoy as he ascends in a balloon on the level, or is it homage to the late film-maker Edward D. Wood: 'A vapor deliquescent, an effervescent liquid, pervading, invading, taking my body, making me fluid. Buoyant I'm sunlight and moonbeams, and carefree I fly to the stars.' Figaro then proceeds to show he passed Astronomy 101 by naming various stars, constellations, and galaxies.

In fact, the (unintentionally?) hilarious, awful-pretentious libretto, the depressing stereotypes of class, race, and gender, and music which panders to lowest-common-denominator audience expectations of how ghostly music, crowd scenes, and romantic trysts in gardens ought to sound suggest the whole thing is a gigantic hoax. A woman dressed as a Valkyrie appears during the Turkish mayhem and shouts: 'This is not opera!' to general mirth. If Corigliano and Hoffman are on the level, and want the audience to enjoy the spectacle and feel for the characters, this is indeed not opera. But if they intended to construct a complex, multi-layered invitation to semiotic meditation on the nature of music, history, and life from a post-historic perspective, their work is in fact a sobering and subtle deconstruction of the human and musical stereotypes that they so blatantly and absurdly present. That Corigliano has in fact written a magnificent, original work inspired by the AIDS health crisis — his First Symphony — suggests he and Hoffman may in fact be mocking their audience, although they could never admit it.

The circumstances under which *The Ghosts of Versailles* was composed tell us much about why it appeared almost simultaneously with Francis Fukuyama's *The End of History and the Last Man*. Since bourgeois liberalism is the final form of state and our material problems are solved (a few technicalities aside) ennui and possibly self-destructive efforts to escape it are the only possible fates for people 'at the end of history.' Fukuyama's insights remarkably fit the boredom expressed by the ghosts in the opera who (coincidentally?) are 'living' in our time. In other words, a post-historic audience is signified by a crowd of ghosts, because the ghosts in the opera function as the audience, thus merging the two groups.

If our problems are solved — us being the people who go to the Metropolitan Opera, not people in Bosnia or Harlem — can art emerge from life where only ghosts exist? Whereas Mozart wrote six operas and hundreds of other works between 1780 and his death in 1791, Corigliano and Hoffman, commissioned to write an opera in 1980 celebrating the Met's centennial in 1983, finally produced it in 1991! Why did it take so long? Research — into operatic and political history — plus the necessity of having parts of the work approved by the Met as the composition progressed.[36] It is no wonder *Ghosts* took about as long to prepare as the average doctoral dissertation or scholarly book these days: it had to fit institutional requirements and be approved by a committee. And in fact, the ponderous erudition underlying what is at least partially an *opera buffa* is reminiscent of contemporary scholarship which struts its conventionality using a mountain of footnotes.

The Ghosts of Versailles was a big hit at the Met and will be revived in the 1994-1995 season. Its popular success makes sense because it feeds the appetite of post-historic people who wish to experience 'history' as nostalgia for romantic and heroic times, people, and places — *Gone with the Wind* would make a fabulous opera if we could only forget about 'political correctness' and keep the slaves singing and smiling. Yet this very success explains why conventional opera has little hope as a creative rather than a performing art. Great opera, like any meaningful music, literature, or art, must connect with the real-life experience of its audience. Women trapped in hopeless marriages to older men was a problem in the nineteenth century; 'mad scenes' were vicarious escapes. Nationalistic operas by Verdi and Wagner quickened the patriotic pulse. But nowadays kings and the church are no longer relevant issues; if we need soldiers, we hire mercenaries; if marriages fail, divorce is the answer. It is logical that Benjamin Britten, whose mature operas *Peter Grimes*, *Billy Budd*, and *Death in Venice* deal with his own homosexuality, are perhaps the most moving of modern times. The works of Kurt Weill and Hans Werner Henze, however powerful and beautiful, are too revolutionary for opera's bourgeois audience. Prosperous narcissists preoccupied with physical fitness, mental health, and material status are unlikely to care much for an art form which presupposes the mutual dependence of characters who cannot simply walk away from each other.

Opera is also comatose if not dead because it is no longer written by opera composers. Instead, academic musicians who win foundation grants or teach in conservatories or universities write opera on the side of their regular compositions. Their career success depends on appealing to fellow professionals rather than to a general public. Someone — more likely, some institution — commissions an opera of a serious composer whose fee is assured and who is more concerned to be respectable than theatrical. The post-historic composer is in the same situation as the post-historic intellectual: he panders to a self-satisfied, estranged elite.

The composer's situation is impossible. If he satisfies the professoriat, he denies the public which wants to hear the same old tunes or reasonable facsimilies thereof. Corigliano and Hoffman had the sense to give the Metropolitan Museum of Opera the same old tunes, literally in many cases, presented in a context which comfortably distanced the audience from any potentially threatening political or social reality through humor and a complex, multi-layered libretto verging on the incomprehensible. (As King Louis remarks at one point — 'I always had trouble understanding the fourth act of *Figaro* and this is even worse!') They also dropped the right musical footnotes to satisfy the professoriat.

Still, *Ghosts* is an apt framework for some nice tunes and fancy stage effects. The loveliest melodies are given neither to the ghosts nor to the revolutionaries, but to the fictional characters from *The Marriage of Figaro*. *Ghosts* achieves further alienation by making art seem more 'real' than even second-hand reality. And the loveliest tune of all, 'O thieving time, give me back my stolen years,' is profoundly moving to an operatic audience which is disproportionately elderly or homosexual — people affected by the AIDS epidemic. This quartet may also serve as a requiem for a civilization that can only live in its past as it builds more and better security systems — like the one in the Met's garage — to preserve its dream world from the barbarians within and without. Marie Antoinette's willing death gives the lie to the fictional Beaumarchais' hope that we can reconstruct 'history as it should have been,' freeze 'thieving time,' and exorcise revolution from our newer and better Versailles. Thus ends an opera that manages to deconstruct political and musical history, not to mention itself and its audience, as it goes along. In so doing, it questions the very post-historical world it so effectively signifies.

Professor of History, Penn State. Versions of this paper were presented at the Congress of the International Association of Semiotics Societies, Berkeley, California, June 1994, and the Semiotics Society of America, Philadelphia, October 1994. The opening quotation is from Metternich's Memoires (8 vols.: Paris, Plon, 1881-84), 3:455.

ENDNOTES

1. Alexandre Kojève, *Introduction to the Reading of Hegel's Phenomenology of Mind*, trans. James Nichols, Jr. (New York: Basic Books, 1969), 43-44, 191, 254.

2. Roderick Seidenberg, *Post-Historic Man: An Inquiry* (Chapel Hill: University of North Carolina Press, 1950), 29-30.

3. Francis Fukuyama, *The End of History and the Last Man* (New York: Basic Books, 1992), xi.

4. Herodotus, *The Histories*, trans. Aubrey de Selincourt (Baltimore: Penguin Books, 1954), 524.

5. Immanuel Kant, *Perpetual Peace*, trans. Ted Humphrey (Indianapolis: Bobbs-Merrill, 1983), 29-30.

6. Herodotus, *The Histories*, esp. 168, 254, 96-100, 599.

7. William Pencak, *History, Signing In: Studies in History and Semiotics* (New York: Peter Lang, 1993).

8. Charles S. Peirce, *Collected Papers*, eds. P. Weiss, A. Burks, and C. Hartshorne, 8 vols. (Cambridge, Mass.: Harvard University Press, 1931-1958), 7. 769; 6. 312. References to volume and paragraph.

9. *Ibid.*, 6. 290.

10. *Ibid.*, 6. 292.

11. *Ibid.*, 1. 51; Charles Peirce, *Historical Perspectives on Peirce's Logic of Science*, ed. Carolyn Eisele (Berlin: Mouton de Gruyter, 1985), 1117-1119.

12. Thorstein Veblen, *The Theory of the Leisure Class* (New York: Macmillan, 1899); *The Higher Learning in America* (New York: Viking, 1935; 1st ed. 1918), esp. 12-13, 80, 85, 88, 98.

13. Herbert Marcuse, *One-Dimensional Man* (Boston: Beacon Press, 1964).

14. Fukuyama, *End of History*, 312, 330.

15. Vincent Descombes, *Modern French Philosophy*, trans. L. Scott-Fox and J. M. Harding (Cambridge: Cambridge University Press, 1980), 31.

16. Jean-Francois Lyotard, *Economie libidinale* (Paris: Minuit, 1974); Jacques Lacan, *Écrits: A Selection*, trans. Alan Sheridan (London: Tavistock, 1977); Georges Bataille, *Visions of Excess: Selected Writings 1927-1939*, trans. A. Stoekl, C. Lovett, D. Leslie, Jr. (Manchester: Manchester University Press, 1985); Jean Baudrillard, *De la séduction* (Paris: Donoel/Gonthier, 1979); Michel Foucault, *Politics, Philosophy, Culture: Interviews and Other Writings, 1977-1984* (New York: Routledge, 1988), 36; Thomas R. Flynn, 'Foucault and the Spaces of History,' *Monist* 74 (1991), 165-187.

17. John Taylor, *Circus of Ambition: The Culture of Wealth and Power* (New York: Warner Books, 1989); Tom Wolfe, *Bonfire of the Vanities* (New York: Farrar, Straus, Giroux, 1987).

18. Carl Becker, 'Everyman His Own Historian,' *American Historical Review*, 37 (1932), 221-236; *The Heavenly City of the Eighteenth-Century Philosophers* (New Haven: Yale University Press, 1932), 47.

19. Eric Voegelin, *Über die Form des Amerikanischen Geistes* (Tubingen: J. C. B. Mohr, 1928), esp. 32-52.

20. Eric Voegelin, 'Reason: The Classic Experience,' *Southern Review* 10 (1974), 237-264; *Science, Politics, and Gnosticism* (Chicago: Henry Regnery, 1968), 108.

21. Eric Voegelin, 'History and Gnosis,' in Bernhard Anderson, ed., *The Old Testament and Christian Faith* (New York: Herder and Herder, 1969), 64-89; 'The Eclipse of Reality,' in Maurice Natanson, ed., *Phenomenology and Social Reality* (The Hague: Martinus Nijhoff, 1970), 185-194.

22. Smithsonian Institute Exhibition of Eastern European Protest Poster Art; National Museum of American Art, Exhibition of Chicano Protest Art; both viewed by author, June 1992, in Washington, DC.

23. See especially Michel Foucault, *Discipline and Punish: The Birth of the Prison*, trans. Alan Sheridan, (New York: Pantheon, 1977); *Madness and Civilization: A History of Insanity in the Age of Reason*, trans. Richard Howard (New York: Mentor, 1965).

24. Harold Innis, *The Bias of Communication* (Toronto: University of Toronto Press, 1951); Marshall McLuhan, *The Gutenberg Galaxy: The Making of Typographic Man* (Toronto: University of Toronto Press, 1962)

25. See references to Foucault in n. 16 above; James Miller, *The Passion of Michel Foucault* (New York: Simon and Schuster, 1993), 15, 315-316.

26. Michel Foucault, *The Archaeology of Knowledge*, trans. A. M. Sheridan-Smith (New York: Harper and Row, 1972), 21, 161-164.

27. Eugen Rosenstock-Huessy, 'Farewell to Descartes,' in *I Am An Impure Thinker* (Norwich: Argo Books, 1970), 1-19; *Out of Revolution: Autobiography of Western Man* (Norwich: Argo Books, 1969; originally published 1938), 24, 125, 151, 477, 490, 625-627.

28. Walter Benjamin, 'Theses on the Philosophy of History,' in *Illuminations*, trans. Harry Zohn (New York: Schocken Books, 1969), 253-264.

29. *Ibid.*, 253.

30. Max Weber, 'Politics as a Vocation,' in Hans Gerth and C. Wright Mills, trans., *From Max Weber* (New York: Oxford University Press, 1946).

31. For my comment on Benjamin, I rely on Lutz Niethammer, *Posthistoire: Has History Come to an End?*, trans. Patrick Camiller (London: Verso, 1992), esp. 4-5, 101-134, who contrasts Benjamin most favorably with his post-historicist contemporaries.

32. *Ibid.*, 139, 142.

33. John Corigliano and William T. Hoffman, *The Ghosts of Versailles*, Metropolitan Opera videotape, has all the references to the opera.

34. Alex Ross, 'The Ghosts of the Met,' *The New Republic*, March 9, 1992, 29-33.

35. Lanford Wilson, 'Ghost Writer,' *Opera News*, January 4, 1992, 16-20.

36. Michael C. Nott, 'Corigliano to Versailles,' *Opera News*, January 4, 1992, 9-11.

Chapter XVII

Ethereal Semiotics:
Origins of an Electronic World

David K. B. Zeeman*

Governments could really take steps to keep the ethereal peace without owning
the entire ether as well as the earth beneath.

Electrical World Magazine, on the Ether, 1906[1]

This is the history of an 'electronic environment.' The idea is by no means
new. A growing number of books and articles have been published
concerning 'cyberspace,' the electronic environment named by philosopher
William Gibson.[2] Cyberspace is the environment perceived by people who
interact with others through electronic communications technology (i.e.
radios, telephones, and computers). The space is not real, in any tangible
sense. It is a 'place' association that the mind assigns to an otherwise
imperceptible and meaningless flow of electrons.

The electronic environment discussed in this article is the manifestation
of cyberspace inspired by wireless telegraphy (early radio) a half-century
before computers dominated access to this intangible location. For this
reason, instead of cyberspace, I will call this environment the 'ether,' as it
was called in the early twentieth century.

The ether, alternatively referred to as the 'æther,' the 'luminiferous
ether,' and the 'electric fluid,' is a theoretical medium that permeates all
space and transmits electromagnetic energy. In the early twentieth century,
the scientific community needed the ether to explain how electrical charges
could 'jump' across the space between two metal filaments. The charge had
to travel through something. The ether was the best explanation available
at the time.

As a concept, the ether evolved considerably throughout the centuries.
The Renaissance philosophers and the great physicists of the eighteenth and
nineteenth centuries accepted without question the existence of the universal
medium. Its structure and nature, however, were bickered over for

generations. Until physicist James Clerk Maxwell unified this chaotic discourse, perceptions of the ether remained numerous, varied, and staunchly defended. As a manifestation of cyberspace the ether became a medium of communication, presenting a number of new problems above and beyond the academic issue of defining it.

When it was discovered that one could use electricity for the purpose of communication, wireless telegraphy, which ultimately evolved into modern radio, was born. At the turn of the twentieth century, however, wireless telegraphy was a very new and largely undefined technology. Furthermore, the technology could produce a very limited number of frequencies, or channels. Research and development of wireless was too slow to accommodate the growing number of transmitting operators, creating tremendous interference problems. The technology was incapable of 'tuning-out,' or selecting higher frequencies, allowing virtually anyone to intercept or obliterate another's message.

The economic, social, and political value of the ether lay in its ability to convey private information quickly over vast distances without the use of wire or cable connections. Interference hindered development of the ether as a viable 'resource,' creating friction between many groups which sought to define and exploit it for their own purposes.

In the context of wireless telegraphy, the ether became contested between two such groups: the amateurs and the United States government. The amateurs were a gathering of public sector hobbyists who used the ether as a field for play and experimentation. The government used it to convey and control military and political information. This paper explores the ether as a shifting sign of the scientific, esthetic, and political intentions of different communities of interpreters.

A Scientific Ether

We can begin to understand the ether by shedding light on its origins. The word *æther* had its roots in the Greek, meaning 'blue sky,' or 'upper atmosphere.'[3] Johannes Kepler, baffled by such natural events as tides, magnetism, and lightning, speculated that some sort of a medium fills and connects everything in the 'interstellar void.' He believed this medium could transmit the energy necessary for such electromagnetic phenomena. René Descartes used many of Kepler's ideas to develop his *Mechanical Philosophy*, which likened the universe to a giant clock-like machine. It was in this framework that Descartes named Kepler's universal medium the 'ether.' Descartes described it as the 'subtler matter' between all matter in the universe.[4]

This definition of the word, thus brought into the world of science, changed considerably throughout the centuries as scientists studying electromagnetic phenomena argued over the ether's structure and internal dynamics. For example, Sir Isaac Newton likened the ether to air: 'just as air contains "aqueous vapor" so the ether may contain various "ætherial spirits" adapted to produce the phenomena of electricity, magnetism, and gravitation.'[5] André Marie Ampère attributed a more 'liquid' nature to the 'luminiferous ether,' claiming both electricity and magnetism to be 'mutually saturating fluids.'[6] Scientists became entralled with defining an ether they had yet to apply practically.

In the late nineteenth century, a young Cambridge student by the name of James Clerk Maxwell redefined, or rather 'undefined,' the ether once and for all. His attitude toward the ether was much more cautious than Newton's or Ampère's. He was concerned that the physical metaphors scientists used to describe the mechanics of the ether were complicating their work. Maxwell stated that '[they] could not specify the nature of the motion of these media, and not prove the media would produce the effects they were meant to explain.'[7] He made little pretense of detailing the ether's nature, describing it generally and carefully as a 'material substance of a more subtle kind than visible bodies, supposed to exist in those parts of space which are apparently empty.'[8]

Maxwell suggested that electrical and magnetic effects arose by some unknown occurrence within the ether. They were physical, and therefore observable, manifestations of processes hidden from our direct senses. This lack of definition enabled Maxwell to conceptualize an 'electromagnetic spectrum,' a continuum, free from the confining attributes of 'gasses' and 'fluids.' The spectrum could transmit waves of electromagnetic force at the speed of light. In 1873, with his *Treatise of Electricity and Magnetism*, Maxwell published the dynamical equations that became the foundation of applicable and theoretical knowledge for wireless technology.

The Ether as a Sign of Communication
In the late 1820's a portal to the ether opened in the spark of Michael Faraday's 'electromagnetic induction.' The British physicist transmitted an electrical charge without wires, a flash which jumped across a tiny gap between two metal spheres. For Faraday, induction was hardly an

electronic environment. Rather it was an observable electromagnetic phenomenon, the culmination of two centuries of scientific research.

While the scientific definition of the ether evolved throughout the mid-nineteenth century, another conception of it slowly formed with the development of wireless technology. Not long after Faraday's experiments, telegraph engineers conceived of using electromagnetic *conduction* for communication purposes. Faraday's 'induction' involved both a wire connection and the air to complete an electrical circuit. Early experiments in conduction proved the wire connection unnecessary: water and the earth, in contact with the air, could serve as a complete circuit.[9]

In 1838, the German professor C. A. Steinheil was the first to suggest using conduction technology to transmit telegraphic signals.[10] From that point on, electromagnetic conduction, in the context of communications, was called wireless telegraphy. Thus, the ether, in the context of interactive communication (wireless), became an electronic environment.

Over the next sixty years, wireless technology remained largely an academic concern. Following James Clerk Maxwell's prediction of electromagnetic waves, the 'Maxwellians' — G. F. Fitzgerald, Oliver Heaviside, Oliver Lodge, and Heinrich Rudolph Hertz — brought wireless technology to an almost marketable form.[11] The insulated academic community, however, seemed to have no interest in turning the technology into a commodity. This lack of interest opened the door for the man most responsible for the commercial development of wireless: the Italian inventor Guglielmo Marconi.[12]

Marconi brought wireless telegraphy to a point of popular accessibility. He developed the technology to make it cheap, easy to use, and available for commercial (and therefore, wide scale) application. Once wireless reached this point, the governments of the great powers and the general public were made aware of the ether's inherent value, and strove to develop it for their own purposes.

A Political Ether

In a September 22, 1899 article, the *New York Times* reported the first presentation of wireless technology in the specific context of political interest. The Marconi Wireless Company was contracted by the United States War Department to conduct a number of military tests.[13] At a time when people naively hoped that wireless would bring the nations together, the political and military aims of the great powers were defining wireless, and the ether, in an entirely different manner.

The practical application of wireless in the world's navies was irresistible: communication between ships without wires would drastically improve logistic and tactical efficiency. Early wireless, however, was generally uniform in its complexity throughout the world, allowing most systems to achieve the same number of frequencies in a range we now call 'HF,' or high frequency. In this range anyone with a simple receiver could intercept important messages. Anyone with a transmitter could disrupt them. Privacy could not be guaranteed since access to the ether was limited to a definite number of frequencies. For political and military application, this proved a significant factor.

America's naval victories in the 1898 Spanish-American War prompted Congress to boost the annual navy budget to $77,000,000.[14] This great expenditure marked a new era in American military history, an era which included the protection of a vast sphere of influence ranging from Cuba, South America, and across the Pacific Ocean to the Philippines. The American navy was clearly modernizing, stepping into the international arena to take its place among the great fleets of the world.

Wireless telegraphy was included among the modernization efforts of the navy. By May 14, 1901, the Naval Bureau of Equipment planned to integrate wireless technology as a means of signaling between warships at sea. Awaiting future tests, the Bureau scaled down its homing pigeon program, intending to replace the birds once a workable wireless system became available.[15]

A 'workable' system, however, proved more elusive than expected. In March 18, 1902, the British battleship *Revenge*, which was fitted with a wireless system, accidentally received a number of private transmissions from the Marconi Company, toward which the American navy leaned toward as a potential contractor.[16] On November 30, 1902, the Italian navy, while on maneuvers in the Mediterranean, intercepted British signals, causing considerable embarrassment for the Empire. In response to the event, a *Times* reporter stated, 'it was found impossible to prevent any signal from being obliterated by the interference of willfully obstructive signals sent out by an invisible enemy.'[17]

As early as 1902, then, it was clear that the practical application of wireless for political and military purposes would not be simple. Governments were too proprietary in their desires to develop the ether in a constructive manner.   The problem of interference indicated to the great powers that an international agreement over the use of wireless was needed.

The catalyst for such an agreement was the role of wireless during the Russo-Japanese War in 1904.   The 111-day conflict served as a test-situation for wireless telegraphy, its first application in a combat situation.   On April 16, Russia put a ban on wireless news coverage in the war zone.   Count Cassini, the Russian Ambassador to the United States, sent a note to both the British and American governments, stating:

> Neutral steamers having on board correspondents who might communicate war news to the enemy by means of perfected [wireless] apparatus . . . will be looked upon as spies and the steamers furnished with wireless telegraphy seized as prizes of war. [18]

Four months later, the *Times* presented the story behind Russia's aggressive policy.   The only operating wireless coverage of the war came from the *London Times*, whose correspondents transmitted news of battles and troop maneuvers from the steamer *Haimun*.   The reporters had been covering the war for two months when on April 15, the Russian cruiser *Bayal* stopped and boarded their ship.   The correspondents were informed that one of their news transmissions interfered with Japanese tactical signals.   The Japanese intercepted the message and used the information to their advantage while landing troops at Chi-nam-Pho.   The Russians took this as an act of sabotage and ordered the *Haimun* and its relay station in China dismantled.

This incident demonstrated that wireless could play a profound role in national security, prompting governments worldwide to place greater emphasis on the direction of internal wireless operations.   On May 28, 1904 the United States government began consolidating departments which used wireless telegraphy along the Atlantic and Pacific coasts, sparking accusations that it was planning a monopoly over access to the ether.   When the *New York Times* questioned the Navy Department on the matter, an official replied:

> Frequently the Government systems clash with those of private individuals and companies. In time of war this would be a serious matter and necessarily for the purposes of defense the Government would be forced to insist on exclusive rights. . . . We can conceive of some sort of right of way through the air. [19]

Other governments responded to the use of wireless in the Russo-Japanese War by expanding their own wireless programs. By 1906, thirty-five nations integrated wireless telegraphy into their armed forces, the United States leading the way with 88 stations, Great Britain following with 44.[20] With so many nations competing for space in the ether, it became clear that some form of international agreement was needed to ease tensions and to define wireless and the ether better in the specific contexts of war and diplomacy.

On September 26, 1906, the International Law Institute in Ghent, Belgium, adopted a code of procedure for the use of wireless in war time. For example, belligerents could prevent a neutral state's transmissions within the designated war zone, as Russia did to the British correspondents in 1904. Neutral states, however, had the right either to disrupt or let alone frequencies that crossed through their borders.[21]

Thus, by 1906 the ether became yet another 'territory' of contention. National governments had shaped the ether to resemble their own world, the tension-filled period before World War I. With this definition firmly in place, the ether became what Foucault has called a 'space of contention.'[22] However, while governments scrambled to control the ether, a growing number of young men and women began staking their own claims to it. In the spirit of the great powers themselves, they vied to protect those claims.

A Public Ether

In a January 31, 1909 article entitled 'Boys Forge Ahead Wireless Work,' the *New York Times* defined an entire class of young people called 'amateurs,' or 'hams,' who took to the ether in droves with their homemade wireless sets. Unlike national governments, the individual amateurs' interest in wireless technology was based largely on the fact that it was fun and exciting.[23] Other influences attributed to that interest were popular culture and the psychology of radio. Above all, wireless was a medium of communication that brought distant people of similar backgrounds and interests into an 'ethereal' community.

Throughout the first decade of the new century, amateur enthusiasts slowly grew in number as the technology became cheaper and more available. New York City, already the financial and commercial center of the world, became the locus of the infant radio industry. As early as 1906, wireless components and related technologies could be found in the crowded emporium of Hugo Gernsbeck's Electro-Importing Company.[24] Both amateur and inventor alike could find what was needed here, but wireless parts could certainly be obtained by other, far more interesting means.

Many young people built their wireless sets from scratch, using sophisticated parts such as Quaker Oats boxes, copper wire, and assorted wood and brass pieces to tune in different frequencies. With an aerial, a solid piece of galena crystal, and a thin, 'cat's whisker' feeler, there was a slight chance of receiving some kind of radio signal. Around 1920 the necessary manufactured components cost the amateur only $2.00 and perhaps another $4.00 for a reasonable pair of commercial headphones.[25] The headgear, however, could be conveniently pilfered from any number of public telephone booths, a sort of 'rite of passage' before the real deviant behavior could commence.

Once assembled, the amateur's wireless set opened up a portal to an electronic environment, a new 'space' to explore and define. A good deal of an amateur's time was spent tuning in to reach clear transmissions, which essentially meant eavesdropping on other messages. He (almost all amateurs were male) could hear wireless tests by the great inventors, secret reports by the government, private communication from ship to shore, and fellow amateurs sending out friendly (and often obscene) messages. If he had no transmitter, or for some reason was unable to respond, amateur protocol would prompt him to mail a 'contact card' to the sender, including the time and date of the confirmed reception.[26] This way, amateurs were not only able to improve their systems with a listening, critical audience, they were establishing a network of friends, rivals, and information, above and beyond established channels of communication. The amateurs were quite unconsciously laying the foundations of their own unique subculture.

But how did this subculture perceive the ether? To answer this question we must look at three specific influences upon the amateur mind: popular culture, the psychology of radio, and the actions of other amateurs within the ether.

Popular Culture

The technological boom of the late nineteenth century resulted in an economic demand for skilled engineers to reproduce discoveries and to custom-design machinery. Thus, the beginning of the twentieth century saw a greater emphasis on jobs requiring skills in physics, math, and electrical mechanics. For the younger generation of this time, wireless was both an exciting new hobby and a potential key to future success in the business world. Many parents encouraged their sons and daughters to tinker with the new technology, viewing such behavior as a wonderful way to gain the skills necessary for a high-paying job.[27]

By 1911, children's stories and the new genre, 'science fiction,' reflected this emphasis on science by actively including wireless telegraphy in their storylines. A favorite, *Tom Swift and His Wireless Message*, indicated that young people could become heroes or great inventors with the new technology. As early as 1907, however, popular culture had begun celebrating the amateur hobby. In a massive front-page exposé, the public interest section of the *New York Times* presented an article entitled, 'New Wonders with Wireless — And By a Boy!' The 'boy' was twenty-six year old Walter J. Willinborg, an engineer at the Stevens Institute in Hoboken, New Jersey. He was interviewed at his home station, where he demonstrated his ability to disrupt frequencies with a 'wizard's skill.' The *Times* reporter wrote of the hobby:

> For intrigue, plot, and counter plot, in business or in love or science, take to the air and tread its paths, sounding your way for the footfall of your friend's or enemy's message. There is a romance, a comedy, and a tragedy yet to be written. There will be only two scenes. One the station of a wireless plant, and the other the ether that encompasses the unseeing and unseeable, the thing through which ghosts tiptoe by night and fade into security by day — the air. It is only known to the spark that is sent to the wires over the wireless station, and leaps from there into the void.[28]

Described as 'romantic' and 'intriguing,' the wireless telegraph had been heartily endorsed by the nation's largest newspaper and promoter of popular culture. According to the article, even frequency jamming was presented as good, clean fun. Not once, for instance, does the reporter question or scold the 'young Mr. Willinborg' for irresponsible behavior while operating in the ether.

Psychology of Radio

While popular culture motivated many young people to take to the air, wireless technology itself influenced their behavior once they interacted within it. In 1935, when radio broadcasting was a well-established medium of communication, psychologists Hadley Cantril and Gordon W. Allport published their *The Psychology of Radio*. It gave some clue as to the affects of the medium upon the listener, and the listener's reaction to it. They concluded that:

> [Radio] places a greater premium upon the use and interpretation of the human voice, it skeletonizes the personality of the speaker or performer, it develops the use of imaginative completion of the situation in the minds of the listeners . . . it frees the listener from the necessity of conventional politeness toward public performers . . .[29]

With its audio bias, wireless barred all other forms of sensory stimulation. Colors, textures, and the intricacies of body language fell by the wayside as sound, either in the dots and dashes of Morse Code or in the tones of the human voice, became the primary method of communication. The 'skeletonization' of the speaker's personality, consequent on the removal of other stimuli, and the freeing of 'conventional politeness' toward public performers, may be indicative of how the wireless medium itself helped foster a certain anti-social behavior among the amateurs.

Wireless brought freedom to the amateurs. In a sense, the mind was set loose to roam the ether, leaving the body safely behind. In the ether, the 'skeletonization' of the personality manifested itself in what the amateur could do there: listen, talk, and interrupt other frequencies. Among these choices, jamming other frequencies was the most enjoyable. It fostered a sense of power. With his body safely behind the walls of his parents' attic, the amateur could disregard whatever social norms he pleased, especially politeness, making irresponsible behavior a concrete possibility. Thus, while the ether brought young people of similar interests and backgrounds together, it also acted as an arena for youthful aggression and playful sparring. Such playful behavior ultimately clashed with political interests.

Ether as Contested Arena

From roughly 1908 to 1911, the *New York Times* gave considerable news coverage to the 'amateur issue,' documenting several cases where amateur 'pranks' sparked negative reactions from the military and business sectors. In a February 14, 1908 article, the *Times* made reference for the first time to friction between naval operations and 'persons operating with no serious object.' Secretary of the Navy Metcalf called for regulation, citing an incident where President Theodore Roosevelt was incapable of transmitting due to the workings of local stations. He recommended 'making punishable the breaking in or interfering with wireless stations while they are transmitting messages.'[30]

In a January 28, 1910 editorial entitled 'Mischief in "Wireless",' the *Times* expressed doubt as to 'whether irresponsible boys and young men, or any operator of wireless instruments, should be allowed to work them at all times and places.' The editorial cited an example of amateur 'abuse' in the case of the steamer, *Bremen*. The passenger ship had approached the New England coast and signaled another ship, the *Nantucket Shoals*, for information on weather conditions. The message the *Bremen* received baffled her navigator and the transmitted information was deemed untrue. The *Bremen* returned to New York and looked into the matter. Her captain discovered that the *Nantucket Shoals* had been sunk a week before the *Bremen*'s arrival in New England, and that the message received was a prank sent by amateurs. The captain was quoted as saying, 'I might have changed my course as a result of those messages, and lost my ship and its human freight.'[31]

Two days later, the *Times* printed another article about amateur mischief. On January 20, the amateur wireless operators of Montclair, New Jersey were 'accused of sending profane and indecent messages through the air.' In addition, two members of the group, Arthur P. Morgan and A. B. Cole, were under investigation for stealing government 'codes' and transmitting false information to naval stations. The boys protested, claiming that none of their systems could achieve the transmitting distance of which the government accused them.[32]

Ether as Property
Incidents where amateur behavior conflicted with government interests were used as evidence in Congress to promote the regulation of the ether. In 1910, the Roberts Bill swiftly passed the House, advocating restricted public use of the ether. The legislation was based on the notion that 'air is not free,' and that 'if [amateur] use of it becomes dangerous to navigation or results in obstructing commerce, it can and should be prevented.'[33]

In a 'letter-to-the-editor,' an amateur named T. J. Styles from Yonkers, New York, protested against the passing of the Roberts Bill. He felt that regulation of the ether was a clear violation of his rights as a property owner:

By the old Roman law, which our modern real estate laws have for their basis, the owner of land owned not only the surface, but all above and below it — up to the sky and down to the earth's centre. To vest legitimately in a wireless board, then, the proposed jurisdiction, it would seem but proper that all those individuals who are the rightful owners of the atmosphere over their respective properties transversible by wireless messages should be consulted on the matter.[34]

Styles's argument indicated how serious the amateurs were in their claims. This argument is essentially based on the same principal of 'taxation without representation' that the colonists used to declare independence from Great Britain. It also resonates with the anti-corporate rhetoric of contempory Populists and Progressives. Styles's logic is simple and irrevocably American: if the Congress wanted to monopolize the air, and if said air was above his property, he should have some say in that process.

The next day, the *Times* responded to Styles's argument by stating that the claims of the government were valid and in the interest of all Americans. The *Times* then took away the very basis of his argument:

Of course, the talk about everybody's owning all the air above his house or land, and his right to do in it anything he chooses, is nonsensical. There is no such right, and never was, in common law or any other law. If only by suppression of the amateur operators can the business or wireless telegraphy be made practicable and convenient, then the amateurs must be suppressed.[35]

This was the first use of the word 'suppression' in the context of the amateurs and it remained the strongest statement ever made by the *New York Times* against them. If the *Times* had any influence on popular opinion, then this editorial polarized the issue once and for all. The amateur's days of freedom in the ether were almost at an end.

On July 23, 1912, President Taft signed the first sweeping wireless regulation, the Radio Act of 1912. The new laws required all wireless operators to be licensed. Amateur public presence in the ether was restricted to 200 meters or less.[36] The days when young 'wizards' such as Walter J. Willinborg could legally reach out their senses across the Atlantic and beyond, searching for a kindred ethereal spirit to converse with, were over.

Play/Not-Play Dynamics in the Ether

Gregory Bateson's *A Theory of Play and Fantasy*, provides an excellent diagnostic approach to describe the conflict between the amateurs and the government.[37] In his efforts to understand the many complexities of verbal communication, Bateson gives a wonderful definition of the abstract concept of 'Play.' He states that 'playing,' is an '[engagement] in an interactive sequence of which the unit actions or signals [are] similar to but not the same as those of combat.' In other words, 'Play' is a non-harmful imitation of combat, or 'Not Play.'

From the amateurs' perspective, their 'pranks' in the ether constituted 'play.' However, when amateur pranks interfered with government and commercial operations, the message received by the government was definitely that of 'Not Play' — a combative challange to government authority and the public welfare. With the government interpreting the amateurs' 'playful' signals as 'not play,' the amateur became a threat to national security and a target for suppression.

Thus, we can define the amateur/government conflict over the ether as a dynamic of communication between two distinct communities of interpreters, a relatively youthful subculture of hobbyists and an established institution with vested, political interests to protect [see Chart A].

Conclusions

As a medium, the ether has been considered both a substance and a channel for communication. The scientific view of the ether, before Maxwell 'undefined' it, held it as material which explained how electricity could travel through the air without connections. In the context of wireless telegraphy, the ether was a conduit for electronic signals. In the most basic sense, the two views were similar; both saw the ether as a medium for transmitting forms of energy.

However, as wireless telegraphy became popularly accessible, the non-academic view of the ether changed. Governments viewed unauthorized use of the ether as breach of national security, a hole which needed to be filled by regulating its use. For the general public, it was clear that the ether was something to be fought over, like property. This view ultimately shaped people's perception of the ether as they took to the air themselves.

Post-modern philosopher Michel Foucault offered a diagnostic approach for what he termed the 'history of spaces.' Space, in this context can include a physical location, such as a 'frontier,' or it can denote a paradigm with a specific discourse that separates it from other disciplines. Once 'discovered,' a space becomes peopled with settlers, developers, students, and followers, each trying in some way to exploit the inherent value of the space for her own purposes. As the value of the space becomes known to the dominant political powers they will attempt to incorporate it.[38]

It would be simple to fit the subjects of this paper into Foucault's model. The 'space' would be the ether; the governments of the great powers, the 'power structure.' The general public, specifically the amateurs, would be the settlers, viewing the ether as a space of 'contention' and freedom, a technological frontier to replace the vanishing American West. However, the historical reality suggests that the incorporation of the ether-space occurred before the amateurs took to the air: governments adopted the International Wireless Treaty by 1906. Most amateurs didn't take to the air until a few years later. And it is not fair to assume that the incorporation of the ether by the United States government constituted an act of aggression against its citizens. The State viewed the ether as a limited resource, and the government was obliged to control its use for the good of the whole nation. Progressive President Theodore Roosevelt proposed regulating the ether as he did the trusts and unspoiled wilderness. In an age of increasing international hostility (1899-1912), the government saw military predominance in the ether as necessary. Commercial uses were considered secondary. The amateurs, pending good behavior, were allocated what was left over.

In a recent publication, Anne Balsamo explains the anti-social behavior of the computer hacker who inhabits the cyberspace of today. She writes:

> Cyberspace offers an enticing retreat for white men from the burdens of their cultural identities. In this sense, it is apparent that although cyberspace seems to represent a territory free from the burdens of history, it will, in effect, serve as another site for the technological, and no less conventional inscription of the gendered, race-marked body.[39]

Although the body is non-existent in cyberspace, the hacker will bring his white, masculine, middle-class traits, or 'bio-political' traits, into it through his actions. The nature of cyberspace itself is thus shaped.

The ether was the cyberspace of 1907. The amateurs were socialized into their aggressive behaviors from the time they were children. All around them, the great powers vied for control of the ether. Individualism and Social Darwinism were the credos of the day, Andrew Carnegie and the cowboys of the West its heroes. The territorial metaphor assigned to the ether was already in place. As the amateurs gained access to the ether, their behavior was appropriate to it. Jamming frequencies, eavesdropping, and sending 'naughty' messages constituted individuals' efforts to 'homestead' on a frontier that was swiftly becoming closed to the common person [see Chart B].

James Clerk Maxwell pointed out that metaphors, although useful for visualizing abstract theories, ultimately confine those theories to the metaphors themselves. The spatial metaphors of 'territory,' 'resource,' and 'frontier' doomed the ether to be fought over as a limited commodity. As a commodity to be purchased, that part of the ether not required for government purposes was sold to the highest bidder. Today, broadcasting has largely replaced the interactive nature of wireless. Public and classical radio stations enjoy token space amid the democratic pluralism of popular music, sports broadcasts, and talk shows. A once-contested and experimental ether now signifies a regulated national culture in which different groups can harmlessly vent their anxieties. . . . signing out . . .

Chart A

Play/Not-Play Communication Dynamics in the Ether

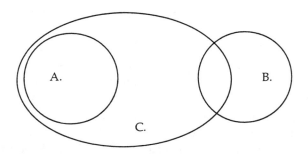

A. **Play**

Engagement in an interactive sequence of which the unit actions or signals were similar to those but not the same as those of combat. Amateurs establishing their network of friends, rivals, and information above and beyond established channels of discourse. This includes chatting, eavesdropping, signal jamming, and impersonation.

B. **Not-Play**

Engagement in an interactive sequence of which the unit actions or signals were threatening.

Commercial, political, and military conflicts over use of the ether, both at the national and international level. Interference of any kind seen as dangerous to national security.

C. **Play/Not-Play**

Amateur engagement in an interactive sequence of which their actions or signals (play) threatened commercial, political, and military interests (not-play).

What the amateurs interpreted as harmless pranks, the government interpreted as threatening.

Chart B

Semiotic Breakdown of the Ether

What did the Ether mean to Hams?

Communicator	Audience
The 'Ether' (radio spectrum)	Amateur Operators

A. Icon: The ether is a theoretical medium that permeates all space and transmits electromagnetic waves.

B. Index: The ether is a medium of human communication, accessed through wireless telegraphy (electromagnetic conduction).

C. Symbol: A new 'space'/ frontier to explore and define. A 'space of freedom' in Foucault's sense, allowing for the expression of individuality and the gathering of like minds. A space to exorcise playful aggressive traits.

What did the Ether mean to the U.S. Government?

Communicator	Audience
The 'Ether'	U.S. Government

A. Icon: (same as above)

B. Index: (same as above)

C. Symbol: The ether, accessed through wireless systems, gave the U.S. armed forces tactical advantages. Amateur use of ether represented a 'hole' in national security, a possible venue for anti-American propaganda. With a only a small number of allocated frequencies the ether was viewed as a limited resource that needed regulation.

* David K. B. Zeeman is a master's candidate in Math Education at Beaver College. Earlier versions of this paper appeared as a senior honors thesis at the Pennsylvania State University and as a paper given at the Semiotics Society of America conference in October, 1994.

ENDNOTES

1. Quoted in *New York Times*, September 10, 1906, 6:3.

2. William Gibson is the author of the novel, *Neuromancer* (New York: Ace Books, 1984); for publications concerning 'Cyberspace' that I have read, please see: Howard Rheingold's *Virtual Reality* (New York: Summit Books, 1991) and Ann Balsamo's 'The Virtual Body in Cyberspace,' *Research in Philosophy and Technology* (Atlanta: Georgia Institute of Technology, 1992).

3. Sir Edmund Whittaker, *A History of the Theories of Aether and Electricity* (New York: Harper, 1951), vol. 2, p. 3.

4. *Ibid.*, pp. 4-6.

5. *Ibid.*, pp. 19-21.

6. John Hendry, *James Clerk Maxwell and the Theory of the Electromagnetic Field* (Boston: Adam Hilger, 1986) p. 65.

7. W. D. Niven, ed. *The Scientific Papers of James Clerk Maxwell* (New York: Dover, 1965), vol. 2, p. 764.

8. *Ibid.*, vol. 2, p. 763.

9. Ellison Hawks, *Pioneers of Wireless* (New York: Gino Press, 1974), p. 60.

10. *Ibid.*, p. 65.

11. See: Bruce J. Hunt. *The Maxwellians* (Ithaca: Cornell Univ. Press, 1991).

12. Susan Douglas. *Inventing American Broadcasting: 1880-1920* (Baltimore: Johns Hopkins Univ. Press, 1987) p. 8.

13. *New York Times*, September 22, 1899, 2:5.

14. *Ibid.*, April 30, 1902, 8:1.

15. *Ibid.*, May 15, 1901, 6:4.

16. *Ibid.*, March 19, 1902, 3:4.

17. *Ibid.*, November 30, 1902, 18:7.

18. *Ibid.*, April 16, 1904, 1:1.

19. *Ibid.*, May 29, 1904, 5:1.

20. *Ibid.*, August 5, 1906, 2:6.

21. *Ibid.*, September 27, 1906, 7:1.

22. Thomas Flynn, 'The Spaces of History.' *The Monist* 116 (1991), 155-177, has a discussion of Foucault's theory of 'space.'

23. *New York Times*, January 31, 1909, 18:1.

24. Felix Barnouw, *History of Broadcasting in the United States* (New York: Oxford Univ. Press, 1966), p. 28. Science fiction's highest literary award, the 'Hugo,' was named after this inventor, writer, and science enthusiast.

25. Robert Sumners, *Radio Broadcasting* (Belmont, Cal.: Wadsworth, 1967), p.40.

26. *Ibid.*, p. 42.

27. Douglas, *Broadcasting*, esp. p. 190, provides an excellent account of the impact of science and the popular media on early twentieth-century American society.

28. *New York Times*, November 3, 1907, pt. 5, 1:1.

29. Hadley Cantril and Gordon W. Allport, *The Psychology of Radio* (Salem: Ayers, 1986), p. 14.

30. *New York Times*, February 14, 1908, 4:3.

31. *Ibid.*, January 28, 1910, 8:2.

32. *Ibid.*, January 30, 1910, 4:6.

33. *Ibid.*, 8:2.

34. *Ibid.*, January 31, 1910, 6:5.

35. *Ibid.*, February 1, 1910, 8:4.

36. Douglas, *Broadcasting*, p. 234.

37. For Bateson's theory, see: Gregory Bateson, 'A Theory of Play and Fantasy,' *Semiotics: An Introductory Anthology* (1985) 129-143.

38. Thomas Flynn, 'The Spaces of History,' 155-177.

39. Balsamo, 'The Virtual Body' p. 23.

Chapter XVIII

A Nineteenth-Century Proposal for Worldmaking in a New Millennium: John C. Calhoun, the Concurrent Majority, and a Defense of Multiculturalism and Political Correctness

William Pencak*

'Why was the unitary national state idea so great and so good? Primarily because it prevailed,' wrote historian Robert Binkley in the midst of the second of two world wars which demonstrated the fruits of organizing Europe into a system of national-states. As Binkley has shown, nineteenth-century Europe abounded with efforts at alternatives, ranging from the Concert of Europe to the dual monarchy of Austria-Hungary, which do not correspond to 'the constitutional law fiction of absolute state sovereignty.'[1] A moment's reflection will convince us that the national sovereign state is something new under the sun, born perhaps with the French Revolution, always imperfectly realized — the Concert of Europe brought back Louis XVIII — and in any case of dubious legitimacy to those forcibly incorporated under its rule. 'The nation' and 'nationalism' are frequently signifiers which justify one group of people taking advantage of another.

History has shown the nation is either too big or too small: too big to satisfy the ethnic and other minorities almost every state includes, too small to confine the multinational flow of commerce and capital which dictates which nations will flourish or fade. Lest one should think the advanced western nations at the end of the twentieth century exempt from such strictures, we need only point to Northern Ireland and to Scottish nationalism in Britain. To what extent are urban African Americans, Latinos, Native Americans, and gays represented in what claims to be their United States? If Bosnia is, thank God, an exception, so, alas, is Switzerland.

On a theoretical level, however, the problem of how a state can incorporate diverse yet conflicting groups has been solved. John C.

Calhoun (1782-1850), South Carolina Senator and for seven years Vice-President of the United States, provided the answer with his notion of the 'concurrent majority.' Calhoun defines this as giving 'to each interest or portion of the community a negative on the others. . . . Without this there can be no systematic, peaceful, or effective resistance to the natural tendency of each to come into conflict with the others; and without this there can be no constitution' (C, 28).[2] The only alternatives are arbitrary power exercised by some over others, or a chaotic war of all against all.

In contrast, Calhoun argues, the concurrent majority 'tends to unite the most opposite and conflicting interests and to blend the whole in one common attachment to the country. . . . Each sees and feels that it can best promote its own prosperity by conciliating the good will and promoting the prosperity of the others. . . . And hence, instead of faction, strife, and struggle for party ascendancy, there would be patriotism, nationality, harmony, and a struggle only for supremacy in promoting the common good of the whole' (C, 38).

Which interests should have a veto over the others? In a perfect 'organism' — '*every* interest will be truly and fully represented,' but in any case 'a few great and prominent interests' must be accounted for to avoid tyranny or anarchy (C, 21). The examples Calhoun provides suggests he was not just, pardon the double entendre, whistling Dixie. The veto of any member of the Polish nobility over the actions of the legislature 'lasted in this form more than two centuries, embracing the period of Poland's greatest power and renown' (C, 55). The six peoples of the Iroquois confederacy selected seven delegates each to all their meetings, with unanimous consent required for action. The dependence of patricians and plebeians in ancient Rome, the former represented in the Senate, the latter by the tribunes and their veto power, was jointly responsible for the republic's greatness. Calhoun even cites the Anglo-American jury, where twelve people must agree unanimously on a verdict, to show the efficacy of an institution which compels consensus and compromise rather than majority rule.

A Disquisition on Government, from which Calhoun's examples are taken, ought to be read semiotically. Never does he mention the conflict between slave and free states in the United States: he appears in the guise of a noble Roman — as he did in the statue the city of Charleston ordered from Europe just before his death, lost at sea, subsequently rescued, then destroyed during the Civil War.[3] Or else he appears as an isolated intellectual — as in the statue which still towers with lordly disdain over

Charleston in empty space on the street that bears his name. His grave also symbolizes this detachment: it is a monument in Charleston's St. Philip's Churchyard where the name Calhoun appears between two stone scrolls on a raised coffin lacking other ornamentation. Grounding his observations in abstract principles supported by examples scattered throughout history, Calhoun sought to convince people he was presenting an objective analysis of the South's case based on eternal principles of political philosophy, which therefore could not be refuted. Only in his incomplete *Discourse on the Constitution and Government of the United States* does the passion behind the theory appear: that a plural executive, a southern tribune to check the northern legislative majority, was required to 'make the Union a union in truth — a bond of mutual affection and brotherhood — and not a mere connection used by the stronger as the instrument of dominion and aggrandizement, and submitted to by the weaker' (C, 103-104).

An institutionalized concurrent majority had four advantages. First, it would force different groups to compromise their differences rather than strive to prevail over their rivals. 'Each portion, in order to advance its peculiar interests, would have to conciliate all others by showing a disposition to advance theirs, and for this purpose, each would select those to represent it whose wisdom, patriotism, and weight of character would command the confidence of the others' (C, 53-53). This actually worked in a modified way immediately after Calhoun's death. The United States held together in the 1850s because northern Presidents Franklin Pierce and James Buchanan, out of weakness if not wisdom, attempted to acquire slave territory in the Caribbean and open the west to slavery. The nation fell apart when Republican Abraham Lincoln insisted slavery be confined to its existing boundaries. The union lasted while the North placated the South.

Second, a concurrent majority would raise the general level of morality. It would 'exert a powerful influence toward purifying and elevating the character of government and the people' (C, 32). Statesmen would have to embody 'truth, justice, integrity, and fidelity' to appeal to those outside their own constituency. On the contrary, where a majority dictates to a minority, there is 'strife between parties for the high and glittering prize of governmental honors and emoluments — falsehood, injustice, fraud, artifice, slander, and breach of faith are freely treated as legitimate weapons.' Neither political parties nor a 'free' press — which Calhoun considered 'the means of controlling public opinion and of molding it . . . [to] carry on the warfare of party' — could adequately protect minority interests. By encouraging the worst traits in human nature to achieve victory in elections rather than consensus among identifiable groups, the parties and the press debased a nation's moral character. A concurrent majority would uplift it. (C, 58).

Third, a concurrent majority would produce a limited, conservative government which maximized human freedom. The state could only act where no interest objected, thus leaving 'necessarily all beyond it open and free to individual exertions.' 'This enlarges and secures the sphere of liberty to the greatest extent which the condition of the community will admit.' Practically speaking, diverse concurrent majorities would only agree on measures for 'the protection of the community,' since what masqueraded as scheme for the 'general welfare' usually disguised the special interest of a part that formed a powerful minority (C, 46).

Finally, and paradoxically, a concurrent majority would create a stronger and more genuine nationalism than a state which insisted on unlimited obedience to a centralized administration. People only acquiesced to the government of a numerical majority 'in form, with that reluctance and hostility ever incident to enforced submission to what is regarded as injustice and oppression.' In states governed by concurrent majorities, however, people 'willingly and cheerfully, under the impulse of an exalted patriotism . . . acquiesce in what the common good requires.' Hence ancient Rome and modern Britain, 'the most remarkable and perfect of their respective forms of constitutional government,' were also the most enduring, powerful, *and* free societies of all times (C, 69).

Calhoun's arguments for a concurrent majority pushed him, and inexorably compel those who accept his logic, beyond mere toleration for cultural minorities. They require any nation desiring freedom rather than force to honor diversity and respect it regardless of the numerical majority's disdain. To update Calhoun's language, states based on the concurrent majority must practice political correctness. The majority, or coalition of dominant minorities, must forbid hate speech or actions which would demean any constituent group in the nation. Such behavior is the moral equivalent of treason, as it disrupts the necessary 'good will' and 'harmony' among interests requisite for national survival.

Calhoun gave a powerful example in a speech he made in 1836. By flooding the South with anti-slavery literature, abolitionists could legitimately be censored and denied use of the mails: 'Will any rational being say that the [censorship] laws of eleven [southern] States of this

Union, which are necessary to their peace, security, and very existence, ought to yield to the laws of the General Government regulating the post-office, which at best is a mere accommodation and convenience' (2:527).[4] Similarly, by passing tariffs which taxed southern agriculture for the benefit of northern industry, the North threatened the prosperity, hence the existence, of the South. Southern states had the right to nullify such laws which violated the express purpose of the constitutional compact: to advance the general welfare, rather than the welfare of a part, and each constituent concurrent majority could only judge its own welfare for itself.

On the other hand, 'personal liberty laws' passed by Northern states to nullify federal measures requiring the return of fugitive slaves were not permissible, unlike the acts of southern legislatures which nullified protective tariffs or efforts to limit slavery expansion. For Calhoun, the difference was clear-cut. The North was engaging in 'hostile acts' (4:528) intended to undermine the very existence of the South. Limitations on expansion demanded 'the interposition of the Government and the passage of an act to prevent the citizens of the slave-holding states from emigrating . . . in order to give' Northerners 'the exclusive right of settling' (4:479-480). The southern slaveholders, on the contrary, asked for 'no action of the Government, demanded no law, to give them any advantage,' but only desired 'a broad and equal' opportunity to relocate themselves.

A real moral as well as political difference thus exists between minorities defending themselves from discriminatory practices and the majority which seeks to enforce such laws. The minority demands respect to maintain its existence within the national polity. A hostile majority is practicing what has come to be called cultural genocide — it insists the minority may only survive if it changes its character and becomes part of or subservient to the majority. Put another way, the South at no time insisted free white Northerners confine themselves east of the territories. The South was not trying to bring free labor to an end as a means of production, despite the preferences of many Southerners for slavery. Similarly, c.1995, African Americans, Native Americans, Latinos, and gays are not insisting white, straight Americans adopt their ways of life; they are insisting on protection which ensures their right to exist without assimilation to their persecutors' norms.

Such underrepresented or ignored concurrent majorities are Calhoun's true heirs. Belligerent nationalist Southerners who pretend to be conservatives (while defending the capitalist order Calhoun deplored as leading to class strife and governmental tyranny) are raiding the past in a sleight-of-hand trick to bolster what is basically a defense of wealth, power, and repression. They demand 'states' and 'community' rights from the federal government, but fail to grant to concurrent majorities within their own communities the same rights they claim for themselves. Arbitrarily to limit legitimate communities to those which are geographically coherent or possess existing political status ignores the real communities to which people declare allegiance. Therefore, it is precisely those communities defended by today's 'conservatives' which are illegitimate according to Calhoun's theory. They question and threaten the existence of rival communities which do not question or threaten theirs. Gays do not question the right of straights to make love their way; Latinos do not insist Anglos remove English from official documents; pro-choice advocates do not insist people stop having children. Members of communities who are denied equality today may use Calhoun's theory to defend their right to be full members of the polity against those who praise Calhoun without having understood him.

Calhoun's philosophy is irrefutable if we accept his reasonable premise that man is 'a social being . . . he has never been found, in any case or country, in any state other than social.' Calhoun took exception to the political theory of the enlightenment which maintained 'that all men are born free and equal.' They are instead 'born subject, not only to parental authority, but to the laws and institutions of the country where born.' Calhoun could thus insist that the integrity of the social constituents of a nation was more important than preservation of the rights of individuals within those constituencies.

But theoretically, Calhoun would have no trouble explaining as well how his system preserved personal freedom which did not threaten the body politic. He could answer objections in two ways. First, once individuals declared themselves no longer represented by members of a recognized concurrent majority, they would have to be recognized as a concurrent majority of their own. Second, where concurrent majorities were effectively in place, these recognized groups would therefore make sure to cultivate the affections of individual members (or of smaller groups) to prevent infinite splintering of the social order. A principle that worked on the national level to reconcile interests would work within concurrent majorities to maintain internal peace.

To bolster his theory, Calhoun could have pointed to a deal arranged by upcountry, predominantly small farming South Carolina to dominate the state's assembly, whereas the slaveholding lowcountry, although numerically inferior, controlled the Senate. It was Calhoun's father Patrick who had been instrumental in ensuring the backcountry received its due. Calhoun was thus carrying on the work of his biological father in addition to proposing the only solution that would have saved the similar compromise of interests America's Founding Fathers had hoped, erroneously, would be adequately preserved by the United States Constitution.[5]

Skeptics might, and did, ask Calhoun: what about the slaves? Where was their concurrent majority? Calhoun replied that 'the Southern States are an aggregate of communities, not of individuals. Every plantation is a little community, with the master at its head, who concentrates in himself the united interests of capital and labor, of which he is the common representative' (3:180). Calhoun insisted 'that in few countries is so much left to the share of the laborer and so little exacted from him or . . . more kind attention paid to him in sickness or infirmities of all age.' He asserted that since masters genuinely represented their slaves in the South, an effective concurrent majority was formed of labor and capital.

The North, on the other hand, where capitalists ran roughshod over the interests of labor, was another story. Calhoun warned that under the new industrial order, 'wages must sink more rapidly than the prices of the necessaries of life, till the operatives will be reduced to the lowest point — when the portion of the products of their labor left to them will be barely sufficient to preserve existence' (6:25-26). No group would accept such conditions: 'With the increase of this difference' between rich and poor, 'the tendency to conflict between them will become stronger; and as the poor and dependent become more numerous in proportion, there will be . . . no want of leaders among the wealthy and ambitious, to excite and direct them in their efforts to obtain the control' (4:360-351). No wonder the historian Richard Hofstadter considered Calhoun 'the Marx of the Master Class,' although his fervent hope was that the republican constitutional innovation of the concurrent majority could derail both sectional and class conflict and save the Union. These were cataclysms to which Southern fire-eaters and Marxist radicals, respectively, looked forward.[6]

Calhoun's theory was sound. Its application to the case he cared about, however, was not only dead wrong, but almost perversely inverted. If masters had truly represented their slaves, hundreds of thousands would not have run away during the Civil War and many thousands fought against the South with such ferocity. If workers truly detested capitalists, if northern laborers felt industrialists had reduced them to hopeless penury, they would not have enlisted by the thousands for Lincoln or, after the Civil War, organized predominantly through unions and legitimate political activism until labor, too, became recognized as a sort of concurrent majority.

Calhoun's perceptual errors, however, ironically confirm his theory. Had Southern masters lived up to Calhoun's idealization, they would have indeed represented their slaves, who then would have been the military asset a South too beguiled by its own defense of slavery had predicted. The South lost the support of its slaves precisely because it refused to practice within its borders the very concurrent majority Calhoun had urged so persuasively on the North. On the other hand, the South came so close to winning because politics which reconciled slaveholding and small farming interests among whites created a fervent Southern nationalism. Conversely, had Calhoun and Marx been right, the modern United States and Western Europe would not possess the most free and stable societies on the globe, which they do because they inadvertently followed his advise and reconciled their workers.

Yet if Calhoun was wrong about masters and slaves, and capitalists and workers, it is impossible not to sense that the old senator was prescient about what would happen to the United States when it tried, however imperfectly, to achieve equality for African Americans. This movement, after a false start during Reconstruction, began in earnest in the 1950's. As Calhoun predicted, integration and equal rights would be seriously complicated because they were imposed on an unwilling minority (or perhaps even majority) through poorly-thought-out and badly implemented programs by a vast bureaucracy. Few efforts were made to obtain for civil rights legislation the concurrent majority consensus necessary to ensure the harmony and good will of opposing groups.

Please substitute 'liberal' for 'profligate' in what follows to understand Calhoun's foresight. Once the South was vanquished, he predicted that 'the blacks and profligate whites that might unite with them would become the principal recipients of federal offices and patronage and would, in consequence, be raised above the whites of the South in the political and social scale.' The result: a nation which would 'become the permanent abode of disorder, anarchy, poverty, misery, and wretchedness' (6:309-311). Calhoun sensed that a movement for equality relying on the power of big government rather than social consensus would inevitably become involved in the political struggle for patronage and pelf. It would be diverted from helping the unfortunate and securing their rights and opportunities into enriching the relevant politicians and interest groups.

Hence the United States election of 1994: a reaction against affirmative action, the welfare state, and social programs — the 'federal offices and patronage' — which, despite thirty years of spending unprecedented in human history, have failed to achieve their purposes while our cities approximate the confusion Calhoun envisioned. Please note that I am holding neutral the moral desirability of racial equality. Assuming the civil rights' movement's goals were laudable, it may now be argued convincingly that it never achieved its potential because groups critical for its success — the white middle and upper classes — were never adequately placated.

Thus, Calhoun's theory accounts for the collapse of a situation he would have deplored. Ironically, the likely aftermath of the present scene, given the contemporary false conservatives' rejection of multiculturalism and political correctness, will be to substitute repression for social programs. This will only provoke rage on the part of those excluded from the new dominant majority.

We cannot reject Calhoun's concurrent majority without risking the exclusion of groups who, having little or no stake in the social order, will vent their anger against it. *Time Magazine* (May 19, 1952) astutely noted that incorporation, rather than exclusion, has historically been the case in the United States:

> Calhounism survives in a great and much-maligned American institution, the smoke-filled room, where party leaders can do what the ballot box cannot do; measure the intensity with which various groups will react for or against (especially against) certain proposals. The majority may be mildly in favor of a policy, and a minority (sectional or otherwise) may be fanatically against it. Under those circumstances, the American politician will often withhold support until he can find a way of placating the minority.

Party brokers in smoke-filled rooms are less powerful in the 1990s than in the 1950s, but their places have been taken by PAC spokespeople in smoke-free environments.

If, as seems likely c.2000, the nation-state may be but a passing, unsuccessful phase of political organization — the Western European states think so, and the former Soviet bloc is proving it every day — then it is worthwhile to consider Calhoun's 'concurrent majority' as an alternative organizing principal. It may serve as a useful model in three areas: pluralist societies such as the United States, where loyalties may be religious and sexual as well as geographical, ethnic, and racial; multi-ethnic states such as Bosnia and Russia; and the worldwide community of nations.

Some may argue that Calhoun is unrealistic. On the contrary, in every society where a modicum of liberty coexists with political stability, it is precisely to the extent that a polity institutionalizes, or renders customary, some version of a concurrent majority. And there is hope for even the worst cases. History's most successful concurrent majorities arose from desperate attempts to save divided states. Calhoun notes that in Rome and Britain concurrent majorities did not arise from rational planning or a peaceful disposition. Rather, 'the constitutions of both originated in a pressure occasioned by conflicts of interest between hostile classes or orders and were intended to meet the pressing exigencies of the occasion, neither party, it would seem, having any conception of the principles involved or the consequences to follow' (C, 78-79). At a critical point, these nations followed the 'wise' course of 'concession and compromise' rather than permit 'deep hatred . . . accompanied by faction, violence, and corruption, which distracted and weakened government,' to continue (C, 71,73). A nation whose very existence is threatened by internal strife is thus a better candidate for thorough reform according to Calhoun's principles than one in which minorities are successfully repressed or moderately appeased.

Like the Founding Fathers — whose example Calhoun hoped to follow in providing a constitutional innovation to preserve a nation tottering on the brink of ruin — Calhoun realized that liberty was a rare plant, a flower precariously balanced between the abysses of anarchy and tyranny. Liberty 'is a reward to be earned, not a blessing to be gratuitously lavished on all alike — a reward reserved for the intelligent, the patriotic, the virtuous and deserving, and not a boon to be bestowed on a people too ignorant, degraded, and vicious to be capable either of appreciating or enjoying it' (C, 42-43).

In his writings, Calhoun did not stress that the concurrent majority is the political application of the religious injunction to love one's enemies as oneself — for your sake as well as theirs. But Calhoun's theory does show the coincidence of religious morality, reasoned political thought, and enlightened self-interest. The world, as he knew, would honor his solution more in the breach than in the observance. But in my opinion, only one other theorist ranks with Calhoun in providing an irrefutable case as to what must be done to realize a political ideal. Plato told us what we needed for a just society. The price to be paid was isolation from outside influence and a loss of personal freedom. But we don't want justice: we want a good life. Calhoun told us what was required for a peaceful society, or world. The price is that groups must restrain themselves from interfering with the behavior of others they perceive as immoral. Rather, they must tolerate the 'immoral' concurrent majority and wait for a subsidiary concurrent majority to demand its place in the sun, which must in turn be recognized as legitimate by all. But we don't want peace either: we want to win.

*William Pencak is Professor of History, Penn State.

ENDNOTES

1. Robert C. Binkley, *Realism and Nationalism, 1852-1871* (New York: Harper & Row, 1941), 184, 157.

2. John C. Calhoun, *A Disquisition on Government and Selections from the Discourse*, ed. C. Gordon Post (Indianapolis: Bobbs-Merrill, 1953). References to this work in the text are indicated by 'C' followed by page numbers.

3. The statue is depicted in Lacy K. Ford, 'Recovering the Republic: Calhoun, South Carolina, and the Concurrent Majority,' *South Carolina Historical Magazine*, 89 (1988): 146-159.

4. *The Works of John C. Calhoun*, ed. Richard K. Crallé (6 vols.; Charleston, SC: Walker & James, and New York: D. Appleton & Co., 1851-56), references to this collection indicated in text by volume and page.

5. Ford, 'Recovering the Republic,' 146, 148.

6. Richard Hofstadter, *The American Political Tradition and the Men Who Made It* (New York: Alfred A. Knopf, 1948), 67-91.

INDEX

William Pencak is Professor of History at Penn State.
Photo: Lita L. Schwartz/Urban Images.